# The Chronological
# Life
# *of*
# Christ

## Volume 2

# The Chronological

# Life of Christ

## Volume 2
## From Galilee to Glory

# Mark E. Moore

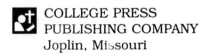
COLLEGE PRESS
PUBLISHING COMPANY
Joplin, Missouri

Cover Design: Mark A. Cole

**Library of Congress Cataloging-in-Publication Data**

Moore, Mark E. (Mark Edward), 1963–
    The chronological life of Christ / Mark E. Moore.
        p.   cm.
    Includes text from: The NIV harmony of the Gospels / Robert L. Thomas,
    editor and Stanley N. Gundry, associate editor.
    Includes bibliographical references and index.
    Contents: v. 2. From Galilee to glory.
    ISBN 0-89900-775-9 (pbk.)
    1. Jesus Christ—Biography.  2. Jesus Christ—Chronology.  3. Bible. N.T.
Gospels—Harmonies, English.  I. Bible. N.T. Gospels. English. New
International. 1996.  II. Title.
BT301.2.M58  1996
226'.1077—dc20
                                                    96-12594
                                                        CIP

# DEDICATED TO MY STUDENTS,

Who give hands and feet and sometimes wings to my words.

To the likes of:

Rob Maupin

Greg Morrell

Barry Smith

Jon Weece

Brian Williams

**I love you guys; happy Sabbath!**

# ABBREVIATIONS

| | |
|---|---|
| *ABW* | Archaeology in the Biblical World |
| *AL* | Alliance Life |
| *Ant* | Antiquities of the Jews |
| *ATJ* | Asbury Theological Journal |
| *ATR* | Anglican Theological Review |
| *AUSS* | Andrews University Seminary Studies |
| *BA* | Biblical Archaeologist |
| *BAR* | Biblical Archaeology Review |
| *BETS* | Bulletin of the Evangelical Theological Society |
| *BibSac* | Bibliotheca Sacra |
| *BibT* | Bible Today |
| *BJRL* | Bulletin of the John Rylands University Library of Manchester |
| *BR* | Bible Review |
| *BT* | Bible Translator |
| *BW* | Biblical World |
| *CBQ* | Catholic Biblical Quarterly |
| *ChHist* | Church History |
| *ChicSt* | Chicago Studies |
| *ChrCen* | Christian Century |
| *CJ* | Concordia Journal |
| *CQ* | Covenant Quarterly |
| *CS* | Christian Standard |
| *CSR* | Christian Scholar's Review |
| *CT* | Christianity Today |
| *CTJ* | Calvin Theological Journal |
| *CTM* | Concordia Theological Monthly |
| *CTR* | Criswell Theological Review |
| *CurTM* | Currents in Theology and Mission |
| *DJ* | Discipleship Journal |
| *EvQ* | Evangelical Quarterly |
| *ExpT* | Expository Times |
| *GR* | Gordon Review |
| *GTJ* | Grace Theological Journal |
| *GWPA* | Gospel Witness and Protestant Advocate |
| *HeyJ* | Heythrop Journal |
| *HibJ* | Hibbert Journal |
| *HTR* | Harvard Theological Review |
| *IEJ* | Israel Exploration Journal |
| *Int* | Interpretation |
| *ITQ* | Irish Theological Quarterly |
| *JAMA* | Journal of the American Medical Association |
| *JBL* | Journal of Biblical Literature |
| *JES* | Journal of Ecumenical Studies |
| *JETS* | Journal of the Evangelical Theological Society |
| *JHLT* | Journal of Hispanic/Latino Theology |
| *JJS* | Journal of Jewish Studies |
| *JPSP* | Journal of Personality and Social Psychology |
| *JPST* | Journal of Psychology and Theology |
| *JQR* | Jewish Quarterly Review |
| *JSNT* | Journal for the Study of the New Testament |
| *JTS* | Journal of Theological Studies |
| *JTSA* | Journal of Theology Southern Africa |
| *LexTQ* | Lexington Theological Quarterly |
| LXX | Septuagint |

| | | | |
|---|---|---|---|
| MT | Masoretic Text | SwJT | Southwestern Journal of Theology |
| *NovT* | Novum Testamentum | | |
| NT | New Testament | *TB* | Tyndale Bulletin |
| *NTS* | New Testament Studies | *TheolEd* | Theological Educator |
| OT | Old Testament | *TrinJ* | Trinity Journal |
| *PEQ* | Palestine Exploration Quarterly | *TS* | Theological Studies |
| | | *VE* | Vox Evangelica |
| *Pres* | Presbyterian | *War* | Jewish Wars |
| PRS | Perspectives in Religious Studies | *WTJ* | Westminster Theological Journal |
| RB | Revue Biblique | *ZNW* | *Zeitschrift für die neutestamentliche Wissenschaft und die Kunde der ältern Kirche* |
| *RestQ* | Restoration Quarterly | | |
| *RevExp* | Review & Expositor | | |
| SJT | Scottish Journal of Theology | | |
| *ST* | Studia Theologica | | |

Note: not all of these are cited in Vol. 2.

## Key to Marginal Icons

 Parables

 Prayer (major teachings about/examples of)

 Fulfilled Prophecies

 Deity of Christ (claims of/witnesses to)

 End-time Teachings

 Healings and other Miracles

 The Kingdom/Church

# TABLE OF CONTENTS

# INTRODUCTION

He made history in April of 1996. For the very first time, *Time*, *Newsweek*, and *US News and World Report* all featured the same cover story: Jesus Christ. If nothing else, these pieces show that there are still plenty of misconceptions and half-truths grinding in the gossip mill about this man. So there you have it . . . not much has changed since Jesus gathered dust in the soles of his sandals on Palestinian soil. He is still the buzz at barber shops and corner cafes. He is still talked about and against. He pricks our curiosity. He sparks our imagination. And often he even earns our ire.

Who is he, *really?* You know he's no politician. But he still kisses babies and transforms nations. He's no social activist. But he is the genesis of who knows how many hospitals, orphanages, and innumerable acts of kindness. He's certainly not an entertainer. But whose daytimer is more crowded? A psychotherapist? Hardly. But how many of us "Humpty Dumpties" has he put back together again?! This peasant carpenter has built himself a kingdom immeasurably greater than his earthly enemies could ever have imagined.

Who is he, *really?* If you eavesdrop in ivory towers you hear scholars batting about this phrase, "the search for the Historical Jesus." The upshot is they try to strip the Gospels of the miraculous and the "mythical" and then read between the lines for what the author was *really* saying. In most of their presentations Jesus turns out to be a cynic philosopher; a zealot rebel; or worse, an anemic, albeit clever, do-gooder that would make a fine next-door neighbor (you know, the "Mr. Wilson" type).

Well, here is the good news and the impetus behind this book: The Gospels, as we have them, present the historical Jesus. We don't have to play hide-and-go-seek with the sources. We don't have to psychoanalyze a hypothetical church. We don't even have to interpret the scissors-and-paste mural of some second-century editor. The Gospels you hold in your hand, miracles and all, tell the truth about Jesus. Who is he, really? He is the Lord, Jesus Christ, who died for our sins and rose for our justification. Now that's worth writing about!

This second volume of *The Chronological Life of Christ* picks up with the last three months of Jesus' life here on earth. No story has been told as much as this one. Yet it is never boring, never passe. It bears repetition well. Like a dazzling display of lightning, it still takes your breath away each time you see it. So this story still casts its spell on the audience. It still endures and endears, transforms us and transports us in time to dusty roads and olive groves and sometimes to the skirts of heaven. It is my prayer that this work helps you hear this story again, perhaps for the very first time.

As with Volume 1, this is **a companion to the NIV harmony** by Thomas and Gundry.[1] That harmony prints the Gospel text in four columns, but we have squeezed it into one. **The texts of all four Gospels** have been combined and printed in a different typeface to read as a single "story line." By simply using the superscripted letters MT,MK,LK,JN,AC to represent Matthew, Mark, Luke, John and (in a few cases) the book of Acts respectively, the reader can quickly identify which Evangelist said what. This will allow you to read all four Gospels at once. By comparing and combining the individual testimonies we can reconstruct the scene with fuller and more colorful detail.

Because of Him,

Mark E. Moore

# PART EIGHT (Continued)
# THE LATER JUDEAN MINISTRY OF CHRIST

Any average "Joe" can correctly choose between bad and good. The real challenge is to choose the best over the better. Martha is a mirror image of many of our best church workers. She is actively engaged in good work to the neglect of more important priorities. The story is simple; its lessons run deep.

§ 104
**Jesus' Visit with Mary and Martha**
(Lk 10:38-42)

Lk 10:38-40

³⁸As Jesus and his disciples were on their way, he came to a village where a woman named Martha opened her home to him. ³⁹She had a sister called Mary, who sat at the Lord's feet listening to what he said. ⁴⁰But Martha was distracted by all the preparations that had to be made. She came to him and asked, "Lord, don't you care that my sister has left me to do the work by myself? Tell her to help me!"

The setting is the village of Bethany. It was a suburb less than two miles east of Jerusalem, on the other side of the Mount of Olives. This is the first time (mentioned) that Jesus is in the home of Mary and Martha, the sisters of Lazarus. This is surely not the first time they have met. They are close friends of Jesus (Jn 11:1-3). We suspect then, that Jesus had an open invitation to the home of his friends Lazarus, Mary, and Martha.[1] For the past year and a half, Jesus has been traveling in Galilee and its surrounding areas. Now he is back down in Judea and he can rekindle this friendship.

We would like to imagine Lazarus meeting Jesus at the Feast of Tabernacles and telling Mary and Martha about it. They send Lazarus back to Jerusalem the next day to invite Jesus to come over for dinner. He is too busy to come during the feast. When it is over, though, Jesus travels about Judea, finally winding his way over to Bethany for a meal

---

[1] It is possible that Simon the Leper (Mt 26:6) is a fourth member of the family. If so, then we might suspect that he is married to Mary or Martha. It is also possible that Mt 26:6 took place in an entirely different home, or that Simon the Leper is Lazarus.

in the home of these dear friends. Since Lazarus is not mentioned, we suggest perhaps he was one of the seventy-two Jesus sent out.

Mary and Martha have worked together[2] to prepare a banquet for their friend and famed rabbi, Jesus. That was no small task, considering his smallest entourage consisted of the Twelve. Mary and Martha apparently have a large home, representing considerable wealth. We wonder what kind of business Simon (the Leper, Mt 26:6) is engaged in and how his sickness affects his standard of living. Or perhaps it is Lazarus who is the main bread-winner of the home. If that is the case, then his raising, a mere two months from now, will be a considerable favor for the family.

Once Jesus finally arrives, Mary walks out and leaves her sister to do all the work while she sits down at Jesus' feet and listens to him teach. Not only is this rude to leave her sister, it is culturally inappropriate. She is assuming the role of a disciple, a characteristically male position (cf. Lk 8:1-3). As Martha races back and forth between the kitchen and the banquet hall, she gets more and more upset with her sister. Finally, she spews out her frustration all over Jesus with these words: "Lord, don't you care that my sister has left me to do the work by myself? Tell her to help me!" With this, she not only blames her sister, but Jesus for her frustration.

Although Martha is somewhat rude (due to her frenzy) and a bit presumptuous to tell Jesus what to do, her request is still reasonable. She wants Mary to *help* her [*synantilambanō*]. The word means "to do her fair share." It is the kind of word you would use to describe two oxen in the same yoke, both pulling their own weight. Now that's just good old Judeo-Christian work ethic.

Lk 10:41-42

[41]"Martha, Martha," the Lord answered, "you are worried and upset about many things, [42]but only one thing is needed.[a] Mary has chosen what is better, and it will not be taken away from her."

[a]42 Some manuscripts *but few things are needed — or only one*

We can almost hear the chuckle as Jesus corrects Martha: "You are worried and upset about many things." Isn't this a sound-bite from our own morning news?! We are a frantic and frenzied people. And like Martha, most of what we worry over are just dishes.

There are some manuscripts at verse 42 which read: "There are only a few things that are needed." If this is the correct reading, Jesus could

---

[2]Martha uses the melodramatic word "abandoned" (v. 40), indicating that at first Mary was helping her.

be speaking about the dinner preparations. He is telling Martha that she is making too much of a "to-do." But the present text is most likely correct. Jesus is not talking about the meal but about his teaching: "The only thing necessary is the Word of God."[3]

The conclusion is clear. Martha had the sublime privilege of sitting at Jesus' feet listening to him, but she is worried about getting the meal "just so." She missed him. In five short months he will be gone. Likewise, we often go through life worrying about trivial matters and missing our divine appointments. Mary, on the other hand, takes advantage of God-incarnate in her living room.[4] Because her ears are open now, the Friday before Jesus is crucified she will be perceptive enough to anoint him for his burial (cf. § 141).

Prayer is so important and powerful. Why is it that we know so little about it and do it so poorly? We're not alone. Jesus' first followers struggled with prayer too. As the Master prayed, they watched with admiration and perhaps even a bit of envy. He prayed so well and so often! Luke, particularly, stresses Jesus' prayer life (3:21; 5:16; 6:12; 9:18, 28; 11:1; 22:32, 41; 23:34). On this occasion, when Jesus returns from one of these stolen moments with the Father, his disciples come with a request: "Teach us to pray." They too wanted the intimacy Jesus had with God.

**§ 105a**
**A Model Prayer**
(Lk 11:1-4)

[1]One day Jesus was praying in a certain place. When he finished, one of his disciples said to him, "Lord, teach us to pray, just as John taught his disciples."

Lk 11:1

Most of this section sounds familiar. In fact, verses 2-4 and 9-12 are lifted straight out of the Sermon on the Mount. This does not mean Luke edited and rearranged Matthew's material.[5] After the tour of the 72, there

---

[3]R.W. Wall suggests that this links Jesus' words to the Manna of Deut 8:3. He proposes that the three pericopes of Lk 10:25-28, 29-37, and 38-42 are linked consecutively to Deut 5-6; 7; and 8, showing that Jesus is to the church what Moses was to Israel. ("Martha and Mary [Luke 10:38-42] in the Context of a Christian Deuteronomy," *JSNT* 35 [1989]: 19-35).

[4]We will find these same two women again in John 11 demonstrating the same characteristics: Martha, taking care of business and Mary offering Jesus worship.

[5]A. J. Banstra, "The Original Form of the Lord's Prayer," *CTJ* 16 (1981): 15-37, evaluates five different suggestions concerning the two versions of this prayer. (1) Jesus gave a similar prayer on two different occasions, faithfully recorded by Matthew and Luke. (We accept this position here). (2) Matthew's version is more original and Luke edited it down. (3) Luke's version is more original and Matthew expanded it liturgically. (4) The prayer, in both forms, was created by the early church and not actually original with

would be crowds of unfamiliar faces. What the Twelve heard a year ago up in Galilee, these Judeans may be hearing for the very first time today.

The crowd remembers well how John taught his disciples to pray. It was not uncommon for a rabbi in those days to teach certain emphases and even liturgies of prayer. John apparently taught certain features of prayer which were uniquely his. This student seems to be asking Jesus to point out his unique strategies and emphases of prayer. After all, they seem to work pretty well. One striking feature of Jesus' prayers is that he always refers to God as Father (cf. Jn 20:17; Rom 8:14-17), with one notable exception in Mark 15:34. While Palestinian Jews did consider God their "Father" (cf. 2 Sam 7:14; Psa 103:13), they were reluctant to address him as "Abba." Thus, Jesus opened up a new intimacy between his disciples and their God.[6]

There are several lessons here in verse 1. (1) Written or memorized prayers, and especially the Lord's prayer, should still be practiced alongside extemporaneous prayer. They are focused; each line is packed with meaning. They generally contain deep theology in beautiful language. They are well-rounded, and thus can become a springboard for extemporaneous prayers. They are also communal. That is, they belong to the church. Thus, we are reminded that we do not pray in isolation from other believers. (2) We would do well to seek out and imitate "prayer masters." They may guide us in our journey toward the face of God. (3) Prayer can be taught. It does not always come naturally. It may require practice and perhaps a bit of experimentation.

Lk 11:2-4 *with*
Mt 6:9-13

[2]He said to them, "When you pray, say:
'{Our[MT]} Father,[a] {in heaven[MT]}
hallowed be your name,
your kingdom come.[b] {Your will be done on earth as it is in heaven.[MT]}
[3]Give us each day {today[MT]} our daily bread.

---

Jesus. (5) Both Matthew and Luke changed the actual words of Jesus to fit their own "worshiping communities." Banstra accepts this fifth solution, suggesting that Matthew's version is more appropriate to Jewish Christians and Luke's version is more appropriate to Gentile Christians. However, several cautions are in order. First, Banstra's conclusions are based on his presuppositions of redaction criticism and copying between the Gospels, neither of which has been adequately proven. Second, both versions of the prayer show signs of careful poetic composition. Thus, it is impossible (and precarious) to identify one as "more original." Third, Jesus was an itinerant preacher. One would expect variant forms of similar addresses.

[6]Cf. J. Jeremias, *The Prayers of Jesus* (Naperville: Allenson, 1967), p. 97. However, W.A. VanGemeren, "'ABBA' in the Old Testament?" *JETS* 31/4 (1988): 385-398, points out that an intimate relationship with a "Father-God" is found in the OT as well as in the NT Thus, we don't have a dichotomy between the two testaments. But Jesus certainly heightens our relationship with God.

⁴Forgive us our sins,
for we also forgive everyone who sins against us.ᶜ
And lead us not into temptationᵈ {but deliver us from the evil one.ᴹᵀ}'"

ᵃ2 Some manuscripts *Our Father in heaven*    ᵇ2 Some manuscripts *come. May your will be done on earth as it is in heaven*    ᶜ4 Greek *everyone who is indebted to us*    ᵈ4 Some manuscripts *temptation but deliver us from the evil one*

[vv. 2-4 = Mt 6:9-13, see comments on § 54f]

There are very few differences between the Lord's prayer in Matthew and in Luke: (1) Matthew's version is longer and more liturgical (see text above for Matthew's additions). (2) Matthew uses "bread today," Luke uses "daily bread." Thus, in Matthew the request for bread seems more immediate. (3) The forgiveness of our fellows in Matthew is past tense "as we have forgiven;" whereas in Luke it is present/future, "for we also forgive." And (4) Matthew uses the word "transgressions" whereas Luke uses "sins."

Jesus has just told the disciples how to pray. Now he encourages them to do it. Sometimes it is difficult to believe God will actually listen to us. After all, can my puny little prayers actually move a sovereign God? Apparently they do. That's the point of this parable.

**§ 105b
Exhortation
to Pray**
(Lk 11:5-13)

Lk 11:5-8

⁵Then he said to them, "Suppose one of you has a friend, and he goes to him at midnight and says, 'Friend, lend me three loaves of bread, ⁶because a friend of mine on a journey has come to me, and I have nothing to set before him.' ⁷"Then the one inside answers, 'Don't bother me. The door is already locked, and my children are with me in bed. I can't get up and give you anything.' ⁸I tell you, though he will not get up and give him the bread because he is his friend, yet because of the man's boldnessᵃ he will get up and give him as much as he needs."

ᵃ8 Or *persistence*

This parable made a lot more sense in Palestine than it does to us. For instance, we would consider it rude for a friend to show up at our house in the middle of the night. But if you are traveling a long distance by foot, it may be unavoidable. Furthermore, if you want to avoid the oppressive Palestinian heat, you would purposely travel at night. It may also sound rude to wake up a neighbor in the middle of the night. This is especially true when we consider the fact that many Palestinian families slept together in the same room on a single mat. If the father gets up to get the bread, he would rouse the wife and kids. Part of their culture, however, was the understanding that a visitor was not simply hosted by a family, but by the whole community. Therefore, this neighbor would have the right to ask his friend to provide for the visitor. And in smaller communities, he could hardly hide the fact that their family had just done their baking for the week.

This parable is similar to the one found in Luke 18:1-8 about the unjust judge who was pressured into giving in to a persistent widow. So what is Jesus saying? Is it that we must be pushy and persistent before God will give us what we ask? Certainly not! This is not a parable of comparison, but one of contrast. It is the classic Jewish logic, from lesser to greater: if even a tight-fisted neighbor will give in to your bold request, how much more will God delight in giving good gifts to his children. This matches exactly what follows in verses 9-13. It also makes sense in light of Jesus' opening line of the parable. "Suppose one of you" was understood as "Can you imagine anyone . . . ?" The answer is obviously, "No!" No one would actually act like the sleeping man of this parable; even less would God act like that. Therefore, we can approach God with confidence because he is our loving father who delights in granting our requests.[7]

Lk 11:9-13

[9]"So I say to you: Ask and it will be given to you; seek and you will find; knock and the door will be opened to you. [10]For everyone who asks receives; he who seeks finds; and to him who knocks, the door will be opened.

[11]"Which of you fathers, if your son asks for[a] a fish, will give him a snake instead? [12]Or if he asks for an egg, will give him a scorpion? [13]If you then, though you are evil, know how to give good gifts to your children, how much more will your Father in heaven give the Holy Spirit to those who ask him!"

[a]11 Some manuscripts *for bread, will give him a stone; or if he asks for*

[vv. 9-13 = Mt 7:7-11, see comments on § 54h]

Luke differs only slightly from Matthew's wording. In verse 11, Matthew uses the bread/stone illustration, whereas Luke uses the egg/scorpion illustration. Viner suggests that the curled up scorpion perhaps looked like an egg.[8] Luke also uses the singular "heaven" (classic Greek

---

[7]A.F. Johnson, "Assurance for Man: The Fallacy of Translating *Anaideia* by 'Persistence' in Luke 11:5-8," *JETS* 22/2 (1979): 123-131, correctly points out that *anaideia*, in the LXX, Greek and early Christian literature always meant "shameless" or "impudence" (with one possible exception of "persistence" in Jer. 8:5). Furthermore, this "impudence" may be a characteristic of the sleeper rather than the knocker. That is, he may get out of bed, not because his friend kept knocking but because he wants to avoid being shamed by the community the next day (cf. Nolland, pp. 625-626). Nevertheless, the primary thrust of this parable is not persistent prayer, but bold prayer.

[8]T. Viner, "Stories Jesus Told: The Friend at Midnight," *CS* (Feb. 3, 1991): 17.

description), while Matthew uses the plural "heavens" (classic Hebrew description). Both of these are only minor differences. There is one other difference of a bit more substance. Instead of the Father giving "good gifts" as in Matthew, Luke says he will give the "Holy Spirit." Now that is the best gift we could get (cf. Acts 1:4; 2:33; Lk 24:49)!

The point is obvious. You expect even a stingy neighbor to give you what you need to entertain guests, even if you ask in the middle of the night. How much more will God, our loving Father, be willing to give us everything we need for nourishment, especially his Holy Spirit. So go ahead and ask! You are sure to get what you need.

§ 106
**Beelzebub and the Sign of Jonah**
(Lk 11:14-36, cf. § 61-62, Mt 12:22-45; Mk 3:20-30)

We've read these words before (§ 61-62). Matthew and Mark used them to describe a nasty confrontation in Galilee. Luke uses the same words to describe a similar skirmish in Judea. We shouldn't be too surprised. Luke and Matthew also use the same words to describe the sending out of the seventy-two in Judea (Lk 10) and the sending of the Twelve in Galilee. We will notice this phenomenon throughout Luke's "central section."

The religious leaders, even here in Judea, can no longer deny that Jesus has done great miracles. Nor can they afford to ignore this man and his movement. They can either admit Jesus' power is from God and submit to his Lordship, or relegate his miraculous power to Satan. But they are not about to admit Jesus was right. Their only alternative is to lambast him. As they do, Matthew records for us Jesus' warning. Blasphemy against the incarnate Christ is somewhat excusable. But blasphemy against the Holy Spirit is not. They are dangerously close to the point of no return.

## JESUS AND BEELZEBUB

Lk 11:14-23 *with* Mt 12:22-25, Mk 3:22-23

[14]Jesus was driving out a demon that was {blind and[MT]} mute. When the demon left, the man who had been mute spoke, and the crowd was amazed. [15]But some of them {Pharisees[MT]} {and teachers of the law[MK]} said, "{He is possessed;[MK]} By Beelzebub,[a] the prince of demons, he is driving out demons." [16]Others tested him by asking for a sign from heaven.

[17]Jesus knew their thoughts and said to them {in parables[MK]}: "Any kingdom divided against itself will be ruined, and a house {or city[MT]} divided against itself will fall. [18]If Satan is divided against himself, how can his kingdom stand? I say this because you claim that I drive out demons by Beelzebub. [19]Now if I drive out demons by Beelzebub, by whom do your followers drive them out? So then, they will be your judges. [20]But if I drive out demons by the finger {Spirit[MT]} of God, then the kingdom of God has come to you.

[21]"When a strong man, fully armed, guards his own house, his possessions

are safe. ²²But when someone stronger attacks and overpowers him, he takes away the armor in which the man trusted and divides up the spoils.

²³"He who is not with me is against me, and he who does not gather with me, scatters."

ª15 Greek *Beezeboul* or *Beelzeboul*; also in verses 18 and 19

[vv. 14-23 = Mt 12:22-30; Mk 3:22-27, see comments on § 61]

Matthew describes a couple of things that Luke does not. First, the attack is led by the Pharisees. Second, it ends with a discussion on the blasphemy of the Holy Spirit, a frightening and powerful narrative. Luke's rendition, however, is a bit more vivid, especially in describing the plunder of a strong man's house.

The Pharisees accuse Jesus of being Satanic. It is a serious charge and potentially true. Jesus cannot ignore it. In fact, he musters some of his best logic to answer this accusation.

*ARGUMENT #1: "Any kingdom divided against itself will be ruined."* Jesus' power is being used against Satan's kingdom. If he belongs to Satan, he would be working for him, not against him. This would be like cutting off one's nose to spite one's face. It is not that Satan *couldn't* order out a demon but that he *wouldn't*.

*ARGUMENT #2: "By whom do your followers drive them out?"* Let's say, for the sake of argument, that Jesus was Satanic because he cast out demons. Would this same argument not also apply to the other Jewish exorcists (cf. Acts 19:13-14)? Their hypocrisy is evident. Their condemnation of Jesus falls back upon themselves.

*ARGUMENT #3: "The kingdom of God has come to you."* If they follow Jesus' logic, they have to be pierced with fear at this point. If there is even a remote possibility that Jesus' power is from God, they have just committed fierce blasphemy. "Has come" is not the normal verb for "come." It means to "arrive, catch up" or even, as in 1 Thessalonians 4:15, "preceded." Bottom line: God's kingdom is sitting on their doorstep!

*ARGUMENT #4: "When someone stronger attacks and overpowers him, he takes away the armor . . ."* This too is a frightening proposition for Jesus' critics. He has just disarmed Satan and divided up his spoils. He has entered Satan's domain, beat him, stripped him of his power, and robbed him of his possessions. Who's next?!

## DEMONS IN ARID PLACES

Lk 11:24-26 *with*
Mt 12:44-45

²⁴"When an evilª spirit comes out of a man, it goes through arid places seeking

rest and does not find it. Then it says, 'I will return to the house I left.' [25]When it arrives, it finds the house {unoccupied,[MT]} swept clean and put in order.[9] [26]Then it goes and takes seven other spirits more wicked than itself, and they go in and live there. And the final condition of that man is worse than the first. {That is how it will be with this wicked generation.[MT]}"

[a]*24 Greek unclean*

[vv. 24-26 = Mt 12:43-45, see comments on § 62]

This whole argument started when Jesus cast a demon out of this mute man. He has become the center of attention. Jesus even uses him to illustrate the desperate situation of the entire nation. Jesus does the guy a favor. He cleans him up by casting out the demon. That is good. But if this fellow doesn't fill his body with something else, the demon, unsatisfied being a vagabond, is likely to return with his buddies to their newly renovated abode. Then this man will be even worse off. Likewise, the Jewish nation receives a great blessing in Jesus' presence. But if they don't accept him as Lord, they are in for a rude awakening. Their plight will be worse than it was before he came.

[27]As Jesus was saying these things, a woman in the crowd called out, "Blessed is the mother who gave you birth and nursed you."
[28]He replied, "Blessed rather are those who hear the word of God and obey it."

Lk 11:27-28

This woman actually blesses the body of Mary, specifically her womb and her breasts. She was blessed with the privilege to bear Jesus and to raise him as a son (Luke 1:28-35, 42-55). God certainly respected her faith and piety. Yet she, like John the Baptist, was less than the least in the kingdom of God. Jesus' introductory conjunction, *menoun*, is a way of saying, "Yes, BUT." Jesus affirms what she has said, but points out its inadequacy. True blessedness is in hearing and keeping the word of God. There is no spiritual blessing apart from obedience to the word. This is like Matthew 12:46-50 (§ 63) — Jesus' family seeking him. Both sections say that Jesus' true family, those who listen and obey, stand in stark contrast to the Pharisees.

---

[9]The word for "put in order" [*kosmeō*] might be understood as "decorated" or "furnished." The picture is not of a house that is desolate with bare walls and no furniture. Rather, the opposite is true. It is ready to be lived in Such is the nature of our human hearts. They are prepared for spiritual habitation.

## SIGN OF JONAH

Lk 11:29-32 *with*
Mt 12:39

[29]As the crowds increased, Jesus said, "This is a wicked {and adulterous[MT]} generation. It asks for a miraculous sign, but none will be given it except the sign of Jonah. [30]For as Jonah was a sign to the Ninevites, so also will the Son of Man be to this generation. [31]The Queen of the South will rise at the judgment with the men of this generation and condemn them; for she came from the ends of the earth to listen to Solomon's wisdom, and now one[a] greater than Solomon is here. [32]The men of Nineveh will stand up at the judgment with this generation and condemn it; for they repented at the preaching of Jonah, and now one greater than Jonah is here.

[a]*31 Or something;* also in verse 32

[vv. 29-32 = Mt 12:38-42, see comments on § 62]

Things are really heating up now. The crowds gather around to check out the hubbub. Jesus has just answered the accusation made about him in verse 15. Now he gets back to the request that some others in the crowd made — for a sign from heaven, v. 16.

How dare they ask for a sign from heaven! Oh, there is nothing wrong with wanting a little verification. That was the whole purpose of miracles (cf. Jn 20:31). Jesus has already done a slug of miracles. Why on earth would they ask for more? Precisely because they are bent on unbelief.

Now, this is surprising since they are supposedly the people of God. Even pagans know better than that. For instance, the Ninevites and the Queen of Sheba knew a good thing when they heard it. Yet these Jews stand here blaspheming Jesus. Their shameful behavior will be exposed on judgment day even by these pagans. They will get a sign, alright. It won't be from heaven. It will be from the belly of the earth when Jesus resurrects.[10]

Lk 11:33-36

[33]"No one lights a lamp and puts it in a place where it will be hidden, or under a bowl. Instead he puts it on its stand, so that those who come in may see the light. [34]Your eye is the lamp of your body. When your eyes are good, your whole body also is full of light. But when they are bad, your body also is full of darkness. [35]See to it, then, that the light within you is not darkness. [36]Therefore, if your whole body is full of light, and no part of it dark, it will be completely lighted, as when the light of a lamp shines on you."

[v. 33 = Mt 5:15, see comments on § 54c]
[vv. 34-36 = Mt 6:22-23, see comments on § 54g]

---

[10]E.H. Merrill, "The Sign of Jonah," *JETS* 23/1 (1980): 23-30.

Jesus teaches that the lamp of the body is the eye. Yet eyes don't produce the light.[11] Rather, they are the vehicle through which light enters the body. Jesus is the light. And he's right before their very eyes. Most people love light. In fact, they put lamps on stands so they can light up the whole house. These guys are trying to "put him out." Their eyes are beholding the light of the world, yet their bodies are not being enlightened because their eyes are bad. They have blinders on. Their shades are pulled to keep out the light. They demonstrate their blindness by seeking yet another sign and ignoring those already given.[12] In a nutshell Jesus says, "Open your eyes and take an honest look at me! I will shine in you if you allow me in" (cf. Eph. 5:13,14). We can either open our eyes and be enlightened (v. 36), or we can shut our eyes and become blind and dark (v. 34). "There is none so blind as those who will not see."

With this, Jesus concludes his argument. So Luke ends with talk about light. Matthew's presentation ends with talk about fruit (Mt 12:33-37). In both narratives, Jesus ties a knot on the encounter by distinguishing between the motives of those who listen and those who won't.

This is now the third event in Jesus' later Judean ministry which parallels an event in his Galilean ministry (cf. § 102a & 106). It would appear that Jesus is now doing in the southern country what he did up in Galilee. Since his time is running out, he must move more quickly.

In section 77 we watched as Jesus quarreled with the Pharisees about this very issue of ceremonial washing up in Galilee. Matthew 15:1 and Mark 7:1 identified them as Pharisees from Jerusalem. Therefore, this may very well be the same group of guys that accosted Jesus before, only this time they have home-court advantage.[13]

**§ 107**
**Woes to the**
**Pharisees and**
**Teachers of the**
**Law**
(Lk 11:37-54;
cf. § 77 & 137a)

---

[11]The ancient Greek and Hebrew understanding of vision was that the eye did, in fact, produce light (cf. Plato, *Timaeus*, 45b-46a). For a summary of ancient testimony see D.C. Allison, "The Eye is the Lamp of the Body," *NTS* 33 (1987): 61-83.

[12]S.R. Garrett, "Lest the Light in You be Darkness": Luke 11:33-36 and the Question of Commitment," *JBL* 110/1 (1991): 93-105.

[13]There are approximately nineteen pericopes in which Jesus confronts the Pharisees (Mt 9:32-34; 12:22-24; 21:33-46; 22:31-40; 22:41-46; 23:1-36; Mk 2:15-17; 2:23-26; 3:1-6; 7:1-8; 8:11-13; 10:2-9; 12:13-17; Lk 5:17-26; 7:36-50; 14:1-6; 15:1-7; 16:14-15; 17:20-21; 19:37-40). These controversies may reflect the continuing debate between Christians and the Pharisees after the fall of Jerusalem in A.D. 70 (cf. R. A. Wild, "The Encounter Between Pharisaic and Christian Judaism: Some Early Gospel Evidence," *NovT* 27/2 [1985]: 105-124).

The Pharisees were the religious right-wing. Originally they were a group of laymen who sought to separate themselves from the impurity of their society by applying OT principles to all aspects of their lives. Their motives, at first, were very good. However, in their zeal for purity they built a "hedge about the law" through many and minute oral traditions. Unfortunately, the further they went, the more interested they became in rituals and the less interested they became in people. This led to the kind of corruption that Jesus is about to rebuke.

Because Jesus did not follow their rules (i.e., the oral traditions) in Sabbath regulations, ritual washings, and fasting, he became a frequent target for their criticism and schemes:

1. They charged Jesus with blasphemy when he claimed to forgive sins (Mt 9:3ff; Mk 6:2ff; Lk 5:21).
2. They scorned his frequent friendship with sinners (Mt 9:11; Mk 2:16; Lk 5:30; 15:1).
3. They accused him of breaking their oral traditions by not fasting (Lk 5:33); violating Sabbath regulations (Mt 12:2, 10; Mk 2:23; 3:2; Lk 6:5-7; 13:14ff; Jn 5:10-18; 9:13); and not washing (Mt 15:1-20; Mk 7:1-23; Lk 11:37-41).
4. They accused Jesus of working for/under Satan (Beelzebub) (Mt 9:34; 11:19; 12:24ff; Mk 3:22; Lk 11:14).
5. They charged him with deception (Mt 27:62ff; Jn 7:12), sedition against Rome (Mt 27:18; Lk 23:1-2), and threatening to destroy the temple (Mt 26:59-61; 27:39-40; Jn 2:19).
6. They mocked him (Jn 7:48), even calling him a Samaritan and demon-possessed (Jn 8:48).
7. They aligned themselves both with the Herodians (Mk 3:6) and with the Sadducees (Mt 16:1) to trap (Lk 11:53-54), arrest (Jn 7:30-32, 44-45; 8:20), and kill Jesus (Mt 27:62; Jn 8:59; 18:3).

Lk 11:37

[37]When Jesus had finished speaking, a Pharisee invited him to eat with him; so he went in and reclined at the table.

Jesus is invited to brunch.[14] This is somewhat odd considering the animosity between Jesus and the Pharisees. Perhaps he secretly desires to trap Jesus and hides his desire behind a hospitable invitation. After all, in just a little bit, the pharisaic party will openly attempt to trap Jesus (vv. 53-54). On the other hand, the Feast of Tabernacles had driven a wedge between the Jewish leaders. Many of them believe in Jesus and

---

[14]This *ariston* was likely served between 10 and 11 a.m., right after morning prayers (cf. Lk 14:12).

many others are taking an honest look at him (Jn 7:45-52; 10:19-21; cf. 12:42). We can't really be sure where this Pharisee is. He may not even know himself.

It seems kind of rude to be invited to someone's house for dinner and then rip his party apart like this. But based on their previous encounters, Jesus is more than justified for such a strong and straight discourse against the Pharisees. In about four months, Jesus will repeat, in almost identical words, much of this present rebuke in the temple itself, the Tuesday before he is murdered (Mt 23).

Lk 11:38-41

[38]But the Pharisee, noticing that Jesus did not first wash before the meal, was surprised. [39]Then the Lord said to him, "Now then, you Pharisees clean the outside of the cup and dish, but inside you are full of greed and wickedness. [40]You foolish people! Did not the one who made the outside make the inside also? [41]But give what is inside ⌊the dish⌋[a] to the poor, and everything will be clean for you. [cf. Mt 23:25-26]

[a]41 Or *what you have*

Jesus didn't wash before he ate. This washing was not for physical cleansing but for ceremonial cleansing. Furthermore, it was not a regulation of the Scriptures but a tradition of the Elders. All the Jews were supposed to wash their hands with at least a half an eggshell of water, poured over the hands with the fingers pointing down so as to wash the sin off the hands downward rather that washing them up your sleeves (cf. Butler, p. 239). They accuse Jesus of ritual uncleanness. Jesus accuses them of spiritual uncleanness. They are clean on the outside but filthy on the inside. Jesus' teaching is clear and simple: Clean up the inside and your outside will be clean too.[15]

Verse 41 creates a problem for the translator. There are several possibilities: (a) "Give the inward things as alms/charity . . ." (b) "Care for the inward things . . ." (c) "Give alms to the inward things." Nevertheless, the meaning of Jesus' statement is clear: Clean up the inside and the outside will be clean as well. How do we clean up the inside? By giving our wealth to the poor. Jesus, sitting at this sumptuous banquet, suggests this Pharisee's time and money would be better spent on benevolence to the poor than ostentatious show. If you think that's rude, just wait until you hear what Jesus says next!

---

[15]J. Neusner, "'First Cleanse the Inside,'" *NTS* 22 (1975-76): 486-495, explains the complex Halakhic background of this particular rule.

Lk 11:42-44

⁴²"Woe to you Pharisees, because you give God a tenth of your mint, rue and all other kinds of garden herbs, but you neglect justice and the love of God. You should have practiced the latter without leaving the former undone. [cf. Mt 23:23]
⁴³"Woe to you Pharisees, because you love the most important seats in the synagogues and greetings in the marketplaces [cf. Mt 23:6-7].
⁴⁴"Woe to you, because you are like unmarked graves, which men walk over without knowing it." [cf. Mt 23:27-28]

WOE #1: MAJORING IN THE MINORS, MINORING IN THE MAJORS. The Pharisees were careful to tithe even their garden herbs. The picture is ridiculous — a long-robed, phylactery-laden cleric out in his yard counting rue[16] or mint leaves. Matthew 23:24 says it well, "You blind guides, you strain out the gnat and swallow the camel." How proficient we often become in perfecting the little niceties and ignoring the major truths. There are no more important characteristics of God than his justice and his love. How often we ignore them for minutiae. We have perfected the use of the microscope and forgotten about the telescope.

WOE #2: SELF-AGGRANDIZEMENT. These guys are concerned about titles. They love it when their very presence brings a hush over the crowd. They demand doors be opened to them and peons move out of their way to let them to the front of the line. They have worked hard for their places of honor and are going to see that they get it.

WOE #3: UNMARKED TOMBS. For a Jew, one of the quickest ways to become defiled is to touch a dead body. That includes stepping on a tomb (cf. Num 19:16). These Pharisees walk about defiling people as if they were unmarked tombs. The crowds encounter their religious leaders without ever knowing they are becoming defiled. Faithless clergy unwittingly spread their disease of unbelief. The laity trust in their leadership, but it leads them to destruction, not salvation.

Lk 11:45-46

⁴⁵One of the experts in the law answered him, "Teacher, when you say these things, you insult us also."
⁴⁶Jesus replied, "And you experts in the law, woe to you, because you load people down with burdens they can hardly carry, and you yourselves will not lift one finger to help them" [cf. Mt 23:4].

The scribes, or lawyers, were usually also Pharisees. Just as cardiologists are specialized doctors, so the scribes were expert Pharisees. They were the upper crust. They felt superior, not only to the general populace, but even to the other Pharisees. It was their job to copy, interpret and answer questions about the Mosaic law. Since they spent so much time

---

[16]"Rue was a small shrub about two feet high, and is said to have been used to flavor wine, and for medicinal purposes" (McGarvey, p. 313).

with the OT text, they were the scholars, the Bible answer men. As is often the case, this knowledge and intellect led to arrogance. Jesus is berating the Pharisees without making a distinction between them and the scribes. That is a little too close to home. So this scribe asks Jesus to differentiate between the two groups. Jesus never pulls a punch . . . watch!

WOE #4: LOADING BURDENS DIFFICULT TO BEAR. Since they know the law so well, they are the ones to enforce and bind the law on the general populace. Since they are experts, they can find loopholes for themselves. However, they won't expend even the slightest effort to help others with their burden. Luke uses a medical term for "lift a finger," which means to touch lightly a sore place or to touch to find a pulse. These scribes will not even lightly touch the loads they mercilessly cast on other people.

[47]"Woe to you, because you build tombs for the prophets, and it was your forefathers who killed them. [48]So you testify that you approve of what your forefathers did; they killed the prophets, and you build their tombs. [49]Because of this, God in his wisdom said, 'I will send them prophets and apostles, some of whom they will kill and others they will persecute.' [50]Therefore this generation will be held responsible for the blood of all the prophets that has been shed since the beginning of the world, [51]from the blood of Abel to the blood of Zechariah, who was killed between the altar and the sanctuary. Yes, I tell you, this generation will be held responsible for it all" [cf. Mt 23:29-36].

Lk 11:47-51

WOE #5: KILLING THE PROPHETS. Being a son implied taking on the same characteristics, occupation, and philosophy of your father. As their ancestors had killed and beaten many of the prophets, so these scribes would have done the same thing (cf. 1 Kgs 19:10, 14; Jer 7:25-26; Mal 3:10). And in the case of Jesus, they will demonstrate the same hatred of truth and stubbornness of heart that their forefathers taught them.

They deny being prophet killers. They say, "We would never have killed the prophets. Indeed, we are honoring the prophets by building elaborate tombs in their memory." But Jesus says these elaborate tombs are extensions of their fathers' work, not an objection to it.

The words, "God in his wisdom said," are not found in the OT. Jesus is not quoting Scripture, but creating it. He is relating what God said to him personally. Because this generation killed Jesus, the fulfillment of all prophets, they stood guilty of the blood of Jesus as well as all the others.[17] By killing Jesus, they summarized all the murders and beatings

---

[17]Abel represents the first martyr. Zechariah represents the last OT martyr, according to the canonical order of the OT books (see notes on Mt 23:33-36, § 137a). It would be like

of their forefathers. Their heinous act was the pinnacle of rebellion against God.

Lk 11:52-53

⁵²"Woe to you experts in the law, because you have taken away the key to knowledge. You yourselves have not entered, and you have hindered those who were entering." [cf. Mt 23:13]

⁵³When Jesus left there, the Pharisees and the teachers of the law began to oppose him fiercely and to besiege him with questions, ⁵⁴waiting to catch him in something he might say.

WOE #6: HIDDEN KEYS. The scribes had the keys of knowledge which allowed people to enter the kingdom. In other words, they knew (or should have known) the correct interpretation of the Scriptures. But they kept it hidden, neither entering themselves nor allowing others to enter.

Jesus identifies the Pharisees' major problems. These six pitfalls are not so different than those of today's clergy. One might call them "occupational hazards."[18]

As Jesus leaves the house, the Pharisees and scribes go after him. They are trying to defend their own intelligence and credibility, by discrediting Jesus. After all, he had no formal education. He should be easy to defeat. But Jesus defies their understanding and preconceived ideas. He wins at all levels.

**§ 108a**
**Warnings and**
**Promises for**
**Disciples**
**(Lk 12:1-12)**

Once again we notice that Luke's words are also found in Matthew (and Mark) in the Galilean ministry. This may mean Matthew and/or Luke edited some accounts together to come up with their own story line. But a more natural explanation is that Jesus said many of the same things at least twice. So the same words can describe equally well the gist of what he said in both Galilee and Judea.

Lk 12:1

¹Meanwhile, when a crowd of many thousands had gathered, so that they were trampling on one another, Jesus began to speak first to his disciples, saying: "Be on your guard against the yeast of the Pharisees, which is hypocrisy."

News spread fast of Jesus' big blowout at the Pharisee's house (§ 107). Often the community was allowed to sit in and observe these feasts. So it

---

us saying, "From Genesis to Revelation." Or we might use the English translation for our advantage and say, "All the prophets, from A-Z."

[18]Liefeld (p. 956) labels them as follows: Hypocrisy (vv. 39-41), imbalance (v. 42), ostentation (v. 43), impossible demands (v. 46), intolerance (vv. 47-51), and exclusiveness (v. 52).

is no real surprise that a large crowd assembles when they hear the news of this heavyweight bout. The word Luke uses to describe this multitude (*myriadon*) is also found in Acts 21:20. (There it refers to many thousands of Jews who had accepted Christ.) This may be the largest crowd found in the Gospels. And they are not passive. They walk all over each other trying to get a front row seat.

Even the inner circle of disciples are still simmering over this confrontation. Jesus first addresses his closest followers, warning them against the leaven of the Pharisees. He uses the same words which he spoke after a similar confrontation back in Galilee (Mt 16:5-6; Mk 8:14-15; § 81a). This leaven, pervasive in influence, is the hypocrisy of the Pharisees.[19] McGarvey (p. 316) says hypocrisy "causes the bad man to hide his badness for fear of the good man, and the good man to hide his goodness for fear of the bad man."

[2]"There is nothing concealed that will not be disclosed, or hidden that will not be made known. [3]What you have said in the dark will be heard in the daylight, and what you have whispered in the ear in the inner rooms will be proclaimed from the roofs.

[4]"I tell you, my friends, do not be afraid of those who kill the body and after that can do no more. [5]But I will show you whom you should fear: Fear him who, after the killing of the body, has power to throw you into hell. Yes, I tell you, fear him. [6]Are not five sparrows sold for two pennies[a]? Yet not one of them is forgotten by God. [7]Indeed, the very hairs of your head are all numbered. Don't be afraid; you are worth more than many sparrows.

[8]"I tell you, whoever acknowledges me before men, the Son of Man will also acknowledge him before the angels of God. [9]But he who disowns me before men will be disowned before the angels of God."

[a]6 Greek *two assaria*

Lk 12:2-9

[vv. 2-9 = Mt 10:26-33, see comments on § 70b]

Verses 2-3 are identical to Matthew 10:26-27, but the setting is different. In Matthew, Jesus is saying, "Don't be afraid to speak out for me

---

[19]C.L. Mitton points out that yeast and leaven are different. Leaven was a lump of dough with yeast in it. Part of it was saved and "cured" for the next baking. By that time it had fermented and could be mixed with the new batch of dough to cause it to rise. Each year, during the feast of unleavened bread, the entire community got rid of all their leaven. This "renewal" of leaven prevented disease from spreading. Based on this practice, leaven is used figuratively in four ways in the NT: (1) Leaven of the Pharisees, Sadducees and Herod (Mt 8:15; 16:6; Lk 12:1). (2) The kingdom of God grows like leaven (Mt 13:33; Lk 13:21). (3) "A little leaven leavens the whole lump" (Gal 5:9; 1 Cor 5:5). (4) Renewal of the Christian life (1 Cor 5:6-7). See C.L. Mitton, "Leaven," *ExpT* (1972-73): 339-343.

in the face of opposition and persecution." What Jesus told the Apostles in private they are now to preach publicly. Here in Luke, the subject is our "hidden commitments." The Pharisee in Luke 11 who invites Jesus to dinner acts like a friend. But his hidden commitments come out by vv. 53-54. Likewise, the Pharisees will rally together with the Sadducees and Herodians to execute Jesus within four months. Since the crowds like Jesus, these Pharisees must treat him with civility in public. But their private animosity and criticism will not long be hidden.

Jesus knows about their death plots. But that is not so scary. All the Pharisees can do is kill the body. Eternity is still in the hands of the Father. The question is, do you cower to bullies who can kill you, or to God who can cast you into hell?[20] The disciples will have to answer that question for themselves soon enough. To help them make their decision, Jesus reminds them that God loves them immensely. In fact, he has even numbered the hairs of their heads. If God watches over the little sparrows, how much more will he protect his precious children? That's the promise. On the other side of the coin is a warning: If you choose to deny Jesus on earth, even because of lethal opposition, he will deny you in heaven. The conclusion: Don't fear men who hate you. Rather, fear the Father who loves you.

Lk 12:10-12

[10]"And everyone who speaks a word against the Son of Man will be forgiven, but anyone who blasphemes against the Holy Spirit will not be forgiven.

[11]"When you are brought before synagogues, rulers and authorities, do not worry about how you will defend yourselves or what you will say, [12]for the Holy Spirit will teach you at that time what you should say."

[v. 10 = Mt 12:31-32; Mk 3:28-30, see comments on § 61]
[vv. 11-12 = Mt 10:18-20 (cf. Mk 13:11 & Lk 21:14-15), see comments on § 70b]

We're still talking about choosing sides. Jesus gives another warning and another promise. Warning: If you speak out against Jesus, it is blasphemy. Fortunately, it's forgivable. You see, it is somewhat understandable that one would misunderstand the incarnation. It is, after all, an incredible concept. The problem is, they are not just rejecting Jesus, but

---

[20]H.K. Moulton, "Luke 12:5," *BT* 25 (1974): 246-247, makes an interesting point. The word "He" (referring to God, RSV), is not in the Greek text. Hence this verse could be rendered, "Fear the one who can cast you into hell after *they have done* the killing." In other words, God is not responsible for the killing, wicked men are. This argument has some weight to it since "the verb *apokteino*, I kill, occurs 74 times, and never once is God the subject, except indirectly in Rev. 2:23 and 19:21" (p. 247).

the Holy Spirit who is validating Jesus through signs and wonders. Now we're going clear back to the exorcism of 11:14-15. Remember how some said Jesus did it by the power of Beelzebub? They said Jesus' works were done by an evil spirit when, in fact, they were done by the Holy Spirit. It's not that the Holy Spirit gets his feelings hurt and refuses to forgive anyone who insults him. Rather, they have already rejected Jesus and the Scriptures that speak of him. The last knot in their rope of hope is the Holy Spirit. If they dismiss him, it's a long way down!

So the Pharisees stand opposed to Jesus AND the Holy Spirit. On the other side of the fence were disciples who were ready to follow Jesus. If they do, they are walking into a hornet's nest. They will encounter the same violent opposition facing Jesus right now. They will be arrested and brought before religious and civil authorities. They are not prepared to handle that kind of confrontation. So, here's the promise: "Don't worry. The Holy Spirit will intervene and give you the right words at the right time."

[13]Someone in the crowd said to him, "Teacher, tell my brother to divide the inheritance with me."

[14]Jesus replied, "Man, who appointed me a judge or an arbiter between you?" [15]Then he said to them, "Watch out! Be on your guard against all kinds of greed; a man's life does not consist in the abundance of his possessions."

**§ 108b**
**Warnings on**
**Wealth and**
**Worry**
(Lk 12:13-34)

It was not uncommon for great rabbis to be consulted about civil matters. After all, the Jews did not separate civil and religious affairs. Because Jesus was not officially part of the religio-political structure, he did not technically have the legal authority to order this man to pay his brother his share of the inheritance. However, Jesus did have both authority from God and credibility with the crowds. He could have forced this brother to pay. But that would have derailed his ministry.

Jesus is not unconcerned about finances or civil justice. But he is not willing for these things to take priority over his ministry as Messiah. He is unwilling to "take the case" which would almost surely result in an avalanche of similar requests and further the misconceptions of a political Messiah.[21]

He speaks, rather, to the motive of the man, which is most likely evil. There were definite laws concerning the inheritance. If the man has a legitimate case then it could most likely be won through the proper channels. Instead, it looks like the man is trying to swindle what is not

---

[21]Cf. T. Gorringe, "A Zealot Option Rejected? Luke 12:13-14," *ExpT* 98 (1986-87): 267-270.

his by making a boisterous demand for it. It is quite possible that he is a younger brother, protesting the eldest brother's double portion which was his God-given right.

Greed, or covetousness, is literally, "wanting-more-ish-ness." It is the insatiable desire for excess. How convicted must those of us be who fill our homes with trinkets and gadgets, all the while convincing ourselves that we must have them. As Jesus says, life does not consist of or stem from what we have, but from our relationship with God.

Lk 12:16-21

¹⁶And he told them this parable: "The ground of a certain rich man produced a good crop. ¹⁷He thought to himself, 'What shall I do? I have no place to store my crops.'

¹⁸"Then he said, 'This is what I'll do. I will tear down my barns and build bigger ones, and there I will store all my grain and my goods. ¹⁹And I'll say to myself, "You have plenty of good things laid up for many years. Take life easy; eat, drink and be merry."'

²⁰"But God said to him, 'You fool! This very night your life will be demanded from you. Then who will get what you have prepared for yourself?'

²¹"This is how it will be with anyone who stores up things for himself but is not rich toward God."

Such are men who plan carefully, deal wisely, store shrewdly, but do not place investments in spiritual things. At just the time he can comfort himself in all his luxury (v. 19), God demands his soul. The Bible considers such a man a fool. It is not that he is stupid, but that his priorities are mixed around. Rather than investing in financial security, we ought to invest in eternity.

When he dies, all these stores of grain will go to his heir(s). Who knows whether they will be managed well or squandered? Many fortunes have been lost by the reckless management of an heir. Ecclesiastes 2:18-19 says, "I hated all the things I had toiled for under the sun, because I must leave them to the one who comes after me. And who knows whether he will be a wise man or a fool? Yet he will have control over all the work into which I have poured my effort and skill under the sun. This too is meaningless." The quality of our earthly labors is most clearly seen with a tombstone in front of it.

Lk 12:22-32

²²Then Jesus said to his disciples: "Therefore I tell you, do not worry about your life, what you will eat; or about your body, what you will wear. ²³Life is more than food, and the body more than clothes. ²⁴Consider the ravens: They do not sow or reap, they have no storeroom or barn; yet God feeds them. And how much more valuable you are than birds! ²⁵Who of you by worrying can add a single hour to his life? ²⁶Since you cannot do this very little thing, why do you worry about the rest?"

[27]"Consider how the lilies grow. They do not labor or spin. Yet I tell you, not even Solomon in all his splendor was dressed like one of these. [28]If that is how God clothes the grass of the field, which is here today, and tomorrow is thrown into the fire, how much more will he clothe you, O you of little faith! [29]And do not set your heart on what you will eat or drink; do not worry about it. [30]For the pagan world runs after all such things, and your Father knows that you need them. [31]But seek his kingdom, and these things will be given to you as well.

[32]"Do not be afraid, little flock, for your Father has been pleased to give you the kingdom."

*[a]25 Or single cubit to his height*

[vv. 22-32 = Mt 6:25-34, see comments on § 54g]

The crowds are allowed to eavesdrop, but Jesus' words are directed primarily to his followers. Those who have been with him for a while have already heard this sermon.[22] Aside from a few minor variations, the words and message are identical to Matthew 6:25-34 in the Sermon on the Mount.[23] Apparently this is a difficult lesson. Jesus had to repeat himself to get his point across. Simply put, we are not to worry about wealth but about the kingdom of God.

This young man who asks Jesus to settle his inheritance dispute is a good example of how NOT to live. The rich farmer in Jesus' parable is another good example of how NOT to live. Both of them are consumed with wealth rather than the kingdom. So Jesus said, "Don't worry about

---

[22]The identical wording of Mt 6:25-34 and Lk 12:22-34 does not necessarily indicate that one of them copied the other and changed the words around. (The words of Luke 12:22-31 follow those of Lk 12:32-34 in Matthew's arrangement). It is more likely that the words of Jesus were memorized and passed on orally with little or no variation. Then Matthew and Luke wrote these words down. But they are in two different sermons. This is not surprising. First, Jesus was an itinerant preacher, and money is a subject that merits repetition. Thus, Jesus said these same things on a number of occasions. Second, both sermons are too short to be word for word renditions of Jesus' entire sermon. Hence, both passages use identical words to give an accurate synopsis of what Jesus said on two different occasions.

[23]The following are the minor changes between Matthew and Luke:
1. Luke uses "consider" (v. 24) rather than "see." For Luke this is more than a casual glance. It requires contemplative meditation to understand God's care for humans above the birds.
2. Luke uses "raven" (v. 24) rather than "birds." A raven was an unclean animal in the OT (Lev 11:15). Perhaps Jesus' use of the word "raven" would subtly suggest God's care for even the unclean things of the world (i.e., people). Luke, as a Gentile, would be interested in that!
3. Instead of the talk about not worrying for tomorrow, Luke says, "Do not be afraid, little flock, for your Father has been pleased to give you the kingdom." This is more tender and demonstrates Luke's characteristic concern for the least and the lost.

wealth, God will take care of it." He uses two illustrations to show just how. We worry so much about food. But take the ravens as an example. God even feeds these unclean birds! How much more will he feed the people he loves so dearly? We also fret over our clothes. But look at the wild flowers. They are beautiful! If God robes such transitory flowers with such beauty, how much more will he take care of you?!

We must not worry. Why? Well, for one thing, it is practical atheism. It shouts our doubts in the goodness of God. He says he will care for us out of his great love. But our worry calls him a liar. This makes us look like the pagans who do not know God (v. 30). Second, worry accomplishes nothing. It's like an old rocking chair that gives us something to do, but gets us nowhere. Jesus said it won't even add a single hour to your life. The figure of speech is literally, "It won't add 18 inches to your life-span." Mixing the metaphors of time and distance, we picture a man walking through life. He comes to the end. All his worry won't even give him one more step. In fact, it's likely to take a few steps off! Third, we can only pursue one thing at a time. When we run after wealth, we cannot pursue God (v. 31, cf. Mt 6:24).

Lk 12:33-34

³³"Sell your possessions and give to the poor. Provide purses for yourselves that will not wear out, a treasure in heaven that will not be exhausted, where no thief comes near and no moth destroys. ³⁴For where your treasure is, there your heart will be also."

[vv. 33-34 = Mt 6:19-21, see comments on § 54g]

Luke 12:33 complements Matthew 6:19. Instead of laying up treasures for ourselves (Mt 6:19), we are called to take those same possessions, sell them, and give the proceeds to the poor (Lk 12:33). That is the means by which we invest in our own account in heaven.

This is not the same as our garage sales. When we sell our goods, it is at severely reduced rates in pawn shops and auctions. For us, real financial security is in banks and bonds. In Jesus' day, their real financial security was in stores of jewels, cloth, precious metals, flocks and stores of food. When they sold these possessions it was at the current rate of exchange, not 10% of its original value.

Brought up to the twenty-first century, what Jesus is suggesting is that we don't keep stockpiling for our own financial future when there are people out there who need our help today. Furthermore, his words are not figurative. Jesus speaks literally when he says that we make financial investments into our eternal future through benevolence now. Truly, we can't take it with us, but we can send it on ahead (vv. 16-21)!

Is it primarily for the benefit of the poor that we sell our possessions? We think not. Our meager contributions will hardly eradicate poverty. It will always be around (Deut 15:11; Mt 26:11). Primarily, Jesus is speaking to the disciples for their own benefit. They need to be released from the encumbrance of material things. Wealth is a great danger to the Christian. It confuses the mind, blinds the heart and distorts proper priorities.

Now, Jesus did not say, or imply, that we are to sell all our possessions. But certainly we need to live by humble means, giving the rest to the poor. We are expected to earn our own living and work if we are able (Prov 6:6-8; 2 Cor 12:14; 1 Tim 5:8; 2 Thess 3:6-15; 1 Thess 4:10-12; Col 3:22-25; Eph 6:5-9). This would include providing for our own living: Home, clothes, transportation; as well as that of our families (1 Tim. 5:8). We need a balance. As Proverbs 30:8-9 states, "Give me neither poverty nor riches, but give me only my daily bread. Otherwise, I may have too much and disown you and say, 'Who is the Lord?' Or I may become poor and steal, and so dishonor the name of my God."

In conclusion, we are not being called to monasticism or self-abnegation. What Jesus is saying is simple:

1. Real life is not in our stores of wealth (vv. 22-23).
2. Don't worry about your basic needs, God will provide. He knows you need all these things (vv. 24-30).
3. Spend your time seeking spiritual things (vv. 31-32).
4. Give your excess away so that you can invest in eternal treasures (vv. 33-34).

We can only give our attention to so many things. In the previous passage, Jesus warns about giving our attention to earthly wealth. Here he gives the positive alternative: Give your attention to Jesus' coming. This material is similar to that found in the Olivet Discourse (Mt. 24:45-51), which clearly speaks of the Second Coming of Christ. But here it may refer more immediately to the impending cross of Christ.

**§ 108c
Warning: Be
Prepared for
Jesus' Coming
(Lk 12:35-48)**

[35]"Be dressed ready for service and keep your lamps burning, [36]like men waiting for their master to return from a wedding banquet, so that when he comes and knocks they can immediately open the door for him. [37]It will be good for those servants whose master finds them watching when he comes. I tell you the truth, he will dress himself to serve, will have them recline at the table and will come and wait on them. [38]It will be good for those servants whose master finds them ready, even if he comes in the second or third watch of the night."

Lk 12:35-38

To be "dressed ready for service" was more than wearing a cummerbund. The word "dressed" is actually "gird your loins." The men in Palestine wore long, flowing robes which would get tangled up in their legs when they tried to work. The solution was to reach down between your ankles, gather up the bottom half of the robe and tuck it into the front of your sash (belt). It looked like a huge diaper. But at least you were then ready to work, run or fight (cf. 1 Kgs 18:46; also Eph 6:14 and 1 Pet 1:13). Furthermore, the verb "be" is a present imperative, indicating continued action. Thus, we are to continually be dressed — continually prepared — to serve the Master.

Not only are we to "gird our loins," we are to keep our lamps lit (cf. Mt 25:1-13). These "lamps" were small dishes which could be held in the palm of your hand. You would simply fill the dish with oil and lay a wick in a groove made for the purpose. These little lamps were quite portable. But you had to take care to keep the wick trimmed and the bowl filled with oil.

Both being dressed and trimming your lamp was easy enough to do. But it did require diligence to stay prepared for the Master's arrival from the wedding banquet.[24] The word "return" (v. 36) means to "depart." It carries the connotation of breaking up camp. In other words, the wedding party is over and he is coming home with his new bride. There was no way to tell when the man might come home. The party could last a few hours or a few days. Therefore, the return of the Master might be deep into the night — the second or third watch (9 p.m. to 3 a.m.). It wasn't especially difficult, but it did take diligence. Likewise, those who wait diligently for Christ, even in the unexpected and uncomfortable times will receive a special blessing when he comes.

Once the Master of this parable does come home, there is an odd reversal of roles. The master was not supposed to serve the servants. That was just unheard of. But as a reward for their diligence, he does. This is precisely what Jesus did for us. The Son became the servant (cf. Lk 22:27; Jn 13:1-17).[25] This would only happen in the kingdom of God.

Lk 12:39-40

[39]"But understand this: If the owner of the house had known at what hour the thief was coming, he would not have let his house be broken into. [40]You also

---

[24]P.E. Deterding, in his provocative article, "Eschatological and Eucharistic Motifs in Luke 12:35-40" *CJ* (1979): 85-93, traces the motifs of Passover, the Messianic banquet, the parousia, and the Lord's Supper. He believes that they can all be found in this text. Thus, (a) Luke 12:35-40 predicts the Lord's Supper as well as the parousia, and (b) the Passover, Lord's Supper, and the Second Coming should be viewed in light of one another since they share similar motifs and metaphors.

[25]This is in contrast to Lk 17:7-10 where a different point is being made (Liefeld, p. 966).

must be ready, because the Son of Man will come at an hour when you do not expect him."

The words "broken into" are literally "dug through." Palestinian houses were built out of adobe-type bricks. Therefore it would be easier to dig through the wall than to break in the door. Now, if we knew when a thief was coming, it would be easy to keep him out (cf. Mt 24:42-44). Likewise, if we knew when Jesus was coming, it would be easy to be prepared for him. Our love for Jesus is not shown primarily in getting ready for his coming but in staying ready for his coming. He will come suddenly and unexpectedly (cf. Mt 24:36-25:30; 1 Thess 5:1-2; 2 Pet 3:10; Rev 3:3). We had better be prepared.

<sup></sup>

Lk 12:41-46

⁴¹Peter asked, "Lord, are you telling this parable to us, or to everyone?"

⁴²The Lord answered, "Who then is the faithful and wise manager, whom the master puts in charge of his servants to give them their food allowance at the proper time? ⁴³It will be good for that servant whom the master finds doing so when he returns. ⁴⁴I tell you the truth, he will put him in charge of all his possessions. ⁴⁵But suppose the servant says to himself, 'My master is taking a long time in coming,' and he then begins to beat the menservants and maidservants and to eat and drink and get drunk. ⁴⁶The master of that servant will come on a day when he does not expect him and at an hour he is not aware of. He will cut him to pieces and assign him a place with the unbelievers. "

Peter, in his typical style, acts as spokesman for the group. Jesus, in his typical style, answers Peter's question with a question (cf. Mt 24:45-51). Peter is really asking about position. That is, "Are we alone your special servants?" Jesus answers by speaking about responsibility. That is, "If I have given anyone responsibility he needs to see that it is carried out." It really does not matter if the servant is Peter alone, the Apostles alone or everyone standing there. The point is, if Jesus has given you a task, you'd better worry about keeping faithful to the task instead of worrying about what others are doing or have been given to do. Elsewhere, however, Jesus specifies that the command to watch applies to everyone (Mk 13:37).

In the kingdom of God, as in all successful organizations, those who execute responsibility well are given more and more responsibility. In a sense, Jesus is answering Peter's question about position. "Do your job well," says Jesus, "and you will be given more to do." As he says elsewhere, "He who is faithful in little will be given much" (Lk 16:10).

Responsibility is easy to carry out when the boss is watching and the first few minutes after he leaves. But when the boss is away for weeks or months at a time, it is easier to slip into irresponsibility. Then comes the true test of an employee's character. Likewise, in the realm of the kingdom of God, many have thought, "Jesus has been away so long. Surely I still have time to straighten up my life before the Lord returns." Read carefully and observe! Our love for Christ is not primarily shown in getting ready for his coming, but in staying ready for his coming.

This talk about cutting someone to pieces is surely hyperbole,[26] although it was not uncommon among ancient nations (cf. 1 Sam 4:12; Dan 2:5; Heb 11:37). Yet we must recognize that the characters in the story represent the false teachers and religious hypocrites who will endure eternal judgment (cf. Acts 20:29-30; Mt 7:15-23).

Lk 12:47-48

[47]"That servant who knows his master's will and does not get ready or does not do what his master wants will be beaten with many blows. [48]But the one who does not know and does things deserving punishment will be beaten with few blows. From everyone who has been given much, much will be demanded; and from the one who has been entrusted with much, much more will be asked."

High handed sin (cf. Num. 15:30-31) will be severely punished. Those who know better and still do wrong, or who know what is right and do not do it, will fall under heavy condemnation. Luke uses a savage word for "beat" which can also be translated "skin," "flay," or "flog."

Sins of ignorance (Num 15:27-29; Psa 19:12) will be punished lightly but will still be punished.[27] Why? Because the servant should

---

[26]P. Ellingworth, "Lk 12:46—Is There an Anti-Climax Here?" *BT* 31/2 (1980): 242-243, suggests that we soften such strong language by translating *dichotomesei* as: "Cut off *from God's people*." He suggests that this reflects Lev 17:10 and aligns better with the second half of Lk 12:46, ". . . and assign him a place with the unbelievers." But M. A. Beavis, "Ancient Slavery as an Interpretive Context for the N.T. Servant Parables with Special Reference to the Unjust Steward (Lk 16:1-8)" *JBL* 111/1 (1992): 37-54, shows that such savage language accurately describes the kind of treatment many slaves endured across the Roman Empire.

[27]This does not imply that the punishment will be pleasant or tolerable. It is still hell. But this does clearly seem to teach degrees of punishment. Some theologians have taken this to indicate a position called annihilationism (e.g., Clark Pinnock, John Stott, Edward Fudge, Michael Green, Russell Boatman). Basically, this position asserts that God will punish evildoers for an appropriate time in a literal hell and then their souls will be extinguished forever. The arguments for this position include: (1) Based on 1 Tim 6:15-16, human immortality is found only in connection with God's divine Spirit and a resurrected body (1 Cor 15:50-54). Thus, if humans are eternal in hell, God must sustain them there just as they are sustained here on earth. This would create an uncomfortable, eternal metaphysical dualism in which God would never completely redeem the universe. (2) The Bible teaches that sinners will be destroyed (Psa 37:2, 9-10, 20, 38; Mal 4:1-2; Mt 3:10-12; 10:28; Gal 6:8; 1 Cor 3:17; Rom 1:32; Phil 1:28; 3:19; 2 Pet 2:1, 3, 6; 3:6-7; etc.). While these passages may figuratively speak of eternal hell, so might the word "eternal" in other passages hyperbolically speak of utter and eternal annihilation (e.g., Mt 25:46; Mk 9:48; Rev 14:11). (3) Annihilationism pictures God as just, rather than a vindictive despot who creatively but sadistically tortures the damned well beyond any reasonable period of time. Thus, Annihilationism becomes an effective apologetic against those who charge God with being the author of an eternal Auschwitz.

have learned the master's will. All people know something of God (Rom 1:20), and will be judged according to their level of understanding (Rom 2:12-13). Ignorance is no excuse.

<sup>49</sup>"I have come to bring fire on the earth, and how I wish it were already kindled! <sup>50</sup>But I have a baptism to undergo, and how distressed I am until it is completed! <sup>51</sup>Do you think I came to bring peace on earth? No, I tell you, but division. <sup>52</sup>From now on there will be five in one family divided against each other, three against two and two against three. <sup>53</sup>They will be divided, father against son and son against father, mother against daughter and daughter against mother, mother-in-law against daughter-in-law and daughter-in-law against mother-in-law."

**§ 108d**
**Warning:**
**Trouble is**
**Coming**
(Lk 12:49-53)

[vv. 51-53 = Mt 10:34-36, see comments on § 70b]

Jesus brought all kinds of good things to the earth. But it was not all picnics and rose gardens. In this passage Jesus counts the cost for the world and for himself.

The cost for Jesus will be Calvary and all it entails: alienation from the Father, becoming sin for us, rejection by his own people, physical torture, public abuse, etc. Jesus calls it a baptism (cf. Mk 10:38-39), that is, an inundation in suffering.

The cost to the world is both fire and division. This fire almost certainly refers to judgment. Because Jesus was tortured, Jerusalem comes under God's curse (Mt 27:25; Lk 23:28-31). This will be clear enough in A.D. 70 when the city is destroyed. Even beyond that, Jesus is the judge (Jn 5:22, 27), and his words are the standard by which men are judged. While this fire signifies judgment, it can also include cleansing. That which is not burned by the fire will be purged by it.

The second cost to the world is that Jesus will cause divisions. Because there is no "neutral zone" with Jesus, he will divide even the most intimate family relationships. One must be decisively for him or against him. The result is tragic, but inevitable if we are to have the benefits he brings.

Jesus did bring peace on the earth (Lk 2:14; 7:50; 10:5), but his peace is only promised to Christians. Unbelievers can't have it. Furthermore, it is a peace of the inner life (Jn 14:27; 16:33), since Christians are often roughly handled in this hostile world. According to this passage, that rough treatment will sometimes come from family (cf. Micah 7:6).

§ 108e
Warning on
Interpreting the
Signs of the
Times
(Lk 12:54-59)

[54]He said to the crowd: "When you see a cloud rising in the west, immediately you say, 'It's going to rain,' and it does. [55]And when the south wind blows, you say, 'It's going to be hot,' and it is. [56]Hypocrites! You know how to interpret the appearance of the earth and the sky. How is it that you don't know how to interpret this present time?"

[vv. 54-56 = Mt 16:2-3, see comments on § 80]

In Judea, a cloud rising in the west means rain from the Mediterranean. A south wind coming up through the desert of the Negev brings a heat wave. Any amateur weatherman in Palestine knows that. Why are people so good at observing weather patterns but so poor at observing spiritual signs of the times? Anyone paying the least bit of attention will recognize Jesus, especially through his miracles and through the prophets. It's not that tough. The signs are obvious.

These signs have direct reference to Jesus' first coming, not his second. The emphasis on the Second Coming of Jesus is not to interpret the signs of the times but to live in readiness and hopeful expectation of the Master's return.

Lk 12:57-59

[57]"Why don't you judge for yourselves what is right? [58]As you are going with your adversary to the magistrate, try hard to be reconciled to him on the way, or he may drag you off to the judge, and the judge turn you over to the officer, and the officer throw you into prison. [59]I tell you, you will not get out until you have paid the last penny."[a]

[a]59 Greek lepton

[vv. 57-59 = Mt 5:25-26, see comments on § 54e]

While Matthew uses these words to talk about human relationships, Luke alludes to the divine. According to Matthew, we are to make friends with a litigating neighbor. In Luke, we are to make friends with the Christ who will take us before the Father (cf. Psa 2:12), either for adoption or for judgment. Time is ticking away. We had better reconcile quickly. We had better settle out of court!

§ 109
Repent or
Perish
(Lk 13:1-9)

REPENT OR PERISH; TURN OR BURN! These slogans are harsh and narrow, even repulsive. But they are also true and straight from the lips of Jesus. His warning is both clear and merciful. If someone is driving his car off a cliff, who would not shout, "REPENT OR PERISH." If the Scriptures are right, we must warn people about hell.

¹Now there were some present at that time who told Jesus about the Galileans whose blood Pilate had mixed with their sacrifices. ²Jesus answered, "Do you think that these Galileans were worse sinners than all the other Galileans because they suffered this way? ³I tell you, no! But unless you repent, you too will all perish. ⁴Or those eighteen who died when the tower in Siloam fell on them — do you think they were more guilty than all the others living in Jerusalem? ⁵I tell you, no! But unless you repent, you too will all perish."

Lk 13:1-5

Outside of Luke, there is no record of Pilate's massacre of these Galileans. Therefore, we have no specific details. We do know that Pilate governed Judea, a perilous area for revolt, from A.D. 26-36. He was in constant conflict with the Jews. "According to his contemporaries, Philo (*Embassy to Gaius* 38) and Josephus (*Antiquities* 18.55-62; *War* 2.169-174), Pontius Pilate was a cruel and violent man" (Evans, p. 205). He is no stranger to conflict with the Jews.

According to this passage, Pilate executed some Galilean rebels while they were in Jerusalem offering sacrifices.[28] That was done easily enough. The Roman garrison was stationed in the tower of Antonia at the N.W. corner of the temple. From their vantage point, they could survey the activities in the temple. Apparently these Galileans stepped out of bounds and the soldiers were ordered to slaughter them right inside the temple as they were performing their sacred sacrifices. That would be odious to the Jews. It sounds like these "tattletales" want Jesus to do something about it. After all, a real Messiah would certainly retaliate against Pilate.

Such an event would also be confusing to the Jews who believed that a person suffered because of sin. Perhaps they want Jesus to explain why such a bad thing happened to good people. Or perhaps they expect him to denounce his fellow Galileans as evil. But Jesus never does buy into that (cf. Jn 9:1-3). Rather, he teaches that judgment is universal and universally harsh. Jesus reiterates the point with a second example of a structural catastrophe at the Pool of Siloam (the details of which we are equally ignorant). Neither of these groups suffered because God was punishing them for sin. They were simply at the wrong place at the right time. Nevertheless, all of us will come under God's judgment unless we repent. And that will be worse than being slaughtered by a sword or crushed by a building.

⁶Then he told this parable: "A man had a fig tree, planted in his vineyard, and he went to look for fruit on it, but did not find any. ⁷So he said to the man who took care of the vineyard, 'For three years now I've been coming to look for fruit

Lk 13:6-9

---

[28]Josephus states that Galileans, in particular, were prone to revolt (Josephus, *Life* 92.17).

on this fig tree and haven't found any. Cut it down! Why should it use up the soil?'

⁸"'Sir,' the man replied, 'leave it alone for one more year, and I'll dig around it and fertilize it. ⁹If it bears fruit next year, fine! If not, then cut it down.'"

Jesus illustrates his previous teaching with a parable: Once upon a time there was a farmer who owned a vineyard. He augmented his grape crop by planting a few fruit trees among the vines. So far so good. He waited for this one fig tree to mature. It did. He waited for it to produce figs. It didn't. He waited a second year, and even a third. Nothing! It's time to cut it out and replace it with something more productive. The farmer's hired hand, who cared for the tree all this time, hates to see his hard work go to waste. So he pleads for a stay of execution for this fruit-less fig tree for just one more year. It's granted. But this will be its last chance.

This was a bad tree. Besides being unproductive, it sucked up valuable resources. Jesus' antagonists are just like that. Not only are they not bearing fruit by accepting Jesus; they are actually hindering his progress!

Like the tree in the story, we have been placed in good ground. Added to that, God has nourished us like a fertilized tree. Then God waits patiently, beyond any reasonable time, for us to produce fruit. Now God's patience is immense but not inexhaustible. He will not allow the "Christian" to remain unfruitful. Thus we come full circle: "REPENT OR PERISH." Judgment is coming on all — the eighteen who died in the collapse of the Tower of Siloam, the Galilean rebels offering their sacrifices in the temple, and everyone who bears no fruit.

**§ 110
Sabbath
Healing of a
Woman Bowed
Double**
(Lk 13:10-21)

Lk 13:10-13

Here we go again. We have yet another Sabbath controversy (cf. § 49-51). Jesus is in the synagogue, teaching on the Sabbath. He sees a woman with a physical need and moves to meet that need. However, as we have seen, healing was not allowed on the Sabbath according to the oral tradition. Thus, another big blowup is just around the corner.

¹⁰On a Sabbath Jesus was teaching in one of the synagogues, ¹¹and a woman was there who had been crippled by a spirit for eighteen years. She was bent over and could not straighten up at all. ¹²When Jesus saw her, he called her forward and said to her, "Woman, you are set free from your infirmity." ¹³Then he put his hands on her, and immediately she straightened up and praised God.

Jesus is apparently the guest lecturer for the day in this synagogue. It was common for the synagogue ruler to ask a guest, especially one as prominent as Jesus, to give the message of the day.

While Jesus preaches, he suddenly notices a "crippled" woman in the audience.[29] The word was a medical term for curvature of the spine.[30] Luke, the physician, notes that she has suffered this way for eighteen years. All of this seems normal enough. What is odd, however, is that this sickness is caused by a demon. We are not saying that this was the demon of "crippling," as if curvature of the spine is its specialty. Nor are we saying this is an exorcism rather than a healing. What we are suggesting is that physical problems can be the work of evil spirits beyond mere natural causes. This doesn't mean that we blame demons for every sniffle and hangnail, but the text seems clear enough. This problem is brought about by an evil spirit. And there are several examples in the OT of spirits controlling a particular condition of a human (spirit of a deep sleep, Isa 29:10; spirit of whoredoms, Hos 4:12, 19). If this is true, then healing of all types becomes a frontal attack of the kingdom of God against the work of the Devil (cf. Acts 10:38).[31]

Lk 13:14-16

[14]Indignant because Jesus had healed on the Sabbath, the synagogue ruler said to the people, "There are six days for work. So come and be healed on those days, not on the Sabbath."

[15]The Lord answered him, "You hypocrites! Doesn't each of you on the Sabbath untie his ox or donkey from the stall and lead it out to give it water? [16]Then should not this woman, a daughter of Abraham, whom Satan has kept bound for eighteen long years, be set free on the Sabbath day from what bound her?"

The ruler of the synagogue doesn't have the guts to speak to Jesus directly. Instead, he yells at the crowd. It's almost as if he is blaming the woman for coming and being healed. He is way out of line. First, the woman does not come to be healed. Jesus calls her out of the crowd. If anyone is to be blamed it is Jesus, not this poor woman. Second, he turns an occasion of celebration into a fight. Third, he is more concerned about nitpicky rules than the health and freedom of one of God's precious children.

The synagogue ruler is angry because the rules of the Sabbath, based on Exodus 20:9-10 — to do no work — have been violated. The traditions of the Pharisees clearly state that no action could be taken to heal

---

[29]The first word of this sentence *idou*, which means "behold," is left untranslated by the NIV. It seems to imply that Jesus suddenly noticed this woman's condition in the middle of his sermon. She was likely sitting with the other women, separated from the men.

[30]J. Wilkinson, "The Case of the Bent Woman in Luke 13:10-17," *EvQ* 49 (1977): 195-205.

[31]J. B. Green, "Jesus and a Daughter of Abraham (Lk 13:10-17): Test Case for a Lucan Perspective on Jesus' Miracles," *CBQ* 51 (1989): 643-654.

on the Sabbath beyond what was necessary to save someone's life. So if a person fell down a flight of stairs, for instance, you could stop the bleeding on the Sabbath, but you could not set their broken bones until the sun had gone down.

There are several important injunctions concerning the Sabbath: (a) Do no work, Exodus 20:9-10. (b) Do not plow or harvest, Exodus 34:21. (c) Do not kindle a fire, Exodus 35:3; Numbers 15:32-36. (d) Do not prepare food, Exodus 16:23. (e) Do not prepare wine, Nehemiah 13:15. (f) Do not carry a load, Nehemiah 13:15. (g) Do not trade or sell, Nehemiah 13:16; Amos 8:5. These, however, were not to be negative but positive. The Sabbath was given to man as a gift, not a punishment. It had a twofold purpose. First, it gave people an opportunity to rest. This was especially appealing to women and slaves. Second, it gave people an opportunity to worship. They were to recognize God's provisional care and to set aside a day specifically for him.[32]

Jesus now moves from the lesser to the greater. If the Pharisees could work in order to preserve an animal, certainly Jesus could work to renew a "Daughter of Abraham," that is, a Jewess. Of course, in a sense, Jesus is comparing apples to oranges. The Pharisees were doing only that which was necessary to preserve the life of their animals. And what Jesus does for this woman was nonessential. That is, it could have waited until the next day. So, according to pharisaic logic, Jesus is still guilty. But the whole point is that Jesus refuses to be subject to human logic and man-made traditions. He certainly would not forfeit an immediate opportunity to help someone in order to avoid offending a misguided and hypocritical system. It is incredible how insidious our hypocrisy can become in clerical robes.

Jesus also makes it clear that her sickness is being caused, or at least kept, by Satan. That is, one of his demons has held her captive for eighteen years in this physical infirmity. The fact that Jesus heals her points to the overpowering of Satan and the breaking in of the kingdom of God.[33]

---

[32]As Christians, we are not under the covenant of the law (Col 2:14; Gal 5:2-6; Eph 2:14-16; Rom 14:5-9). Therefore, we are not obligated to keep the Sabbath as a term of salvation. But it is still a gift to us, especially the continual Sabbath rest in the abiding presence of our Lord, Jesus Christ (Heb 4:9-11). Moreover, the Sabbath principle still applies to our lives. If we don't rest at regular intervals throughout our life, it will likely be taken off at the end in one lump sum.

[33]Luke has carefully crafted this section to show that this incident is paradigmatic for the restoration of Israel through the coming kingdom of God. This woman represents the true Israel, which is about to flourish in a kingdom like a mustard seed (Lk 13:18-21), in contrast to the unfruitful fig tree of Israel's religious establishment (Lk 13:6-9). The careful chiasm of Lk 12:49-13:35 highlights many of Luke's favorite themes, such as the

[17]When he said this, all his opponents were humiliated, but the people were delighted with all the wonderful things he was doing.

Lk 13:17

This was such a sound victory for Jesus that his opponents were immediately humiliated. They tucked their tails between their legs and scampered off. We are not told, but surely they redoubled their efforts to eliminate this troublemaker. This is, after all, precisely what they did the last time Jesus healed someone on the Sabbath (Mt 12:14; Mk 3:6; Lk 6:11). The crowd, on the other hand, loved these "wonderful things" (lit., "beautiful things"). They delighted in the healing of this woman, the exposing of hypocrisy and the breaking in of the kingdom of God. All in all, it was a good day.

[18]Then Jesus asked, "What is the kingdom of God like? What shall I compare it to? [19]It is like a mustard seed, which a man took and planted in his garden {field[MT]} {ground[MK]}. {[I]t is the smallest seed . . . [y]et when planted, it grows and becomes the largest of all garden plants.[MK]} It grew and became a tree, and the birds of the air perched in its branches."
[20]Again he asked, "What shall I compare the kingdom of God to? [21]It is like yeast that a woman took and mixed into a large amount[a] of flour until it worked all through the dough."

Lk 13:18-21 *with* Mt 13:31; Mk 4:31-32

[a]21 Greek *three satas* (probably about ½ bushel or 22 liters)

Now Jesus gives two similar illustrations of the kingdom. Both talk about something little growing big and having great effect. The kingdom of Christ is like that. It had humble beginnings, even going back to a manger. But today, there is no greater institution, no greater power, no greater army than that of the kingdom of God.

[vv. 18-19 = Mt 13:31-32 & Mk 4:30-32, see comments on 64e]

MUSTARD — This well-known garden herb has a minute seed, but in good soil it can reach a height of ten feet (the average being about four feet). Small birds can, in fact, rest in its branches. This may be a prophetic picture of protection in the Messianic kingdom (Eze 17:23; 31:6, 12; Dan 4:12, 14, 21-22). Thus, two attributes of the kingdom are elucidated: Its incredible increase and its provision of protection.

[vv. 20-21 = Mt 13:33, see comments on 64f]

---

coming of Christ, the temple, demons, *dei*, divided response, etc. For more details, see D. Hamm, "The Freeing of the Bent Woman and the Restoration of Israel: Luke 13:10-17 as Narrative Theology," *JSNT* 31 (1987): 23-44 and R.F. O'Toole, "Some Exegetical Reflections on Luke 13:10-17," *Biblica* 73 (1992): 84-107.

LEAVEN — Whereas the men did the planting of the seeds, the women did the baking of the bread. Jesus' illustrations are from daily experiences of the working class. His audience would know exactly what he was talking about. The "large amount of flour" is literally "three *sata — pecks.*" That would make enough bread to feed a large family for more than a week. What woman had not marvelled at this incredible permeating power of yeast? The kingdom of God is like that. Quietly, imperceptibly, it spreads, permeates and raises the whole lump. The Jews expected the Messianic kingdom to come with clashing cymbals and spectacular power. God chose quiet, subtle permeation.

**§ 111**
**Feast of**
**Dedication**
(Jn 10:22-39)

Jesus returns to Jerusalem for the Feast of Dedication. He was here just two months ago for the Feast of Tabernacles. So he takes up the discussion right where he left off, talking about the Good Shepherd and his sheep (cf. Jn 10:1-21).

Jn 10:22-24

²²Then came the Feast of Dedicationª at Jerusalem. It was winter, ²³and Jesus was in the temple area walking in Solomon's Colonnade. ²⁴The Jews gathered around him, saying, "How long will you keep us in suspense?³⁴ If you are the Christ,ᵇ tell us plainly."

ª*22* That is, Hanukkah    ᵇ*24* Or *Messiah*

The Feast of Dedication was celebrated on the 25th of Kislev, roughly equivalent to our December. It was an eight-day memorial celebrating the rededication of the temple in 165 B.C., 3 years to the day after it had been defiled by Antiochus Epiphanes (cf. 1 Macc 4:36-59; 2 Macc 10:1-8). Although it was not one of the official pilgrim feasts, it still drew a healthy crowd. The most notable feature of the feast was the special lighting of the temple and many of the private homes in Jerusalem. That's why they sometimes called it "The Feast of Lights."

Jesus is walking around the Portico of Solomon, which covered the east side of the temple (cf. Acts 3:11; 5:12). It would be a logical shelter from the cold winter wind and rain, as well as the largest place to gather a crowd. He is accosted (literally encircled) by the Jewish leaders. Their question appears reasonable enough, but is designed to trap Jesus. They want Jesus to confess clearly if he thinks he is the Messiah. That way they can accuse him openly of blasphemy (cf. Mk 14:60-64).

---

³⁴Lit., "How long will you lift up our souls." It is equivalent to our idioms: "Keep us hanging" or "Hold us in suspense."

[25]Jesus answered, "I did tell you, but you do not believe. The miracles I do in my Father's name speak for me, [26]but you do not believe because you are not my sheep. [27]My sheep listen to my voice; I know them, and they follow me. [28]I give them eternal life, and they shall never perish; no one can snatch them out of my hand. [29]My Father, who has given them to me, is greater than all[a]; no one can snatch them out of my Father's hand. [30]I and the Father are one."

[a]29 Many early manuscripts *What my Father has given me is greater than all*

Jesus has already clearly stated who he is. In fact, this was the purpose of his last three sermons in John (Jn 5:16-47; 6:32-59; 7:14-30). Furthermore, his deeds have been an unmistakable declaration of his deity. But these leaders' hard hearts have closed their eyes and ears. So they ask Jesus to clearly declare his identity.[35] But if he does, they will neither listen nor understand. Jesus is the Messiah, but he is a far cry from what that word conjures up in the current Jewish mind. Therefore, he chooses to allow his deeds to declare his identity rather than his words.

Jesus responds with this allegory of sheep (cf. comments on Jn 6:37-40 in § 76a). It's quite a slap in the face for Jesus' present audience. He claims to be the true shepherd of God's people. These guys were only false shepherds. Worse than that, they are thieves. Worse than that, they will not be allowed in to have their way with the sheep. This allegory is primarily a rebuke to these faithless clergymen. But for the flock, these words could hardly be more comforting. We are eternally secure in Christ Jesus. No power on earth can separate us from his love (cf. Rom 8:38-39). As his sheep, we hear his voice and follow. As our shepherd, he knows us personally and leads us to eternal life. We will never perish because he protects us.[36]

In regard to the doctrine of eternal security, we make the following observations:

1. This is the clearest declaration in the Scriptures of eternal security. Yet the point of the passage is not whether a believer can "fall away" but whether (s)he can be "snatched away." Certainly the Christian need fear no power in the universe which might separate him from Christ (Rom 8:35-39). At the same time we dare not ignore those passages which warn believers about falling back into unbelief (Mt

---

[35]The word translated "plainly" (Gk. *parresia*) also implies boldness. Perhaps this is a gentle dig at Jesus, calling him a coward if he won't come right out and claim to be the Messiah.

[36]The NIV has a note in the margin at verse 29. Some ancient manuscripts read: "What my Father *has given me is greater than all*." The question is, "What is greater than all?" If it is the Father (NIV), then that explains why he is able to protect his flock. If it is the flock (marginal note), then that explains why Jesus is so adamant about their protection.

10:22; 24:13; Jn 15:1-6; Rom 11:20-22; 1 Cor 9:24-27; 10:1-13; Gal 5:1-4; 1 Tim 1:18-19; Heb 6:4-8; 10:26-31; 2 Pet 2:20-22; Jude 6).

2.  This is an allegory in the middle of a heated debate. That fact should shape how we interpret the text. In other words, we should be cautious about reading too much into specific details of the text. Rather, we should concentrate on the major point(s) of comparison.

3.  It is not actually true that all sheep listen to their shepherds. Every Palestinian shepherd knew the heartbreak of sheep that wandered off and died. Even Jesus knew that heartbreak with Judas (Jn 17:12; 18:9).

4.  Psalm 95:7-10 offers an interesting parallel to this text. Israel is called the flock of God and yet was warned to listen to him lest they be forbidden to enter his rest.

5.  Originally, this was not spoken primarily to believers but to unbelievers. Therefore, its original function was not to comfort but to rebuke the would-be sheep poachers.

6.  Our perseverance in Christ is not solely or even primarily dependent upon our own efforts. He is our shepherd and takes seriously his obligation to protect and keep his own flock. He is responsible for bringing us into the flock (Jn 6:44) and sustaining us in the flock (Jn 10:27-30). Christ is supremely capable of keeping us. Furthermore, we must be careful that this text does not become a battleground and lose its ability to comfort believers.

7.  Our conclusion may well depend on our starting point. If we begin reading "eternal security" texts[37] that may well be our conclusion. On the other hand, if we start with "apostasy" texts,[38] we will likely conclude that a person can walk away from Jesus. Caution: The goal of Bible study is not to defend a doctrine but to be obedient to the Word. We mustn't ignore any passage on either side of this debate.

Jn 10:31-39

[31]Again the Jews picked up stones to stone him, [32]but Jesus said to them, "I have shown you many great miracles from the Father. For which of these do you stone me?"

[33]"We are not stoning you for any of these," replied the Jews, "but for blasphemy, because you, a mere man, claim to be God."

---

[37]E.g., Ps 89:30-35; Jn 4:14; 5:24; 6:37-40; 10:27-30; Rom 8:29-39; 11:29; 14:4; 1 Cor 1:8; 2 Cor 1:21-22; 5:4-5; Eph 1:13-14; 4:30; Phil 1:6; 1 Thess 5:23-24; 2 Tim 1:12; 2:19; 4:18; Heb 6:17; 7:25; 1 Pet 1:3-5; 1 Jn 2:18-19; 3:6; 5:12-13; Jude 24.

[38]E.g., Josh 24:19-20; Neh 1:7-9; Ps 95:7-10; Mt 10:22; 13:1-9, 18-23; 18:21-35; 24:13; Lk 12:42-46; Jn 15:1-6; Rom 11:20-22; 1 Cor 9:24-27; 10:1-13; 15:1-2; Gal 5:1-4; 6:7-9; Col 1:19-23; 1 Tim 1:18-19; 4:1; 2 Tim 2:11-13; 4:10; Heb 3:1-19; 4:1-13; 6:4-8; 10:26-31, 36-39; 12:15-17; 2 Pet 2:20-22; Jude 6; Rev 2:5, 7, 10, 11, 17, 26; 3:5, 12, 21; 21:7.

³⁴Jesus answered them, "Is it not written in your Law, 'I have said you are gods'ᵃ? ³⁵If he called them 'gods,' to whom the word of God came — and the Scripture cannot be broken — ³⁶what about the one whom the Father set apart as his very own and sent into the world? Why then do you accuse me of blasphemy because I said, 'I am God's Son'? ³⁷Do not believe me unless I do what my Father does. ³⁸But if I do it, even though you do not believe me, believe the miracles, that you may know and understand that the Father is in me, and I in the Father." ³⁹Again they tried to seize him, but he escaped their grasp.

ᵃ*34* Psalm 82:6

This is the second time they have tried to stone Jesus.³⁹ The last time was three months ago at the Feast of Tabernacles (Jn 8:59). Jesus does not come right out and say, "I am the Messiah," or "I am Jehovah." But the implication is clear enough that the Jews are ready to stone him for blasphemy (cf. Jn 5:17-18; 8:58-59; 10:30-33). Had Jesus not actually been God's Son, they would have been Scripturally justified in doing so (Lev 24:16).

They can't kill Jesus legally since the Romans just recently stripped the right of capital punishment from the Jews. But they are so mad right now that doesn't really matter. They are prepared to assassinate him anyway.

In vv. 32-33, it appears that Jesus and the Jews are talking about two different things: Miracles vs. Testimony. Jesus is determined to reveal his identity, not through verbal declaration, but through miraculous deeds. He knows they will not accept a mere verbal claim of deity. Thus, he demonstrates who he is by what he does (cf. § 46, healing the paralytic).

As his defense, Jesus calls them back to Psalm 82:6, where the judges of Israel were called *Elohim*.⁴⁰ Since they functioned on God's behalf, they were backed by God's authority. Because they were backed by God's authority, they were granted God's title — *Elohim*. Now, Jesus is NOT saying that he is a mere judge of God or an underling worker of God. No, claiming to be God's Son is tantamount to saying, "I share God's character, position and authority." In short, he is claiming equality with God.

---

³⁹The NIV "They picked up stones" is literally, "They *carried* stones." There were probably no stones laying around the Portico of Solomon. Therefore, this probably indicates that they ran over to the portion of the temple still under construction and each carried back an armload of rocks.

⁴⁰A. Hanson, "John's Citation of Psalm 82 Reconsidered" *NTS* 13 (1964-65): 363-367, points out that there are other valid interpretations of this passage (none without difficulty). Even the Jews had three different interpretations of Ps 82. (a) According to the *Tractate Berakoth* in the Babylonian Talmud, God is the speaker and the judges of Israel

Jesus' argument, once again, is from lesser to greater. If they didn't scream and "holler" about earthly judges being called gods, why should they object if Jesus claims equality with God (cf. Jn 5:18; 10:33; 19:7, 12)? After all, he proves it through a sinless life and miraculous deeds. These earthly judges only received a word from God. They only listened to God. But Jesus has actually seen God (Jn 1:18). He is set apart by God, sent to earth from heaven, and does the work and miracles of God. Hence, he has every right to claim equality with God. His argument is rational. Unfortunately, it is delivered to an irrational audience. They try to seize him, but once again he eludes their grasp, not because he is sneaky, but because he has God's protection. It is not yet time (cf. Jn 7:6, 30; 8:20; 13:1; 19:28).

In verse 35, Jesus makes this comment, "And the Scripture cannot be broken." It is a minor addition which adds practically nothing to the meaning of the text, but it tells us an awful lot about Jesus' view of the Bible. He apparently believed in the inspiration, infallibility, and inerrancy of the Scriptures. And if he really did come down from heaven as he claimed, then he would be in a pretty good position to know.

---

are called "gods" as his representative. This is the view adopted here and defended by S. L. Homcy, "'You Are God's'? Spirituality and a Difficult Text," *JETS* 33/4 (1989): 485-491. (b) According to a fragment found at Qumran (11QMelch), "the speaker is Melchizedek, an angelic being, God's representative; those addressed are the evil angels." Hanson, himself, adopts this view, suggesting that Jesus was that Melchizedek. He puts it this way: "If to be addressed by the pre-existent Word justifies men in being called gods, indirect and mediated though that address was . . . far more are we justified in applying the title Son of God to the human bearer or the pre-existent Word, sanctified and sent by the Father as he was, in unmediated and direct presence" (A. Hanson, "John's Citation of Psalm 82" *NTS* 11 [1965]: 158-162). (c) According to the Tractate *'Aboda Zarah*, God was addressing the Israelites at the base of Mt. Sinai. J.H. Neyrey, "'I Said: You are Gods': Psalm 82:6 and John 10," *JBL* 108/4 (1989): 647-663, defends this third view. Psalm 82, he says, does not refer to judges (or even angels or Melchizedek as some claim). Rather it refers to the Israelites at the base of Mt Sinai. That is the most common Midrashic interpretation. These Jews received the Torah which purified them. Thus, it was believed, they became immune to death (like the original Adam). Hence, they were called gods (Ps 82:6). But because they sinned by worshiping the golden calf, they would be killed (Ps 82:7). The logic is still from lesser to greater. If Israelites can be called gods because of their holiness at Sinai, how much more can Jesus who is consecrated by God? Jesus answers their charge of making himself equal to God. He says, "I didn't make myself equal to God. God made me equal by consecrating me."

# PART NINE
# THE LATER PEREAN MINISTRY

§ 112
**Jesus Moves from Jerusalem to Perea**
(Jn 10:40-42)

⁴⁰Then Jesus went back across the Jordan to the place where John had been baptizing in the early days. Here he stayed ⁴¹and many people came to him. They said, "Though John never performed a miraculous sign, all that John said about this man was true." ⁴²And in that place many believed in Jesus.

After a second near-stoning in Jerusalem at the Feast of Dedication (Jn 10:31-33), Jesus eludes his would-be assassins and escapes to Perea on the east side of Jordan. This territory was in Herod Antipas' jurisdiction. Thus the Jerusalem leaders would not legally be able to arrest him. Besides, the locals have an enduring affection for John the Baptist which was naturally transferred to Jesus, especially after his benevolent miracles. Thus Jesus was safe among the crowds.

§ 113a
**Question about Entering the Kingdom**
(Lk 13:22-30)

Lk 13:22-25a

We have interrupted Luke's flow of thought by inserting John 10:22-42 between Luke 13:21 & 22. While that's helpful for a harmony, we must also pay attention to Luke's context. Reading Luke alone, this question, "Will many people or few enter the kingdom?" naturally follows on the heels of Jesus' teaching about the expansion of the kingdom of God. On the one hand, it looks big. But on the other hand, it's hard to get in (cf. Mt 7:13-23).

²²Then Jesus went through the towns and villages, teaching as he made his way to Jerusalem. ²³Someone asked him, "Lord, are only a few people going to be saved?"

He said to them, ²⁴"Make every effort to enter through the narrow door, because many, I tell you, will try to enter and will not be able to. ²⁵Once the owner of the house gets up and closes the door, you will stand outside knocking and pleading, 'Sir, open the door for us.'"

Luke says that Jesus is on his way to Jerusalem. But we learn from John that he just escaped from there. Furthermore, it will be another three months before he returns. Thus we read Luke to say, "Jesus' mind and heart are pointed decisively in Jerusalem's direction" (cf. Lk 9:51; 13:33-34; 17:11; 19:28, 41).

During Jesus' itinerant preaching tour of Perea, someone asks this simple and logical question: Are few or many going to be saved? The rabbis' opinions differed. Even Jesus gives a yes/no answer. Yes, few are going to enter because the gate is narrow (vv. 24-28). On the other hand, many will be saved (vv. 28-30). It seems that few Jews will be saved, but many Gentiles (cf. Rom 11:11-15). Perhaps Jesus is reiterating what he has taught in parables. That is, the kingdom starts small but multiplies immensely (Lk 13:18-21; cf. § 64e, 64f).

Entering through the narrow gate is no easy task. The Greek word for "make every effort" is *agonizō*, from which we get the word "agonize." It was used to describe the extra effort a person exerts when involved in an athletic contest or a fight. Getting into the kingdom is tough. Jesus never promised that we could waltz right in! It requires effort, struggle and persistence. We need to think clearly about Jesus' preaching on salvation. It is a gift that we cannot merit; it is NOT a gift that is free or easy. Many will stand outside the door once it has been shut only to be utterly disappointed that (s)he did not make the effort to enter when the gettin' was good (cf. Mt 7:13-23). Jesus is that narrow door, not because he is narrow minded, but because he is the only way to the Father (John 14:6).

It almost sounds like some people will try to get in but just not have what it takes. That is NOT what Jesus is saying. He means that there is a time for repentance. If you wait too long, it may be too late. In fact, closing the door may be a symbol of death. While there is life, the opportunity is generally open. Once a person dies, the door is closed forever (Heb 9:27). Many will appeal to God to let them in after it is too late, perhaps even after their death. But the time for repentance will be over.

Lk 13:25b-27

"But he will answer, 'I don't know you or where you come from.'
[26]"Then you will say, 'We ate and drank with you, and you taught in our streets.'
[27]"But he will reply, 'I don't know you or where you come from. Away from me, all you evildoers!'"

We enter the kingdom, not by deeds, but through relationship with Jesus. When Jesus says, "I don't know you or where you come from" he is saying, "I don't have a relationship with you or even with your family."[1] That was a powerful sentiment in Jewish ears. Only family members will have the door opened to them.

---

[1]Packett suggests that we change the punctuation from *"Ouk oida humas, pothen este"* ("I don't know you, where you are from") to *"Ouk oida humas. Pothen este?"* ("I don't

It is not as if these people are total strangers. They know the master of the house. The practice of eating and drinking was a significant gesture in their culture. There was a certain bonding attached to it. In addition, the master of the house had taught in their streets. They had achieved a certain level of relationship and were counting on that to get them into the house. Again, the door is only opened to family. In a parallel passage, Matthew 7:21-23, they relied on their works. They claimed to be servants. Here they claim to be friends. However, only family will be allowed in.

Everyone but "family" will be "sent away" [*apostete*]. In its noun form this word is translated "apostasy." It is the utter renouncing of someone or something. In other words, the owner of the house will have nothing to do with them. Why? Because they were lackadaisical? Because they missed the boat? NO! Because they were "workers of unrighteousness." Those who do not enter the kingdom have a sin problem, not a time-management problem. So they committed some heinous crime? Yes! They rejected Jesus. In the eyes of any father, rejection of his son is the greatest possible offence.

[28]"There will be weeping there, and gnashing of teeth, when you see Abraham, Isaac and Jacob and all the prophets in the kingdom of God, but you yourselves thrown out. [29]People will come from east and west and north and south, and will take their places at the feast in the kingdom of God. [30]Indeed there are those who are last who will be first, and first who will be last."

Lk 13:28-30

The theme of family relationship continues in v. 28. None of these past heroes were perfect. In fact, some of them were not even very good. But they all trusted God for their salvation rather than their own works. The picture here is of the Messianic banquet so hoped for by the Jews. For them, the only thing worse than missing this Messianic banquet was to peer through the windows to see their spot filled by a profane Gentile. This would be a painful portrait for these Palestinian Jews (on "weeping and gnashing of teeth" see Mt 8:12; 22:13; 24:51; 25:30).

Here we find the second answer to the man's questions: Will many or few be saved? Many! They will come from all parts of the earth. This was prophesied numerous times (Isa 2:2; 19:16-24; 25:6-12; 60:8-14; 66:18-24; Hos 1:10-11; Zech 14:16-21). The Jews rejected their own Messiah. The Gentiles flocked to him.

---

know you. Where are you from?") This has the advantage of smoothing a somewhat awkward phrase and making a nice transition into vv. 26-27 (E. B. Packett, "Luke 13:25" *ExpT* 67 [1955-56]: 178).

The last (Gentiles) will be first (above the Jews).[2] This was one of Jesus' favorite sayings. In all contexts it deals with God's economy versus man's. People prioritize things differently than God. We honor visible, tangible works. God honors a pure heart and a true family relationship. We will be surprised at the judgment when God strips us all of our deeds and ostensible armor of false righteousness. We will stand with Jesus alone or we will stand outside the door . . . alone.

**§ 113b**
**The Pharisees**
**Warn Jesus**
**about Herod**
(Lk 13:31-35)

[31]At that time some Pharisees came to Jesus and said to him, "Leave this place and go somewhere else. Herod wants to kill you."

[32]He replied, "Go tell that fox, 'I will drive out demons and heal people today and tomorrow, and on the third day I will reach my goal.' [33]In any case, I must keep going today and tomorrow and the next day — for surely no prophet can die outside Jerusalem!"

Herod Antipas was a sad case (see notes on § 71 a-b). He's the one who executed John the Baptist. And it looks here like he has his sights set on Jesus. After all, both men are part of the same movement (Lk 9:9). He is even convinced that Jesus is some kind of "reincarnation" of John (Mt 14:1-2). To make matters worse, Jesus is more popular than John ever was. In fact, some members of Herod's own court are following him (Lk 8:3; cf. Acts 13:1). It's not surprising that Herod tries to catch up with Jesus (Lk 9:9; 23:7-12).[3] If he does, it will spell certain death for Jesus. Now, Jesus is not afraid to die. That's why he came. But it must be in Jerusalem, not Machaerus.

Herod was not popular among the Jews. The Pharisees especially hated him. In fact, they even hated his supporters, the Herodians. But more than Herod and his cronies, the Pharisees hated Jesus (Lk 5:17, 21, 30; 6:2, 7; 7:30; 11:38-54; 14:1-6). That's why they aligned with these strange bedfellows (Mt 22:14-16; Mk 3:6). The two groups worked together to eliminate this pest. That being the case, why in the world would the Pharisees warn Jesus that Herod was about to get him? Perhaps these are good Pharisees, not the bad ones who aligned with Herod. There are, after all, some noble Pharisees (e.g., Nicodemus, Joseph of Arimathea, Gamaliel). But it is unlikely that they are numerous

---

[2]The Gentiles were last in rank. That is, they were viewed as unclean. Moreover, they were the last to receive the Gospel. Throughout the book of Acts the Jews were always the first to hear. Because they rejected Jesus, their seats at the Messianic banquet were filled by Gentiles (Acts 13:46; 18:6; 19:8-9; 28:28).

[3]J.B. Tyson, "Jesus and Herod Antipas," *JBL* 79 (1960): 239-246, traces Herod's pursuit of Jesus.

enough or bold enough at this late stage in Jesus' ministry to warn him about Herod.

More likely, this is part of their game plan. Although Luke does not charge them with deception, it seems likely that they have ulterior motivations for trying to get Jesus to leave. First, they are losing the battle in Perea. People are following Jesus in droves and the longer he stays in the area the worse it gets. Second, they want him in Jerusalem. Jesus seems to have a stronger hold in Galilee and Perea than he has in Judea. And the Pharisees have a stronger hold in Judea, especially in the capital, Jerusalem. They almost got him last time. With one more shot, they just might get their man.

Jesus knows what they are really saying. He sees their hearts. That is precisely why he responds the way he does. He calls Herod a fox. In the OT a fox indicated a small, insignificant schemer (Neh 4:3; S of S 2:15). Furthermore, Jesus uses the feminine "she-fox." Many believe that he was exposing Herod's wife as the mover and shaker behind his schemes. Jesus obviously is not intimidated by this insignificant, henpecked schemer.

Jesus understands, with impressive clarity, the sovereignty of God. His steps are ordained. Herod is hardly going to thwart God's plans! And Jesus is hardly going to be derailed by petty threats.[4] We would do well to learn this lesson. God is in control. We, as his people, rest in his hand. If we are obedient, we find ourselves in his protection. As with Jesus, this does not mean that we will never be harmed. But God's plans will never be thwarted in the lives of his obedient children.

The Pharisees must feel naked when Jesus talks about dying at Jerusalem. He reveals their shameful desires. He admits his own destiny of destruction. You would think he would feel sorry for himself. But his grief is poured out on Jerusalem. All the beauty of Zion, the hope and aspirations of Jerusalem are embodied in this man standing before them. Yet they eagerly hasten him to Jerusalem, the executioner's house.

[34]"O Jerusalem, Jerusalem, you who kill the prophets and stone those sent to you, how often I have longed to gather your children together, as a hen gathers her chicks under her wings, but you were not willing! [35]Look, your house is left to you desolate. I tell you, you will not see me again until you say, 'Blessed is he who comes in the name of the Lord.'[a]"

Lk 13:34-35

[a]35 Psalm 118:26

---

[4]"Three days" undoubtedly reminded Luke's readers of the resurrection. But it probably means nothing more than a short period of time.

Here is utter pathos.[5] Matthew (23:37-39) will repeat these same words just a few days before Jesus' death. Matthew also gives a fuller account of their killing of the prophets (23:29-36). True to form and history, Jerusalem rejects its Christ, nails him to a cross, washes its hands and says, "There, now we shall have some peace!" Little do they know the impending doom which they have brought upon themselves (v. 35).

Jerusalem[6] will be left "desolate" (lit., abandoned, empty). This carries two implications. First, Jesus is their Messiah. When they kill him, there is no other in which to hope.[7] Second, within one generation, the city will pay for their heinous crime against the Son of God (Mt 24:1ff.; Lk 19:41-44; 21:20-24). In A.D. 70 the Roman armies surrounded Jerusalem and tore it down stone by stone, but not before internal strife had ripped her to pieces. Factions and civil war within, the Roman armies without, the city of Jerusalem had never before, nor since, experienced such horror and devastation.

Jesus says that they will not see him again until they cry, "Blessed is he who comes in the name of the Lord" (Ps 118:26). In three months the crowds outside of Jerusalem will shout these very words, welcoming Jesus at the triumphal entry. But even after that Jesus repeats this prophecy (Mt 23:37-39). In other words, it is not yet fulfilled at the triumphal entry. Should we look figuratively to 70 A.D. when Jesus comes in judgment against the city? That hardly fits the jubilant tone of their declaration. Thus we conclude that this must ultimately refer to his Second Coming, when every knee shall bow and every tongue confess that he is Lord (Phil 2:9-11; Mt 24:30-31; Rev 1:7). Perhaps this may even suggest the salvation of many Jews (Rom 11:25-27) who jubilantly receive Jesus at his Second Coming.[8]

---

[5]This is the first of four instances that Luke records where Jesus weeps over Jerusalem (13:31-35; 19:41-44; 21:20-24; 23:27-31).

[6]The word "Jerusalem" is used three times in a row. That is a powerful repetition (epizeuxis).

[7]K. Baltzer, "The Meaning of the Temple," *HTR* 58 (1965): 263-277, argues that "house" should be understood as temple. After all, *oikos* is the most common word in the LXX for temple. And while Luke usually uses *hieron*, when his material parallels Mt or Mk he uses *oikos* for temple (6:4; 19:46). Furthermore, he suggests that Jesus embodies the *shekinah* glory of God (Lk 9:28-36; Acts 7:55; 9:3-5). Hence, when Jesus leaves the temple (or is rejected by God's people), the glory [*kabod*] of God has departed. In other words, when Jesus leaves the house (i.e., temple), so does their God.

[8]D.C. Allison, "Mt 23:39 = Lk 13:35b as a Conditional Prophecy," *JSNT* 18 (1983): 75-84, points out that in the context of Ps 118:26 these words are jubilant praise, but in the context of Mt 23:39 and Lk 13:35 they spell doom. How shall we handle this paradox?

This is the last of three times that Jesus ate with a Pharisee (Lk 7:36; 11:37; 14:1). The first time it ended in a fight when Jesus allowed the sinful woman to anoint his feet. The second time it ended in a fight because Jesus neglected to wash his hands before he ate. So we are not too terribly surprised that this meal ends with Jesus thrashing both the host and his guests over their self-seeking seating charts.[10]

**§ 114**
**Dinner with a**
**Pharisee and**
**Healing of**
**Dropsy**
**(Lk 14:1-24)[9]**

[1]One Sabbath, when Jesus went to eat in the house of a prominent Pharisee, he was being carefully watched. [2]There in front of him was a man suffering from dropsy. [3]Jesus asked the Pharisees and experts in the law, "Is it lawful to heal on the Sabbath or not?" [4]But they remained silent. So taking hold of the man, he healed him and sent him away.

[5]Then he asked them, "If one of you has a son[a] or an ox that falls into a well on the Sabbath day, will you not immediately pull him out?" [6]And they had nothing to say.

Lk 14:1-6

[a]5 Some manuscripts *donkey*

Luke prepares his readers for the impending bout by noting two details. First, the banquet is in the home of a *prominent* Pharisee, literally, "One of the rulers of the Pharisees." Quite possibly he is a member of the Sanhedrin or perhaps the ruler of the synagogue in which they had worshiped that Saturday. Second, it takes place on a Sabbath. That has spelled trouble before (cf. § 50-52, 100c, 110).

We don't know the motives of this prominent Pharisee (whether he was benevolent or malevolent toward Jesus). But the result of his invitation is that Jesus is carefully scrutinized by the whole group of Pharisees. This word for "carefully watched" is used two other times by Luke (6:7,

He suggests that the text does not mean, "When the Messiah comes the people will bless him," but "When Israel blesses him, the Messiah will come." He defends this passage as conditional prophecy by several supporting evidences: (a) The Jews did believe the coming of Messiah was contingent on their purity and/or repentance. (b) *Heos* often sets up a contingent Greek sentence. (c) This structure seems to be consistent in Rabbinic literature for conditional sentences. (d) This respects both the promised salvation of Ps 118 as well as the context of judgment in Mt 23 and Lk 13. (e) Acts 3:19-21 and 2 Peter 3:11-12 both allude to ushering in the coming of Christ.

[9]Lk 13 and 14 should probably be read as twin towers of controversy with the Pharisees. There are significant parallels: (a) 13:10-17 & 14:1-6 are Sabbath healings. (b) 13:22-30 & 14:15-24 describe who makes it into the kingdom. (c) 13:31-35 & 14:25-35 present the suffering of Jesus, Jerusalem and the disciple.

[10]J.T. Carroll, "Luke's Portrayal of the Pharisees," *CBQ* 50 (1988): 604-621, traces the evolution of Jesus' controversy with the Pharisees. While there were always some Pharisees who supported Jesus and his followers (e.g., Jn 3:1-2; Acts 5:33-40; 23:6-10), according to Luke, things went from lukewarm to red-hot, especially during Jesus' final trek to Jerusalem (Lk 5:21, 26; 6:1-11; 7:29-30, 36-50; 11:37-54; 12:1; 14:1-6, 7-11, 12-14, 15-24; 15:1-2; 16:14-31; 17:20-21; 18:9-14).

20:20). Both times it describes the Pharisees trying to catch Jesus doing something wrong.

There in the crowd is a man with dropsy. Today this disease is called edema. Simply put, the guy is retaining water. It sounds benign enough. But edema often indicates a heart or liver disorder. Depending on the cause, edema can be curable, but other times it is fatal. Either way, he looks pathetic.

Why is he at the feast? He may have been planted in the crowd to cause another controversy (cf. Lk 5:17; 6:7). More likely, however, he is just one of the many sick people who followed Jesus hoping to be healed. While the spectators gather in the courtyard to gawk at this sumptuous feast, this fellow gets swept in with them.

The question Jesus asks is so simple (v. 3). The answer is so obvious! Yet the Pharisees keep silent. They want Jesus to break the traditions by healing (cf. § 51 & 110). But now they are in a catch-22. They can't say it's lawful to heal on the Sabbath. They would have nothing to pin on Jesus and they would contradict their own traditions. But neither can they say it's unlawful. That would contradict logic, compassion and all that is good and just. It would expose their hypocrisy and their devotees might just convert to following Jesus. Their solution is silence.

Jesus' response is to heal the fellow right in their face. Feathers are about to fly. Jesus doesn't want this guy caught in the cross fire (cf. Jn 5:1-18; 9:1-34). So he sends him away. Then he turns to deal with the Pharisees. He reminds them that they also heal on the Sabbath. If they would save a son or an ox, certainly Jesus can save this man with dropsy.[11] The clear difference is that the Pharisees will only do what is necessary to save a life on the Sabbath.[12] Jesus goes beyond this by providing healing on the Sabbath which could have waited until Sunday. Therein lies the rub. Jesus clearly and purposely breaks their Sabbath traditions in favor of God's greater concern for mercy and compassion.

Jesus' logic overpowers them. The phrase, "They had nothing to say" is literally, "They were not able to answer against these things." They are not tongue-tied, they are hog-tied. They know they have been outwitted. They want to contradict Jesus in the worst way, but they are thoroughly unable to do so.

---

[11]Some manuscripts have "ass" instead of "son."

[12]In the Dead Sea Scrolls, "Cairo Damascus Covenant" 11:13-15, it was forbidden by the Qumran sect to give help to an animal on the Sabbath, either in birth or by pulling it out of a ditch. It was allowed, however, in both the OT and the rabbinic law (*Shabbath* 128b).

Lk 14:7-11

[7]When he noticed how the guests picked the places of honor at the table, he told them this parable: [8]"When someone invites you to a wedding feast, do not take the place of honor, for a person more distinguished than you may have been invited. [9]If so, the host who invited both of you will come and say to you, 'Give this man your seat.' Then, humiliated, you will have to take the least important place. [10]But when you are invited, take the lowest place, so that when your host comes, he will say to you, 'Friend, move up to a better place.' Then you will be honored in the presence of all your fellow guests. [11]For everyone who exalts himself will be humbled, and he who humbles himself will be exalted."

The Jewish banquet was laid out across a horseshoe shaped table which was about six inches off the ground. Around the table were cushions or low couches on which three men could recline. The host sat at the top of the "horseshoe." The place of honor was at his right hand and the number two seat was at his left. This seating chart went back and forth across the table to the lowest "seat."

There was a very definite pecking order in these feasts. You might get away with sliding up a spot or two. But if you got too audacious, the host would have to ask you to give way to his more prominent guest. That would be embarrassing.

These men are like children arguing over who gets to sit in the front seat of the car. It is ridiculous, selfish and arrogant. Jesus' attention is riveted on this ludicrous scene of grown men fighting for positions on cushions.[13]

He says, "Don't take the best seat you can get. Take the lowest seat." That is good advice not only spiritually but socially (cf. Prov 25:6-7). Instead of being singled out for demotion, you will be singled out for promotion. We imagine that everyone is noting where we sit and how important we are. The truth is that most people are so embroiled in their own quest for recognition that they have little time or energy to see you are sitting in a lower position than they. Even when they do, they probably will not say, "What a dope, he's in a low position." They will likely say, "That is odd, he could be in a much higher seat if he chose to be." The result of self-humiliation is often public acclamation.

Jesus is not just talking about banquet etiquette. This rule applies to every arena of our lives, from parking places to company parties. If we act arrogantly, God will surely bring someone along to put us in our place. We may get away with a little bit for a little while, but eventually, this childish self-seeking will be the cause of great embarrassment.

The contrast is also true. If we humble ourselves by taking a lower

---

[13]Luke uses an imperfect verb, indicating that this scene continued for some time. Jesus "was noticing" (*epechō*, meaning "to latch onto").

position we will eventually be properly recognized among our peers. The secret is really in letting someone else recognize you rather than promoting and exalting yourself.

God's economy is not only different than ours, it is often opposite of ours. And when life is over, God will turn the totem pole upside down. Those who were on the top will be on the bottom and those on the bottom will be on the top. God is able to do this because he judges the heart whereas we are only able to judge appearance and performance. God knows the depths of a person, whether his motive is pure or poor.

Lk 14:12-14

> [12]Then Jesus said to his host, "When you give a luncheon or dinner, do not invite your friends, your brothers or relatives, or your rich neighbors; if you do, they may invite you back and so you will be repaid. [13]But when you give a banquet, invite the poor, the crippled, the lame, the blind, [14]and you will be blessed. Although they cannot repay you, you will be repaid at the resurrection of the righteous."

This next bit of advice is directed to the host. In essence, it is the same as the advice to the guests. Instead of being ostentatious and self-seeking, be humble and giving. How? "Stop continually inviting"[14] important people to your parties. Now there is nothing wrong with having friends or relatives over for dinner. But if they are the only ones you ever invite, you have a problem. A tremendous amount of money was spent on these banquets. It was spent on people who could provide for themselves. Those who really needed it never got invited.

We all recognize the importance of investments. If we spend all our money now, we won't have any to enjoy later. Giving to the poor is really an investment. We are choosing to forego the enjoyment of recognition by our peers so that we will be recognized by God. He will reward well at the resurrection.

Lk 14:15-20

> [15]When one of those at the table with him heard this, he said to Jesus, "Blessed is the man who will eat at the feast in the kingdom of God."
> [16]Jesus replied: "A certain man was preparing a great banquet and invited many guests. [17]At the time of the banquet he sent his servant to tell those who had been invited, 'Come, for everything is now ready.'
> [18]"But they all alike began to make excuses. The first said, 'I have just bought a field, and I must go and see it. Please excuse me.'
> [19]"Another said, 'I have just bought five yoke of oxen, and I'm on my way to try them out. Please excuse me.'
> [20]"Still another said, 'I just got married, so I can't come.'"

---

[14]That is the implication of the Greek present imperative.

Jesus has just finished talking about the believer's reward at the resurrection of the righteous (v. 14). This naturally triggers one pious Pharisee to think about the Messianic banquet (Isa 25:6-12; 65:13-16). This fellow is on target. Unfortunately, many of those around the table are not going to share in the Messianic feast (cf. 13:28-30); not because they are not invited, but because they refuse to come when they are invited. Jesus' rebuke comes in the form of a parable. He'll tell this story again the Tuesday before he dies (Mt 22:1-14). It will have a slightly different emphasis and a few differing details. But the punch line is the same.

God is giving a banquet for his Son Jesus. The invitations are extended far and wide announcing the upcoming feast (v. 16). Once the meal is prepared, a second invitation is sent (v. 17): "Come with haste to the celebration." Everybody who's anybody is invited — all the rich and famous. (Figuratively this symbolizes the Jews.) But they reject it unanimously [*apo mias*]. With one accord they send the servant away.

Three excuses are given.[15] The first two are similar. What idiot would buy a piece of property without first checking it out?! The fact is, both of these men have already checked out their purchases. They are using them as excuses not to come. To make matters worse, this is an evening banquet, which started at sundown. They could not have checked out their purchases in the dark. This makes their excuses even more feeble and offensive. The third fellow seems to have a valid excuse. He just got married and wants to spend time with his wife. Normally, these feasts were not integrated, and so these newlyweds could not be together. Deuteronomy 24:5 offers some support for his excuse. There it says that a newly married man is exempt from military service for a year so that he can stay at home and please his wife (see also 1 Cor 7:33). His excuse is the most valid; yet it is also the most curt.

[21]"The servant came back and reported this to his master. Then the owner of the house became angry and ordered his servant, 'Go out quickly into the streets and alleys of the town and bring in the poor, the crippled, the blind and the lame.'
[22]"'Sir,' the servant said, 'what you ordered has been done, but there is still room.'
[23]"Then the master told his servant, 'Go out to the roads and country lanes and make them come in, so that my house will be full. [24]I tell you, not one of those men who were invited will get a taste of my banquet.'"

Lk 14:21-24

The Jews reject their own Messiah, so salvation goes out to the Gentiles (cf. Acts 28:28; Rom 11:1-24). In the parable there is a sense of

---

[15]The word "make excuses" can also mean, "To shun, reject, or refuse."

urgency about the invitation — the food is getting cold. Obviously, the Messianic banquet is not getting cold or stale, but there is still an urgency about this invitation. God has mapped out the span of this age. As the divine clock winds down, our opportunity to invite others in grows thin. Furthermore, each man's days are numbered. If a person does not come quickly, the opportunity to respond may very well be squandered.

Therefore, the servants are sent everywhere. Four different words are used for road. The first two in v. 21 indicate two types of city streets. The second two in v. 23 indicate country roads. The streets were broad and wide, the alleys were narrow, and the country lanes (v. 23) were simply shrubs or fences in which vagabonds found shelter. In other words, they were to scour the streets for guests.

They were to invite everyone — the poor, crippled, blind and lame. Some of these would have been excluded from full participation in Jewish worship because of their physical imperfections. This makes the invitation all the more precious. The master, intent on filling the banquet hall in honor of his son, sends the servants out for yet another round. Only this time the servants are not merely *inviting* people, they were to *"make them* come." The servant, of course, could not physically force someone to come. But he could emphasize the urgency and importance of the invitation. Likewise, we as evangelists need to express the urgency of the invitation to come to Jesus. There is a great celebration awaiting those who do.

This parable weaves together the sovereignty of God and the response of men. We see that our coming to Christ was not due to our own cleverness, perception, or worthiness. We were called by God and compelled through his servants. On the other hand, some will be excluded because of their callous rejection. In response, God hardens their hearts as a sovereign act of judgment (v. 24, Isa 6:9-10; Mt 13:15; Jn 12:40; Acts 28:26-27; Rom 11:1-24). Then it is too late to come.

**§ 115
Counting the
Cost of
Discipleship**
(Lk 14:25-35)

In these days of equal rights and extreme materialism, it is difficult to speak of the radical costs of being a disciple of Jesus. We have confused free grace with cheap works. True enough, we cannot earn salvation as if we were twisting God's arm with good deeds. At the same time, salvation is not free! It costs us our family, our marriage, our children, our possessions, our position, our time. Nothing short of everything is acceptable.

²⁵Large crowds were traveling with Jesus, and turning to them he said: ²⁶"If anyone comes to me and does not hate his father and mother, his wife and children, his brothers and sisters — yes, even his own life — he cannot be my disciple. ²⁷And anyone who does not carry his cross and follow me cannot be my disciple."

[vv. 25-27 = Mt 10:37-38, see comments on § 70b; also Mt 16:24; Mk 8:34; Lk 9:23]

The big blowout at the Pharisee's house (§ 114) attracts a good bit of attention, resulting in yet another huge crowd. That is just what happened the last time Jesus ate with a Pharisee (Lk 12:1). Because these feasts were semi-public, and Jesus' feast speeches were so pointed, they stirred up community interest.

As this entourage moves along, Jesus suddenly, and even heatedly, turns on the crowd. This stern admonition is a reaction to the shallow admiration of the crowd. Still today Jesus has many fans but few advocates. It is popular to talk about him in a semi-scholastic way, or to follow, to a minimal extent, the Judeo-Christian ethic. It is quite another thing, however, to be a true disciple. Jesus explains the difference.

To be a disciple demands total allegiance. We must love Jesus more than even our families. "Hate" is obviously an exaggeration. But compared to our love for Jesus our love for even our family looks like hate. Especially in Jesus' day, neglect of family obligations in deference to Jesus would be viewed as hate. We're talking about priorities. Who is more important? If anyone other than Jesus tops our list, we are not ready to be his disciple.

Furthermore, a disciple must pick up his cross daily (lit., his own cross). When a man picked up his cross, he embarked on a one-way journey from which he would not return. The cross is not merely a burden, a ministry, or an inconvenience. Nor is it even a willingness to die for Jesus. It is in instrument of execution which brought horror to Jesus' audience.¹⁶ You see, crucifixion was an ugly reminder of Roman domination. To make matters worse, Deuteronomy 21:22-23 specifies that anyone who hangs on a tree is cursed. These Jews must have been somewhat scandalized by Jesus' bold demand . . . so should we. But the truth remains, every Christian is subject to a death sentence for life (cf. Gal 2:20-21; 2 Cor 5:14-21; Phil 3:4-11).

---

¹⁶D.R. Fletcher, "Condemned to Die," *Int* 18 (1964): 156-164.

Lk 14:28-30

²⁸"Suppose one of you wants to build a tower. Will he not first sit down and estimate the cost to see if he has enough money to complete it? ²⁹For if he lays the foundation and is not able to finish it, everyone who sees it will ridicule him, ³⁰saying, 'This fellow began to build and was not able to finish.'"

This is the first of two parables Jesus tells about counting the cost. The word "estimate" originally meant "to count with pebbles." It indicated a meticulous reckoning of the specific cost. It is no mere estimation; it is an explicit calculation.

The foundation is generally the most important and most costly part of a building. But it is only the beginning. Many disciples just get started in the faith and run out of steam. It is like the rocky ground in the parable of the soils. The seed quickly sprouts, but has no root. So as soon as the sun gets a little hot, it withers.

One reason to count the cost is to avoid ridicule. The foolish builder becomes a laughingstock to the whole city, as his unfinished foundation stands as a monument to his stupidity.

Lk 14:31-33

³¹"Or suppose a king is about to go to war against another king. Will he not first sit down and consider whether he is able with ten thousand men to oppose the one coming against him with twenty thousand? ³²If he is not able, he will send a delegation while the other is still a long way off and will ask for terms of peace. ³³In the same way, any of you who does not give up everything he has cannot be my disciple."

This second parable deals with fighting rather than building. You can either fight, run or talk. If you aren't big enough to fight, and can't afford to run, you had better start talkin'! The point is, before you get into a fight, you had better consider carefully if you have what it takes to finish it. Likewise, before you come to Jesus, you had better carefully consider whether you have what it takes to stick it out for the long haul. It is the faithful, not the flashy, who will be saved!

In the world, we ask, "Does he have what it takes to win?" In the church, God asks, "Has he given up everything to be saved?" The world calls us to gain; Christ call us to die. This certainly does not mean that we retain no possessions. But it does indicate renouncing those possessions as your own.[17] God is now in control of our stock. It is at his disposal to use as he chooses.

---

[17]Such is the implication of the word *apotassetai* ("give up"). The present tense probably implies a continual abandonment even under one's own management. T.E. Schmidt, "Burden, Barrier, Blasphemy: Wealth in Mt 6:33, Lk 14:33, and Lk 16:15," *TrinJ* 9 [n.s.] (Fall 1988): 171-189, has an insightful analysis of Jesus' "money talk" and our neglect to either listen to or apply his commands.

[34]"Salt is good, but if it loses its saltiness, how can it be made salty again? [35]It        Lk 14:34-35
is fit neither for the soil nor for the manure pile; it is thrown out.
   "He who has ears to hear, let him hear."

[vv. 34-35 = Mt 5:13, see comments on § 54c; also Mk 9:50, § 91]

This is a famous saying of Jesus.[18] Only here, verse 35 adds an extra
detail about being thrown on the manure pile. Sodium chloride (i.e., salt)
is an extremely stable chemical. It cannot actually "lose its saltiness."
Therefore, we must be talking about some kind of counterfeit salt. It
looks like salt but has none of its properties. It was so worthless that it
did not even have chemical nutrients which could be useful on a com-
post pile.[19] It is totally useless filler.
   This is important stuff. That's why Jesus calls his audience to wake
up and pay attention with this Hebraism: "He who has ears to hear, let
him hear."

This is the great "Lost and Found" chapter of the Bible. It is a single        **§ 116**
explosive discourse, started by the first two verses. Jesus tells three para-        **Parables of**
bles, back to back, about the great joy of finding something lost. This        **Lost and**
passage is especially poignant on the heels of the banquet in the        **Found**
Pharisees' house (Lk 14:1-24).        (Lk 15:1-32)

[1]Now the tax collectors and "sinners" were all gathering around to hear him.        Lk 15:1-2
[2]But the Pharisees and the teachers of the law muttered, "This man welcomes
sinners and eats with them."

   It all started when the Pharisees kept grumbling about Jesus frater-
nizing with "sinners."[20] They contemptuously state, "This man welcomes
sinners and eats with them." Their statement is true, but derogatory.
They are insinuating that because Jesus eats with them he is like them.
You know, "Birds of a feather flock together." Jesus has a reputation of

---

[18]W. Nauck interprets the major "salt" sayings of the NT (Mk 9:49-50; Lk 14:34-35; Mt
5:13; Col 4:6) against the backdrop of a proverb on salt from the Rabbinic treatise *Derek
'Erec Zuta*. He proposes that each text is best understood by interpreting the metaphor of
salt as wisdom and industriousness in the context of discipleship. This fits well our present context of judiciously counting the cost of following Jesus and wisely listening to
(i.e., obeying) Jesus' words (W. Nauck, "Salt as a Metaphor," *ST* [1952]: 165-178).

[19]E.P. Deatrick, "Salt, Soil, Savior," *BA* 25 (1962): 41-48.

[20]Notice that the NIV places the word "sinners" in quotations. This editorial addition
accurately reflects the Pharisees' attitude about Jesus' friends without Luke, himself,
buying into it.

welcoming sinners (cf. Lk 7:29, 34, 37). He even calls Matthew, a tax collector, to be one of his special Apostles (Mt 9:9-13). He goes so far as to eat in his house! Later on he will eat with Zacchaeus, a chief tax collector!

But when Jesus eats with sinners, they don't defile him; he cleans them up. It's like when Jesus healed the leper. Instead of Jesus being defiled, the leper was cleansed. Oh what joy that was to Jesus, to search and find and save a sinner.

### THE LOST SHEEP (cf. Mt 18:12-14); Emphasis: The Lost

Lk 15:3-7

³Then Jesus told them this parable: ⁴"Suppose one of you has a hundred sheep and loses one of them. Does he not leave the ninety-nine in the open country and go after the lost sheep until he finds it? ⁵And when he finds it, he joyfully puts it on his shoulders ⁶and goes home. Then he calls his friends and neighbors together and says, 'Rejoice with me; I have found my lost sheep.' ⁷I tell you that in the same way there will be more rejoicing in heaven over one sinner who repents than over ninety-nine righteous persons who do not need to repent."

Jesus' Jewish, agricultural audience has no trouble picturing this parable. There are sheep all around them. And everyone knows that sheep get lost. It was a common problem. They kind of wander aimlessly as they graze. Pretty soon they look around and they are all alone. Typically a lost sheep will lay down and bleat until it is found. Often looking for a lost sheep was a group effort. Thus, each person in the audience had probably been on a "sheep hunt" if not for themselves, for a friend or neighbor.

They knew the joy of finding a sheep. Not only were sheep a valuable agricultural commodity, they were semi-pets. They each had their own name and were clearly dependent on the care of the shepherd. Thus, the shepherd and his sheep had a tender relationship. If it is natural to look for lost sheep, how much more should we expect God to look for lost people (cf. 1 Pet 2:25)? Jesus is doing exactly what we would expect God to do — seeking and saving the lost. This is all the more true when we understand that "sheep" in the OT was a symbol for God's people (cf. Ps 23:1ff; 119:176; Ezek 34:1ff; Zech 11:16-17; Isa 40:11; 53:6; Jer 23:1).

So the shepherd leaves the ninety-nine sheep to look for one. Presumably he leaves them with his helpers. No one was foolish enough to leave a flock of sheep unattended in an open field. Once he finds the little lost lamb, he puts it on his shoulders. This was a popular picture in the early church:

We cannot go through any part of the catacombs, or turn over the pages of any collection of ancient Christian monuments, without coming across it again and again. We know from Tertullian that it was often designed upon chalices. We find it ourselves painted in fresco upon the roofs and walls of the sepulchral chambers; rudely scratched upon gravestones, or more carefully sculptured on sarcophagi; traced in gold upon glass, molded on lamps, engraved on rings; and, in a word, represented on every species of Christian monument that has come down to us.[21]

There is joy in finding what was lost. This is so natural, so human, so divine! Just as we rejoice over something lost that has been found, so too, does God. If we have $1,000 in the bank, but lose a $20 bill, we will look until we find it. And when we find it we are more thrilled about the $20 being found than over the fact that we still had $1,000 in the bank. All God's people are precious. But there is still something especially joyful to God about "finding" a lost soul. "The Lord is not slow in keeping his promise, as some understand slowness. He is patient with you, not wanting anyone to perish, but everyone to come to repentance" (2 Pet 3:9).

## THE LOST COIN, Emphasis: The Search

Lk 15:8-10

[8]"Or suppose a woman has ten silver coins[a] and loses one. Does she not light a lamp, sweep the house and search carefully until she finds it? [9]And when she finds it, she calls her friends and neighbors together and says, 'Rejoice with me; I have found my lost coin.' [10]In the same way, I tell you, there is rejoicing in the presence of the angels of God over one sinner who repents."

[a]8 Greek *ten drachmas*, each worth about a day's wages

Several observations about this parable bring it to life. First, the coin this woman lost was a drachma. It was worth about a day's wage. Second, considering that women generally did not work, this was either given to her by her husband or was part of her dowry. Jeremias suggests that her dowry may have been worn as a headdress from which one of the coins was lost.[22] Either way, it would be a precious resource to her and a large embarrassment if she lost it. She lights a lamp to look for it. Either her house had few windows, or she is not willing to wait for the morning light — she must find it now! Besides, when you are living on

---

[21]Vincent, *Word Studies in the New Testament*, Vol. 1, p. 383.

[22]Jeremias, *Parables of Jesus* (Philadelphia: Westminster, 1972), p. 134, contra J.D.M. Derrett, "Fresh Light on the Lost Sheep and the Lost Coin," *NTS* 26 (1979-80): 36-60.

dirt floors, the longer something is lost, the more likely it is to stay that way. We also notice that the Greek word for "friends" is feminine. We can't be sure that she ever told her husband, but she does tell her sewing circle. Jesus has thus put the "lost and found" in terms that both men and women can understand.

### THE LOST SON, Emphasis: The Restoration

Lk 15:11-16

[11]Jesus continued: "There was a man who had two sons. [12]The younger one said to his father, 'Father, give me my share of the estate.' So he divided his property between them.

[13]"Not long after that, the younger son got together all he had, set off for a distant country and there squandered his wealth in wild living. [14]After he had spent everything, there was a severe famine in that whole country, and he began to be in need. [15]So he went and hired himself out to a citizen of that country, who sent him to his fields to feed pigs. [16]He longed to fill his stomach with the pods that the pigs were eating, but no one gave him anything."

Charles Dickens said, of this parable, "It is the finest short story ever written." This is the most famous parable of the trilogy and the climax of the series. It is also the longest parable Jesus ever told. It has two parts. The first is about the son who wanders and the second is about the son who doesn't. The first son gets lost abroad, the second gets lost at home. The second son is equally important because it brings us back to vv. 1-2 where the Pharisees (the sons who did not wander) complain about Jesus socializing with the lost sons.

The story opens with the younger son prematurely demanding his inheritance. The inheritance of a Jewish man was divided according to the number of sons he had, plus one. If he had three sons, it was divided into four parts; four sons, five parts; etc. The oldest son got the extra part, called the "double portion" (Deut 21:17). This man had two sons. The estate was then divided into three parts. One third was to go to the younger son at the death of his father.[23] Until that time, however, he has absolutely no right to claim his inheritance. In fact, to demand his inheritance early was like saying, "Drop dead, Dad."[24] This impudent young buck is declaring that he can no longer live under his father's roof. Only by his father's graciousness does he receive anything.

We might also note that the father divides it between them. The older son gets his share too — although perhaps only in promissory

---

[23]J.D.M. Derrett, "Law in the N.T.: The Parable of the Prodigal Son," *NTS* 14 (1967-68): 56-74, points out that some of the estate would be set aside for maintenance of the farm and unmarried females. Thus, his share would probably be more like $2/3$ rather than $1/3$.

[24]E.H. Hiehl, "'The Lost' Parables in Luke's Gospel Account," *CJ* 18 (1992): 244-258.

notes rather than in tangible coins like his brother. Nonetheless, the fact that he already has received what is his, makes his complaining at the end of the parable offensive.

The younger son, eager for independence, travels far in search of greener grass. Hard times hit. They hit especially hard for such a foolish fellow who has squandered his resources. He is desperate! So he hires himself — literally, "attached himself" — to a local hog farmer. He thrusts himself on a citizen of that country who probably neither needed nor wanted him. Thus, he is given the lowest job, and one ultimately odious to the Jew — feeding pigs. It would be difficult to paint, for a Jew, a picture of deeper depravity than this.

Just when it seems that things can't get any worse, they do. He gets so hungry that he is prepared to eat the carob pods which belonged to the pigs. They were edible, but only as a last resort. A diet of carob pods is mentioned in other Jewish literature as that of direst need, the most extreme poverty. They are shaped like a pair of miniature horns and thus derive the name *keration*, meaning "little horns."

[17]"When he came to his senses, he said, 'How many of my father's hired men have food to spare, and here I am starving to death! [18]I will set out and go back to my father and say to him: Father, I have sinned against heaven and against you. [19]I am no longer worthy to be called your son; make me like one of your hired men.' [20]So he got up and went to his father.

"But while he was still a long way off, his father saw him and was filled with compassion for him; he ran to his son, threw his arms around him and kissed him."

Lk 15:17-20

This whole sad situation slaps the boy back into reality. He "came to his senses." This phrase indicates a return to sanity. The young man wisely chooses to return home. He would clearly be better off as a slave to his father than a slave to this pig farmer. As he approaches the farm, the father sees him and runs to greet him. In the Middle East, running was an act of indignity. This father ignores the proper protocol in excitement for his son. Jesus does not indicate whether the father is standing and waiting or just happens to look up and see him at the end of the drive. What Jesus does say, however, is that the father takes the initiative for reconciliation. He throws himself on his son's neck with many kisses [*katephilesen*], ignoring the filth and stench of the swine, the tattered clothes and unshaven face.

[21]"The son said to him, 'Father, I have sinned against heaven[25] and against you. I am no longer worthy to be called your son.ª'

Lk 15:21-24

---

[25]"Against heaven" is a Hebraism, meaning "Against *God*." It may also indicate that his sins had "reached to heaven" (Liefeld, p. 984).

²²"But the father said to his servants, 'Quick! Bring the best robe and put it on him. Put a ring on his finger and sandals on his feet. ²³Bring the fattened calf and kill it. Let's have a feast and celebrate. ²⁴For this son of mine was dead and is alive again; he was lost and is found.' So they began to celebrate."

ᵃ*21* Some early manuscripts *son. Make me like one of your hired men.*

Originally the son thought of becoming a servant in his father's house. He has his whole speech memorized verbatim (vv. 18-19). But before he is even able to get half of it out of his mouth (v. 21), his father starts barking out orders to the servants and lavishes on the boy all the trappings of an honored son.

The robe, ring, and sandals are more than signs of comfort, they are signs of sonship and freedom. The robe was such as would be given to an honored guest. The ring is a sign of authority. And the sandals represent freedom since slaves went about barefoot. His father clearly restores him to the place of an honored son. In short, he is "alive again." This word for "resurrection" is an obvious allusion to the effects of sin. This parable has the seeds of NT theology — being dead in sin but alive in Christ (Rom 6:4, 9, 11; 7:4; 8:10-11; Eph 2:5; Col 2:13).

Lk 15:25-32

²⁵"Meanwhile, the older son was in the field. When he came near the house, he heard music and dancing. ²⁶So he called one of the servants and asked him what was going on. ²⁷'Your brother has come,' he replied, 'and your father has killed the fattened calf because he has him back safe and sound.'

²⁸"The older brother became angry and refused to go in. So his father went out and pleaded with him. ²⁹But he answered his father, 'Look! All these years I've been slaving for you and never disobeyed your orders. Yet you never gave me even a young goat so I could celebrate with my friends. ³⁰But when this son of yours who has squandered your property with prostitutes comes home, you kill the fattened calf for him!'

³¹"'My son,' the father said, 'you are always with me, and everything I have is yours. ³²But we had to celebrate and be glad, because this brother of yours was dead and is alive again; he was lost and is found.'"

This begins the second part of the parable, concerning the older brother. This conclusion to the discourse brings us back to verses 1 and 2 where the Pharisees are upset because Jesus is spending time with publicans and sinners.

The older brother hears the music [*symphonias*] and dancing [*choron*] on his way in from the field. He is obviously curious. There is a surprise party for somebody. Perhaps he thinks it's for him. When a servant says that his lost little brother has come home and is the one being honored, he becomes angry and refuses to go in. His little brother has belligerently demanded his inheritance, dishonored his father, squandered his estate, and shamed his family. The older brother is justified (logically and legally) in his anger. But the letter of the law does not always coincide with the spirit of the law. He misses compassion and forgiveness, which far outweigh retribution.

His father goes out to the elder brother.[26] For the second time that day he goes out to retrieve a lost son. But the elder brother, jealous of the party going on inside, is not yet ready to give up his own private pity-party. His opening comment, "Look!" sets the tone for this encounter. Not only does he chide his brother, but by extension he criticizes his own father. "This son of yours," sticks out like a sore thumb. He is not willing to call the prodigal his own brother. He also levels several accusations against his brother that he can't even know for sure are true. For instance, the story never mentions his hiring prostitutes.

The father's response is gentle and reasonable. The older brother has and will get his just reward. That's not even an issue. The primary issue is not justice, but gladness. His brother[27] was lost, but now has been found (Eph 2:1-5).

Again we end this third parable with a note of great joy at finding that which was lost. We do not learn, however, what happened with the older brother. Did he, or did he not, enter the house with his father and begin rejoicing over his brother's return? Perhaps Jesus does not tell because the story has not yet ended. Jesus stands in the middle of the prodigals: tax collectors and sinners. The Pharisees stand on the fringe. The story is still in progress. The outcome is not yet determined.

To understand the context of chapter 16, we must go back to 15:1-2.[28] Jesus has surrounded himself with tax collectors and sinners. The Pharisees stand on the perimeter, criticizing. Chapter 15 is a series of three parables directed toward the Pharisees. They tell of God's initiative in seeking the lost. On the other hand, chapter 16 talks about man's initiative. We have here a pair of parables. The first is directed toward the

**§ 117a**
**Parable of the**
**Shrewd**
**Manager**
(Lk 16:1-13)

---

[26]The father going out to meet his son is the climax of each half of the parable according to G.W. Ramsey, "Plots, Gaps, Repetitions, and Ambiguity in Luke 15," *PRS* 17 (1990): 33-42.

[27]"Very few translations reflect the interesting fact that Luke has the father use *exactly the same turn of phrase* in his reply; '. . . ho adelphos sou houtos . . .' (v. 32)" (T. Corlett, "'This *Brother* of yours,'" *ExpT* 100 [1989]: 216).

[28]The NIV leaves out an important word: "Also." "And Jesus also said to the disciples . . ." This connects chapter sixteen with 15:1, 2. M.R. Austin, "The Hypocritical Son," *EvQ* 57 (1985): 307-315, goes so far as to say that the parables of the lost sheep and coin are a pair, and the parables of the prodigal son and the prodigal steward are a pair and should thus be read in connection to each other.

disciples, the second goes back to the Pharisees. The first tells us how to use our money to get to heaven. The second tells us how to use our money to get to hell.

Lk 16:1-4

[1]Jesus told his disciples: "There was a rich man whose manager was accused of wasting his possessions. [2]So he called him in and asked him, 'What is this I hear about you? Give an account of your management, because you cannot be manager any longer.'

[3]"The manager said to himself, 'What shall I do now? My master is taking away my job. I'm not strong enough to dig, and I'm ashamed to beg — [4]I know what I'll do so that, when I lose my job here, people will welcome me into their houses.'"

Once upon a time there was this wealthy man who put one of his servants in charge of his household affairs. Now, this servant was probably not a freeman but neither was he a busboy. It was his job to distribute his master's goods — food, salaries, etc. It was a highly trusted position, which he apparently abused. Someone ratted on him. That put him in a precarious position. He would be out of his cushy pencil-pushing job. His options were few and unattractive.

A person in such a high position can't just be dispatched immediately. He still has to collect the paperwork, close out the inventories and clean out his desk. He uses this small window of opportunity to his advantage. Jesus commends him for that. He does not necessarily condone what he does but how he does it.

Lk 16:5-9

[5]"So he called in each one of his master's debtors. He asked the first, 'How much do you owe my master?'

[6]"'Eight hundred gallons[a] of olive oil,' he replied.

"The manager told him, 'Take your bill, sit down quickly, and make it four hundred.'

[7]"Then he asked the second, 'And how much do you owe?'

"'A thousand bushels[b] of wheat,' he replied.

"He told him, 'Take your bill and make it eight hundred.'

[8]"The master commended the dishonest manager because he had acted shrewdly. For the people of this world are more shrewd in dealing with their own kind than are the people of the light. [9]I tell you, use worldly wealth to gain friends for yourselves, so that when it is gone, you will be welcomed into eternal dwellings."

[a]6 Greek *one hundred batous* (probably about 3 kiloliters)     [b]7 Greek *one hundred korous* (probably about 35 kiloliters)

By reducing the debts he would certainly make friends. As the household manager, he still had the authority to do that. This "bill" was actually a written document, signed by both parties as a contract for payment. Once it was turned back over to the debtor he was free from his obligation. The account was "paid in full." This may not have been ethical, but it was legal.

Derrett suggests that he was not reducing the actual debt owed but simply knocking off the interest (i.e., "usury") that had accrued on the loan. If this was the case, he would have rightly following OT law (Exod 22:25; Lev 25:36-37; Deut 15:7-8; 23:19-20).[29] Although this act would have lowered the master's income, it would have raised his reputation. To that extent it would have been a wise move for both the manager and the master.

The master commended the manager. Surely he was not pleased with being defrauded, but he couldn't help but be impressed with the shrewd servant's scheme. In those days, servants did sometimes defraud their masters and those they helped were obliged to scratch their backs in return.[30]

Are we to believe that Jesus used a bad person as a good example?[31] Why not? Even an enemy can be pleasantly impressed with the skill of his opponent.[32] What parent hasn't used this kind of logic? It goes something like this: "If that rotten Billy Schmutz can be nice to his kid sister, surely you can do as much!"

---

[29]J.D.M. Derrett, "Fresh Light on St Luke 16:1, The Parable of the Unjust Steward," *NTS* 7 (1961): 198-219. However, Derrett's deductions are based on the Mishnah tractates which were not codified until the third century. Furthermore, the parable does not suggest that the servant reduced the usury from the payment. In fact, the term "unrighteous manager" [*ton oikonomon tes adikias*] seems to speak against the view that the manager was a noble character. J. A. Fitzmyer, "The Story of the Dishonest Manager," *TS* 25 (1964): 23-42, offers an alternate explanation. He suggests that the steward reduced the debt by the amount of his commission. Both Fitzmyer and Derrett would thus interpret the steward's actions as legal and commendable. This alleviates the tension of a master praising a dishonest deed. But both theories appear to go beyond the evidence available concerning ancient contracts and the job of managers.

[30]Cf. John S. Kloppenborg, "The Dishonoured Master (Luke 16:1-8a)" *Biblica* 70 (1989): 474-495.

[31]Some have difficulty with Jesus commending a bad person. Hence, they interpret Jesus' words as irony. They understand Jesus something like this: "Yeah, right, you go ahead and try to make friends with filthy lucre. Just see if they can help you in eternity." The manager is thus an example of what NOT to do (cf. D.R. Fletcher, "The Riddle of the Unjust Steward: Is Irony the Key?" *JBL* 82 [1963]: 15-30).

[32]There are a number of examples in Greco-Roman literature where a trickster servant was honored for outwitting his master. These come especially from the lives of Aesop and Plautus. See M.A. Beavis, "Ancient Slavery as an Interpretive Context for the New Testament Servant Parables with Special Reference to the Unjust Steward (Lk 16:1-8)," *JBL* 111/1 (1992): 37-54. Some have even suggested that Jesus is the rogue in this story who is accused of mishandling the affairs of God (cf. W. Loader, "Jesus and the Rogue in Luke 16:1-8a: The Parable of the Unjust Steward," *RB* 96/4 [1989]: 518-532).

Jesus is not exalting the man's dishonesty, his wastefulness, his laziness or his pride. He is commending his ability to use his present and temporary power and resources to make preparation for what was coming. We who are children of light should do no less. We must use our power, resources and abilities to prepare for eternity. We do that in at least two ways. Primarily, we use our resources and abilities to make investments into eternal things (Mt 6:19-21, 33). We win friends (specifically God) who can help us when we are helpless (e.g., judgment) so that we will have a comfortable place when we lose our job (i.e., when we die). Secondly, we evangelize the lost, using whatever resources and skills we have so that they too can prepare for the future. Both of these points will be further illustrated in the second parable (vv. 19-31).

The children of light (Eph 5:8) can be so naive! We are afraid that if we are shrewd, we are being unchristian. We feel we should not use secular abilities or procedures in the work of the kingdom. But Jesus said, "Be as shrewd as serpents and as innocent as doves" (Mt 10:16). We ought to be impressive examples of sagacity to this world!

This "shrewd use of resources" must also include our money, especially for Americans who have been entrusted with so much of it! The wisest use of money is not temporal pleasure, but eternal security. Present investments in the poor will be honored by God in eternity. Just how that might happen is explained in the second parable in vv. 19-31.

Lk 16:10-13     [10]"Whoever can be trusted with very little can also be trusted with much, and whoever is dishonest with very little will also be dishonest with much. [11]So if you have not been trustworthy in handling worldly wealth, who will trust you with true riches? [12]And if you have not been trustworthy with someone else's property, who will give you property of your own?
[13]"No servant can serve two masters. Either he will hate the one and love the other, or he will be devoted to the one and despise the other. You cannot serve both God and Money."

[v. 13 = Mt 6:24, see comments on § 54g]

This is axiomatic. The stock boy who pilfers from the grocery store will embezzle from the company if he ever gets to be the CEO. The person who foolishly spends his/her last five bucks will probably do no better if (s)he wins the lottery. The converse is also true. The child who saves his allowance will likely have a healthy IRA as an adult. The woman who tithes her puny alimony will likely tithe a substantial inheritance check that she may acquire.

If this is true, then God can certainly tell how we will handle spiritual wealth by the way we handle material wealth. If we honor God with our finances, then we can be entrusted with larger spiritual responsibilities and riches. But if God does not have control of our pocketbooks, then it is unlikely that he has full control of any other part of us.

Our hands are only big enough to carry a cross. Everything else must be subsumed under that burden — our jobs, hobbies, and entertainments. To the secular man, nothing is sacred; to the spiritual man, nothing is secular (Edersheim, 2:275). All our resources, time and talents belong to God to be used in the building of his kingdom.

## TRANSITIONAL TEACHINGS ON WEALTH:

§ 117b
The Story of
Lazarus and
Dives
(Lk 16:14-31)

These "transitional teachings" may look like a random collection clustered here somewhat out of place. They are, after all, found in Matthew's account in different contexts. But they have two important functions in this pericope. First, they form a transitional bridge between the two parables on wealth; the first being directed primarily to the tax collectors, the second to the Pharisees. Second, they summarize four practical results of the Pharisees' love for money: (1) They value things that God hates (v. 15). (2) They attempt to violently overtake the kingdom of God (v. 16). (3) They set aside the Word of God especially where it conflicts with their financial interests (v. 17). (4) And they divorce their wives.

Lk 16:14-18

[14]The Pharisees, who loved money, heard all this and were sneering at Jesus. [15]He said to them, "You are the ones who justify yourselves in the eyes of men, but God knows your hearts. What is highly valued among men is detestable in God's sight.
[16]"The Law and the Prophets were proclaimed until John. Since that time the good news of the kingdom of God is being preached, and everyone is forcing his way into it. [17]It is easier for heaven and earth to disappear than for the least stroke of a pen to drop out of the Law.
[18]"Anyone who divorces his wife and marries another woman commits adultery, and the man who marries a divorced woman commits adultery."

The Pharisees, because of their love for money, sneered at Jesus' teaching. The Greek word has the connotation of turning one's nose up or even snorting at. People today are no different. They mock Jesus because they value things that God detests: power, physical beauty, financial independence, position, illicit passion. The people of Hollywood, Wall Street and the Playboy Mansion are the boast and envy of the world. But what they have has not gotten them one inch closer to things that really matter. In fact, with such temporal things, they have built a barrier between themselves and God.

[v. 16 = Mt 11:12-13, see comments on § 57]

There are three primary interpretations of this verse. First, it may be a compliment to all those following after Jesus.[33] Hendricksen says,

> But what is necessary is that men vigorously press forward into the kingdom, and this is exactly what since the days of John the Baptist, courageous men have been doing. Entrance into the kingdom requires genuine self-denial, earnest endeavor, untiring energy, utmost exertion.[34]

However, Jesus' primary audience is the Pharisees, not his followers (v. 14). In addition, this word "forcing" [*biazetai*] indicates violence and opposition, not merely force. This is even more obvious in Matthew 11:12.

Second, J. Cortes (following F. Godet's 1889 commentary) suggests that v. 16 means something like this: "The law and the prophets (were in effect) until the time of John [the Baptist]; since then the good news of the kingdom of God is being proclaimed [by Jesus], and everyone is *insistently urged* to enter it (the kingdom)."[35] This does have the advantage of explaining the word "all." After all, neither "all" of the Pharisees opposed Jesus, nor "all" of Jesus' followers pursued him relentlessly. But "all" people were urged strongly to enter the kingdom. In addition, the word *biazetai* can mean "urge strongly." It is used that way in the LXX. And in NT times it was practically synonymous with *parabibazomai*, which means to "urge strongly" (cf. Lk 24:29 & Acts 16:15). While this interpretation is possible here (even though "urge strongly" is not the primary definition of *biazetai*), it hardly fits Matthew 11:12. Since these two are such close parallels, it seems best to find an interpretation that fits both passages.

As we suggested on Matthew 11:12, this is neither a compliment to Jesus' preaching nor to his followers. It is an insult to the Pharisees. The kingdom of God was promised through the prophets up to the time of John. Now it is here. What do the Pharisees do with it? As a whole, they oppose it violently.

[v. 17 = Mt 5:18, see comments on § 54d]

Jesus just nailed the Pharisees for opposing the kingdom proclaimed by the prophets. Now he puts the nail in the coffin. The reason the

---

[33]This is the unanimous view of the early church fathers according to F. W. Danker, "Lk 16:16 — An Opposition Logion," *JBL* 77 (1958): 231-243.

[34]W. Hendricksen, *The Gospel of Luke* (New Testament Commentary; Grand Rapids: Baker, 1978), p. 774.

[35]J.B. Cortes, "On the Meaning of Luke 16:16," *JBL* 106/2 (1987): 247-259.

Pharisees oppose the present work of God (v. 16) is because they ignore the previous revelation of God in the Scriptures (v. 17). But they won't be able to stop the growth of the kingdom any more than they can rewrite the Bible. The declarations of God stand for eternity. Those who stand against Jesus stand against the Scripture and its Author. One of them will fall. Can you guess which one?

[v. 18 = Mt 19:9 & Mk 10:11, see comments on § 122; also Mt 5:32, § 54e]

The Pharisees would deny that they ignore the Scriptures. So Jesus gives one of many examples of how they do. Let's take the subject of divorce. The Bible says "God hates divorce" (Mal 2:16). But the Pharisees weaseled their way out of the law. This "allowed" them to abuse women and gain financially. The results of divorce are hardly different today: Women's freedom and finances suffer while men's raise. God still hates it.

Back to the issue at hand. Jesus told his disciples this parable about using money to get into heaven (Lk 16:1-13). He then turns his attention back to the Pharisees (v. 14) with a miscellany of "money talk." This sets up our last parable in this series. It describes how one might use money to go to hell.

### THE STORY OF LAZARUS AND DIVES:

If this story is a parable it is an unusual one. For instance, it has no introduction like other parables. And unlike other parables, it names one of its players, Lazarus (which means "God helps"). Such a symbolic name would be appropriate in this parable.[36] It seems curious, though, that it comes so close to the actual raising of Lazarus (Jn 11:1-44; § 118). Thus some interpret this story as a literal description of Lazarus' experience in the grave. However, the Lazarus of Jn 11 was apparently a well-to-do fellow, not a pauper like this guy. In addition, this story has certain characteristics of a parable and follows a string of parables. Therefore, it is probably best to treat it as a parable. As such, we should be cautious about gleaning from these verses a picture of the intermediate state of the dead since not all details of a parable are intended to be

---

[36]R. Bauckham, "The Rich Man and Lazarus: The Parable and the Parallels," *NTS* 37 (1991): 225-246, points out that in stories of people raising from the dead, the individuals are almost always named. Furthermore, it would be necessary here to name Lazarus since the descriptions of the rich man and the poor man are reversed after they die.

interpreted. Besides, this parable is not about the dead but about the living. Jesus has been speaking to the Pharisees who loved wealth more than they loved the prophets. This parable is designed to show them the eternal consequences of their present use of wealth. Thus, this is the flip-side of the previous parable. Its theme is "reversal." In the end, God will more than even the score.[37]

Lk 16:19-24

[19]"There was a rich man who was dressed in purple and fine linen and lived in luxury every day. [20]At his gate was laid a beggar named Lazarus, covered with sores [21]and longing to eat what fell from the rich man's table. Even the dogs came and licked his sores.

[22]"The time came when the beggar died and the angels carried him to Abraham's side. The rich man also died and was buried. [23]In hell,[a] where he was in torment, he looked up and saw Abraham far away, with Lazarus by his side. [24]So he called to him, 'Father Abraham, have pity on me and send Lazarus to dip the tip of his finger in water and cool my tongue, because I am in agony in this fire.'"

[a]23 Greek *Hades*

This rich man had the best and was not afraid to flaunt it. His purple clothes were the most expensive of the day and his table was stuffed with delicacies. Lazarus, in stark contrast, was a beggar. He was apparently lame since his friends had to carry him each day to the place where he begged for alms. Rather than sumptuous clothes, he was decorated with open ulcers. The dogs, odious to the Jews, came and licked (and snipped at) his sores. This was utter degradation.

As you would expect, even in their funerals there was a considerable contrast between Lazarus and Dives.[38] The body of the rich man was undoubtedly anointed and wrapped and placed in an expensive tomb. The body of the poor man was probably tossed with contempt on the flames of the city dump (Gehenna). But then we get a glimpse of "The Other Side."

---

[37]Jesus' story was not unique. It has a number of parallels in ancient literature: The Egyptian story of Si Osiris (cf. R. Baucham, "The Rich Man and Lazarus," *NTS* 37 [1991]: 225-246); The Cynic story of Micyllus (cf. R. F. Hock, "Lazarus and Micyllus: Greco-Roman Backgrounds to Luke 16:19-31," *JBL* 106/3 [1987]: 447-463); and the Jewish Apocrypha in 1 Enoch 22 (cf. L. Kreitzer, "Lk 16:19-31 and 1 Enoch 22," *ExpT* 103 [1992]: 139-142). However, just because these stories use the same theme or basic plot is no reason to assume that they are necessarily dependent on each other. Jesus, in particular, was perfectly capable of developing this theme independently. What this does mean, however, is that Jesus' audience would recognize the basic story line of this parable.

[38]The early church named the wealthy character Dives, which is the Latin word for "rich man," or Neves (cf. K. Grobel, ". . . 'Whose Name was Neves,'" *NTS* 10 [1963-64]: 373-382).

The NIV's "hell" is literally "*hades*." The Greeks believed it was a place of continued human consciousness where the good were comforted and the evil were tormented. That is the picture Luke paints for us here. But that is also the picture of "*sheol*" in the OT. Thus, *hades* is an appropriate translation in the LXX for the Hebrew word *sheol*.

Hades is not the ultimate destiny of the wicked. That would be the lake of fire, which is not yet in use (Rev 20:11-15). Rather, it is a temporary place of imprisonment for disembodied souls and a precursor to future reward or punishment. At the final judgment Hades is going to be forced to give up its dead (Rev 20:12, 13). Then Hades, with his bride, Death, will be permanently destroyed (Rev 20:14; 1 Cor 15:26). It seems that in the final state (i.e., New Jerusalem and the lake of fire) that the experiences of those in Hades will be intensified. In other words, those who are in torment will find their suffering multiplied. Those who are being comforted will find inexpressible joy.

Lk 16:25-31

25"But Abraham replied, 'Son, remember that in your lifetime you received your good things, while Lazarus received bad things, but now he is comforted here and you are in agony. 26And besides all this, between us and you a great chasm has been fixed, so that those who want to go from here to you cannot, nor can anyone cross over from there to us.'
27"He answered, 'Then I beg you, father, send Lazarus to my father's house, 28for I have five brothers. Let him warn them, so that they will not also come to this place of torment.'
29"Abraham replied, 'They have Moses and the Prophets; let them listen to them.'
30"'No, father Abraham,' he said, 'but if someone from the dead goes to them, they will repent.'
31"He said to him, 'If they do not listen to Moses and the Prophets, they will not be convinced even if someone rises from the dead.'"

The issue here is really not egalitarianism on the other side of the grave. A poor man may, in fact, find himself in torment and a rich man may find himself in comfort. The reason the rich man was in torment was because of his gross financial neglect of the poor. He is not suffering because he was rich but because he was unrighteous with his riches.

He is now experiencing a hellish torment from which there can be no reprieve, especially by Lazarus, the one he had refused to help in his time of suffering. Now he would like to at least save his brothers from this same terrible fate. Unfortunately, Lazarus can't help his brothers any more than he could help Dives.

We like to think that miracles are sure ammunition for evangelism. They are not. Jesus' most astounding miracles didn't convince everyone. If someone is not inclined to listen to the prophets, they will not be moved by a miracle, even one as great as a resurrection.

Here we get a glimpse of what goes on beyond the grave. The punch of this text, however, is in the here-and-now. If this parable tells the truth we had better be about the business of evangelism. Let us stand with the prophets on this side of the grave, announcing the good news of Jesus and warning about the dangerous reality of hell. But even more directly, this passage warns us that our present financial management has eternal repercussions. Neglect of the poor will have frightfully severe consequences.[39] H. Kvalbein rightly says, "A life of affluence and luxury closes your ears to the Word of God and your eyes to the need of your neighbor."[40]

§ 117c
**Miscellaneous Lessons on Discipleship**
(Lk 17:1-10)

Here Jesus talks about rights that a disciple does not have. We do not have the right to "do our own thing" if it causes another to sin (vv. 1-2). We do not have the right to keep our mouths shut when we see another sinning (v. 3). We do not have the right to be judgmental or to bear a grudge (v. 4). And we do not have the right to feel smug or complacent in our work for the Lord (vv. 7-10).

These miscellaneous lessons are collected here by Luke without his usual chronological markers.[41] They may represent an actual day's teaching. But more likely, they are a collection of common themes of Jesus which reflect the kind of discussions he had during his later Judean/Perean ministry. There is a similar collection in Matthew 18, with many identical sayings (cf. § 91-92).

Lk 17:1-6

[1]Jesus said to his disciples: "Things that cause people to sin are bound to come, but woe to that person through whom they come. [2]It would be better for him to be thrown into the sea with a millstone tied around his neck than for him to cause one of these little ones to sin. [3]So watch yourselves.

"If your brother sins, rebuke him, and if he repents, forgive him. [4]If he sins against you seven times in a day, and seven times comes back to you and says, 'I repent,' forgive him."

---

[39]The message of this parable got through to Albert Schweitzer. He was both a renowned concert organist and a famous professor of NT in the University of Strasbourg. But in 1913 he gave all that up to become a medical missionary in equatorial Africa. In his own words: "The parable of Dives and Lazarus seemed to me to have been spoken directly to us! We are Dives . . . so do we sin against the poor man at our gate" (*On the Edge of the Primeval Forest* [1922]).

[40]H. Kvalbein, "Jesus and the Poor: Two Texts and a Tentative Conclusion," *Themelios* 12 (1986-87): 86.

[41]Liefeld notes that "the introductory words 'Jesus said to his disciples' are similar to those in other places where there apparently is no attempt to establish a chronological sequence (e.g., 12:22, 54; 13:6; 16:1)" (p. 993).

⁵The apostles said to the Lord, "Increase our faith!"
⁶He replied, "If you have faith as small as a mustard seed, you can say to this mulberry tree, 'Be uprooted and planted in the sea,' and it will obey you."

[vv. 1-2 = Mt 18:6-7, see comments on § 91]

The phrase "things that cause people to sin" is all one Greek word [*skandalon*] meaning "stone of stumbling." It was an obstacle that tripped people up. We might relate it to a raised crack in the sidewalk. They are bound to come, sometimes purposely, sometimes inadvertently, but come they will. It is not too surprising to find them coming through unbelievers; you would expect that. But they are all the more deadly when they come through believers because they come as a surprise. Paul talks at length about this in Romans 14 and 1 Corinthians 8-10 in relation to eating meats sacrificed to idols. It is imperative that Christians monitor their own behavior so as not to be a stumbling block to others.

There is a heavy consequence for causing anyone to sin, but especially the little ones. Jesus is probably speaking more directly about children than "spiritual babes" (cf. Mt 18:6-7). Children may not be able to understand our theological platitudes, but they certainly watch our behavior closely. The key is laid out in verse three: "Watch yourselves!" Because you can be sure that the kids are!

We do not have the right to privacy of our own actions. Nor do we have the right to privacy if a brother is sinning. We are obliged to go to the brother in love, in purity, and in gentleness and rebuke him. Matthew 18:15-20 gives three specific steps to follow when rebuking a brother [see comments on § 92]. The steps are simple enough to follow, but they are seldom carried out. Why? For one thing, we don't want to hurt anybody's feelings. You know, that's the stuff that splits churches. Besides, we really don't want people prying into our business. So we leave them alone, hoping they will extend the same courtesy to us and praying that the problem just kind of goes away. But the result is a church with sin swept under its carpets. This places a dark spiritual cloud over the assembly which hinders our worship, fellowship and evangelism.

[vv. 3-4 = Mt 18:21-22, see comments on § 92]

Two things are noteworthy in verses 3-4. First, Jesus uses a ridiculously high number of times that a person would sin against you. This just doesn't happen. A person would leave town before they got abused this way. To make matters worse, Jesus has them doing it daily! The point is essentially, "No matter how much a person sins against you," you are to forgive them. Of course, the way Jesus phrases it is more fun to listen to. Second, we notice that Jesus does not say, "If they repent," but "If they *say*, 'I repent.'" We are not to be the judge of whether or not another person repents. We can't see their heart or motives. We must accept that person's confession.

If we take Jesus' words literally and implement them practically, this is tough stuff! No wonder the disciples cried, "Increase our faith!" (literally, "impart to us faith"). They asked for an instant, spontaneous fix of faith. But generally that is not how faith is developed. Most often it comes through the grist and grit of difficult circumstances, the monotony of our daily existence, and the raw exposure of our own imperfections.

Part of the problem is that we want great faith; but Jesus just wants growing faith. The Greek text does not have the word "small" in verse six. It simply says "faith *as* a grain of mustard seed." Elsewhere, the mustard seed has been likened to the kingdom of God (Lk 13:18-21). It illustrates how something starts out little but ends up big. But the emphasis is not only on its littleness but on its potential for growth. Such is faith. It naturally gets bigger. If we put it to use, it will increase thousands of times its original size. In other words, it doesn't matter where you start; it matters where you're headed.

Growing faith can do wondrous things, like moving mulberry trees. That would be an impressive feat since the mulberry tree grows to a height of 35 feet. But Jesus has no interest in tossing trees around, or even mountains for that matter (cf. Mt 17:20; 21:21; Mk 11:23). Our greatest obstacles are not trees but principalities and powers. The true faith-work of the Christian is obeying God and sharing the gospel.

Lk 17:7-10      [7]"Suppose one of you had a servant plowing or looking after the sheep. Would he say to the servant when he comes in from the field, 'Come along now and sit down to eat'? [8]Would he not rather say, 'Prepare my supper, get yourself ready and wait on me while I eat and drink; after that you may eat and drink'? [9]Would he thank the servant because he did what he was told to do? [10]So you also, when you have done everything you were told to do, should say, 'We are unworthy servants; we have only done our duty.'"

This illustration is so clear, it needs little comment but one small warning. We must think with the mindset of the first century where slavery was a common and accepted practice.[42] In our culture these words

---

[42]According to M.A. Beavis, the ratio of slaves to free was 1 in 5 in the empire and 1 in 3 in the city of Rome. They were clearly treated as property and sometimes subjected to harsh treatment and cruel tortures (cf. M.A. Beavis, "Ancient Slavery as an Interpretive

sound offensive. Jesus is not approving the practice of slavery but merely using it as a sermon illustration to make a spiritual point concerning our own relation to God.

When you own a slave you expect that slave to do all he is told. When it is done, you don't expect to thank a slave for doing what he is told. No matter how well a slave carries out his duties, he is of no real profit to the master until he exceeds his duties. When a slave goes beyond the expectations of the master, he then becomes profitable.

We, like the slave, are of no real profit to God unless we exceed the expectations (which none of us do). Thus, we are all unprofitable servants. The bottom line: There is no room for smugness or complacency for a servant in the kingdom of God. "The demands of vv 1-6 may be heavy, but their fulfillment creates no claim upon God. This is nothing more than the duty we owe him" (Nolland, p. 841).

This passage is the centerpiece of John's Gospel. It looks backward to the previous signs of Jesus, and looks forward to the last and greatest sign, the resurrection. This is the pinnacle of Jesus' public ministry and the passage to his passion. Here we see, as never before, both Jesus' humanity and his deity.[43]

**§ 118a
The Sickness
and Death of
Lazarus**
(Jn 11:1-16)

Jn 11:1-6

¹Now a man named Lazarus was sick. He was from Bethany, the village of Mary and her sister Martha. ²This Mary, whose brother Lazarus now lay sick, was the same one who poured perfume on the Lord and wiped his feet with her hair. ³So the sisters sent word to Jesus, "Lord, the one you love is sick."

⁴When he heard this, Jesus said, "This sickness will not end in death. No, it is for God's glory so that God's Son may be glorified through it." ⁵Jesus loved Martha and her sister and Lazarus. ⁶Yet when he heard that Lazarus was sick, he stayed where he was two more days.

Here in verse one, John introduces his readers for the first time to Lazarus, Mary, Martha, and their hometown of Bethany. According to verse two, John assumes his audience is already familiar with these siblings. Perhaps John expected them to have already read the two synoptic accounts of Mary and Martha. In Luke 10:38-42 we read about Mary sitting as a student at Jesus' feet, leaving the kitchen duties to Martha. Naturally, Martha complained and asked Jesus to make Mary help. In a

Context for the N.T. Servant Parables with Special Reference to the Unjust Steward (Lk 16:1-8)," *JBL* 111/1 [1992]: 37-54.

[43]For an excellent Rhetorical analysis of Jn 11:1-44, see M. W. Stibbe, "A Tomb with a View: Jn 11:1-44 in Narrative-Critical Perspective," *NTS* 40 (1994): 38-54.

surprising twist, Jesus refuses to make Mary get up and help because she had "chosen the better." The second story, specifically mentioned in verse two, would take place just one week before Jesus was crucified. It was when Mary lavishly anointed Jesus' feet with an entire pint of very expensive ointment (Mt 26:6-13; Mk 14:3-9; Jn 12:1-8).

So, before John even tells the story, his audience knows a good little bit about these women. It is understood that they were close friends of Jesus. It is also understood that they were women of faith; Martha of the practical kind, Mary of the lavish, worshipful kind. We know little of Lazarus, but apparently he was a man of means and prominence (cf. v. 19).

Lazarus becomes critically ill. It couldn't have come at a worse time. Jesus has been skirting the boundaries of Judea since the Jerusalem Sanhedrin put a contract out on him after the last two feasts. His demise is only about two months away.[44] Now Lazarus needs him in Bethany, just two miles from Jerusalem, the heart of this hotbed of danger.

Banking on their friendship, Mary and Martha send a messenger(s) to Jesus. They don't actually ask Jesus to come to Bethany. They simply inform him that Lazarus is on his deathbed. The sisters are polite enough not to presume their family is more important than Jesus' ministry. At the same time, they are certainly hoping that Jesus will break away from his busy travel itinerary to come and heal their brother. Apparently, they even wait until his condition is critical so as not to saddle Jesus with a frivolous request or to have him come to Bethany only to find Lazarus has already recovered. It has come to the point that if Jesus does not intervene, Lazarus is obviously going to die. In fact, they wait too long because about the time the messenger arrives to inform Jesus of Lazarus' condition, he has already died.[45]

John does not tell us exactly where Jesus is, but it was somewhere in Perea, on the other side of the Jordan (Jn 10:40), near where John the Baptist had been baptizing. It probably took a good two days for the messenger to get to Jesus. Surprisingly, Jesus sends him back home with

---

[44]Jesus has already attended the Feast of Dedication, December A.D. 29. He still has a fairly lengthy itinerant ministry in Perea as recorded in Lk 17-19; Mt 19-20. Therefore, we speculate that this event took place about one month after Dedication and two months prior to Jesus' death.

[45]We have recreated the chronology as follows: (1) About two days before Lazarus dies, a servant is sent to Jesus. (2) He gets to Jesus two days later and informs him of Lazarus' imminent death. (3) The servant returns to Bethany two days after Lazarus' death with Jesus' promise that Lazarus would not die (v. 4). (4) On the same day, Jesus and his disciples set out for Bethany. (5) They arrive two days later, when Lazarus has been dead four days (v. 17, 39).

the words, "This sickness will not end in death. No, it is for God's glory so that God's Son may be glorified through it" (cf. 9:3). However, when he returns to Bethany, Lazarus is already dead.

Now this message must have puzzled the sisters, especially the part about Lazarus' sickness (and now death) bringing glory to God and Jesus. However, this enigma does not shake their faith. Instead of accusing Jesus of error, they interpret his words figuratively (vv. 23-24). But even that is an indication of their weak faith. Jesus' words are literal; they just can't imagine him raising Lazarus from the dead. Now surely they know that he has raised Jairus' daughter (Mt 9:18-25; Mk 5:21-43; Lk 8:40-56) and the widow's son at Nain (Lk 7:11-17). But those "raisings" took place before rigor mortis set in. This is a qualitatively different miracle.

According to verse eleven, Jesus knew when Lazarus died. Perhaps he understood this by divine omniscience. It is also possible that this messenger was immediately sent back to Jesus to inform him of Lazarus' death. They either invite Jesus to the funeral or tell him not to bother coming because it was now too late and/or too dangerous.

⁷Then he said to his disciples, "Let us go back to Judea."

⁸"But Rabbi," they said, "a short while ago the Jews tried to stone you, and yet you are going back there?"

⁹Jesus answered, "Are there not twelve hours of daylight? A man who walks by day will not stumble, for he sees by this world's light. ¹⁰It is when he walks by night that he stumbles, for he has no light."

Jn 11:7-10

The reason Jesus left Judea was because of the assassination attempt at the Feast of Dedication (Jn 10:31, 39-40; also 8:59). It is obviously dangerous to return. In fact, the next time Jesus goes to Jerusalem, in about two months, he will be executed. The disciples are aware of the danger and thus protest Jesus' suggestion of returning to Judea.

Jesus responds with this enigma about twelve hours in a day. That was the length of the Jewish work day (cf. Mt 20:1-14). In other words, Jesus' work for God is not yet finished (cf. 9:4). Until it is, no one is going to lay a finger on him (2:4; 7:6, 30; 8:20; 12:23, 27; 17:1). Although Jesus is cautious not to get caught, because it is not "his time," no one, even in Jerusalem, is going to prematurely kill him. Jesus is not the one in danger here. It is those who brazenly ignore God's plan (i.e., walk in darkness) that get into trouble.

¹¹After he had said this, he went on to tell them, "Our friend Lazarus has fallen asleep; but I am going there to wake him up."

¹²His disciples replied, "Lord, if he sleeps, he will get better." ¹³Jesus had been

Jn 11:11-16

speaking of his death, but his disciples thought he meant natural sleep.

[14]So then he told them plainly, "Lazarus is dead, [15]and for your sake I am glad I was not there, so that you may believe. But let us go to him." [16]Then Thomas (called Didymus[46]) said to the rest of the disciples, "Let us also go, that we may die with him."

Again Jesus is misunderstood, not because his words are taken figuratively, but because they are taken literally. The disciples are glad Lazarus is sleeping. This is generally a good sign for recovery. But that's not the kind of sleep Jesus is talking about. By "sleep," he means "death" (cf. Gen 47:30; 2 Sam 7:12; Mt 27:52; Acts 7:60; 1 Thess 4:13).[47] That is especially appropriate for believers for whom death will be a happy experience (Ps 116:15; Lk 16:22; 23:43; Jn 14:2; Phil 1:21, 23; 2 Tim 4:6).

Because of the disciples' crass literalism, Jesus blurts out the coarse reality: *Lazarus is dead!* Jesus may seem insensitive, rejoicing over the death of a friend. But he is able to see the end from the beginning. He not only knows that he will bring Lazarus back to life, but that by doing so the disciples will gain new ground in their faith.

Thomas stands out as leader of the group. (This led Edersheim to speculate that Peter and his fishing partners took some time off while they were so close to Galilee to take care of family and business). Aside from the four lists of Apostles (Mt 10:2-4; Mk 3:16-19; Lk 6:14-16; Acts 1:13), Thomas is only mentioned two other times. After the resurrection, Thomas went fishing with Peter (Jn 21:2). And of course the most famous "Thomas passage," is John 20:24-28, where he doubted that Jesus had risen from the dead, something that could also be said of the other ten Apostles prior to seeing Jesus. (See the comments in § 179 about the unfair term "Doubting Thomas.")

This "Doubting Thomas" has enough faith to die with Jesus! He clearly understands the danger of Jesus returning to Judea and is willing to go stand by him in execution. Some have said that his confession was bogus because when it does come time to die with Jesus, he (and the others) ran away (Mt 26:56). But Peter said the same thing (Mt 26:35), and no one doubts his sincerity. Like most of us, Thomas' and Peter's intentions were better than their actions.

---

[46]A Greek word meaning "Twin." We can only guess whether this was a literal description of Thomas.

[47]As Hendriksen (p. 143) points out, the euphemism of "sleep" for "death" is not an adequate basis for the doctrine of "soul-sleep." Although the soul is "asleep" to *this* world (Job 7:9, 10; Isa 63:16; Eccl. 9:6), it is very much awake in its own world (Lk 16:19-31; 23:43; 2 Cor 5:8; Phil 1:21-23; Rev 7:15-17; 20:4).

[17]On his arrival, Jesus found that Lazarus had already been in the tomb for four days. [18]Bethany was less than two miles[a] from Jerusalem, [19]and many Jews had come to Martha and Mary to comfort them in the loss of their brother. [20]When Martha heard that Jesus was coming, she went out to meet him, but Mary stayed at home.

[21]"Lord," Martha said to Jesus, "if you had been here, my brother would not have died. [22]But I know that even now God will give you whatever you ask."

[23]Jesus said to her, "Your brother will rise again."

[24]Martha answered, "I know he will rise again in the resurrection at the last day."

[25]Jesus said to her, "I am the resurrection and the life. He who believes in me will live, even though he dies; [26]and whoever lives and believes in me will never die. Do you believe this?"

[27]"Yes, Lord," she told him, "I believe that you are the Christ,[b] the Son of God, who was to come into the world."

[a]*18* Greek *fifteen stadia* (about 3 kilometers)     [b]*27* Or *Messiah*

When Jesus arrives, Mary and Martha are in their fourth day of mourning. For a Jew, mourning may last a full year. For the first day, of course, there is heavy mourning, which decreases incrementally on the third and seventh days. Mourning continues for twelve months but continues to get lighter until the end of the year, when it is stopped. They are joined by some of the prominent "Jews" from Jerusalem who would be more than a little familiar with Jesus, especially after the Feasts of Tabernacles and Dedication. No doubt many of these Jews are amiable to the "Jesus band" as are Mary, Martha, and Lazarus (v. 45). But some apparently are not (cf. v. 46).

When the rumor arrived that Jesus was on his way, Martha ran out to intercept him before he even came into town. She's not upset with Jesus but sad for Lazarus when she says, "If you had been here, my brother would not have died." Yet even in her mourning, Jesus brings a sense of hope: "But I know that even now God will give you whatever you **ask**." This word "ask" is interesting. Hendricksen (pp. 148-149) says:

> She used a word for prayer (*aiteō*, to ask) which Jesus never employed with reference to his own requests. The term which Martha used is proper upon the lips of an inferior asking a favor of a superior (4:9, 10; 14:13; 15:7, 16; 16:23, 24, 26). The term which Jesus employed with respect to his own requests generally implies the equality of the two persons (*erotaō*).

Jesus had sent the messenger back to Martha with the promise that Lazarus would not die and that through his sickness both he and God would be glorified. But Lazarus is now dead. She could not blame Jesus for not healing Lazarus. After all, the message had gotten to him too late. But the message Jesus sent back does not seem to gel with the fact that Lazarus has died. Therefore, Martha, unshaken in her faith in Jesus, interprets his words spiritually to mean that Jesus would raise up Lazarus on judgment day.

Jesus is our hope on judgment day, and what a blessed hope he is! He is indeed the "Resurrection and the Life" (Jn 6:39-40, 44, 54; 1 Cor 6:14; 15:20-28; 2 Cor 4:14; see also Acts 4:2; 23:6; 24:15; Rom 6:5; 1 Cor 15:42; Phil 3:10-11; Rev 20:5-6). So here we have the fifth of Jesus' "I AM" statements in John. It triggered something in Martha. She utters a confession of Christ that rivals even Peter's great confession (Mt 16:16-18).

### Confessions of Christ in John

| John the Baptist | Look, the Lamb of God, who takes away the sin of the world (1:29). |
|---|---|
| Andrew | We have found the Messiah (1:41). |
| Philip | We have found the one Moses wrote about (1:45). |
| Nathaniel | Rabbi, you are the Son of God; you are the King of Israel (1:49). |
| Samaritans | This man really is the Savior of the world (4:42). |
| Simon Peter | You have the words of eternal life. We believe and know that you are the Holy One of God (6:68-69). |
| Martha | I believe that you are the Christ, the Son of God, who was to come into the world (11:27). |

Martha's hope and confession still fall short of what Jesus actually promises her. Ultimately Jesus' gift of eternal life is far greater than a resuscitation of Lazarus' life. But this miracle in John 11 is one of the important evidences that Jesus is, indeed, able to grant us eternal life. In other words, if he can raise Lazarus today, he can raise us in the future.[48]

Jn 11:28-37    [28]And after she had said this, she went back and called her sister Mary aside. "The Teacher is here," she said, "and is asking for you." [29]When Mary heard this, she got up quickly and went to him. [30]Now Jesus had not yet entered the village, but was still at the place where Martha had met him. [31]When the Jews who had been with Mary in the house, comforting her, noticed how quickly she got up and

---

[48]J.P. Martin suggests that Lazarus' raising not only anticipates and verifies Jesus' resurrection, but together, these two events assure John's readers that they too will be raised on the last day. Thus, this story has strong eschatological and exhortational import aside from its historicity ("History and Eschatology in the Lazarus Narrative, John 11:1-44" *SJT* 17 [1964]: 332-343).

went out, they followed her, supposing she was going to the tomb to mourn there.

³²When Mary reached the place where Jesus was and saw him, she fell at his feet and said, "Lord, if you had been here, my brother would not have died."

³³When Jesus saw her weeping, and the Jews who had come along with her also weeping, he was deeply moved in spirit and troubled. ³⁴"Where have you laid him?" he asked.

"Come and see, Lord," they replied.

³⁵Jesus wept.

³⁶Then the Jews said, "See how he loved him!"

³⁷But some of them said, "Could not he who opened the eyes of the blind man have kept this man from dying?"

It seems Mary is not aware that Jesus has come until Martha returns. She pulls Mary aside privately and informs her that Jesus has come. As we might suspect, she immediately bolts for the door. Her friends who had come from Jerusalem to console her are concerned when she runs out of the house so quickly. They follow her to see if she might need a shoulder to cry on or a strong arm to hold her. She leads them right to Jesus.

For whatever reasons, Jesus is still outside the city limits. Perhaps he is at the "graveyard." Perhaps he was avoiding the popularity and danger that come with entering the city. Or perhaps he wants to have a private interview with Mary as he had with Martha. After all, Jesus had asked for her (v. 28).

When Mary arrives, she falls at his feet. She seems to be comfortable there (cf. Lk 10:39; Jn 12:3). She repeats verbatim the words of her sister. She too believes that Jesus could have healed her brother. How often, in the previous week, must these sisters have repeated these words to each other: "If only Jesus were here!" It is interesting that with the same words, Martha sparks Jesus into a theological discussion, but Mary moves his heart!

How the human is mixed with the divine in this text! Jesus knows that Lazarus is going to be alive again just moments from now. There will be laughter and celebration. But he is still caught up in the emotion of the moment. His dear friend is dead, and Mary lies crumpled at his feet in a puddle of tears. The commiserating crowd looks on her plaintively with sympathetic tears rolling down their own cheeks. Jesus is moved.

The two words used to describe Jesus' emotions are strong. The first, *embrimaomai*, is generally used for anger, not sadness (Mt 9:30; Mk 1:43; 14:5). It literally means "to snort like a horse." The second word, *tarassō*, means "to be stirred up" or "agitated." It is used to describe a storm-tossed sea (Isa 24:14, LXX). Jesus isn't just sad; he is bothered.

We can only guess, but surely he is angered by death itself, as a result of the fall in Eden. Surely he is angry at Satan, not only for spoiling the pristine utopia of Eden, but for continuing to ravage the precious people who now surround him. And surely he is agitated by their lack of faith and understanding that the one who created life itself is standing before them. And some of these very Jews who now weep with Mary will rejoice over Jesus' beaten body just two months from now, just two miles from here.

At Jesus' request he is shown to the tomb of Lazarus. Again, a flood of emotion sweeps over our Lord as he is caught in the currents of humanity. Verse 35 records with such simplicity the profound reality of Jesus' humanity: "Jesus wept." Unlike the Jewish mourners, who wailed ostentatiously (some with dubious sincerity), Jesus' tears are quiet and controlled (cf. Heb. 5:7).[49] Yet they still catch the attention of the crowd. They are an obvious indication of Jesus' affection for Lazarus. This crowd shares the sentiments of Mary and Martha: "It's a shame he wasn't here earlier. Surely he could have done something about this and saved us all this grief." Little do they know how lucky they are to be here now and how fortunate it is that Jesus was not here earlier.

Jn 11:38-44

[38]Jesus, once more deeply moved, came to the tomb. It was a cave with a stone laid across the entrance. [39]"Take away the stone," he said.

"But, Lord," said Martha, the sister of the dead man, "by this time there is a bad odor, for he has been there four days."

[40]Then Jesus said, "Did I not tell you that if you believed, you would see the glory of God?"

[41]So they took away the stone. Then Jesus looked up and said, "Father, I thank you that you have heard me. [42]I knew that you always hear me, but I said this for the benefit of the people standing here, that they may believe that you sent me."

[43]When he had said this, Jesus called in a loud voice, "Lazarus, come out!" [44]The dead man came out, his hands and feet wrapped with strips of linen, and a cloth around his face.

Jesus said to them, "Take off the grave clothes and let him go."

Jesus stands before a cave, probably cut out of limestone.[50] A large stone has been rolled down into a "V" shaped groove in front of the

---

[49]The word used to describe Mary's weeping (v. 31, 33) as well as the Jews' (v. 33) is *klaio*, which indicates a "loud mournful cry." The word used to describe Jesus' weeping, *dakryo*, simply indicates the shedding of tears.

[50]Edersheim measures the average vault at about 6 feet wide, 9 feet deep, and 6 feet high. They generally had "niches" for eight bodies, three on each side and two at the back, opposite the entrance. They also often had smaller niches cut for ossuary boxes which contained the bones of family members after their bodies had fully decayed.

opening to keep out scavengers. It would also serve to partially "trap" the stench of the decaying body inside. The spices and perfumes wrapped in linen strips around the body also helped. But even seventy-five pounds, which was not abnormal for an honorable burial (Jn 19:39), was not sufficient to cover up the odor. So when Jesus orders the stone to be removed, Martha protests. It would have been an offensive odor as well as an offensive action. One of the worst insults against a Jew would be to disturb his grave. Although moving the stone alone would not commit any such offense, it was a needless step in the wrong direction.

Jesus could remove the stone merely by speaking the word. He could empower Lazarus to kick it out of the way when he comes out of the tomb. The stone is not the barrier; it is their lack of faith, their unexpectant hearts. By having them remove the stone, he is eliminating two barriers at once.

Removing the stone is the first preparation for the miracle; his prayer is the second. He prays, not for his own benefit but for the crowd's. He doesn't ask God to perform this miracle, but thanks him for already having done it. This clarifies two important things: (1) *Jesus is sent from God.* God has granted him divine power and always listens to him. Jesus is not merely God's man, he is the God-Man. (2) *This miracle is evidence, not entertainment.* Lazarus is going to die again. These people will have to go through all this grief again. Although they appreciate having Lazarus back and are impressed with Jesus' power, if they don't accept him as Lord then they are missing the point.

Jesus calls out in a loud voice, "Lazarus, come out!" Perhaps the loud voice was so that Lazarus could hear him, being all wrapped up and stuffed in the back of a cave. That is unlikely, however, since Lazarus' soul is probably not even located in the decaying corpse at the moment. More likely Jesus shouts for the crowd, partially as a signal of authority and partially to be heard above the din of moans and sniffles.

Here he comes, wrapped from head to toe. Some have suggested that since his feet were bound that he could only have "hopped" out of the cave rather than walking out. That adds a bit of humor to the narrative. So does the fact that Jesus has to tell them to unwrap his head (so that he could breathe?).[51] And one must wonder who was more surprised to see whom — Mary and Martha or Lazarus?

---

[51]Both the stone and the grave clothes serve to foreshadow Jesus' own resurrection. W.E. Reiser, "The Case for the Tidy Tomb: The Place of the Napkins of John 11:44 and 20:7" *HeyJ* 14 (1973): 47-57, says that the napkins not only connect the two events but contrast them. He suggests that for Lazarus, the napkin was a sign of death, for Jesus it was a sign of life and the key piece of evidence for John believing in Jesus' resurrection (Jn 20:6-8).

As the feeding of the 5,000 was the high point of the Galilean ministry, so the raising of Lazarus is the high point of the Judean ministry and a prelude to Jesus' own resurrection. "Each of the seven signs [of John] illustrates some particular aspect of Jesus' divine authority, but this one exemplifies his power over the last and most irresistible enemy of humanity — death" (Tenney, p. 114). Not only has Jesus raised him from the dead, he has reversed the effects of four days of decomposition. Furthermore, the Jews believed that the soul of the deceased person "hovers around the body for three days" (Hendriksen, p. 146) but then leaves when it sees that all hope is gone.

The crowds are predictably impressed. This will create a fervor which will peak at the Passover two months from now. People will be talking about it. They will want to see both Jesus and Lazarus, who, in our day, would surely be swamped with radio and TV talk-show interviews.

**§ 119**
**Sanhedrin's**
**Decision to**
**Assassinate**
**Jesus**
**(Jn 11:45-54)**

The raising of a dead man created quite a stir. The shock waves reached Jerusalem. They even rocked the inner sanctum of the Sanhedrin. Caiaphas spoke for the whole group when he said, "This guy has got to go." In fact, he prophesied for the entire nation. Jesus did have to die, but for very different reasons than this unwitting prophet suggested.

Jn 11:45-48

⁴⁵Therefore many of the Jews who had come to visit Mary, and had seen what Jesus did, put their faith in him. ⁴⁶But some of them went to the Pharisees and told them what Jesus had done. ⁴⁷Then the chief priests and the Pharisees called a meeting of the Sanhedrin.

"What are we accomplishing?" they asked. "Here is this man performing many miraculous signs. ⁴⁸If we let him go on like this, everyone will believe in him, and then the Romans will come and take away both our place[a] and our nation."

ᵃ48 Or temple

It is not surprising that many put their faith in Jesus, nor is it surprising that most of the leaders didn't. They all agreed that Lazarus' resuscitation was a momentous event that the religious authorities should know about. Not only was it of theological interest, it was of political interest. This miracle created a fervor among the crowds that could potentially be dangerous. The Romans kept a close watch on the Jews because they were prone to revolt. They had proved that a number of times — even during Jesus' lifetime. This gave the Sanhedrin all the more reason to arrest (Jn 7:30-32, 44-45; 10:39) and kill Jesus (Jn 5:18; 8:59; 10:31). It was simply an issue of national security.

So some of the eyewitnesses inform the "powers-that-be" in Jerusalem. They call an emergency session of the Sanhedrin. They come to three conclusions: (1) Jesus is doing many astounding miracles. (2) Their efforts to stop him have been miserable failures. Not only has he eluded their grasp (Jn 7:44-45; 8:59; 10:39), but more and more people are believing in him (Jn 7:31, 40-41; 8:30; 9:36; 10:19-21). (3) If they don't stop him the Romans will. Interestingly enough, Caiaphas' logic in forcefully stopping Jesus, will be reversed by Gamaliel who will advise this same Sanhedrin to let the Apostles alone lest they should find themselves fighting against God (Acts 5:38). Both Caiaphas and Gamaliel were likely in both meetings. One can't help but wonder what all went into this one hundred and eighty degree turn.

The third conclusion was a sad misunderstanding of Jesus' mission. The common Jewish expectation was for an earthly, political Messiah. They wanted one who would throw off the shackles of Rome and regain Jewish independence (if not dominance). The Pharisees shared such an expectation and preached such a hope. But now that they see it coming, they don't want it at all. The risk of a bloody revolution is just too great. Furthermore, after all their grumbling against Rome, if the truth be told, they kind of like things just as they are. They don't want their authority to be challenged or stripped by some would-be Messiah.

This meeting of the Sanhedrin carries several insidious conclusions about its members. (1) They care more about their positions than they do about the kingdom of God. (2) They don't trust God to fight for them against an ominous enemy. (3) Their conclusions are wrong because they are thinking according to the flesh, not the spirit. (4) They are deceiving the Jewish populace, which thinks they are seeking the best interest of the people and the truth of the Scriptures. (5) They do not want the Messiah. They would obviously prefer to discredit Jesus' miracles and scriptural claims to messianic identity. But since they can't, they will abandon their own messianic hopes in lieu of their socio-political positions.

To make matters worse, this was all due to their misconception about the Messiah. Jesus' kingdom was no threat to Rome. Pilate saw that (Jn 18:33-38). Yet because of their hatred for Jesus, they came in direct confrontation with Rome through Pilate. And because of their execution of Jesus, they came in direct confrontation with God through Titus. In A.D. 70 the wrath of God demolished their city, even the holy temple, as Jesus predicted (Mt 24:2; Lk 21:20; 23:27-31). Because the temple was destroyed, animal sacrifices ceased. Thus the Sadducean party disbanded along with the Sanhedrin. In their attempt to save their positions and places, they destroyed them. This is part of the paradox of the kingdom (Mt 10:39).

Jn 11:49-54

⁴⁹Then one of them, named Caiaphas, who was high priest that year, spoke up, "You know nothing at all! ⁵⁰You do not realize that it is better for you that one man die for the people than that the whole nation perish."

⁵¹He did not say this on his own, but as high priest that year he prophesied that Jesus would die for the Jewish nation, ⁵²and not only for that nation but also for the scattered children of God, to bring them together and make them one. ⁵³So from that day on they plotted to take his life.

⁵⁴Therefore Jesus no longer moved about publicly among the Jews. Instead he withdrew to a region near the desert, to a village called Ephraim, where he stayed with his disciples.

Caiaphas reigned as High Priest from A.D. 18-36. He was the son-in-law of Annas, who reigned as High Priest from A.D. 7-14. Because the Jews accepted the High Priest for life, the populace still looked to Annas for leadership. This can be seen in the fact that Jesus' first trial was before Annas before he was taken to Caiaphas. But the Romans did not want any one individual becoming entrenched in power. That's why they frequently replaced the High Priest. This may be the meaning behind the words, "that year" (v. 49).

Caiaphas was a typical Sadducee — boisterous and rude.[52] Josephus (himself a Pharisee), has this to say of Sadducees:

> The Pharisees are affectionate to each other and cultivate harmonious relations with the community. The Sadducees, on the contrary, are, even among themselves, rather savage in their conduct, and in their inter-course with their peers are as ungentle as they are to aliens (*War* II:166).

Caiaphas, as High Priest, prophesies without intending to (cf. 1 Pet 1:10-12). He is used by God in spite of himself. He would probably feel a little scandalized if he realized the true meaning of his words and just how right he was. Jesus' death will be for all the people of Israel. Not only that, John says that Jesus' blood cleansed the whole world (1 Jn 2:1-2)!

The secret plots of the Sanhedrin become more public. They begin, in earnest, an organized effort to capture, convict, and kill Jesus. Someone (perhaps Nicodemus) sends a warning to Jesus. Consequently, he lays low in Ephraim for a while. Archaeologists have not been able to

---

[52]His behavior demonstrates his corrupt character: Mt 26:3, 57; Lk 3:2; Jn 11:49; 18:13, 14, 24, 28; Acts 4:6.

definitely locate Ephraim, but being near the wilderness, it would afford Jesus the opportunity for a "quick get-away." The next two months will be marked by continuous travels and discussions along the road, until the time of his final encounter in Jerusalem. Jesus will keep himself secluded, primarily in rural areas, and keep moving so as to avoid the clutches of the Sanhedrin.

## FINAL JOURNEY TO JERUSALEM

Like Naaman of old, this Samaritan found healing from God's prophet (2 Kgs 5:8-19). At the beginning of his ministry, Jesus said this kind of thing would happen (Lk 4:23-27). Like the Samaritans of John 4, this fellow finds the "savior of the world" and returns to worship him.[53]

**§ 120a
Healing the Ten
Lepers**
(Lk 17:11-19)

[11]Now on his way to Jerusalem, Jesus traveled along the border between Samaria and Galilee. [12]As he was going into a village, ten men who had leprosy[a] met him. They stood at a distance [13]and called out in a loud voice, "Jesus, Master, have pity on us!"

Lk 17:11-13

[a]12 The Greek word was used for various diseases affecting the skin — not necessarily leprosy

After raising Lazarus the Sanhedrin put an all-points bulletin out for Jesus. They wanted to capture him in the worst way. Jesus, knowing it was not yet his time, flees toward Galilee, laying low for a while in a village called Ephraim (Jn 11:54). Spring has sprung and it is time for Jesus' final ascent to Jerusalem. Each of the synoptics mark this final teaching tour (Mt 19:1-2; Mk 10:1; Lk 17:11). Large crowds, including several significant women (Mk 15:40-41), follow Jesus from Ephraim down to Jerusalem. Undoubtedly they are headed to Jerusalem for the Passover feast.

Travelling between Galilee and Samaria, Jesus is about to enter one of these "border" villages, when he is hailed by a group of lepers. These nine Jews and one Samaritan share the same miserable fate (see comments on § 45). Were it not for their cursed disease, they would never be seen together.

Leviticus 14 is a vivid description of leprosy. It is not what we know as Hansen's disease, which is a disease of the nervous system. Leprosy is an infectious skin disease. It was dreaded and incurable. In fact, barring

---

[53]D. Hamm, "What the Samaritan Leper Sees: The Narrative Christology of Luke 17:11-19," *CBQ* 56/2 (1994): 273-287.

an act of God, no one was ever cured of leprosy. To make matters worse, it was generally associated with sin in a person's life. Therefore, lepers were banished from their communities. One of the legal restrictions of a leper was that he could not come close to a healthy person. And if a healthy person inadvertently came too close, the leper was obliged to shout, "Unclean! Unclean!" It was humiliating.

**Lk 17:14-19**

<sup></sup>¹⁴When he saw them, he said, "Go, show yourselves to the priests." And as they went, they were cleansed.

¹⁵One of them, when he saw he was healed, came back, praising God in a loud voice. ¹⁶He threw himself at Jesus' feet and thanked him — and he was a Samaritan.

¹⁷Jesus asked, "Were not all ten cleansed? Where are the other nine? ¹⁸Was no one found to return and give praise to God except this foreigner?" ¹⁹Then he said to him, "Rise and go; your faith has made you well."

Jesus orders them to show themselves to the priests. After all, that was the law for ceremonial cleansing (Lev 14:8-11). It is interesting that Jesus does not immediately heal them. Rather, he waits until they have obeyed his command to go to the priests. In faith, they depart and are cleansed while on their way.

It seems a shame that the only thing holding this group together is leprosy. They can only be friends in illness. Once they are healed, the Samaritan leaves the others. He certainly isn't going to show himself to a Jewish priest! He has his own priest to go to. So, instead of continuing with his nine ex-comrades, he returns to thank Jesus.

Now, the nine are doing just what they were told. They are obeying Jesus as well as the Law. They are doing what is right. However, the Samaritan is doing what is better. That's a tough distinction for Christians as well. Often we are motivated to do what is right, to obey, and to fulfill God's laws. There is certainly nothing wrong with that. But the "better" is to worship Jesus. Again, we see a distinction between ritual and relationship. It is possible to do all the right things and still miss Jesus.

**§ 120b**
**The Coming of the Kingdom and the Son of Man**
**(Lk 17:20-37)**

This passage is essentially the same material as we have in Matthew 24 but given in a completely different setting. It is a different time, a different audience, and a different question is asked. In Matthew 24, the Apostles ask about the beautiful buildings in the temple (cf. Lk 21:5-38). Here it is the Pharisees who question Jesus, not about the temple, but about the kingdom. That is a difficult concept since the kingdom comes in stages. The kingdom was present with Jesus' first appearance (Lk 11:20; 17:21). The kingdom came on the day of Pentecost (Mk 9:1;

16:28). It comes as a millennial kingdom (Rev 20:4). And it will be finally and completely manifest in the New Jerusalem (Rev 21:1-6).

Locating which stage Jesus is talking about is sometimes difficult. Even more so, since Matthew 24 deals predominantly with the destruction of Jerusalem which took place in A.D. 70 (cf. Lk 21:5-38). But here, that does not seem to be the message, even though it uses much of the same language. It appears that similar illustrations and examples were given to describe two different events. That is a little confusing, but not so uncommon in biblical prophecy.

Jesus is asked two questions about the kingdom by two different groups. First the Pharisees ask, "*When* will the kingdom come?" Later in the discussion, his own disciples ask "*Where* the kingdom comes."

Lk 17:20-21

[20]Once, having been asked by the Pharisees when the kingdom of God would come, Jesus replied, "The kingdom of God does not come with your careful observation, [21]nor will people say, 'Here it is,' or 'There it is,' because the kingdom of God is within[a] you."

[a]21 Or among

The Pharisees are as interested in the kingdom as the "Jesus band" is. By and large, both groups shared similar expectations of the Messianic kingdom. It was to be: (1) Political — the Messiah would vanquish all foes of Israel (especially the Romans) with military power. (2) Prosperous — there would be incredible, even divine wealth given to every citizen of Israel. (3) Visible — it was to be announced in a fantastic, loud, flashy manner so that all could see and join in the celebration.

Jesus refers to this third point when he says, "It does not come with 'careful observation'" (i.e., visible signs). It is not going to be something you can observe as a sky rocket or a ticker-tape parade. Unfortunately, their concept was entirely wrong because they were looking for an earthly rather than a spiritual kingdom.

Because the kingdom is spiritual and not physical, it is internal, not external (i.e., "within you").[54] However, this phrase can also be translated "among you" or even "within your grasp."[55] That is probably what Jesus has in mind considering he is speaking to the Pharisees who hardly have the purpose, nature, and heart of the kingdom within them. Thus, Jesus implies that he himself is the manifestation of the kingdom of God even as he stands in their midst. They can accept him if they want to. In

---

[54]K.S. Proctor, "Lk 17:20-21," *BT* 33/2 (1982): 245.

[55]H.J. Cadbury, "The Kingdom of God and Ourselves," *ChrCen* 67 (1950): 172-173 and C.H. Roberts, "The Kingdom of Heaven (Lk 17:21)" *HTR* 41/1 (1948): 1-8.

other words, the Pharisees ask, "When comes the kingdom?" Jesus answers, "Here I am, standing in your midst, available for the asking."

Lk 17:22-29

[22]Then he said to his disciples, "The time is coming when you will long to see one of the days of the Son of Man, but you will not see it. [23]Men will tell you, 'There he is!' or 'Here he is!' Do not go running off after them. [24]For the Son of Man in his day[a] will be like the lightning, which flashes and lights up the sky from one end to the other. [25]But first he must suffer many things and be rejected by this generation.

[26]"Just as it was in the days of Noah, so also will it be in the days of the Son of Man. [27]People were eating, drinking, marrying and being given in marriage up to the day Noah entered the ark. Then the flood came and destroyed them all.

[28]"It was the same in the days of Lot. People were eating and drinking, buying and selling, planting and building. [29]But the day Lot left Sodom, fire and sulfur rained down from heaven and destroyed them all."

[a]24 Some manuscripts do not have *in his day*.

The conversation now shifts from the Pharisees to the disciples but the topic remains the same: "When will all this take place?" Although Jesus, in their midst, represents the presence of the kingdom, the full manifestation of the kingdom will not come until after the passion of Christ (v. 25). Was it fulfilled in Jesus' resurrection? No, because he only appeared to a few and did not manifest himself as lightning flashes across the sky (v. 24). This must refer to the Second Coming. That's consistent with Matthew 24. There Jesus' illustrations about lightning and Noah also refer to his return.

From the days of the Apostles until the present time, there have been people claiming to be the Christ or to have seen the Christ. Even by the time Luke wrote his Gospel, there were rumors that Jesus had already come (2 Thess 2:1-2). It is so tempting to follow them because we want so badly to see the inauguration of King Jesus (v. 22). But we ought not be duped into chasing after them. When Jesus comes, it is going to be as obvious as lightning that flashes from one end of the sky to the other (v. 24).

These verses set the eschatological clock for the rest of the chapter. That is, we are now looking at the Second Coming of Christ. It has many parallels to the destruction of Jerusalem (cf. Mt 24; Mk 13; Lk 21:5-38), but it is seen here in its own context.

All the verbs in vv. 27 and 28 are imperfect, indicating continued past action. In other words, life went on as it had in the past. People were continually involved in life's normal events. As in the days of Noah, it will be business as usual. Just as they were surprised by the flood, people will be caught suddenly by the coming of Christ. As in the days of Lot, life will proceed as it normally does. Just as they were surprised by the fire and brimstone, people will be caught suddenly by the coming of Christ. Jesus will come suddenly and unexpectedly (1 Thess 5:2-3; 2 Pet 3:8-10).

> [30]"It will be just like this on the day the Son of Man is revealed. [31]On that day no one who is on the roof of his house, with his goods inside, should go down to get them. Likewise, no one in the field should go back for anything. [32]Remember Lot's wife! [33]Whoever tries to keep his life will lose it, and whoever loses his life will preserve it."

Lk 17:30-33

The theme of "suddenness" continues. Jesus is going to return so suddenly that you won't even have time to collect your possessions. Those who love Christ will not need them. Those who do not love Christ, will not be spared by them.

Thus we hear warning number one in verses 30-31: Jesus will come so suddenly that you won't have time to gather your possessions. Now we hear warning number two in verses 32-33: The love of your possessions may keep you out of the coming kingdom. Lot's wife loved her city. By looking back to it during its destruction, she lost her salvation. That same principle is now applied to the Second Coming of Christ. Those who love this present world will have no place in the kingdom of Christ.

Jesus summarizes these two warnings with his most frequently cited saying: "Whoever tries to keep his life will lose it, and whoever loses his life will preserve it." Earlier this was applied in an ethical sense to the cost of discipleship (Mt 10:39). Here the application is quite concrete, referring to our love of possessions. The principle is the same: You must make a choice about your allegiance. Will it be to Christ or to this world? This is the disciple's key question from the time we come to Christ until the time he comes to us.

> [34]"I tell you, on that night two people will be in one bed; one will be taken and the other left. [35]Two women will be grinding grain together; one will be taken and the other left.[a]"
> [37]"Where, Lord?" they asked.
> He replied, "Where there is a dead body, there the vultures will gather."
>
> [a]35 Some manuscripts *left. [36]Two men will be in the field; one will be taken and the other left.*

Lk 17:34-37

Jesus' return will come suddenly. With it will come some very sharp divisions in the home and on the job. There will surely be many homes where everyone is saved and many shops where everyone is lost. But the point is that one Christian can't save the whole house. There will be a painfully discriminating judgment when Jesus returns. Therefore, he calls us to be committed to him above our possessions.[56]

The idea of judgment is always connected with the Second Coming. Here it is taken out of the courtroom and put onto the battlefield. The picture Jesus paints is a field of carnage, with slain bodies strewn across it, dotted with scurrying vultures, feasting on the carrion. Where there is a dead body, there is a vulture (cf. Mt 24:28). Likewise, where there is sin there will be judgment. The disciples ask, "Where, Lord? . . . Where will the kingdom manifest itself in judgment?" Jesus replies, "Anywhere and everywhere." It's a PG-13 picture for sure. Jesus paints it again, even more vividly, for John in the book of Revelation:

> I saw heaven standing open and there before me was a white horse, whose rider is called Faithful and True. With justice he judges and makes war. . . . The armies of heaven were following him, riding on white horses and dressed in fine linen, white and clean. Out of his mouth comes a sharp sword with which to strike down the nations. "He will rule them with an iron scepter." He treads the winepress of the fury of the wrath of God Almighty. On his robe and on his thigh he has this name written: KING OF KINGS AND LORD OF LORDS.
>
> And I saw an angel standing in the sun, who cried in a loud voice to all the birds flying in midair, "Come, gather together for the great supper of God, so that you may eat the flesh of kings, generals, and mighty men, of horses and their riders, and the flesh of all people, free and slave, small and great." . . . The rest of them were killed with the sword that came out of the mouth of the rider on the horse, and all the birds gorged themselves on their flesh (Rev 19:11, 14-18, 21).

**§ 121**
**Two Parables**
**on Prayer**
(Lk 18:1-14)

Lk 18:1

Jesus continues his trek from Ephraim to Jerusalem with a rather large entourage. As they walk along, Jesus teaches. On one such occasion, he gives two parables about prayer. The first is directed at his disciples. The point is clear: Pray and do not give up! The second parable is directed at the self-righteous Pharisees. The point is equally clear: Prayer that is self-confident and critical is ineffective with God.

¹Then Jesus told his disciples a parable to show them that they should always pray and not give up.

Right up front Luke gives us the meaning of this parable. That's pretty unusual but it punctuates the importance of persistent petition. We

---

[56]Verse 36 is absent in the oldest Greek manuscripts and thus omitted from most modern translations. It reads, "Two will be in the field; one shall be taken and the other shall be left" (cf. Mt. 24:40). Its inclusion or exclusion makes no real difference in our understanding of the text.

must, however, realize the context of the passage. Jesus has just finished talking about his Second Coming. He has just told his disciples that they would "long for one of his days" (17:22). It is prayer — constant, persistent prayer — that will sustain the disciples of Jesus as they wait for his return. We must "not give up." Sure, it can be tiring as we labor and wait. Persistent prayer is the tool Jesus offers to sustain misunderstood and mistreated disciples (cf. 1 Thess 5:17).

[2]He said: "In a certain town there was a judge who neither feared God nor cared about men. [3]And there was a widow in that town who kept coming to him with the plea, 'Grant me justice against my adversary.'
[4]"For some time he refused. But finally he said to himself, 'Even though I don't fear God or care about men, [5]yet because this widow keeps bothering me, I will see that she gets justice, so that she won't eventually wear me out with her coming!'"

Lk 18:2-5

The parable opens with a villain — an unjust judge. Edersheim (II: 287) describes these village judges as something like the old marshal. They were appointed by the Romans as peace-keeping forces in the smaller towns. They were often corrupt, taking bribes and vying for political position. In walks this widow. That was unusual. In those days, women didn't go to court themselves. They would be represented by a male advocate. But this poor widow has no one willing to plead her case — no husband, no sons, no in-laws. Against proper etiquette, in humiliation, this widow pesters the judge to act as her advocate. She is utterly alone and in serious danger (cf. Mk 12:40; Lk 20:47). Her only hope is an unjust judge. Now that's a pathetic picture.[57] Although her chances of obtaining justice are slim, it's her only shot. So she keeps at it persistently. Eventually her importunity prevails.

The word translated "wear me out," literally means "to strike someone under the eye." We would say, "She gave him a black eye." It is used figuratively in the sense of "putting him to shame."[58] Her persistence scandalizes the judge in several ways. (1) It demonstrates that he is not doing his job, which may hinder his further promotion. (2) She shows that he is unjust, which will sully his reputation in the community. (3) She takes up enormous amounts of his precious time. Even though he fears not God, nor does he respect the opinions of men, the price tag for putting off this woman is just too high and getting higher by the minute.

---

[57]The Bible consistently exhorts God's people to take care of widows (Exod 22:22-24; Deut 10:18; 24:17; 27:19; Job 24:3, 21; Isa 1:17; 10:2; Jer 22:3; Mal 3:5; Mk 12:40; Acts 6:1; 9:41; 1 Tim 5:13-15; James 1:27) precisely because they are so vulnerable.
[58]J.D.M. Derrett, "Law in the NT: The Unjust Judge," *NTS* 18 (1971-72): 178-191.

[6]And the Lord said, "Listen to what the unjust judge says. [7]And will not God bring about justice for his chosen ones, who cry out to him day and night? Will he keep putting them off? [8]I tell you, he will see that they get justice, and quickly. However, when the Son of Man comes, will he find faith on the earth?"

How can this scallywag represent God in this parable? Is Jesus saying that we will get what we want from God if we pester him through prayer? NO! This is a parable of *contrast*, not *comparison*. What Jesus is saying is that if the unjust judge will give in through persistent petition, how much more will a loving Father eagerly grant the requests of his beloved "chosen ones" (v. 7, cf. Mt 24:22; Rom 8:33; 1 Pet 2:9; Rev 17:14)? The point of the story is not that we pester God with prayer until he gives in. The point is that we *are not* pestering God when we pray and so we should not give up.

This would have come as a bit of a shock to Jesus' audience. Jewish theology considered it a bit offensive to "nag" God with our needs.[59] But Jesus told us to do it. Remember the "ask, seek, knock" stuff?[60] Then he gave us a couple of parables to illustrate how to pray persistently (Lk 11:5-8; 18:1-8). As if that was not enough, Jesus showed us how himself (Mk 14:35-42). But what's the point of praying continually if God already knows our needs? Mitchell puts it this way: God does not become more willing to give, but the person more able to receive. Thus, persistent prayer primarily changes the petitioner, not God.[61]

Jesus promises that our prayers will be answered. We will receive justice, and receive it quickly. This does not necessarily mean "immediately" but "in a short span of time." Just wait until Jesus returns (17:29-37; cf. Rev 22:20). It could happen at anytime. And when it does happen it will be swift. Hicks helps with his translation of v. 7: "Will not God vindicate his elect who cry unto him day and night even though he appears to delay over them?"[62] We're gonna have to wait for that day. But mark my words, it will come. Until then, you keep praying!

When Jesus comes, will he find faith? Again, we observe that Jesus is speaking of prayer in relation to his Second Coming. Sure we have to wait. We cannot speed up God's timetable through prayer. But we do consistently recognize his loving care in our lives. The question Jesus

---

[59]Talmud *Berakh* 3.6; 31a.

[60]These three commands are present imperatives, indicating continued action. This is all the more striking since Jesus overwhelmingly used aorist imperatives when teaching on prayer.

[61]C.C. Mitchell, "The Case for Persistence in Prayer," *JETS* 27 (1984): 161-168.

[62]J.M. Hicks, "The Parable of the Persistent Widow (Luke 18:1-8)," *RestQ* 33 (1991): 209-223.

asks is, "Will you be faithful in prayer until I return? Will you make it?" This question is unanswered until this day. And it may be the only question that we are able to answer better than Jesus. It is up to us. Will we be faithful until the return of our Lord? Surely if this widow could persist with this unreliable, unpredictable, unrighteous judge, we can persist with a loving God who always keeps his word.

Lk 18:9-12

⁹To some who were confident of their own righteousness and looked down on everybody else, Jesus told this parable: ¹⁰"Two men went up to the temple to pray, one a Pharisee and the other a tax collector. ¹¹The Pharisee stood up and prayed aboutª himself: 'God, I thank you that I am not like other men — robbers, evildoers, adulterers — or even like this tax collector. ¹²I fast twice a week and give a tenth of all I get.'"

ª11 Or to

Jesus has just spoken about the unrighteous judge. Now he contrasts this self-righteous worshiper with a repentant sinner. The Pharisees considered themselves worthy of God's grace. They believed that by their religious performance, they earned the right to make demands of God and to demean others (cf. vv. 18-30; Mt 23:5-7; Mk 7:6; Phil 3:4-6).

The Pharisee "prayed about himself" (or more accurately, "Prayed TO himself"). The reason this man leaves the temple without his prayer answered is that he prays to himself and not to God. He never asks for anything. All he really does is report how wonderful he is (using the pronoun "I" five times in his prayer) and reports how awful this publican is. He can easily catalogue his ritual prowess. He fasted twice a week and meticulously tithed a tenth (cf. 11:42). The Pharisees fasted on Mondays and Thursdays. The law only required one fast a year (cf. Lev 26:29; Num 29:7). However, the market convened on these days and thus people came to town. Special synagogue services were held and the Sanhedrin convened. It was the perfect time to attract attention.

This was (is) the typical attitude of the Pharisee. Rabbi Simeon ben Jochai said, "If there are only two righteous men in the world, I and my son are these two; if there is only one, I am he!"

Lk 18:13-14

¹³"But the tax collector stood at a distance. He would not even look up to heaven, but beat his breast and said, 'God, have mercy on me, a sinner.'
¹⁴"I tell you that this man, rather than the other, went home justified before God. For everyone who exalts himself will be humbled, and he who humbles himself will be exalted."

The tax collector is a study in contrast. He stands at a distance, recognizing his own unworthiness before God. He refuses to assume the normal posture for Jewish prayer — standing, looking up to heaven.

This man, like a scolded child, is not even willing to look into his father's eyes. While the Pharisee stands at a distance browbeating this tax collector, he beats himself on the chest. Instead of praying to himself, he prays to God. His petition is simple, "God, have mercy on me, a sinner." The Greek text has a definite article and should be read "THE sinner." Whereas the Pharisee elevates himself as a righteous man, the publican elevates himself as THE sinner.

Both men get what they sincerely asked for. The publican is justified. The Pharisee gets NOTHING. That's exactly what he asks and exactly what he thinks he needs. It may be difficult for us to feel the impact of this story because we have already been prepared by Luke to feel compassion for the least and the lost (5:12, 27; 7:34, 37; 15:1-2; 16:20), and disdain for the Pharisee (5:17; 6:2, 7; 7:39; 11:37-54; 15:2; 16:14).[63] But in Jesus' day, the "reversal" of this parable would be shocking. So too in our day, we might feel scandalized if we truly understood whose prayers God really respects.

**§ 122
Divorce,
Remarriage,
Celibacy**
(Mt 19:1-12;
Mk 10:1-12;
cf. Lk 16:18)

As Jesus continues his trek to Jerusalem the crowds get thicker. The Pharisees, always lurking in the background, come to the front with a question. They aren't looking for an answer but an opportunity. They want to trip Jesus up with this sticky wicket of divorce. It was as much of a hot button back then as it is today. Everyone stops. All ears are opened; all eyes are on Jesus. His words are typically stunning. He applies to men, for the first time, the same absolute restrictions on divorce that had always applied to women. This offers women unparalleled protection from the ravages of men who, like these Pharisees, want to have their cake and eat it too.

Mt 19:1-3 *with*
Mk 10:1

¹When Jesus had finished saying these things, he left Galilee and went into the region of Judea to the other side of the Jordan. ²{Again^MK} Large crowds followed him, {and as was his custom, he taught them^MK} and he healed them there.
³Some Pharisees came to him to test him. They asked, "Is it lawful for a man to divorce his wife for any and every reason?"

Since his second year of ministry, every time Jesus attracts a crowd he also attracts Pharisees. They are not disciples, they are informants —

---

[63]In Luke's characterization, the Pharisees and tax collectors are binary opposites (3:12-13; 5:27-30; 7:34; 15:1; 18:11-13; 19:2,10). Culturally, the Pharisees wore white hats while the tax collectors wore black hats. But Luke always has them switched (cf. A.M. Okorie, "The Characterization of Tax Collectors in the Gospel of Luke," *CurTM* 22/1 [1995]: 27-32).

obvious enemies. This is even more true since the Sanhedrin openly plotted to kill Jesus (Jn 11:53) and put out a "warrant" for his arrest not more than a month ago (Jn 11:57). That's what sent Jesus to this area in the first place (Jn 11:54; Lk 17:11).

Their question is designed to trap Jesus (cf. Mt 16:1; Mk 10:2; Lk 11:53). Divorce was a raging debate. In fact, the Talmud devotes an entire chapter to it, entitled *Gittin*. Jesus brought up the subject in Judea a couple of months earlier but there was apparently no opportunity to debate the issue then (Lk 16:14, 18). Now that the Pharisees have finally caught up with Jesus, they accost him with this issue. This time it is open for discussion.

The Pharisees' opinions on divorce were divided into two camps. One followed Hillel, the other Shammai (both of whom had been dead for several decades). Hillel said that a man could divorce his wife if she displeased him for almost any reason.[64] In fact, Akiba, a disciple of Hillel, goes so far as to say that a man could divorce his wife if he found a better looking woman (*Gittin* 9:10).[65] Shammai, on the other hand, said one could only divorce his wife for a serious sexual offense. No matter what Jesus answers, half of the crowd will likely be furious.

Shammai's view is closer to Jesus' than Hillel's. But the two are still miles apart. First of all, Shammai's theology of divorce is based on Deuteronomy 24:1-4, whereas Jesus' is based on Genesis 1-2. Second, Shammai deals with only the legal permission for men, whereas Jesus deals with the spiritual obligations of both men and women. Third, only Jesus places restrictions on remarriage, which the Jews would have seen as a nearly absolute right.

We should also note that it was this very issue which caused John the Baptist to lose his head (Mt 14:3-12). The Pharisees meet Jesus on John's old "stompin' ground" (cf. Jn 10:40-41; Lk 17:11). If they can just get him to say the same things that John did, perhaps Jesus will fall to the same fate as his predecessor. That would please these Pharisees.

---

⁴"Haven't you read," he replied, "that at the beginning the Creator 'made them male and female,'ᵃ ⁵and said, 'For this reason a man will leave his father and mother and be united to his wife, and the two will become one flesh'ᵇ? ⁶So they

Mt 19:4-6

---

[64]Valid reasons for divorce according to the Hillelites would include (1) burning a husband's dinner (*Gittin* 90a), (2) going out in public with her head uncovered, (3) talking with men, (4) spinning in the public streets, (5) speaking disrespectfully of her in-laws in front of her husband, (6) being troublesome or quarrelsome, (7) not bearing children within ten years (Edersheim, II:333-334).

[65]Josephus, who was also a Pharisee and a divorcee, was in the Hillelite camp. He believed that divorce was permissible for almost any reason (*Ant*, 4.253).

are no longer two, but one. Therefore what God has joined together, let man not separate."

ᵃ4 Gen 1:27; 5:2     ᵇ5 Gen 2:24

Jesus never backed down from a good fight. They challenge him with a most difficult and touchy issue and he jumps in feet first with his fists up. His opening retort, "Haven't you read" (cf. Mt 12:3, 5; 21:16, 42; 22:31; Mk 12:10, 26), would be offensive to these Bible scholars who had likely not just read but memorized most of the Torah.

Their theology of divorce is based on the hagglings of oral tradition grounded in Deuteronomy 24:1-4. But Jesus, with typical clarity, goes clear back to the beginning and God's design for a man and a woman. First, he states that God designed a man and a woman to be married to each other (citing Gen 1:27 verbatim from the LXX). They belong together physically, emotionally and spiritually.

Second, the marriage bond involves two things: "Leaving and Cleaving" (Gen. 2:24, also from the LXX). Leaving father and mother, in the Biblical world, was not necessarily setting up a separate household. In fact, that would have been a rare thing, at least in the days of the Patriarchs. Rather, "leaving" meant changing your primary commitments. Mom and Dad no longer receive primary loyalty. The second part of the marriage bond involves becoming one flesh. Although this is not exclusively sexual intercourse, there is no greater picture of physical union than this.[66] Thus marriage is pictured as a covenant (Prov 2:17) which stands on two pillars: (a) commitment and (b) oneness — intimate faithfulness. If either of these is destroyed, the marriage breaks down.

Based upon these two pillars God "joins" a couple. Jesus uses a word that means "yoked together" [synezeuksen]. Thus, they become life-partners, co-laborers. This is God's design from the Garden. It is not particularly Jewish or Christian, it is human. This is God's "creation ordinance": One man with one woman for life.

Mt 19:7-8     ⁷"Why then," they asked, "did Moses command that a man give his wife a certificate of divorce and send her away?" [Deut 24:1-4].

⁸Jesus replied, "Moses permitted you to divorce your wives because your

---

[66]Sexual intercourse, in and of itself, does not constitute a marriage. A marriage requires both intimacy (consummated in sexual intercourse) and commitment. Although 1 Cor 6:16 affirms that sexual intercourse with a prostitute creates a bond that transcends physical contact, it does not go so far as to say that the couple becomes husband and wife. If it did, then Jesus would have been mistaken when he told the woman at the well that the man she was living with was not her husband (Jn 4:18). That is precisely why intercourse outside of marriage is so dangerous. It creates a unity between two people without a commitment of the couple. The consequences are often devastating.

hearts were hard. But it was not this way from the beginning."

The Pharisees debated the meaning of Deut 24:1-4. But they mishandled the text. For starters, Moses did not "command" that a man divorce his wife. Rather, he forbade a man from marrying the same woman twice. This was primarily for the protection of the woman. In such a male dominated society, women were treated as property. This law would keep a man from too quickly dismissing a wife just because they got in a fight. If he lets her go, it is for keeps. He can't snatch her back like a child swapping baseball cards.

The primary question in the Hillel versus Shammai debate is the meaning of "something indecent." Literally, it means "nakedness" or "exposure" specifically of the genitals (and most often in reference to women). It probably does not refer merely to adultery, for the law prescribed the death penalty for adultery (Lev 20:10; Deut 22:22). One hardly needs to divorce a dead woman. And even though the Jews seldom executed people for adultery (especially in NT times), it would be rather incongruous for Moses to establish such a double standard within the written law itself. On the other hand, "something indecent" certainly must mean more than "being ugly" or "being a bad cook" as the Hillelites applied it. It seems reasonable to assume that "something indecent" covers a range of sexual sins including adultery. This would be true for both the Hebrew word and Jesus' application of it, translated with the Greek word *porneia*. Thus, a serious sexual sin breaks the "one flesh" pillar of the marriage covenant.

Back to the Pharisees' question. Although Moses did not *command* divorce, his regulations did *de facto* **permit** it. Now, Moses is not advocating divorce. Rather, he is regulating it. He can't stop it, but he can put some parameters around it. Without legal guidelines, women and children[67] were especially vulnerable to the ravages of what Jesus calls "hard hearts."[68]

⁹"I tell you that anyone who divorces his wife, except for marital unfaithfulness, and marries another woman commits adultery {against her.ᴹᴷ}

Mt 19:9 *with* Mk 10:11

¹²"And if she divorces her husband and marries another man, she commits adultery.

Mk 10:12

¹⁸"And the man who marries a divorced woman commits adultery."

Lk 16:18

---

[67]Perhaps it is only a coincidence, but it seems significant that the next two pericopes following this teaching on divorce deal with children and money, both critical issues where divorce is concerned.

[68]God allowed divorce legislation to accommodate the hard hearts of his people. In much the same way God permitted a monarchy and the building of a temple even though these were not his original intentions either.

This is a most difficult text for a number of reasons. But before deal-ing with the text itself, we ought to set some parameters around our explanation of this text. First, this is a debate between Jesus and the Pharisees. The question, designed to trap Jesus, is specifically about a husband divorcing a wife.[69] Therefore we should probably be as cautious about making universal absolutes from this narrative as we are with other "debate" texts.[70]

Second, when Matthew writes this, the ink is hardly dry from 18:18-35, dealing with forgiving an erring brother and confronting an unrepen-tant brother. Divorce, although a highly personal issue, must not be dealt with alone. Christians are part of a body. Therefore, a couple heading toward divorce have an obligation to seek counsel and support from the broader Christian fellowship to which they are joined.

Third, we must balance both solid exegesis and realistic application. Although the text must reign supreme over our opinions, reason, and culture, any explanation of the text which leads to oppression, bigotry, or legalism is suspect. It is our job not only to explain the text accurately but to apply it with sensitivity. That being said, this verse confronts us with at least two major questions:

### 1. Is Jesus giving permission to divorce if your spouse is unfaithful?

Some say "NO!" This "exception clause" is found only in Matthew 5:32 and 19:9. Some suggest that Matthew would not contain an excep-tion clause which Mark and Luke didn't have because then Matthew's recipients would be allowed to divorce but Luke and Mark's audience would not. However, among the Greeks and Romans, to whom Mark and Luke primarily wrote, it was universally assumed that adultery was adequate grounds for divorce. It just went without saying. In other words, Matthew explicitly states what Mark and Luke can assume.

If we look closely at Matthew 5:32, it doesn't actually say that adul-tery is permission for divorce. It merely says that if a man divorces his wife he forces her to become an adulteress, unless, of course, she had

---

[69]In Jewish circles, it was nearly unheard of that a woman would divorce her husband. In Greco-Roman circles, however, it was more common. This is probably why Mark includes his words (10:12), stating that what goes for the man also goes for the woman. It would be more applicable to Mark's audience than to Matthew's.

[70]C. Blomberg cautions that "Few try to make the pronouncements in various other con-troversy or pronouncement stories absolute (cf., e.g., Matt 19:21; 9:15, and esp. 13:57, a particularly interesting parallel because of its similar exception clause . . .), so one should be equally wary of elevating 19:9 (or Mark 10:11-12) into an exceptionless absolute" ("Marriage, Divorce, Remarriage and Celibacy: An Exegesis of Matthew 19:3-12" *TrinJ* 11NS [1990]: 162).

already been involved in adultery. In other words, if she is already an adulteress, you can't make her one. That logic works well for Matthew 5:32.[71] But it doesn't hold up in Matthew 19:9. Here it is the man who commits adultery by divorcing his wife.

Based on this, we can confidently say that Jesus grants permission, without obligation, to divorce an "unfaithful" spouse. But just what exactly is this "unfaithfulness?" The word used in both Matthew 5:32 and 19:9 is *porneia*. It at least means "adultery" [*moichos*].[72] But it may mean more. Like its OT counterpart [*'ervah*] in Deut 24:1, *porneia* can cover a range of sexual sins. These could include coitus, indecent exposure, homosexuality, molestation, incest, etc. But it would have to be of such a serious nature as to breach the "oneness" of the marital covenant.

But is sexual infidelity the only valid reason for divorce? No. Paul clearly adds another in 1 Corinthians 7:15. If an unbelieving spouse abandons a Christian, the believer is to let him/her go. If a Christian is abandoned by a fellow believer, however, (s)he is to remain celibate and strive for reconciliation (1 Cor 7:11). One might assume that the Christian abandoned by a nonbeliever should also remain celibate (1 Cor. 7:8), unless the sexual temptation is too great to withstand (1 Cor. 7:9). Obviously a second marriage is preferable to fornication.

In conclusion, there are two valid reasons for divorce: (1) Sexual unfaithfulness, which destroys the first pillar of the marriage covenant — "Oneness." (2) Abandonment by an unbelieving spouse, which destroys the second pillar of the marriage covenant — "Commitment." Are there other instances in which Jesus would approve of divorce besides abandonment or adultery? Some confidently say, "Yes."[73] If there are, however, they would have to be serious enough to irreparably damage one of the two pillars of the marriage covenant. Some have suggested that physical abuse, sexual deviancy, insanity, Alzheimer's, extended comatose, alcoholism/drug addiction, etc., might fall into this category. But we need to be cautious here.

---

[71]However, P. H. Wiebe, "Jesus' Divorce Exception," *JETS 32/3* (1989): 327-333, shows that linguistically the exception clause can modify either phrase, "Whoever divorces his wife" or "causes her to commit adultery." Hence, even in Mt 5:32, it could be taken as a valid exception for divorce.

[72]*porn* — root words are used much more commonly for women's sexual misconduct than for men's. This may explain why Jesus uses *porneia* here rather than the more specific word for adultery, *moicheō*.

[73]R.H. Stein, "Is It Lawful For a Man to Divorce His Wife?" *JETS* 22/2 (1979): 115-121 and M. J. Molldrem, "A Hermeneutic of Pastoral Care and the Law/Gospel Paradigm Applied to the Divorce Text of Scripture," *Int* 45 (1991): 43-54.

While recognizing that neither Jesus' nor Paul's discussions are designed to handle all the complexities and possibilities of divorce, they do set God's parameters on this issue. On the one hand, we must be faithful with what the Scripture teaches. On the other hand, we must apply this teaching with sensitivity, compassion, and reason. So, based on the context of Matthew 18:15-35, we offer this caution against dealing too lightly with divorce. Although there may be more valid reasons for divorce than the two mentioned by Jesus and Paul, that is *not* an individual decision. When a couple is experiencing marital difficulty, they have an obligation to the body to seek counsel and prayer. A couple embroiled in conflict will almost invariably magnify their problem(s) and too quickly conclude that their differences are irreconcilable. At that point, godly Christian leaders are probably able to make better decisions than the couple. Since divorce affects the whole body, it hardly seems right for it to be a private decision.

Divorce is always bad (Mal 2:16). It should be recognized as a personal failure and a spiritual defeat. But sometimes in a fallen world we find ourselves with a set of poor options. We don't have the luxury of choosing between good and bad but merely between the lesser of two evils. There are times when divorce is a more reasonable, healthy option than remaining married. But we must weigh our options carefully and only accept divorce as a last resort when all other options have failed.

### 2. Who is guilty of adultery in divorce and remarriage?

Jesus is not saying that divorce is the act of adultery. Rather, he says divorce is *like* adultery. That is, they both break the marriage covenant. It is a metaphor.[74] Jesus often used such figures of speech. For instance, in the Sermon on the Mount, when Jesus first introduced this teaching on divorce (5:32), he surrounded it with other metaphors: Anger = murder; Lust = adultery; "gouge out your right eye;" salt & light, etc.

The woman becomes an adulteress through no apparent fault of her own (Mt 5:32). How? A divorced woman in Jesus' day had few options. The fortunate remarried. The unfortunate were forced into prostitution. Both of these options would include sexual activity which could be labeled "adultery." But what about the woman who remains celibate (perhaps supported by a family member)? If she has not slept with another man either prior to or after the divorce, it is unfair to call her an adulteress. However, she is *treated* like an adulteress and she suffers the same privation and rejection that adulteresses often experience. So for

---

[74]"Adultery" was often used metaphorically in the OT for "idolatry" (Hos 2:4; 4:12; Jer 5:7; Ezek 16:32; 23:37).

all *practical* purposes, her ex-husband forces her to become an adulteress even though she has not committed the crime.

So how is divorce like adultery? Divorce destroys the pillar of "commitment" in marriage. Adultery destroys the pillar of "oneness" in marriage. Either way, the marriage is shot. Thus, both divorce and adultery have the same terrible consequence. Hence, divorce is just as bad as adultery. Now that would come as a shock to these persnickety Pharisees who would never commit adultery but felt perfectly free to divorce whimsically. Furthermore, remarriage, which these fellows felt was their God-given right, destroys any glimmer of hope for reconciliation. Thus, remarriage is also like adultery.[75] Divorce, adultery and remarriage — all three separate what God has joined together.

Does this mean that remarriage is sinful? The early church unanimously responded with a resounding "Yes!" But what would Jesus say? If all attempts at reconciliation have failed, then it might not be sin. It is never ideal. It is a mark of moral failure. It bears the burden of past brokenness. But where divorce is concerned we have no good options. We are sometimes forced, therefore, to choose between the lesser of two evils. That doesn't mean the second marriages won't be good. But they can never be best. Paul would like for all singles to remain celibate. But he knows that many can't handle it (1 Cor 7:8-9). In that case, remarriage is a better option than fornication. In addition, where children are concerned, two parents are generally better than one.

But if a couple remarries, will they not be living in continual adultery? NO! Remarriage is not adultery, it is adultery-like. That is, it puts a nail in the coffin of the first marriage. The "adultery" is tied to the divorce, not the sexual union of the second couple.[76] Some, however, would suggest that because the Greek phrase "commits adultery" is in the present tense, that it means that the couple continues to commit adultery as long as they live together. However, the present tense verb means no more in Greek than it does in English. It simply indicates an event that occurs without any clear indication as to whether it continues or not.[77] Furthermore, the implication of such an idea is atrocious.

---

[75]All parties involved commit adultery: (1) The man who divorces his wife (Mt 19:9), (2) the woman who divorces her husband (Mk 10:12), (3) the woman who is divorced by her husband (Mt 5:32), and (4) the man who marries a divorced woman (Mt 5:32).

[76]"When one further recognizes that remarriage was viewed as a fundamental right by virtually all Jews in antiquity (*m. Git.* 9:3), one should realize that if Jesus had wanted anyone in his audience to understand that he was forbidding all remarriage, he would have had to have said so much more clearly" (C.L. Blomberg, "Marriage, Divorce, Remarriage . . ." *TrinJ* 11NS [1990]: 179-180).

[77]In the Greek language the present tense verb does indicate continued action if it is used

If second-marriage couples are living in a continued state of adultery, then the only solution would be to dissolve that second marriage and seek reconciliation of the first marriage. This may imply (1) committing adultery through a second divorce, (2) dissolving a good marriage to seek a near impossible reconciliation of a bad marriage, (3) traumatizing two relationships, (4) and dividing children of a second marriage.

Furthermore, Jesus recognized the validity of multiple marriages (Jn 4:18), without either approving of them or accusing them of being mere adultery. So did Moses (Deut 24:1-4). We should do the same. This is especially true of those who come to Christ as divorcees (1 Cor 7:17). Destroying a second marriage in a futile attempt to reconcile a first marriage hardly seems a step in the right direction.

**Mt 19:10-12** *with*
**Mk 10:10**

{[10]When they were in the house again[MK]} [10]The disciples said to him, "If this is the situation between a husband and wife, it is better not to marry."

[11]Jesus replied, "Not everyone can accept this word, but only those to whom it has been given. [12]For some are eunuchs because they were born that way; others were made that way by men; and others have renounced marriage[a] because of the kingdom of heaven. The one who can accept this should accept it."

[a]*12 Or have made themselves eunuchs*

The sanctity of marriage and the call to celibacy after divorce is serious stuff. So once they resort to the privacy of their host's house, the disciples question Jesus about this. Perhaps facetiously they say, "If marriage is that tough, it would be better to be single."

But instead of softening the blow, Jesus says, "You are right! It would be better to be celibate, but not everyone can be." Paul would agree (1 Cor 7:7-9). Most people in the modern church just chuckle and say, "Yea, that's not for me!" without ever giving serious thought to the contribution that a single person could make to the kingdom.[78] Relationships are beautiful and they are God's plan. But they take an enormous amount of time and energy that could be used for the work of the gospel (1 Cor. 7:32-35).

---

in the imperative, subjunctive, or infinitive moods. But when used in the indicative mood, as it is here, it does not always mean progressive action; and the only way to tell is through the context (C.D. Osburn, "The Present Indicative of Matthew 19:9," *RestQ* 24 [1981]: 193-203).

[78]The early church took this seriously. There were large groups of people who remained single so they could devote their entire time and attention to the service of the church (W.A. Heth, "Unmarried 'For the Sake of the Kingdom' (Mt 19:12) in the Early Church," *GTJ* 8/1 [1987]: 55-88).

But remaining single does require a gift from God. There are three categories of eunuchs, according to Jesus. The first is a person who was born without the natural capacity for sex. The second is a person who, through surgery (e.g., castration), loses his sexual urges (e.g., Acts 8:27). Third, is a person who determines not to marry for the cause of Christ. While the theology of celibacy for the Catholic priesthood has appropriately been questioned by Protestants and Catholics alike (cf. 1 Tim 4:1-3), the gift of celibacy has been woefully underestimated by evangelicals.

Most single people among our ranks are treated as an unfortunate anomaly. Great attempts are made to "fix them up" as if they were broken.[79] Singles' ministries would do well to give a balanced Biblical perspective rather than falling prey to the unbalanced contemporary persuasion that idolizes sexuality. There are more important things than personal, sexual gratification. The question should not be, "Which would make me happier," but "Would I be more effective for Christ married or single?"

§ 123
**Jesus on Children in the Kingdom**
(Mt 19:13-15;
Mk 10:13-16;
Lk 18:15-17)

Matthew and Mark connect this section with Jesus' teaching on divorce. By doing so, they may intend to highlight the sanctity of the family. Luke, on the other hand, connects it to a couple of parables on prayer — The Widow and the Tax Collector. Both parables show how God hears the prayers of "little people." The disciples have apparently missed this lesson since they forbid these kids to come to Jesus.

Mk 10:13-16 *with*
Mt 19:13-15;
Lk 18:16

{Then^MT} [13]People were {also^LK} bringing little children to Jesus to have him touch them {and pray for them,^MT} but the disciples rebuked them {those who brought them.^MT} [14]When Jesus saw this, he was indignant. He {called the children to him and^LK} said to them, "Let the little children come to me, and do not hinder them, for the kingdom of God {heaven^MT} belongs to such as these. [15]I tell you the truth, anyone who will not receive the kingdom of God like a little child will never enter it." [16]And he took the children in his arms, put his hands on them and blessed them {he went on from there.^MT}

The crowds continue to expand (cf. Mt 19:2; Mk 10:1), placing increasing demands on Jesus' time. Among those clamoring for Jesus' attention and touch are a group of women with their children.[80]

---

[79]In the Bible we find a number of fruitful single men and women including: Jesus, Jeremiah, Paul, Anna, and probably John the Baptist, Lydia, and Mary Magdalene (cf. F. Stagg, "Biblical Perspectives on the Single Person," *RevExp* 74 [1977]: 5-19).

[80]Both Matthew and Mark use the word *paidia*, which was earlier used to describe Jairus' 12-year-old daughter. But Luke uses the word *brephe* (v. 15) which normally signifies an infant (Lk 2:12, 16; Acts 7:19; 2 Tim 3:15; 1 Pet 2:2) and can even be used for an unborn child (Lk 1:41,44). Thus, Jesus' invitation includes a broader age-range of children.

The disciples' motives are probably good. They want to run interference for Jesus and protect him from these demanding mothers and their rambunctious children. Now, anyone who has been in a church service with a bunch of kids can understand the frustration of the disciples. Kids tend to squirm about and make noise and generally distract everyone around them; sometimes with their sweetness, sometimes with their noise. These children are distracting the adults from hearing Jesus.

Jewish children were expected to be quiet and submissive, and were generally equated with servants until they came of age (cf. Gal 4:1-2). Yet they were a cherished part of Jewish society. It was not at all uncommon for parents to take their children to important people to have them place their hands on them and pray for them. But the disciples rebuke them when they should have known better. Clear back in Galilee, Jesus already taught them that children are the epitome of kingdom citizens (cf. § 90, Mt 18:1-5; Mk 9:33-37; Lk 9:46-48).[81]

When Jesus sees what the disciples are doing he becomes angry and tells them to "get out of his way" [mē kōlyete].[82] This doesn't happen very often. Twice it is implied that Jesus was angry with the Chief Priests when he cleansed the temple (Jn 2:14-17; Mt 21:12-13; Mk 11:15-17; Lk 19:45-46). But only one other time is it explicitly stated that Jesus was angry. That was when he healed the man's withered hand on the Sabbath (Mk 3:5). He was angry because the Pharisees prioritized religious ritual over this poor man's need. Thus Jesus got angry with only three groups that we know of: Pharisees, Sadducees, and his disciples. How odd it is then that "sinners" are the target of so much "Christian" venom.[82a]

---

[81]The latter Judean and Perean ministries of Jesus often cover the same issues as Jesus' Galilean ministry, sometimes even with identical words. Here are some of the parallels: (1) Sending out the 72 (Lk 10:1-16) and the 12 (Mt 10); (2) The Model Prayer (Lk 11:1-4, 9-12 & Mt 6:9-13; 7:7-11); (3) Beelzebub and blasphemy of the H.S. (Lk 11:14-36 & Mt 12:22-37; Mk 3:20-30); (4) Conflict with the Pharisees at a meal (Lk 11:37-54; 14:1-24 & Mt 15:1-20; Mk 7:1-23); (5) Warnings for discipleship (Lk 12:1-12; 14:25-35; 17:1-10 & Mt 10:18-33, 37-38; 18:6-7, 21-22); (6) Warnings about money (Lk 12:22-34 & Mt 6:19-34); (7) Warnings about allegiance to Jesus above family (Lk 12:49-53 & Mt 10:34-36); (8) Warnings about discerning the times (Lk 12:54-59 & Mt 16:2-3; 5:25-36); (9) Controversy over Sabbath healing (Lk 13:10-21; 14:1-24 & Mt 12:1-14; Mk 2:23-3:6; Lk 6:1-11); (10) Extended use of Parables (Lk 15-16; 18:1-14 & Mt 13; Mk 4; Lk 8); (11) Raising someone from the dead (Lk 7:11-17; 8:40-56; Mt 9:18-26; Mk 5:21-43 & Jn 11:17-44).

[82]This same Greek construction is also used in the context of baptism (Mt 3:14; Acts 8:36; 10:47; 11:17). However, the connection is circumstantial, not theological. In other words, this verse is not intended to teach or even suggest infant baptism.

[82a]Jesus' emotions betray God's own priorities. Emotions are not human weakness but, in fact, part of our *Imago Dei*. Our weakness comes in our inability to control our emotions or direct them toward the right people and situations (cf. W. Hansen, "The Emotions of Jesus," *CT* [Feb 3, 1997]: 43-46).

There could scarcely be a more tender scene than this. Jesus calling the kids and scooping them up in his arms. They are models for kingdom citizens, not because they are gullible and weak. They are model citizens because (a) they are humble, (b) they do not seek rank or position, and (c) they freely recognize their need for help.

The scene is brief. Jesus must move on. He has a Passover to attend.

**§ 124a**
**Rich Young**
**Ruler**
(Mt 19:16-30;
Mk 10:17-31;
Lk 18:18-30)

This story is simple. An influential young "businessman" is compelled to follow Jesus. But he just can't bring himself to part with his money so he leaves Jesus instead. Few stories are more poignant for the American church. Perhaps that's why we feel it necessary to explain it away. We say, "Boy that's a powerful story for rich people." We don't think it applies to us. You see, the "rich" are people with just a little more money than we have. Or we say, "Well, Jesus doesn't ask everyone to give up wealth, only those for whom it was a problem." Yet we never consider just how much of an obstacle money is in our own pursuit of Christ.

Mk 10:17-18 *with*
Mt 19:16;
Lk 18:18

[17]As Jesus started on his way, a man {a certain ruler[LK]} ran up to him and fell on his knees before him. "Good teacher," he asked, "what {good thing[MT]} must I do to inherit eternal life?"

[18]"Why do you call me good?" Jesus answered. "No one is good — except God alone."

As Jesus weaves his way through Perea toward Jerusalem, he is once again stopped with a question. This urgent young man stands in stark contrast to the children Jesus has just blessed (Mt 19:13-15; Mk 10:13-16; Lk 18:15-17). Even though he is young (probably 20-40), he has already achieved great economic success (Lk 18:23).[83] Furthermore, he is a respected leader in the community (Lk 18:18), probably through the synagogue. He was respectful (Mk 10:17), religious (Mk 10:20), and teachable (Lk 18:18). He appears to be the perfect "prospect."

Unlike the Pharisees, who halted Jesus' progress with a question designed to trap him (Mt 19:3; Mk 10:2), this young man seems to be sincere. After all, he approaches Jesus with utmost respect both in his posture (kneeling), appellation ("Good teacher"), and honesty ("What do I still lack?"). Hence, Jesus "loved" him (Mk 10:21). Furthermore, he asks a good question; no, the *best* question: "What must I do to inherit eternal life?"

---

[83]Although Matthew and Mark simply say that he had many possessions [*ktemata polla*], which does not necessarily mean that he was rich, Luke uses a phrase that could only be applied to the upper class [*plousios sphodra*].

Before Jesus answers his question, he must clarify two important issues: #1 — Who is Jesus, and #2 — How are we saved? Unless he has a basic understanding of these two things, he won't properly understand Jesus' answer to his question.

**Issue #1: Who is Jesus?** The young man addresses him as "Good Teacher."[84] Jesus calls his attention to what that implies. When Jesus says, "No one is good but God alone," he is not saying that he, himself, is not good. Rather, he is calling attention to the fact that he shares God's goodness. Only on that basis and only with that understanding will this young man be able to properly hear the answer to his question.

This "goodness" probably has more to do with Jesus' ability to teach truth than his moral perfection (2 Cor 5:21; Heb 4:15). In other words, he is a good teacher because he has all the right answers. Yet God alone has a corner on the "truth." Therefore, if Jesus always speaks truth then he truly speaks as God's representative (Jn 8:28; 12:49-50). Therefore, this young man had better be prepared to listen well.

Mk 10:19-20 *with*
Mt 19:17-20

{"If you want to enter life, obey the commandments." "Which ones?" the man inquired. Jesus replied,[MT]} [19]"You know the commandments: 'Do not murder, do not commit adultery, do not steal, do not give false testimony, do not defraud, honor your father and mother,[a] {and love your neighbor as yourself.'[b"MT]}

[20]"Teacher," he {the young man[MT]} declared, "all these I have kept since I was a boy. {What do I still lack?[MT]}"

[a][*Mk 10:]19* Exodus 20:12-16; Deut. 5:16-20    [b][*Mt 19:]19* Lev. 19:18

**Issue #2: How are we saved?** The Jews were thoroughly convinced that a person gained God's favor by their own good behavior (Deut 30:15-16). So Jesus first gives the typical Jewish response, "Keep the commandments." He catalogues the fifth through the tenth commandments (Exod 20:12-16; Deut 5:16-20).[85] Then, as Matthew notes, Jesus summarizes the whole list by appending Leviticus 19:18, "You shall love your neighbor as yourself" (cf. Mt 22:34-40).

---

[84]There are significant differences between Matthew's wording and Mark's which D.A. Carson has dealt with in length ("Redaction Criticism: On the Legitimacy and Illegitimacy of a Literary Tool," in *Scripture and Truth*, ed. D.A. Carson and J.D. Woodbridge [Grand Rapids, MI: Zondervan, 1983], 131-137). These differences will not be dealt with here because (1) the purpose of this work is not to deal with the technical aspects of higher criticism, (2) they don't significantly affect the meaning of the passage, and (3) Matthew hints at Mark's wording anyway in v. 17, indicating that the two readings are not antithetical. J.W. Wenham, "Why Do You Ask Me About the Good? A Study of the Relation Between Text and Source Criticism," *NTS* 28 (1982): 116-125, makes a case for Matthew's original text reading "Good Teacher, what good thing must I do."

[85]Mark probably intends for "do not defraud" to be a practical application of the 10th commandment to not covet.

These last six commandments deal only with a person's horizontal relationships (i.e., human to human). This rich, young ruler is blameless in his dealings with other people (v. 20). That does not mean that he is absolutely sinless (Rom 3:23). But a sincere apology and the temple sacrifices made up the shortfall for occasional transgressions. He is impeccably devout and could say with the Apostle Paul, "As for legalistic righteousness, *I am* faultless" (Phil 3:6).

Even though his external righteousness is blameless, his heart and mind are not right. Something is missing, and he knows it. In the depths of his spirit he feels the words of Jesus, "For I tell you that unless your righteousness surpasses that of the Pharisees and the teachers of the law, you will certainly not enter the kingdom of heaven" (Mt 5:20). So when Jesus gives him the classic Jewish answer to "How are we saved?" he responds, "Yeah, yeah, I've heard all that before, but it just hasn't worked. What am I missing?!"

We are saved by grace through faith; not by our own works lest anyone should boast (Eph 2:8). This young man knows that none of his previous good deeds have earned him eternal life.[86] And yet he still clings to legalism for he knows nothing else. Christianity stands alone as the only world religion in which a person is saved by what God does for you rather than what you do for God. Indeed, legalism is a tenacious and pernicious religious idea. I dare say that most who call themselves Christians have not fully given up on it.

{When Jesus heard this,[LK]} [21]Jesus looked at him and loved him. "One thing you lack," he said. "{If you want to be perfect,[MT]} Go, sell everything you have and give to the poor, and you will have treasure in heaven. Then come, follow me." [22]At this the man's face fell. He went away sad, because he had great wealth.

Mk 10:21-22
*with* Mt 19:21;
Lk 18:22

Jesus calls this young man to be a disciple by first ridding himself of all his money. This was an especially surprising demand in light of the fact that the Jews forbade giving away more than twenty percent of your possessions (*Kethub.* 50 *a*). Every disciple is called to follow Jesus in faith. But sometimes there are obstacles that stand between us and Jesus so that we cannot follow him until we rid ourselves of these barriers. For this young man, the barrier was money. For others it may be family, business, reputation or self. Just because the obstacle may be different for us, the demand is no less absolute or radical (Gal 2:20; Mt 10:37-39; Phil 3:7-11).

------------

[86]It is probably significant that this text uses three terms synonymously for salvation talk: Eternal life, entering the kingdom, and saved. At the very least, this indicates that eternal life has a present aspect to it. It lasts forever, but it begins now.

The two stories that closely follow in Luke's account show that not every disciple is called to sell everything and give it to the poor. Zacchaeus gave half of his wealth (19:1-10), and the faithful servants in the parable of 19:11-27 are called to invest their money wisely for the Master (Blomberg, p. 299). In all instances, however, God's view of money is clear: He owns it all. We are merely stewards, using his resources for his purposes. At the same time, the contemporary American church, inundated by a materialistic society, needs to carefully hear Jesus' call to abandon wealth to follow him. We almost certainly underestimate how much of this text actually does apply to us (Jas 2:14-17; 1 Jn 3:17).

One can keep the law and still love anything else (money, sex, power). But when coming to Jesus, we forsake all other loves. This man must make a choice between a relationship with Jesus and a love for his money. "No man can serve two masters. Either he will hate the one and love the other, or he will be devoted to the one and despise the other. You cannot serve both God and money" (Mt 6:24). The primary issue here is not benevolence to the poor, as important as that is, but allegiance to Jesus. His money is standing in his way. Jesus asks him to get rid of it.

The man goes away sad. Luke uses a word that might be rendered literally, "surrounded by grief." Matthew says he was "grieving" [*lypeō*]. His sadness is not that he just "lost his salvation." Certainly, in his mind, he did not choose money over eternal life. Rather, he is sad because his question remained unanswered. He is still looking for a way to gain salvation AND keep his money.

He mistakes salvation as some kind of reward for righteousness rather than a personal relationship with his Messiah. If salvation is seen as a system of reward, then there is no reason a person cannot have riches or power and still be saved. But if salvation is understood as a relationship with Jesus, then you must make a choice about what you will give your time and attention to: money or the Lord.

Mk 10:23-27
*with* Mt 19:23,25;
Lk 18:24

[23]Jesus looked around {at him[LK]} and said to his disciples, "How hard it is for the rich to enter the kingdom of God {heaven[MT]}!"

[24]{When [they] heard this,[MT]} The disciples were amazed at his words. But Jesus said again, "Children, how hard it is[a] to enter the kingdom of God! [25]It is easier for a camel to go through the eye of a needle than for a rich man to enter the kingdom of God."

[26]The disciples were even more amazed, and said to each other, "Who then can be saved?"

[27]Jesus looked at them and said, "With man this is impossible, but not with God; all things are possible with God."

[a]24 Some manuscripts *is for those who trust in riches*

While Jesus watches this young man walk off with his chin in his chest, he says to the disciples, "How hard it is for the rich to enter the kingdom of God." We have become accustomed to this kind of talk. But Jesus' Jewish audience is astonished. You see, they believed, with scriptural support, that wealth was a blessing from God. Of all people, the rich were the most likely candidates for eternal life since God favored them. If they can't make it, then what are the chances for all the "little people"?

The crowd is perplexed. Instead of solving their conundrum, Jesus confuses them further by saying that the rich would no sooner get into heaven than a camel[87] would pass through the eye of a needle. That is obviously impossible! The camel[88] was the largest animal in Palestine and the eye of a needle[89] was the smallest "opening" in common use.

Modern guides in Jerusalem will point to a supposed gate in the wall as the "eye of the needle." It is common to suggest that this gate is what Jesus is referring to here since the camel could just barely squeeze through it and then only on its knees. Aside from the fact that there is no evidence to support such an interpretation, it ruins the metaphor. The point is not that it is difficult for the rich to get into heaven but that it is impossible.[90]

Jesus' audience is stunned. Their question is predictable, "Who then can be saved?" It may appear that Jesus is off on a tangent, but in fact, he is at the heart of the issue. The rich young ruler asked, "What must I do to inherit eternal life?" Jesus points out that no amount of good works will suffice. No amount of law-keeping will "fill the gap" (Mt 19:20). We must abandon all that stands between us and Jesus and trust God alone and completely. Salvation is God's gracious gift (Mk 10:27), which we appropriate through a response of faith (Mk 10:21).

[28]Peter said to him, "We have left everything to follow you!" — Mk 10:28

[28]Jesus said to them, "I tell you the truth, at the renewal of all things, when the Son of Man sits on his glorious throne, you who have followed me will also sit on twelve thrones, judging the twelve tribes of Israel. — Mt 19:28

---

[87]J.D.M. Derrett suggests that "camel" in Aramaic [*gamal*] is a play on the word *gemiluth* meaning "acts of benevolence" which the rich were neglecting ("A Camel through the Eye of a Needle," *NTS* 32 [1986]: 465-70).

[88]In Babylon this idiom is changed to an elephant passing through the eye of a needle since elephants are the largest animal in Babylon.

[89]Luke uses a special word that Matthew and Mark do not, which indicates a surgical needle.

[90]A few of the later manuscripts substitute "rope" for "camel." That does justice to the metaphor and retains the element of impossibility, but the manuscript support is so weak that it makes it an unlikely reading.

²⁹"[N]o one who has left home {or wife^LK} or brothers or sisters or mother or father or children or fields for me and the gospel {the kingdom of God^LK} ³⁰will fail to receive a hundred times as much in this present age (homes, brothers, sisters, mothers, children and fields — and with them, persecutions) and in the age to come, eternal life. ³¹But many who are first will be last, and the last first."

Peter is sharp! He starts to think to himself, "Salvation is gained through total abandonment of this world and total commitment to following Jesus. I've done that!" So, speaking for the Twelve, he points out the obvious to Jesus. Perhaps his motives are a bit selfish and his mindset a bit legalistic, but his logic is sound. Jesus gives him a straightforward, legitimate answer. The Apostles' reward will be fourfold. All other disciples will share the last three of the four benefits:

First, the Apostles will sit on twelve thrones and judge the twelve tribes of Israel (Mt 19:28, cf. Lk 22:28-30). That is, when Jesus returns and judgment begins, the twelve Jewish tribes will be judged by the twelve Apostles. At the same time, Christians will help judge of the rest of the world and even the angels (1 Cor 6:2-3). Jesus calls this the "renewal of all things" [*palingenesia*] (cf. Isa 34:4; 51:6; 65:17; Dan 7:9-14, 18, 27; 2 Pet 3:10-13; Rev 21-22). We will finally get back to God's original plan that started in the Garden.

The second reward, which takes place in this present life (Mk 10:30), is the multiplication of the very things we are asked to give up (homes, brothers, sisters, mothers, children and fields). Matthew and Mark both specify one hundred times the amount. This is 10,000% interest. This promise is literally fulfilled when the church shares its wealth with the body of Christ.

Third, along with this great wealth comes persecution (Mk 10:30). It is part of the package for standing with Jesus (Jn 15:18-25). Finally, beyond the persecutions of this life is the hope of eternal life. That will certainly make all the sufferings we endure here seem as nothing (Rom 8:18).

**§ 124b
Parable: First
Shall Be Last
and the Last,
First
(Mt 20:1-16)**

It is unfortunate that our Bibles begin a new chapter here. This parable is an extension of the previous discussion. That becomes obvious when we read the same words in both Matthew 19:30 and 20:16, "The last will be first and the first will be last." This phrase serves as the "book ends" for the parable.

Thus, this parable illustrates how the first can be last and the last first. But contextually it also rounds out Jesus' answer to Peter about rewards of discipleship. The rich man asked Jesus, "What must I do to inherit eternal life?" Aside from keeping the commandments, Jesus said he would have to give up all his possessions and follow him. The rich young ruler walked away sad, but Peter asked, "Lord, we have done that. So what will we get?" Jesus presents an impressive list. There are benefits to discipleship. But that is not the end of the story. Salvation is by grace through faith. Lest Peter think that he earned these benefits, Jesus tells this story to remind us that what we have in Christ is not because we have earned it but because God is gracious.

[1]"For the kingdom of heaven is like a landowner who went out early in the morning to hire men to work in his vineyard. [2]He agreed to pay them a denarius for the day and sent them into his vineyard.

[3]"About the third hour he went out and saw others standing in the marketplace doing nothing. [4]He told them, 'You also go and work in my vineyard, and I will pay you whatever is right.' [5]So they went.

"He went out again about the sixth hour and the ninth hour and did the same thing. [6]About the eleventh hour he went out and found still others standing around. He asked them, 'Why have you been standing here all day long doing nothing?'

[7]"'Because no one has hired us,' they answered.

"He said to them, 'You also go and work in my vineyard.'"

Mt 20:1-7

During the harvest, a farmer has to hire extra hands to get all the crops into the barn before they spoil in the field. It is a delightful but frantic time. In Palestine, he went to the marketplace where itinerant workers would congregate, waiting to be hired.

Our story opens where the workday begins, at sunrise in the marketplace. There we meet the farmer who hires a group of men and sends them to his vineyard to gather grapes for the day.[91] The going wage was one denarius for twelve hours of work.[92] That's what the farmer promises these hired hands. A few hours into the workday the grapes aren't being gathered fast enough. So the farmer returns to the marketplace to find and hire more workers. Because they are late-comers, he doesn't promise them a denarius but only "what is fair." The farmer continues to hire laborers in this same manner throughout the day: at noon, 3 p.m., and 5 p.m., merely one hour before the workday ends. This is an obvious exaggeration but it paints a vivid picture.

[8]"When evening came, the owner of the vineyard said to his foreman, 'Call the workers and pay them their wages, beginning with the last ones hired and going on to the first.'

Mt 20:8-16

---

[91]The vineyard was a frequent symbol for Israel (esp. Isa 5:1-7).

[92]The soldier's wage seemed to have set the standard. They were paid a denarius a day (Tobit 5:14; Tacitus, *Annales*, 1.17; Pliny 33:3).

⁹"The workers who were hired about the eleventh hour came and each received a denarius. ¹⁰So when those came who were hired first, they expected to receive more. But each one of them also received a denarius. ¹¹When they received it, they began to grumble against the landowner. ¹²'These men who were hired last worked only one hour,' they said, 'and you have made them equal to us who have borne the burden of the work and the heat of the day.'

¹³"But he answered one of them, 'Friend, I am not being unfair to you. Didn't you agree to work for a denarius? ¹⁴Take your pay and go. I want to give the man who was hired last the same as I gave you. ¹⁵Don't I have the right to do what I want with my own money? Or are you envious because I am generous?'

¹⁶"So the last will be first, and the first will be last."

In those days workers were generally paid at the end of each work-day (cf. Lev 19:13). They all line up to get their money. At the front of the line are those hired last. The farmer's foreman begins to dole out the cash. Everyone who has been hired after sunrise has no idea what they are going to be paid, but certainly they expect less than a denarius. What a shock it must be for those who have worked only one hour to receive a full day's pay — twelve times what they worked for!

That excites everybody. They start to figure how much of a bonus they might receive. But when they stretch out their hand, the foreman plops down a single denarius. Those who have labored since sunrise are not just disappointed, they are downright indignant. Like echoes from their childhood, they cry, "It's not fair!" The farmer, with indignation that matches their own replies, "You're right, it is not fair . . . It is gracious. And that is my business and none of your concern!"[93]

In this same way, "Many who are first will be last and many who are last will be first" (19:30). At present, we only get glimpses of this promise. However, when Jesus returns there will be a reversal of man's economy. The totem pole of prestige will be flipped upside down so that those who are on top in this world will be on the bottom in God's kingdom.[94]

Our world honors beauty, wealth and power. These are the people who get to go to the front of the line to receive preferential treatment. But God honors faith, humility, and childlikeness. So when the "king-dom comes," the most unlikely candidates of this world will be treated with equal or greater respect than the present day "biggies." The poor will be rich, the oppressed will be liberated, children will be exalted, the handicapped will be healed, and the uneducated will be informed. But right now, right here, its our job as Jesus' church to implement God's

---

[93]The term "friend" [*hetaire*] is not a term of endearment (cf. Mt 11:16; 22:12; 26:50). It closely parallels our idiom, "Hey buddy!"

[94]This little word "many" indicates that this is not an absolute statement. Not <u>all</u> roles will be reversed in the kingdom of God.

economy as much as we can. Obviously we can't do it all. But when Jesus returns, he will complete the process.

<sup>MK 10:32</sup>They were on their way up to Jerusalem, with Jesus leading the way, and the disciples were astonished, while those who followed were afraid. Again he took the Twelve {disciples<sup>MT</sup>} aside and told them what was going to happen to him. <sup>33</sup>"We are going up to Jerusalem," he said, "and {everything that is written by the prophets about the Son of Man will be fulfilled:<sup>LK</sup>} the Son of Man will be betrayed to the chief priests and teachers of the law. They will condemn him to death and will hand him over to the Gentiles, <sup>34</sup>who will mock him {[and] insult him<sup>LK</sup>} and spit on him, flog him and kill {crucify<sup>MT</sup>} him. Three days later he will rise."

<sup>34</sup>The disciples did not understand any of this. Its meaning was hidden from them, and they did not know what he was talking about.

**§ 125a**
**Third**
**Prediction of**
**Jesus' Passion**
(Mt 20:17-19;
Mk 10:32-34;
Lk 18:31-34)

Lk 18:34

This is a graphic scene. After three particularly potent encounters with the Pharisees (19:3), his disciples (19:13), and this rich young ruler (19:16), Jesus is back on route to Jerusalem. He seems to be walking with a vengeance toward the capital city, his terminal destination. It appears that Jesus is walking out ahead, leading the pack with a furious pace. His disciples follow close behind, astonished, while the more uncommitted crowds lag further behind, afraid. Just what was going through their minds, we may never know. But this is certain, there is something in Jesus' pace and resoluteness that shouts just how serious are these moments and movements. For whatever else this holy city represented to these people, for Jesus it meant death.

He takes the Twelve aside to teach them privately once again (cf. 16:21 and 17:22-23). Away from the crowd, he explains to his faithful band what this is all about. This is the third time Jesus clearly predicts his own death (cf. § 83, 86, 88), although he has alluded to it a number of times. This particular prediction goes beyond the other two by stating the specific involvement of the Gentiles and the specific mode of execution — crucifixion.

There are essentially six elements to this prediction:
1. It must take place in *Jerusalem.*
2. He will be *betrayed.*
3. The *chief priests and teachers of the law* (i.e., Pharisaic and Sadducean leaders) will be responsible for his death.
4. He will be delivered over to the *Gentiles* for a death sentence.
5. They will *mock (insult and spit), flog, and crucify* him.
6. He will *rise on the third day.*[95]

---

[95]Notice that Mt and Lk, in reference to the three days of the resurrection, use the dative case indicating "on" while Mk uses the preposition "after" [*meta*]. This indicates that Jesus was not speaking of a precise chronological measurement.

Many have doubted the integrity of this narrative. Because it is such a specific prediction, they assert that it must have been written after Jesus' death and then credited to Jesus. But if Jesus was who he claimed, and did what the Gospel writers say, then predictive prophecy is a minor miracle for Jesus. The issue boils down to this: Do you believe that Jesus was a mere man or was he God incarnate?

Luke offers two significant contributions to this narrative. First, he reminds the disciples that the prophets predicted his death (v. 31). Certainly Isaiah 53 and Psalm 22 must have come to mind as well as Psalm 16:10; 118:22; Genesis 3:15. Second, he highlights their ignorance, as he did with the second passion prediction (Lk 9:45). This matter was hidden from them. The word [*kryptō*] seems to indicate that God concealed the matter from the Apostles; it wasn't merely that they were obtuse.

**§ 125b
James and
John Ask for
Chief Seats**
(Mt 20:20-28;
Mk 10:35-45;
cf. Lk 22:24-27)

If they weren't Apostles, we would be tempted to dismiss them as selfish fools when James and John ask for special position with Jesus. They think they are en route to the "inaugural ball" when, in fact, they are on their way to an excruciating execution.

<sup>MK 10:35</sup>Then {the mother of<sup>MT</sup>} James and John, the sons of Zebedee, came to him {kneeling down.<sup>MT</sup>} "Teacher," they said, "we want you to do for us whatever we ask."

<sup>36</sup>"What do you want me to do for you?" he asked.

<sup>37</sup>They replied, "Let {grant<sup>MT</sup>} one of us sit at your right and the other at your left in your glory {kingdom.<sup>MT</sup>}"

According to Matthew, it was Salome (Mt 27:55-56 with Mk 15:40), the mother of James and John, who makes this request. Likely the two boys put her up to it, thinking she will have more pull with Jesus. It is likely that Salome was Jesus' aunt (cf. Jn 19:25), and as a woman she might be able to tug his heart strings better than they. Besides, the request looks less selfish coming from their mother. But Jesus sees through their little scheme and speaks directly to James and John.[96]

Their request is open-ended: "Do for us whatever we ask." It appears that they know their request is a bit out of bounds. After all, Jesus has already confronted the whole group about seeking rank and position (§ 90). And he has just reiterated the importance of becoming like children (§ 123), and his own impending death (§ 125a). As usual,

---

[96]Mt 20:22 uses the second person plural "you all," indicating that Jesus was speaking directly to James and John or at least including them in his answer to Salome.

they have not been listening. To make matters worse, they are going to continue to argue about which of them is the greatest even up to the very night Jesus is betrayed (Lk 22:24-27).

Jesus isn't going to fall for their ploy. He asks them, "What is it you want?" They reply, "We want the #1 and #2 seats in the kingdom." They are dangerously close to Jerusalem. This city represents danger for Jesus. But like Superman, Jesus consistently dodges and deflects bullets. Neither plots of the Jews, storms of the sea, nor demonic forces have overpowered him. Undoubtedly the Twelve share the expectation of the crowds that Jesus will establish his kingdom upon arriving in Jerusalem. Therefore, James and John want to beat the others to the punch. They want to seize the highest administrative appointments in the coming Messianic kingdom. And why shouldn't they? They have the majority vote in the inner three!

³⁸"You don't know what you are asking," Jesus said. "Can you drink the cup I drink or be baptized with the baptism I am baptized with?"

³⁹"We can," they answered.

Jesus said to them, "You will drink the cup I drink and be baptized with the baptism I am baptized with, ⁴⁰but to sit at my right or left is not for me to grant. These places belong to those for whom they have been prepared {by my Father.ᴹᵀ}"

Mk 10:38-40 *with*
Mt 20:23

Jesus tries to open their eyes by using two metaphors for suffering: Baptism (Mt 3:11-12) and Cup (Ps 75:8; Isa 51:17; Jer 25:15-28). They aren't headed to Jerusalem for a victory celebration but for suffering. James and John want to be singled out as Jesus' closest associates. Presently that won't mean promotion but persecution. They are ignorantly confident that they can share Jesus' impending experiences.

Indeed, both of them will be baptized with the fire of persecution. James will be the first Apostolic martyr (Acts 12:2). John, on the other hand, will be the last surviving Apostle. According to tradition he was the only one who did not die as a martyr. Although his life was spared, he was not exempt from suffering. In the waning years of his life, he was exiled to Patmos where he saw the vision of Revelation (1:1).

Jesus can promise them persecution but not position. That is his Father's prerogative alone. Although Jesus will be given all authority after his resurrection (Mt 28:18), during his ministry, he lives in submission to his Father (Jn 14:28). Not only that, he submits himself to the physical and spiritual needs of sinful humanity. He comes as a servant and invites his disciples to no greater position.

⁴¹When the ten heard about this, they became indignant with James and

Mk 10:41-45 *with*
Mt 20:28; Lk 22:26

John. ⁴²Jesus called them together and said, "You know that those who are regarded as rulers of the Gentiles lord it over them, and their high officials exercise authority over them. ⁴³Not so with you. Instead, whoever wants to become great among you must be your servant {as the youngest,ᴸᴷ} ⁴⁴and whoever wants to be first must be slave of all. ⁴⁵For even {just asᴹᵀ} the Son of Man did not come to be served, but to serve, and to give his life as a ransom for many."

The ten are predictably upset, not because James and John misconstrue Jesus' teaching but because they beat them to the punch. All twelve want those coveted chief seats. Even after three years of walking with Jesus, watching him serve and taking notes on his sermons, they still don't grasp the basic purpose and method of his ministry — to die as a servant of humanity. You would think Jesus' closest disciples would know better. But even after 2,000 years, the lesson is hardly better understood or implemented.

The problem is simply this: We are imitating the ways of the world (Gentiles), rather than Jesus. We pattern our churches after governments and businesses. We vie for power and position through titles, salaries, recognition, votes, perks, boards and authority. Jesus' heart is broken.

The pathway to greatness in the kingdom is not up some corporate ladder. Rather, it is paved with a basin and a towel (Jn 13:1-17). This is not difficult to understand. Jesus repeats it too much for us to forget it. But our obvious neglect to live it out reveals the difficulty we have with this sublime paradox that the greatest in the kingdom of God is to be a servant (1 Cor 9:19; 2 Cor 4:5; 1 Pet 5:2-3).

Jesus' ultimate example of the theology of humility is around the next corner, at the cross. Liberal theologians have attempted to whisk away Mk 10:45 (and Mt 20:28). It is too clear to be comfortable. But it tenaciously stands its ground. This is Jesus' mission statement: To serve humanity by dying for our sins. The word "ransom" [*lytron*] was commonly used in Greek circles for the price that was paid for the release of a slave. Furthermore, in the LXX it is used for "deliverance" of God's people (Exod 30:12; Ps 49:7-9). Here, the Greek and Hebrew worlds come together as Jesus is pictured releasing captives from their slavery to sin (Rom 6:16-18; Isa 53:10-12).

We also find in Mark 10:45 the preposition "for" [*anti*] which means "in place of." It could hardly be clearer that Jesus died "instead of many" (Titus 2:14; 1 Pet 1:18). His death is a replacement, a substitute for ours.

**§ 126**
**Healing Blind**
**Bartimaeus at**
**Jericho**
(Mt 20:29-34;
Mk 10:46-52;
Lk 18:35-43)

The healing of blind Bartimaeus seems symbolic. On the one hand, it looks back over the last three years and exemplifies Jesus' messianic ministry (Lk 4:18). One the other hand, it looks forward to Jerusalem's blindness (cf. Jn 9:39-41). It points out the paradox. The blind beggar sees, but Israel's leaders are blind.

[46]Then they came to Jericho. As Jesus and his disciples, together with a large crowd, were leaving {approached[LK]} the city, a blind man, Bartimaeus (that is, the Son of Timaeus), {two blind men were[MT]} was sitting by the roadside begging.

Mk 10:46 *with* Lk 18:35; Mt 20:30

[36]When he heard the crowd going by, he asked what was happening. [37]They told him, "Jesus of Nazareth is passing by."
[38]He called out, "Jesus, Son of David, have mercy on me!"
[39]Those who led the way rebuked him and told him to be quiet, but he shouted all the more, "Son of David, have mercy on me!"

Lk 18:36-39

The city of Jericho is located about fifteen miles northeast of Jerusalem. It is one of the major stops on the trade route to Arabia. It would be the last stop for the pilgrims from Syria, Galilee, Decapolis, Mesopotamia, and Arabia as they traveled to Jerusalem for this Passover feast. It was a fertile city full of palms, figs, gardens, and balsams used to heal diseases of the eyes (Strabo 16.2.41), (Carson, p. 435).

As Jesus leads the pilgrim parade out of the city, he encounters two blind men.[97] Mark and Luke only mention one man, Bartimaeus (Mk 10:46). He's the one who apparently shouts out to Jesus. But Matthew informs us that there were actually two men healed that day. He did the same thing with the two Gerasene demoniacs (Mt 9). That's just typical of Matthew's eyewitness detail.

Bartimaeus and his friend sit by the roadside begging. That's about the only way a blind man could make a living in those days. Now, they are blind but not deaf. They hear the tumult as the parade passes. It is a motley crowd, made up of pilgrims heading to Jerusalem, traders and caravaners passing through this commercial capital, Roman soldiers stationed here to keep peace in this strategic city, and merchants trying to take advantage of the excitement inherent in Passover.

---

[97]Matthew and Mark say Jesus healed the men as he left Jericho. Luke says he healed them as he entered. This apparent discrepancy is easily solved. There were actually two sites of Jericho at this time (Josephus, *War* 4.459). They were only about a mile apart. So Jesus healed these fellows as he left the old city but before he came to the new city. Matthew and Mark mention the OT site which was pretty much in ruins, while Luke, more Greek in orientation, mentions the newer site which had been beautifully rebuilt by Herod the Great.

Another possible solution is that Luke placed the stories of Bartimaeus and Zacchaeus topically rather than chronologically making Jesus' Jericho visit climax with Zaccheus' story. Then, to avoid unnecessary confusion, he has Jesus heal the men on the way into the city instead of on his way out. In any event, Mk 10:46 does mention both Jesus entering and leaving the city. Luke follows the first half of the verse while Matthew only mentions the second half.

Bartimaeus asks someone what is going on. They tell him that Jesus is passing through their town. This is headline news! Surely the gossip has not slipped by Bartimaeus' acute ears. Rumor has it that this Jesus raised Lazarus from the dead over in Bethany, not much more than a dozen miles away. Further rumors say that the Sanhedrin is after this guy for blasphemy and insubordination. Bartimaeus cares little about the rumors. All he knows is that anyone who can raise the dead is able to give him sight! That is enough for him.

He begins to shout, "Son of David, have mercy on me!" That's the same phrase the blind man of Galilee used to secure his healing over a year ago (Mt 9:27-31). Because this phrase is used in both accounts and because both involve two blind men, some have suggested that they are actually two versions of the same healing. That is unlikely for several reasons: (1) Matthew was an eyewitness to both accounts and would not likely confuse them. (2) They take place in two different geographical areas, separated by more than a year. (3) The first account ends with a command to keep quiet (Mt 9:30). Bartimaeus may use this same phrase because he heard about the other healing. Or it may just be that both these blind men are more astute in identifying Jesus than is the general populace. Nonetheless, there could hardly be a more kosher Messianic title than this one (Isa 11:1, 10; Jer 23:5-6; Ezek 34:23-24; see notes on § 68).[98]

The front-runners of the crowd are less than impressed with Bartimaeus' outburst. They try to shut him up just like the disciples had with the little children (§ 123). But the more they tried to quiet him, the more of a scene he creates until finally he captures Jesus' attention.

Mk 10:49-52 *with* Lk 18:41; Mt 20:34

[49]Jesus stopped and said, "Call him." So they called to the blind man, "Cheer up! On your feet! He's calling you." [50]Throwing his cloak aside, he jumped to his feet and came to Jesus.

[51]"What do you want me to do for you?" Jesus asked him.

The blind man said, "Rabbi, {Lord,[LK]} I want to see." {Jesus had compassion on them and touched their eyes.[MT]}

[52]"Go," said Jesus, "your faith has healed you."

Lk 18:43

[43]Immediately he received his sight and followed Jesus, praising God. When all the people saw it, they also praised God.

Jesus stops the procession and calls for Bartimaeus. Suddenly, the people who excoriated him start to encourage him. The NIV's "cheer

---

[98]The title, "Son of David" is used primarily in the context of healing (Mt 9:27-31; 12:22-23; 15:21-28; 20:29-34; 21:14-15). Kingsbury suggests that the title is a polemic against Jewish rejection of their Messiah and king. That is, the blind outcasts "saw" their true king, while the religious leaders were blind to him (cf. Jn 9:40-41) ("The Title 'Son of David' in Matthew's Gospel," *JBL* 95/4 [1976]: 591-602).

up" is rather anemic. Every other use of this word [*tharseō*] is by Jesus when he promises someone healing or safety (Mt 9:2, 22; 14:27; Mk 6:50; Jn 16:33; Acts 23:11). There is no doubt, this guy is going to get his sight back. We see that Bartimaeus has full confidence, for he throws off his cloak and runs to Jesus. In other words, he left his most valuable possession on the curb. For a blind beggar that is a dangerous proposition. But he seems certain that he will be able to retrieve it.

Jesus knows what Bartimaeus wants but asks anyway. Apparently Jesus wants to elicit faith from him and a proper response from the crowd. Typical of Matthew, he tells us that Jesus is not content simply to heal Bartimaeus, but that he feels compassion for him and touches his eyes (cf. Mt 9:36; 14:14; 15:32; Mk 1:41). Then Jesus releases him to go his own way. Bartimaeus chooses to join the procession going up toward Jerusalem. Perhaps this will be his very first Passover. What a shock it will be for Bartimaeus to witness with his very own eyes the execution of the one who gave him this new-found sight.

§ 127a
**Salvation of Zacchaeus**
(Lk 19:1-10)

Luke alone tells us about Zacchaeus. For him, this incident is a microcosm of Jesus' ministry.[99] In the last four chapters Luke has stressed the least and the lost. He kept talking about down-and-outers. Now he highlights this "up-and-outer." Like the other outcasts, Jesus welcomes him with open arms. How fitting that Luke concludes this episode with what might be considered a theme for the whole book: "The Son of Man came to seek and to save what was lost."

Lk 19:1-6

¹Jesus entered Jericho and was passing through. ²A man was there by the name of Zacchaeus; he was a chief tax collector and was wealthy. ³He wanted to see who Jesus was, but being a short man he could not, because of the crowd. ⁴So he ran ahead and climbed a sycamore-fig tree to see him, since Jesus was coming that way.

⁵When Jesus reached the spot, he looked up and said to him, "Zacchaeus, come down immediately. I must stay at your house today." ⁶So he came down at once and welcomed him gladly.

News somehow reached Jericho that Jesus was coming. No doubt, the healing of two blind beggars on the outskirts of the old city fanned into flame their interest in Jesus. The crowds migrating to Jerusalem postponed the final leg of their journey. They lined the streets of Jericho awaiting his arrival, hoping to be where the action was. There were

---

[99]J. O'Hanlon, "The Story of Zacchaeus and the Lukan Ethic," *JSNT* 12 (1981): 2-26, shows how this story summarizes Luke's theology in general but especially chapter 18, Jesus' travel narrative, and explicates the sermon on the plain.

various "un-Jewish" elements in the crowd: The Roman peace-keeping forces, the international merchants passing through Jericho, and this small but very powerful chief tax collector.

Zacchaeus was no mere tax collector. He was a chief tax collector in upper management, the most powerful governmental authority of Jericho in the "Revenue Department." He was in charge of a number of men whom he assigned to various duties and customs in the surrounding area (see notes on § 47a for details on tax collection). Furthermore, Jericho was a major trade center on the route between Egypt, Palestine, Arabia, and Syria. In other words, Zacchaeus is a major player in the Roman government.

He is as eager as the crowds to see this Jesus. But he is too short to see over the shoulders of this clamoring crowd. He can't squeeze his way to the front to get a good look at him, and because he is hated, both as a tax collector and a Roman collaborator, no one is inclined to give him preferential treatment. His only recourse is to run up the street to the next tall tree and climb it. It happens to be a sycamore-fig tree (an odd breed with the leaves of a sycamore but the fruit of a fig). This is a bit beneath the dignity of a man of his stature. But he doesn't have a lot of options and his curiosity gets the best of him. It drives him up a tree.

When Jesus reaches the spot, he calls Zacchaeus by name. Perhaps Jesus is familiar with some of the governmental officials of the area. But more likely this is a case of Jesus' divine knowledge. Some of the crowd must be thinking, "Jesus, you don't know who you're talking to!" But the fact that he uses Zacchaeus' name indicates that Jesus knows exactly who he is talking to. Not only does Jesus know him, he wants and needs him ("I *must* stay . . ." [*dei meinei*]). So Zacchaeus responds immediately and eagerly. We are often bewildered and offended at the people God chooses to love and their immediate and affectionate response to him.[100]

Lk 19:7-10     ⁷All the people saw this and began to mutter, "He has gone to be the guest of a 'sinner.'"

⁸But Zacchaeus stood up and said to the Lord, "Look, Lord! Here and now I give half of my possessions to the poor, and if I have cheated anybody out of anything, I will pay back four times the amount."

⁹Jesus said to him, "Today salvation has come to this house, because this man, too, is a son of Abraham. ¹⁰For the Son of Man came to seek and to save what was lost."

---

[100]This passage provides a beautiful allegory for our own conversion: Jesus (1) knows you, (2) wants/calls you, and (3) needs you.

How many in the crowd want Jesus to acknowledge them, even with a simple wave or a wink?! How many would pay for a handshake or an autograph? Suddenly one individual's dream is coming true. Jesus has stopped to single out one man . . . Zacchaeus! But of all the people who *don't* deserve such an honor, he is at the top of the list. This is a frightful error!

The crowds stand outside Zacchaeus' house in a stupor. This jealous, grumbling mob is fit to be tied. Meanwhile inside, Zacchaeus experiences repentance in a tangible way. His conversion could be chronicled in his checkbook.[101]

First, he follows the Law of Moses by repaying four times the amount to all those he has defrauded (Exod 22:1; cf. Lk 3:13). Then he follows the Law of Christ ("the law of love," Gal 6:2; James 2:8) by giving half his wealth to care for the poor. Jesus proclaims that he is saved, not on the basis of his good deeds, but on the basis of his relationship to Abraham (Gal 3:29). His good deeds are only an expression and evidence of his faith (James 2:14-26). Zacchaeus stands in stark contrast to the rich young ruler (Lk 18:18-30; cf. Lk. 12:33).

Jesus concludes with his own mission statement (v. 10). He wants the lost to be found (Lk 15). He wants to heal the sick and release the captives. Whether they are "down-and-outers" like the lepers or "up-and-outers" like Zacchaeus, Jesus came to seek and to save the lost. He is less than impressed with our narcissistic religious programming and sanitized sanctuaries that fail to reach the lost.

This parable is very much like the one Jesus will tell about five days from now, on Tuesday of the final week as he privately teaches the Twelve on the Mt. of Olives (Mt 25:14-30). Although there are several differences

**§ 127b**
**Parable of the Minas**
(Lk 19:11-28; cf. Mt 25:14-30)

---

[101]However, A.C. Mitchell, "Zacchaeus Revisited: Luke 19:8 as a Defense" *Biblica* 71 (1990): 153-176, argues that Zacchaeus is not a repentant sinner, but that Jesus vindicates him as a legitimate son of Abraham before his peers. Furthermore, Luke 19:8 describes Zacchaeus' regular practice of benevolence and is not an act of repentance. Thus, Zacchaeus is defending himself as a faithful Jew rather than making a turn around in his life. If he is right, then the "lost" Jesus came to seek and save, refers to, or at least includes, social outcasts. Thus, this story is not about conversion but Jesus exploding typical stereotypes and subverting our prejudices about "bad" people. See also, A.C. Mitchell, "The Use of *Sukophantein* in Luke 19:8: Further Evidence for Zacchaeus's Defense" *Biblica* 72 (1991): 546-547; R.C. White, "A Good Word for Zacchaeus," *LexTQ* 14 (1979): 89-96; and D.A. Ravens, "Zacchaeus: The Final Part of a Lucan Triptych?" *JSNT* 41 (1991) 19-32. However, D. Hamm argues cogently for the traditional view that Zacchaeus is a repentant sinner ("Luke 19:8 Once Again: Does Zacchaeus Defend or Resolve?" *JBL* 107/3 [1988]: 431-437).

between the parables, the similarities are stronger.[102] Both parables describe how Jesus' disciples should act between his ascension and his Second Coming.

Lk 19:11-15

[11]"While they were listening to this, he went on to tell them a parable, because he was near Jerusalem and the people thought that the kingdom of God was going to appear at once. [12]He said: "A man of noble birth went to a distant country to have himself appointed king and then to return. [13]So he called ten of his servants and gave them ten minas.[a] 'Put this money to work,' he said, 'until I come back.'

[14]"But his subjects hated him and sent a delegation after him to say, 'We don't want this man to be our king.'

[15]"He was made king, however, and returned home. Then he sent for the servants to whom he had given the money, in order to find out what they had gained with it."

[a]13 A mina was about three months' wages.

The closer Jesus gets to the capital city, the more intense is the popular anticipation that he will inaugurate his Messianic Kingship. Even Jesus' closest disciples share this misguided notion of a physical, militaristic kingdom (Mt 24:1-3; Acts 1:6). So to correct this erroneous expectation, Jesus tells the parable of the minas.

The plot is simple enough: A rich man makes an attempt to become king through diplomatic measures with a distant government. While he is gone he places several of his stewards over his financial affairs and expects them to make money for him while he is away. But he is a hated man and so the local council sends a diplomatic delegation to this distant government to appeal that he *not* be made king.

When Jesus tells this parable his audience surely snickers. You see, this very thing took place about twenty-five years earlier. Archelaus succeeded his father, Herod the Great. He became Tetrarch over Judea, Samaria and Idumea. But that wasn't enough for him. So he left his palace in Jericho and traveled to Rome to request the title of King (A.D. 6). The Jews hated him and sent a delegation to plead with Caesar that Archelaus not be made king over them. Archelaus was thus deposed — the Jews won their case. Thus, this crowd would have been shocked to hear that the nobleman in the parable returned as king — the locals lost!

---

[102]Differences: (1) King vs. rich man; (2) amount of money and reward; (3) and hatred for the king. Similarities: (a) The bad servant hides the money rather than deposits it; (b) the king said, "Well done good servant" and "He who has will be given more . . ."; (c) the extra money is given to the servant who earned the most; and (d) both parables end in judgment.

But there is a second historic parallel here — Jesus himself. Many of this very crowd, not much more than a week from now, will shout "Crucify him!" The "nobleman" was rejected by his people who refused to accept him as king. Their petty protest will last only as long as the king is away. When he returns, there will be a reckoning of both the citizens (v. 27), and his own servants (v. 15).

> [16]"The first one came and said, 'Sir, your mina has earned ten more.'      Lk 19:16-23
> [17]"'Well done, my good servant!' his master replied. 'Because you have been trustworthy in a very small matter, take charge of ten cities.'
> [18]"The second came and said, 'Sir, your mina has earned five more.'
> [19]"His master answered, 'You take charge of five cities.'
> [20]"Then another servant came and said, 'Sir, here is your mina; I have kept it laid away in a piece of cloth. [21]I was afraid of you, because you are a hard man. You take out what you did not put in and reap what you did not sow.'
> [22]"His master replied, 'I will judge you by your own words, you wicked servant! You knew, did you, that I am a hard man, taking out what I did not put in, and reaping what I did not sow? [23]Why then didn't you put my money on deposit, so that when I came back, I could have collected it with interest?'"

Ten servants are each given a mina (worth about three months wages). It is a small amount to the nobleman, but enough to test the ability of his servants. One of the ten earns ten minas, an incredible increase of 1000%. Another servant also does extremely well with a 500% increase. Both are commended and rewarded with leadership of an entire city for each mina they earned. They have proved themselves worthy in little so they are given much (Lk 16:10).

A third servant, however, doesn't fare so well. In fact, he doesn't even try. He hides the thing! His excuse is fear. Instead of accepting responsibility for his own failure he begins to blame the king for being a "hard man," taking what was not his, living off the labor of others. But his excuse just won't stand up to scrutiny. If the man is truly afraid of his master, and if the master is as mean as the servant accuses him of being, then the servant is an extraordinary fool for not at least depositing the money for interest. A more likely explanation is that the man hates his master and was sure that he would NOT return as king. Then he could keep the mina for himself after all the nobleman's property had been redistributed.

> [24]"Then he said to those standing by, 'Take his mina away from him and give it      Lk 19:24-28
> to the one who has ten minas.'
> [25]"'Sir,' they said, 'he already has ten!'
> [26]"He replied, 'I tell you that to everyone who has, more will be given, but as for the one who has nothing, even what he has will be taken away. [27]But those

enemies of mine who did not want me to be king over them — bring them here and kill them in front of me.'"

²⁸After Jesus had said this, he went on ahead, going up to Jerusalem.

Now that the nobleman is a king he is going to start acting like one. First he redistributes the wealth wisely. His servants protest that the wealthiest steward gets the extra mina. That may not be fair, but it is a wise business investment. Who wants to invest their money "fairly" rather than "wisely?" Now, if we place our cash in CD's with the highest interest, why should God not grant his resources and rewards to those who execute "kingdom business" most faithfully (1 Pet 4:10; cf. comments on Lk 16:10, § 117a)? If this parable is about the Second Coming of Christ, one might assume that there are levels of reward in heaven.

Second, this king must squelch any potential rebellions. This may be ugly, but in the long run the king will save lives by killing the leaders of this insurrection. In like manner, when Jesus comes there will be judgment and punishment both for those who claim to be his stewards and for those who openly oppose him. Now it would be a mistake to press every gruesome detail of the king in this parable to make it match Jesus. But it would also be a mistake to paint Jesus as eternally turning the other cheek. Jesus is kind and merciful and forgiving. But these traits are balanced with his justice, sternness, and purity. He is not to be tested or trifled with (cf. Mt 24:27-30; Rev 1:13-18; 19:11-18). As Psalm 2:9-12 says:

> You will rule them with an iron scepter; you will dash them to pieces like pottery. Therefore, you kings, be wise; be warned, you rulers of the earth. Serve the LORD with fear and rejoice with trembling. Kiss the Son, lest he be angry and you be destroyed in your way, for his wrath can flare up in a moment. Blessed are all who take refuge in him.

**§ 128a & 141**
**Arrival and**
**Anointing at**
**Bethany**
(Mt 26:6-13;
Mk 14:3-9;
Jn 11:55–12:11)

ᴶᴺ ¹¹:⁵⁵When it was almost time for the Jewish Passover, many went up from the country to Jerusalem for their ceremonial cleansing before the Passover. ⁵⁶They kept looking for Jesus, and as they stood in the temple area they asked one another, "What do you think? Isn't he coming to the Feast at all?" ⁵⁷But the chief priests and Pharisees had given orders that if anyone found out where Jesus was, he should report it so that they might arrest him.

Truly, Jesus was born to die. The culmination of his life is imminent and all the major players have moved into place. While many people have joined Jesus on his final trek to Jerusalem, many more have preceded him to the holy city. They have arrived early for ritual purification in preparation for Passover.

The temple mount is beginning to buzz with excitement as the priests gear up for the most sacred festival of their year. But the excitement generated this year is more intense than ever. In addition to the normal Passover preparations there are constant questions about Jesus. On the one hand the crowds keep asking each other, "Do you think Jesus will show up?" After all, he skipped the last Passover but then attended both the Feasts of Tabernacles and Dedication the previous fall and winter (respectively). On the other hand, the religious hierarchy has put out an A.P.B. for his arrest. They blatantly deny that Jesus is anything but a blasphemer and a rabble-rouser in spite of his many wondrous miracles. Their biggest problem is this raising of Lazarus thing. That is a miracle they just can't deny or evade. Therefore they plan to "undo" it by killing both Jesus and Lazarus. But the populace, if not moved to faith, are at least intensely curious about this rumor of a "raising" and are eager to see both Jesus and Lazarus.

¹Six days before the Passover, Jesus arrived at Bethany, {in the home of a man known as Simon the Leper^MT,MK}, where Lazarus lived, whom Jesus had raised from the dead. ²Here a dinner was given in Jesus' honor. Martha served, while Lazarus was among those reclining at the table with him.

Jn 12:1-2 *with* Mt 26:6; Mk 14:3

Even if this banquet is held on Saturday, Jesus almost certainly arrives in Bethany on Friday since it is doubtful that he traveled any great distance on the Sabbath. Although the "Sabbath Journey" of three-fifths of a mile was set by Oral Tradition, Jesus still honors the Scripture through Sabbath rest. Therefore we reckon the six days of John 12:1 by Roman "exclusive" counting and assume Jesus & Co. arrive in Bethany on Friday. That does not necessitate, however, that the banquet is held on the day of his arrival. It could be held on Friday, with all the preparations being completed before the Sabbath began. Or it could be held on Saturday after the Sabbath ended at sunset.

Aside from this banquet, we also read of the Jews from Jerusalem who discover Jesus' whereabouts and come to see both him and Lazarus (Jn 12:9). When does this take place? Well, we know that the Triumphal Entry, which almost certainly took place on a Sunday, is the next day (Jn 12:12). Therefore we can reconstruct the events this way: Jesus arrives in Bethany on Friday. When Jesus is welcomed into the private home of Simon the Leper, the crowds have no reason to stay in Bethany. They continue their trek to the city of Jerusalem, just two miles over the Mt. of Olives. News of Jesus' whereabouts arrives too late for the Jerusalemites to make it back to Bethany before the Sabbath begins so they wait until Saturday night to go. Then on Sunday they join Jesus' entourage at the

Triumphal Entry. Meanwhile, this banquet takes place either on Friday or Saturday night.[103]

Apparently at least two families join together to honor Jesus: Lazarus' and Simon's. It is theoretically possible that "Simon" is another name for Lazarus. But that is unlikely if our assumption is correct that Lazarus is a prominent man among the Jews of Jerusalem (Jn 11:45-47). Even if he were healed, it is doubtful that a leper could gain such status. There is also speculation that he is Martha's husband, or perhaps her father, since she serves at the banquet. However, it would not be at all uncommon for a woman to serve a meal in a home that was not her own. What seems more likely is that Lazarus and Simon, both of whom have been healed by Jesus, join together in honoring him with a special meal.

Jn 12:3 *with*    [3]Then Mary took {an alabaster jar of[MK]} about a pint[a] of pure nard, an expen-
Mk 14:3; Mt 26:7    sive perfume[.] {She broke the jar and poured the perfume on his head[MK]} {as he
was reclining at the table.[MT]} [S]he poured it on Jesus' feet and wiped his feet
with her hair. And the house was filled with the fragrance of the perfume.

[a]*3* Greek *a litra* (probably about 0.5 liter)

We must remember that this is not the first time this family has fixed a meal for Jesus and his band (cf. Lk 10:38-42, § 104). Mary honored Jesus the first time by sitting at his feet and listening like a good student. This time she will honor him with an expensive and impetuous gift. This alabaster flask likely hung around her neck. It was made of a translucent stone which had been reamed out for its costly contents and then sealed back up. In order to pour out the ointment you would break the neck of the flask.

Inside was a full pint of pure nard, literally "myrrh." Hendriksen (p. 175) says that this particular ointment was "an aromatic herb grown in the high pasture-land of the Himalayas, between Tibet and India." It represented a year's wages, about three hundred denarii. Perfumes were especially important in a culture where water (hence baths) was scarce. But a whole pint of perfume is a bit excessive. She has so much, in fact, that she starts at his head (Mt and Mk) and pours clear down to his feet (Jn). No one needed a whole pint of perfume! Unless, of course, they were dead. It was common to anoint dead bodies heavily and then put

---

[103]Both Matthew (26:2) and Mark (14:1) mention this event along with the Sanhedrin's plot to capture Jesus and Iscariot's premeditated betrayal, which took place two days before the Passover (i.e., Wednesday according to Jewish reckoning). Matthew and Mark are not saying that the anointing took place on Wednesday. Rather, they have structured their narrative rhetorically and "flash back" to this event in Bethany earlier in the week which illustrates so well Judas' avaricious greed.

other spices and perfumes in the folds of the burial cloth to overpower the stench of decomposition. This lavish act is only reasonable in light of Jesus' impending death.

Her lavish worship of Jesus is improper according to human standards. It is wasteful. It could have been used for more practical purposes. Furthermore, she lets down her hair in public, a cultural impropriety in and of itself, and then proceeds to humiliate herself by wiping Jesus' feet with her hair![104] Hence, the disciples protest.

[4]But one of his disciples {the disciples,[MT]} Judas Iscariot, who was later to betray him, objected {some of those present were saying indignantly to one another,[MK]} [5]"Why wasn't this perfume sold and the money given to the poor? It was worth a year's wages.[a]" {And they rebuked her harshly.[MK]} [6]He did not say this because he cared about the poor but because he was a thief; as keeper of the money bag, he used to help himself to what was put into it.

*Jn 12:4-6 with Mt 26:8; Mk 14:4-5*

[a]3 Greek *three hundred denarii*

[6]"Leave her alone," said Jesus. "Why are you bothering her? She has done a beautiful thing to me. {It was intended that she should save this perfume for the day of my burial.[JN]} [7]The poor you will always have with you, and you can help them any time you want. But you will not always have me. [8]She did what she could. She poured perfume on my body beforehand to prepare for my burial. [9]I tell you the truth, wherever the gospel is preached throughout the world, what she has done will also be told, in memory of her."

*Mk 14:6-9 with Jn 12:7*

The disciples, led by Iscariot, begin to object to Mary's act and berate her for it. Judas is motivated by greed. Since he has pilfered from the money bag, he sees here a wasted opportunity. The others, however, have pure motives, misguided as they are. They think they represent Jesus' heart in this matter since he has so often shown interest in the poor. But Jesus once again adds a surprising twist to the story. Just as Jesus had berated Martha's seemingly reasonable critique of Mary's behavior (Lk 10:40-42), so he also berates the disciples' here.

The disciples just don't understand how beautiful this deed is. But they should. Jesus has now clearly predicted his death at least a half-a-dozen times with another six to eight allusions to it. They apparently just haven't been listening. But Mary has. Her deed looks like a burial anointing. Jesus says it is a burial anointing. Therefore one might assume that she means it to be a burial anointing. Perhaps she and Judas are the first two disciples to truly believe that Jesus is going to die; but

---

[104]Many have suggested that this scene and Lk 7:36-50 actually stem from the same story but that both have been embellished in different ways. However, the differences in the stories are just too strong to view them as a single tradition. See § 59 for an explanation of the differences between these two narratives.

how different are their responses. Maybe she isn't quite that perceptive, but if anyone has had a chance to be it is Mary. Of all the disciples, she has listened most carefully to Jesus. And for her perception and devotion, Jesus promises that she will be remembered whenever and wherever the gospel is preached.

Now about the poor, Jesus reminds the disciples that the poor people will always be around. The opportunities to minister to Jesus, however, are numbered. Therefore, this lavish and extravagant gift is not a waste.

The opportunities to minister to the poor are endless. The opportunity to minister to Jesus is limited. What about today? There is nothing wrong with nice church buildings and paying preachers adequately. But these can hardly be equated with gifts lavished on Jesus personally. Now that he is gone it is time for us to redouble our efforts to minister to the poor. This is especially true since Jesus takes it personally when we help the poor (Mt 25:40; cf. Deut 15:11).

Jn 12:9-11    ⁹Meanwhile a large crowd of Jews found out that Jesus was there and came, not only because of him but also to see Lazarus, whom he had raised from the dead. ¹⁰So the chief priests made plans to kill Lazarus as well, ¹¹for on account of him many of the Jews were going over to Jesus and putting their faith in him.

It has been about two months since Jesus raised Lazarus from the dead. The very presence of this man with Jesus is the cause of a mass "conversion" among the Jews. These aren't fairy tales that take place in a distant land. Bethany is in their own backyard and now they have been able to verify this incredible story firsthand. But the chief priests still are not impressed. They are not concerned with the veracity of this miracle story. They are concerned about the security of their positions and the breadth of their influence. Since both Jesus and Lazarus are hindrances to these things, they must be eliminated. The blindness and hypocrisy of these Jewish leaders are colossal. But, unfortunately, they are not unparalleled in other religious institutions where hierarchy and power overshadow the purpose and plans of God.

# PART TEN
# THE FINAL WEEK

This is only the second event of the life of Jesus to be recorded in all four Gospels. The first was the feeding of the 5,000. The disciples know something significant is about to happen. Jesus walked wherever he went. Yet now, less than two miles from his final destination, he mounts a donkey?! Suddenly this Palestinian peasant looks like a conquering king as he rides into the holy city.[1] The crowds are eager . . . but for what?

**§ 128b**
**The Triumphal Entry**
(Mt 21:1-11, 14-17;
Mk 11:1-11;
Lk 19:29-44;
Jn 12:12-19)

Mk 11:1-7 *with*
Mt 21:2;
Lk 19:33-34

## 1. Preparation

[1]As they approached Jerusalem and came to Bethphage and Bethany at the Mount of Olives, Jesus sent two of his disciples, [2]saying to them, "Go to the village ahead of you, and just as you enter it, you will find a {donkey with her[MT]} colt tied there, which no one has ever ridden. Untie it and bring it {them[MT]} here. [3]If anyone asks you, 'Why are you doing this?' tell him, 'The Lord needs it and will send it back here shortly.'"

[4]They went and found a colt outside in the street, tied at a doorway. As they untied it, [5]some people {its owners[LK]} standing there asked, "What are you doing, untying that colt?" [6]They answered as Jesus had told them to {[saying] the Lord needs it,[LK]} and the people let them go. [7]When they brought the colt to Jesus and threw their cloaks over it, he sat on it.

Jesus approaches Jerusalem from Bethany, about two miles to the east. In between the two cities stands the Mt. of Olives at 2,600'. It provides an impressive, panoramic view, especially of the temple courts which lay 300' directly below. In the next few days, Jesus will make a lot of memories on this mountain. Here he will weep over Jerusalem, give the "Olivet Discourse," pray in Gethsemane, and ascend to heaven.

On the eastern slope of the Mt. of Olives is a small village called Bethphage. From there Jesus sends two unnamed disciples (likely Peter

---

[1]Cf. Zech 14 and P.B. Duff, "The March of the Divine Warrior and the Advent of the Greco-Roman King: Mark's Account of Jesus' Entry into Jerusalem," *JBL* 111/1 (1992): 55-71.

and John) to fetch a donkey and her colt.² Matthew mentions that they actually bring two animals.³ Mark explains why. The colt has never been ridden.⁴ If Jesus is going to keep from getting thrown off, they had better bring the colt's mother along to calm its nerves, especially in the midst of this raucous crowd.

Jesus had prepared them for the inevitable — someone was bound to ask why they were taking the animals. They are to say, "The Lord has need of it." The word "lord" might refer to the owner of the animal, who perhaps had come out to follow Jesus.⁵ However, since Luke says "its owners" were standing there and asked the two disciples what they were doing, it is more likely that the word "Lord" refers to Jesus. We must remember that Jesus has spent the last six months in the area of Judea and Perea. He has raised Lazarus from the dead and his seventy commissioned preachers have healed hundreds or perhaps thousands of people in the area. In other words, Jesus was well-known and well-liked. It is therefore, reasonable to assume that Jesus sends the two disciples to one of his local supporters to appropriate the animals on loan.⁶

## 2. *Prophecy*

Mt 21:4-5

⁴This took place to fulfill what was spoken through the prophet:
⁵"Say to the Daughter of Zion,
  'See, your king comes to you,
gentle and riding on a donkey,
  on a colt, the foal of a donkey.'"ᵃ

ᵃ5 Zech. 9:9

---

²According to J.D.M. Derrett, "Law in the New Testament: The Palm Sunday Colt," *NovT* 13 (1971): 241-258, the state could sequester animals from the general public for its own use. 1 Sam 8:17 gives OT support for this practice. Jesus, as David's descendant and Messiah, certainly had this right! Furthermore, rabbis also had this right under certain circumstances. However, unlike the state, Jesus seeks permission to use the animal and promises to return it. Thus the apostles seem to submit to the legal responsibilities of borrowing an animal from Exod 22:14-15.

³Matthew has been accused of misreading the Hebrew parallelism of Zechariah 9:9 (cited in Mt 21:5), which mentions two animals in subsequent lines, where probably only one is signified by parallel phrases. However, Matthew, of all people, knew how to read prophetic poetry. His account is not a result of faulty hermeneutics, but accurate eyewitness detail.

⁴Oxen, donkeys, and colts that had never been ridden were sometimes used for sacred purposes (Num 19:2; Deut 21:3; 1 Sam 6:7).

⁵J.M. Ross, "Names of God: A Comment on Mk 13:3 and Parallels," *BT* 35/4 (1984): 443.

⁶J. Blenkinsopp suggests that the act of untying the colt would have Messianic significance based on the Oracle of Judah (Gen 49:10-11), ("The Oracle of Judah and the Messianic Entry," *JBL* 80 [1961]: 55-64).

The book of Zechariah predicts the Messiah with astounding clarity.[7] This passage in particular was interpreted by many rabbis as Messianic. Matthew shows how this triumphal entry fulfills Zechariah 9:9.[8] He also shows, however, that although Jesus is the Messiah predicted by the prophets, he is not the Messiah expected by the people. They were looking for the king to ride into Jerusalem[9] on a war horse (cf. Rev 6:4; 19:11). What they were promised was a Prince of Peace (Isa 9:6) riding on a donkey — a symbol of kings and of peace (Judg 5:10; 1 Kgs 1:33).

This kind of use of prophecy will continue to the end of the Gospels. Although we have already become accustomed to Jesus fulfilling prophecy throughout the Gospels, we will be overwhelmed by *how much* Jesus fulfills in this last week. Most of it will convey this same message: Jesus is the Messiah predicted by the prophets, but not the Messiah expected by the people.

### 3.  *Praise*

{[36]As he went along,[LK]} [8]A very large crowd spread their cloaks on the road, while others cut {palm[JN]} branches from the trees {in the fields[MK]} and spread them on the road.

Mt 21:8 *with* Lk 19:36; Jn 12:13; Mk 11:8

[37]When he came near the place where the road goes down the Mount of Olives, the whole crowd of disciples began joyfully to praise God in loud voices for all the miracles they had seen.

Lk 19:37

[9]The crowds that went ahead of him and those that followed shouted,
"Hosanna[a] to the Son of David!"
"Blessed is he {the king[LK]} who comes in the name of the Lord!"[b]
{"Blessed is the coming kingdom of our father David!"[MK]}
"{Peace in heaven and glory[LK]} Hosanna[a] in the highest!"

Mt 21:9 *with* Lk 19:38; Mk 11:10

[a]*9* A Hebrew expression meaning "Save!" which became an exclamation of praise; also in verse 15    [b]*9* Psalm 118:26

As Jesus climbs the Mt. of Olives, the people are prepared to proclaim him Messiah and King. This is the second time such a thing has happened. A year ago, when Jesus fed the 5,000 (men), a crowd was prepared to make him king by force (Jn 6:15). That was up in Galilee. This is on the doorstep of the temple.

---

[7]Especially Zech 9:9; 11:13; 12:10; 13:7; 14:4.

[8]The introductory phrase is actually closer to Isaiah 62:11, "Say to the Daughter of Zion, 'See, your king comes to you.'" Since the context of Isa 62:11 is also appropriate to our passages, Matthew may intend for us to see a connection.

[9]Tenney (p. 127) notes that Daughter of Zion is "a personification of the city of Jerusalem" in the OT, especially in the latter prophets (Isa 1:8; 52:2; 62:11; Jer 4:31; 6:23; Lam 2:4, 8, 10, 13; Mic 4:8; Zeph 3:14; Zech 2:10).

It was no accident this crowd is assembled. The Passover pilgrims poured into Jerusalem over this very hill. They had come filled with political and religious fervor. That's especially true this year. Jesus has spent the last six months in an itinerant ministry in Judea and Perea. His entourage of disciples has grown steadily. Furthermore, the rumors of Lazarus have raised quite a stir. In fact, the word on the street is that the Sanhedrin wants to assassinate both Jesus and Lazarus. People are curious, expectant, and jubilant. They want a Messiah very badly. And this man, with his ability to perform such miracles, is their primary candidate.

Some in the crowd laid their garments on the ground. Others cut palm branches (cf. Rev. 7:9; 1 Macc 13:51; 2 Macc 10:6-7) from the trees in the adjacent fields and laid them down for the colt to walk on.[10] Both of these are political and regal gestures. In other words, the crowds welcome Jesus as King in the Holy City (2 Kgs 9:13).

As Jesus crests the Mt. of Olives, this huge multitude breaks into jubilant shouts which echo across the city. Its sheer volume has attracted everyone's attention, and its Messianic implications have generated excitement. From Psalm 118:25-26, viewed by the Rabbis as Messianic, they borrow such phrases as "Hosannah" and "blessed is he who comes."[11] And they add to these such Messianic words as "David," "Kingdom," "Peace," "Glory in the highest." Their message rings out loud and clear. Predictably the Sanhedrin is fit to be tied. Jesus will deal with them shortly.

In addition to the Sanhedrin, this parade of praise no doubt catches the attention of the Roman garrison. They are stationed in Jerusalem as peace-keeping forces. They are especially cautious during Jewish feasts,

---

[10]Today the only palm trees in the area are in Jericho. This has led some to say that they carried these branches from Jericho about 13 miles away. This may have been part of the celebration of Tabernacles. But the text seems to indicate that they cut them right there. Obviously, then, palms used to grow around Jerusalem but have been thoroughly stripped from the area (cf. B.A. Mastin, "The Date of the Triumphal Entry," NTS 16 [1969-70]: 76-82).

[11]The word Hosannah literally means, "Lord, Save." But during Jesus' day the word "hosannah" had, for the most part, lost original meaning and was merely an expression of praise, much like our own use of the word "Amen." However, there is something almost prophetic about the crowd's call for "Hosannah" on the first day of the Passover week. C.H. Johnson, "The Song of Entry," BW 34 (1909): 47, suggested the following reconstruction of the crowd's acclamation of Jesus: "Hosanna, Hosanna, Hosanna, Hosanna to the Son of David; Blessed is he that cometh in the name of the Lord, Blessed is the King that cometh in the name of the Lord; the King of Israel; Blessed is the kingdom that cometh, the kingdom of our Father David; Peace in Heaven and glory in the highest, Hosanna in the highest. Amen."

when the political and religious sentiments of the Jews are at fever pitch. Now they will watch carefully the man who rides into town with such acclamation. We are probably not far off when we picture a thick line of bodies on either side of the path from the base of the mountain to its peak. As Jesus moves down the mountain the crowd falls in line behind him forming an ever-growing, impressive parade heading straight for the temple courts.

### 4. *Ignorance of the Disciples*

[16]At first his disciples did not understand all this. Only after Jesus was glorified did they realize that these things had been written about him and that they had done these things to him.

[17]Now the crowd that was with him when he called Lazarus from the tomb and raised him from the dead continued to spread the word. [18]Many people, because they had heard that he had given this miraculous sign, went out to meet him.

Jn 12:16-18

The disciples are as excited about all this as the crowds are, and for the same wrong reasons. They too share the popular misconceptions about the Messiah. In fact, they won't get it straight until after Jesus is glorified (i.e., ascended). The beauty of this event is not in what it could lead to (an earthly kingdom) but what it comes from (OT prophecies).

### 5. *Pharisees*

[39]Some of the Pharisees in the crowd said to Jesus, "Teacher, rebuke your disciples!"

[40]"I tell you," he replied, "if they keep quiet, the stones will cry out."

Lk 19:39-40

[19]So the Pharisees said to one another, "See, this is getting us nowhere. Look how the whole world has gone after him!"

Jn 12:19

The Pharisees are fit to be tied. They understand the implications of both the actions and words of the crowds. They know both their culture and their Scriptures. They view all of this as blasphemous. Yet Jesus allows it. In the mind of the Pharisee, Jesus has an obligation to call a halt to his disciples before their inadvertent excitement crosses the line into blatant blasphemy.

Far from stopping them, Jesus says, "Their praise is both accurate and inevitable. If they stop the stones will start." They demand that Jesus suppress the crowd. But Jesus stands nose to nose with them and calls their hand. On this day, they are a few cards short. They have neither the popular appeal nor the official power to do anything but stand idly by and watch. The battle lines are drawn and they'll not be idle long.

### 6. *Jesus Weeps over Jerusalem*

Lk 19:41-44

[41]As he approached Jerusalem and saw the city, he wept over it [42]and said, "If you, even you, had only known on this day what would bring you peace — but now it is hidden from your eyes. [43]The days will come upon you when your enemies will build an embankment against you and encircle you and hem you in on every side. [44]They will dash you to the ground, you and the children within your walls. They will not leave one stone on another, because you did not recognize the time of God's coming to you."

We are tempted to rejoice in Jesus' victory over the Pharisees. But Jesus doesn't gloat; he weeps. The word itself indicates deep sobs. His interest is not in winning an argument, but a people. On the surface it seems that he has done just that. But he knows their hearts. Within five days, many of those shouting "Hosanna" will change their tune to "Crucify him!"

As he stands over the city, perhaps looking directly into the temple courts, he pleads for her peace. Not a political peace at the end of a bloody uprising, but peace with their God. That is his ultimate goal, but their eyes are blinded to this. When Jesus refuses to be the Messiah they want, they will kill him. As a result, the vengeance of God will fall full upon the very stones of this city. Within forty years, the Romans will see to it that not one stone remains upon another. Jesus will describe this in more detail in just three days, from this very spot (Mt 24; Mk 13; Lk 21). But for now, his prophetic warning gives way to tears. Surely this would have greatly confused his disciples, if indeed, any of them notice.

### 7. *Entrance into the Temple*

Mt 21:10-16

[10]When Jesus entered Jerusalem, the whole city was stirred and asked, "Who is this?"

[11]The crowds answered, "This is Jesus, the prophet from Nazareth in Galilee."

[14]The blind and the lame came to him at the temple, and he healed them. [15]But when the chief priests and the teachers of the law saw the wonderful things he did and the children shouting in the temple area, "Hosanna to the Son of David," they were indignant.

[16]"Do you hear what these children are saying?" they asked him.

"Yes," replied Jesus, "have you never read,

"'From the lips of children and infants
you have ordained praise'[a]?"

[a]*16* Psalm 8:2

Mk 11:11 *with*
Mt 21:17

[11][Jesus] looked around at everything, but since it was already late, he went out {of the city[MT]} to Bethany {where he spent the night[MT]} with the Twelve.

By the time Jesus makes it through the city gates, everyone is buzzing about him. The NIV translation of verse 10, "The whole city was stirred" is somewhat understated. The word translated "stirred" is used elsewhere in reference to the shaking of an earthquake (Mt 27:51; Rev 6:13). The Jerusalem residents and the Passover pilgrims ask those at the head of the parade, "Who is this?" "Jesus the prophet from Nazareth" is all the answer they need and the one they already suspect.

The sick of the city make their way to the outer court of the temple, the only one in which they were allowed. It was common for the sick and lame to sit at the temple gates and beg from those entering (cf. Acts 3:2). Somehow they find their way to Jesus through the mass of bodies and crooked necks. As if there wasn't enough excitement already, Jesus heals them. Even the children have formed a choir to echo their parents' praise.

The Pharisees, who have already accosted him, are now bolstered by the Sadducees. Since Jesus is taking over their territory in the temple, they must ask him to quit in spite of the fact that he is doing wonderful things! Such hypocrisy is too flagrant to be gentle with. Jesus responds by saying, "Have you never read?!" That's like accusing a preacher of not knowing John 3:16. Based on Psalm 8:2, they should have been more sensitive to the praise of these kids. It is not that this passage is so famous, but that this event is so obvious. What a contrast! On the one hand you have the praise of the people, the sick being healed and children worshiping God. And on the other hand you have the religious leaders wanting to put a stop to it because it is out of their control.

Such hypocrisy deserves more than this minor rebuke. It will, however, have to wait until the next day. Jesus has already used up the bulk of the afternoon with the Triumphal Entry and this healing service. He merely scopes out the problem, returns to Bethany with his inner band of twelve, and sleeps on it. But the fireworks are coming on Monday!

At this point, Matthew condenses his narrative. This has two results. First, it looks as if the cleansing of the temple took place on Sunday afternoon, while Mark clarifies that it took place on Monday. Second, he makes it look like the cursing of the fig tree and the lessons drawn from it took place at the same time. Again, Mark clarifies that there was a twenty-four hour interval between the two.

Mark's twenty-four hour interval is valuable not just for understanding the chronology, but also the theology of this passage. You see, Jesus curses the fig tree on Monday. The disciples don't notice it until Tuesday. Between these two events, Jesus cleanses the temple. Thus we understand that the withered fig tree is a symbol of Israel's future. It is kind of like an enacted parable.

**§ 129a**
**Cursing of the**
**Fig Tree**
(Mt 21:18-19;
Mk 11:12-14)

Mk 11:12-14 *with*
Mt 21:18-19

[12]The next day {early in the morning[MT]} as they were leaving Bethany {on his way back to the city,[MT]} Jesus was hungry. [13]Seeing in the distance {by the road[MT]} a fig tree in leaf, he went to find out if it had any fruit. When he reached it, he found nothing but leaves, because it was not the season for figs. [14]Then he said to the tree, "May no one ever eat fruit from you again." And his disciples heard him say it. {Immediately the tree withered.[MT]}

Early on Monday morning Jesus hikes two miles back to Jerusalem for some unfinished business in the temple. Jesus shouldn't have been hungry yet. Jews normally only ate two meals a day: 10 a.m. and 6-7 p.m. It was still too early for "breakfast." Perhaps in all the excitement of the previous day Jesus missed his supper. That would not be the first time Jesus missed a meal because of business (Mk 3:20; 6:31).

Up ahead, off to the side of the road, Jesus notices a fig tree in full leaf. Passover time was unusually early for fig trees to leaf out. But normally, with the leaves came the green buds which would mature into figs. They are bitter but edible. Jesus goes to the tree looking for the fruit that its leaves promise. But he finds nothing but leaves.

Jesus has been criticized for expecting figs before their time. After all, "It was not the season for figs." That criticism misses the point. The leaves promise there will be green fruit. But there isn't. What's worse, without the green fruit now, there will be no figs later.

Jesus has also been severely criticized for using his divine power to destroy an inanimate object in a fit of anger.[12] This too misses the point. Jesus isn't wreaking vengeance on a deceitful tree. He is using this opportunity to teach his disciples a valuable lesson, especially in light of what he is about to do in the temple. To Jesus people are more valuable than things. He places more value on teaching his disciples than on an inanimate object. This same lesson was to be learned at the loss of 2,000 pigs in Gerasa. Besides, this tree is unproductive. It is taking up space on God's good earth without doing its job. It is absurd to picture nature weeping the loss of its valued comrade through the whimsical anger of Jesus. It is a useless tree.

It has the appearance of a fruit-bearing tree, but it is not. So Jesus curses this unproductive tree as he is about to curse this unproductive nation. The disciples hear him. There is no way they could have predicted from his words — "May no one ever eat fruit from you again" — how immediate and severe the demise of this poor tree will be. Matthew

---

[12]T.W. Manson, "The Cleansing of the Temple," *BJRL* 33 (1951): 259 says, "It is a tale of miraculous power wasted in the service of ill temper (for the supernatural energy employed to blast the unfortunate tree might have been more usefully expended in forcing a crop of figs out of season); and as it stands is simply incredible."

says that it withers immediately. Within twenty-four hours, when they pass this spot again, they will notice that it has withered from its roots (Mk 11:20). Now that is "immediate" in any arborist's book!

Matthew, Mark and Luke place this cleansing at the close of Jesus' ministry. John, however, places it at the beginning of Jesus' ministry. Now, no one will deny that the Gospel writers sometimes place events topically rather than chronologically. But such a radical revision by John, writing after the Synoptics, could be construed as misleading and inaccurate. The most natural assumption, then, is that Jesus cleansed the temple twice, once at the beginning and once at the close of his ministry (cf. Morris, pp. 288ff).

§ 129b
**Second**
**Cleansing of**
**the Temple**
(Mt 21:12-13;
Mk 11:15-18;
Lk 19:45-48;
cf. § 31)

Mk 11:15-17 *with*
Mt 21:12

[15]On reaching Jerusalem, Jesus entered the temple area and began driving out {all[MT]} those who were buying and selling there. He overturned the tables of the money changers and the benches of those selling doves, [16]and would not allow anyone to carry merchandise through the temple courts. [17]And as he taught them, he said, "Is it not written:
    "'My house will be called
    a house of prayer for all nations'[a]?
But you have made it 'a den of robbers.'[b]"

[a] *17* Isaiah 56:7    [b] *17* Jer. 7:11

The first gate Jesus comes to, when entering Jerusalem from the east, leads right into the temple court, that is, the court of the Gentiles. What he sees borders on the bizarre. There are pigeons, and sheep and oxen (Jn 2:14). There are boxes and crates and haggling. There are tables where the Roman currency is exchanged for the kosher sheqel required for the temple tax.[13] It is chaotic and it is infuriating.

At the first cleansing Jesus wove together a whip out of strands of rope. We are not told that he made a whip this time. But there is still a good bit of force needed to overturn the tables of the money changers. Mark adds this interesting tidbit: Jesus "would not allow anyone to carry merchandise through the temple court." Merchants were using the court of the Gentiles as a shortcut to the road leading east over the Mt. of Olives. Jesus' vengeance is not only against those who are selling but also those who are buying.

It is an impressive scene. Businessmen on their hands and knees scrambling to collect their coins scattered across the pavement. Sheep,

---

[13]J. Neusner, "Money-Changers in the Temple: The Mishnah's Explanation," *NTS* 35 (1989): 287-290.

oxen, goats, and pigeons running wildly, frightened by all the turmoil. People pushing and shoving trying to get out of their way. The Sadducees are scowling from the sidelines, furious that Jesus has interfered with their financial gain. But there is really not much they can do about it. The populace supports Jesus, especially after that impressive parade the day before, and hates the obvious corruption of the temple. Were the Sadducees to intervene the people would likely rally and riot in support of Jesus (Mk 11:18). Furthermore, the Roman garrison is watching carefully with their hands on their swords. If a fight breaks out, the Romans could swiftly and eagerly end it.

All of this was so foreign to the original purpose of the temple. Quoting from both Isaiah 56:7 and Jeremiah 7:11, Jesus calls them back to the basics: The temple was to be a place of prayer for all nations. It is notable that the buying and selling takes place in the court of the Gentiles. No one could pray in that place with all the bleating of sheep, jangling of coins and haggling customers. But then Jewish prejudice would consider Gentiles unworthy of prayer anyway. However, the word of God ordained this place as a holy place of prayer and predicted that the Messiah would cleanse it (Mal 3:1-3). [For further comments see § 31.]

**Mk 11:18** *with*
**Lk 19:48**

[18]The chief priests and the teachers of the law heard this and began looking for a way to kill him, for they feared him, because the whole crowd was amazed at his teaching {[and] hung on his words[LK]}.

It is clear that Jesus is winning the multitudes. Both the Sadducean sect (chief priests) and the Pharisaic sect (teachers of the law) want to kill him. They are afraid of the power that Jesus wields over the multitudes. Furthermore, Roman authorities closely monitored the monies of the temple and filched funds through taxation. Thus, Jesus' cleansing of the temple had political and economic ramifications beyond the boundaries of Judaism.[14] These leaders are clearly more concerned about their positions of authority than the possibility that Jesus is their long-awaited Messiah.[15] This arrogance and selfishness will blind them to the bitter end.

---

[14]Cf. J.M. Dawsey, "Confrontation in the Temple," *PRS* 11 (1984): 153-165.

[15]The high priesthood was quite lucrative and had become thoroughly corrupt. Josephus reports that Jesus ben Gamaliel bought the position of high priest with a bribe (*Ant* 20. 213). He also says that some higher ranking priests would beat the lower ranking ones to steal their rightful tithes from them (*Ant* 28. 181 & 206-207). Furthermore, they would sometimes overcharge worshipers up to 25 times the value of a sacrificial animal. This made them feared and hated (cf. C.A. Evans, "Jesus' Action in the Temple: Cleansing or Portent of Destruction?" *CBQ* 51 [1989]: 237-270).

Jesus has just cleansed the temple. Specifically, he drove out the rabble from the court of the Gentiles. Now the proselytes can pray properly. Jesus is their hero. So it's no surprise that one group of Greek converts wants to talk to Jesus.

**§ 130a**
**Some Greeks**
**Want to See**
**Jesus**
(Jn 12:20-36)

Jn 12:20-26

[20]Now there were some Greeks among those who went up to worship at the Feast. [21]They came to Philip, who was from Bethsaida in Galilee, with a request. "Sir," they said, "we would like to see Jesus." [22]Philip went to tell Andrew; Andrew and Philip in turn told Jesus.

[23]Jesus replied, "The hour has come for the Son of Man to be glorified. [24]I tell you the truth, unless a kernel of wheat falls to the ground and dies, it remains only a single seed. But if it dies, it produces many seeds. [25]The man who loves his life will lose it, while the man who hates his life in this world will keep it for eternal life. [26]Whoever serves me must follow me; and where I am, my servant also will be. My Father will honor the one who serves me."

These Greeks are apparently proselytes at the gate. They came up to Jerusalem to worship the God they believed in but had not yet entered the covenant relationship through circumcision. There was obviously something about Philip that attracts them. Perhaps it is his name. After all, he and Andrew are the only two called by their Greek names from the very beginning. Philip takes them to Andrew who is famous for bringing people to Jesus (cf. Jn 1:41; 6:8-9).

Andrew is Peter's brother. He is the only one in the fishing business excluded from the inner three. But next to them he was probably closest to Jesus. Thus, it makes sense that Philip brings these Greeks to Andrew. He would have the best shot at escorting them to Jesus.

Well, Andrew tells Jesus that these Greeks want to see him, but we never find out if they get to. All we are given is Jesus response to "them." Does that refer to Philip and Andrew or to the group of Greeks? Whatever it means, we know that a crowd of Jews surrounding Jesus hears his reply (v. 29).

This response seems pretty unrelated to the request of the Greeks. But it is exactly what they need to hear. They want to become part of God's people, and they will. But they will be included because Jesus dies for their sins, not because they convert to Judaism.

We're not so surprised to see foreigners seeking Jesus. After all, the centurion (§ 55) and the Syro-Phoenician woman (§ 78) have already pursued Jesus. But this present group is a clear sign that the end of the road is just ahead. Jesus reflects on that briefly and packs into his response a few choice warnings for his would-be followers.

Jesus' execution will shake the disciples to their very core. Therefore, they must remember that Jesus' death is as necessary as the death of a wheat kernel. If a wheat seed is not buried in the ground, there will be no harvest. Likewise, if Jesus isn't killed and buried, there will be no resurrection, no church, no Gentile inclusion (cf. Isa 53:10; Lk 24:26; Rom 3:23-25; 5:12-21). And what goes for Jesus, goes for the disciples. They too must die (cf. Mt 10:37-39; 16:24-26; Mk 8:34-38; Lk 9:23-26; 14:26; 17:32, 33). After all, you can't follow Jesus without going where he goes.

Jn 12:27-29

<sup></sup>27"Now my heart is troubled, and what shall I say? 'Father, save me from this hour'? No, it was for this very reason I came to this hour. 28Father, glorify your name!"

Then a voice came from heaven, "I have glorified it, and will glorify it again." 29The crowd that was there and heard it said it had thundered; others said an angel had spoken to him.

Jesus knows what is coming and is disturbed. He expresses his grief in verse 27. How we punctuate this verse makes a difference. The first phrase is certainly a question. But the second phrase may well be a declaration rather than a question as the NIV punctuates it. If we understand it as a question, we hear Jesus say, "Should I really say, 'Father save me from this hour?' No, because that is why I came!" However, if we understand it as a statement, then we hear Jesus say, "Father, I know what is coming and I don't want to go through with it . . . However, I came to accomplish this very thing, so let's get on with it."

This second view would make this statement very much like the prayer of Gethsemane (cf. Mt 26:39; Mk 14:36; Lk 22:42). Jesus is beginning to understand the overwhelming implications of Calvary. It is not surprising that he does not want to go through with it. But he is not driven by self-indulgent desires. He is more interested in his Father's glory than his own comfort. He doesn't have to, but he faithfully executes the Father's plan.

Jesus' prayer is intense! It is full of commitment to the Father and personal pathos. God respects and responds to his Son in this decisive moment with an audible affirmation. This is the third and last time God speaks audibly during Jesus' ministry. Each time was a critical moment: at his baptism (Mk 1:11), transfiguration (Mk 9:7) and now, as he solidifies his commitment to the cross.

Many of the people do not understand the voice and so attribute the sound to thunder (cf. Acts 9:7; 22:9). Others are convinced that the words come from an angel. But Jesus hears it loud and clear, "I have glorified it and will glorify it again." This was no doubt a welcome and timely endorsement from the Father.

[30]Jesus said, "This voice was for your benefit, not mine. [31]Now is the time for judgment on this world; now the prince of this world will be driven out. [32]But I, when I am lifted up from the earth, will draw all men to myself." [33]He said this to show the kind of death he was going to die.

[34]The crowd spoke up, "We have heard from the Law that the Christ will remain forever, so how can you say, 'The Son of Man must be lifted up'? Who is this 'Son of Man'?"

Although these words must be a great comfort to Jesus, they are even more desperately needed by the crowd. They will watch as Jesus is crucified in three or four days. That punishment is only reserved for the vilest of criminals. Jesus is to be the recipient of the wrath of man as well as the wrath of God when the judgment for man's sin falls upon him. It will not look good for Jesus. For those who love him, it will seem like Satan had conquered. For those who hate him, it will look like God has vanquished him (cf. Isa 53:10). Neither is really the truth. Jesus dies willingly, taking the penalty that belongs to us.

The cross of Christ will accomplish a lot. First, through the cross the sins of the world would be judged. For those who accept Jesus, the cross cancels the debt incurred by their sins. For those who reject, the cross would picture their own impending judgment. Second, through the cross, God vanquished the Devil, not Jesus. Satan is, indeed, the prince of this world (Lk 4:6; 2 Cor 4:4; Eph 2:2; 6:12). But at Calvary he was stripped of his power of death and sin. Third, through the cross, Christ would draw all men unto himself. This notorious act of suspending Jesus between heaven and earth would become the focal point of the church. It was this very deed, designed to destroy him, that actually established him as the cornerstone.

Even the crowd recognized this metaphor "lifting up"[16] in reference to his death. Only they believed the Messiah's reign was to be permanent. "How can you be the Messiah," they asked, "if you are going to die?" Now that was a good question in light of Isaiah 9:7 (cf. Ps 110:4; Ezek 37:25; Dan 7:14).

[35]Then Jesus told them, "You are going to have the light just a little while longer. Walk while you have the light, before darkness overtakes you. The man who walks in the dark does not know where he is going. [36]Put your trust in the light while you have it, so that you may become sons of light." When he had finished speaking, Jesus left and hid himself from them.

Jesus is the light (see comments on v. 46). Anyone who accepts

---

[16]"The verb *lifted up* (*hypsoō*) is used in John exclusively to refer to Jesus' death (John 3:14; 8:28; 12:32, 34)" Tenney (p. 131).

Jesus receives his light in them just as a candle might be lit from a bonfire. But in a few short days, darkness will fall (i.e., the crucifixion). Jesus will raise from the dead, but most of his appearances will be private and only to the disciples. True enough, people will still be able to obtain the light (i.e., accept Jesus) through the disciples, but that will be much more difficult. The best time to follow Jesus is as he stands before them.

After saying this he went out from the crowd and hid himself. If this event took place on Monday, Jesus would come out of hiding within sixteen hours. But his big day of discussions on Tuesday would be his last. It is possible that this event took place on Tuesday afternoon. If that is the case, then these are the last public words of Jesus. The next time he shows up before a crowd would be Friday morning in Pilate's Praetorium. They will then shout, "Crucify him!"

## § 130b
## Blind Eyes and
## Dead Hearts
## (Jn 12:37-50)

[37]Even after Jesus had done all these miraculous signs in their presence, they still would not believe in him. [38]This was to fulfill the word of Isaiah the prophet:
"Lord, who has believed our message
    and to whom has the arm of the Lord been revealed?"[a]
[39]For this reason they could not believe, because, as Isaiah says elsewhere:
[40]"He has blinded their eyes
    and deadened their hearts,
so they can neither see with their eyes,
    nor understand with their hearts,
    nor turn — and I would heal them."[b]
[41]Isaiah said this because he saw Jesus' glory and spoke about him.

[a]38 Isaiah 53:1    [b]40 Isaiah 6:10

This section summarizes the entire public ministry of Jesus. He has constantly backed up his claims with miracles (Jn 2:11, 23; 3:2; 4:48, 54; 6:2, 14, 26; 7:31; 9:16; 10:41; 11:47; 12:18; esp. 20:30). But even with these, the Jews, by and large (v. 42), would not believe. The imperfect verb tense "were not believing" describes their continuing unwillingness to turn to Jesus. It is not because the miracles are faulty. Nor is it entirely the fault of the Jews. God has hardened their hearts (Rom 11:25).

The first passage is quoted from Isaiah 53:1. Even in its original context it appears to be a conversation between the Messiah and Jehovah. Even though Jesus preaches the truth and verifies it with miracles, the Jews refuse to believe. The second passage is from Isaiah 6:10 and is part of Isaiah's commission to preach. It is quoted two other times in the NT (Mt 13:14-15 [cf. Mk 4:12; Lk 8:10] and Acts 28:26-27). All four times it appears in the Bible it highlights the hardening of the Jews.

In Matthew the "credit" for the hardening is laid at the preacher's feet. That is, Jesus taught in parables so that the religious leaders would *not* understand his message. In Acts, the "credit" is laid at the listener's feet. They had every opportunity to respond to God's message but did not. And here, the "credit" is laid at God's feet. That's because the hardening of the heart is a progressive and cooperative effort between God and men. As men turn their backs on God, he withdraws his Spirit from them. Thus, they are less likely to repent and turn back to God. This is a frightening proposition. (See comments on Mt 13:14-15, § 64b).

Verse 41 is an astounding statement equating Jesus with Jehovah. It says that Isaiah saw Jesus' glory. But turning back to Isaiah 6:1 it says, "I saw the Lord seated on a throne, high and exalted, and the train of his robe filled the temple." The chapter goes on to describe the praise offered to the preincarnate Christ. Clearly, John viewed Jesus as the very God.

[42]Yet at the same time many even among the leaders believed in him. But because of the Pharisees they would not confess their faith for fear they would be put out of the synagogue; [43]for they loved praise from men more than praise from God.

[44]Then Jesus cried out, "When a man believes in me, he does not believe in me only, but in the one who sent me. [45]When he looks at me, he sees the one who sent me. [46]I have come into the world as a light, so that no one who believes in me should stay in darkness."

Jn 12:42-46

This paragraph is a fitting summary of Jesus' ministry and teaching. First, there was always a mixed response to Jesus even among the leaders (v. 42). Most rejected him but many did not. Those who did believe Jesus often kept their mouths shut so that they would not get kicked out of the synagogue. We might call them cowards. However, we must remember that by being ejected from the synagogue they would have lost their jobs, their families, and their respect in the community. It was a heavy blow. But verse 43 clarifies what was of greatest value to them: The praise of men. Indeed, man's praise is a dangerous thing to desire. It is fickle and demanding and often requires one to reject God's Word and ways.

Second, Jesus highlights two personal characteristics that have epitomized his public ministry: (1) His intimate union with the Father (cf. Jn 1:14; 3:35; 5:18-23; 5:26; 5:36-37; 5:45; 6:27; 6:32; 6:45; 7:16; 8:16; 8:18-19; 8:27-28; 8:41; 10:30; 10:38; 12:49-13:1), and (2) the light he brought to this world (Mt 4:16; Lk 2:32; Jn 1:4-5; 1:7-9; 3:19-21; 8:12; 9:5; 11:9-10; 12:35-36; 12:46). The implication of both of these characteristics is obvious. When we believe in Jesus, we too will experience intimacy with the Father, and we will no longer live in darkness but will walk in the light.

Jn 12:47-50

⁴⁷"As for the person who hears my words but does not keep them, I do not judge him. For I did not come to judge the world, but to save it. ⁴⁸There is a judge for the one who rejects me and does not accept my words; that very word which I spoke will condemn him at the last day. ⁴⁹For I did not speak of my own accord, but the Father who sent me commanded me what to say and how to say it. ⁵⁰I know that his command leads to eternal life. So whatever I say is just what the Father has told me to say."

This paragraph picks up another old discussion. Jesus did not come to judge but to tell us the truth about God (cf. Jn 5:24, 25-47; 8:31, 37, 51; 14:23-24). In fact, his words are the very words of God, (see comments on 7:16; cf. 3:11; 8:26, 28, 38; 14:10). Therefore, when a person rejects Jesus he or she rejects God. Thus, they are judged not by Jesus but by their own rejection of God's word. On the flip side, following the words of Jesus leads to eternal life.

**§ 131**
**Lessons from**
**the Withered**
**Fig Tree**
(Mt 21:19b-22;
Mk 11:19-25;
Lk 21:37-38)

[MK 11:]¹⁹When evening came, they went out of the city.

²⁰In the morning, as they went along, they saw the fig tree withered from the roots. ²¹Peter remembered and said to Jesus, "Rabbi, look! The fig tree you cursed has withered!"

²²"Have faith in God," Jesus answered.

[MT 21:]²¹"I tell you the truth, if you have faith and do not doubt, not only can you do what was done to the fig tree, but also you can say to this mountain, 'Go, throw yourself into the sea,' and it will be done.

[MK 11:]²⁴"Therefore I tell you, whatever you ask for in prayer, believe that you have received it, and it will be yours. ²⁵And when you stand praying, if you hold anything against anyone, forgive him, so that your Father in heaven may forgive you your sins."

Tuesday morning the apostolic band marches back to Jerusalem from Bethany. Peter is the first to notice the fig tree withered from its very roots. The *unstated* lesson of Jesus here is about the position of the Pharisees and Sadducees. Based on the structure of Mark's narrative, we conclude that this fig tree is a symbol of the Jewish leaders (cf. Jer 8:13; Hos 9:10; Mic 7:1-6; Nah 3:12). Their appearance was deceitful. Outwardly they looked like productive trees — they did all the right things. But upon closer inspection, they had no real fruit. As Jesus literally predicted the demise of Jerusalem on Sunday afternoon (Lk 19:41-44), he does so here symbolically with the fig tree.

Jesus' *stated* lesson is about prayer. He prayed against the fig tree with dramatic results. Jesus' disciples can also pray with that same power. But there are two parameters in this text around effective prayer: faith and forgiveness (cf. Mt 6:14-15, § 54f). Without faith in God and forgiving those who have wronged us, our prayers are anemic.

Does this mean that prayer is a *carte blanche* calling card for those who pray in faith? No. If we are correct in assuming that the cursing of the fig tree is a picture of the cleansing of the temple, then we might assume that the prayers Jesus is speaking about are specifically in reference to faithless Israel. Even though the unbelief of the Jewish leaders seems like a daunting obstacle (a mountain), it can be overcome through faithful prayer. Jesus may have even waved his hand toward the Mt. of Olives or even Mt. Zion to illustrate his point.

If we take this passage alone, we could potentially pray for some extravagant and frivolous things (cf. Mk 10:35). A number of other parallel passages place some parameters around our prayers. For example, we should ask:

1.  In faith (Mt 21:22), and obedience (1 Jn 3:22).
2.  With persistence (Lk 11:9; 18:1-6).
3.  According to the will of Jesus (i.e., "In my name"), (Jn 14:13-16; 15:16; 16:23-26; 1 Jn 5:14-15), remaining in him (Jn 15:7).
4.  In cooperation/conjunction with other believers (Mt 18:19).
5.  With unselfish motives (James 4:2-3).

And we are to pray for:

1.  God to send workers into the harvest (Mt 9:38).
2.  The Holy Spirit (Lk 11:13).
3.  That which is necessary in order to bear fruit (Jn 15:16).
4.  Wisdom (James 1:5).

So while we don't believe that we can just ask for any old thing, we mustn't deny the power of prayer. Ephesians 3:20 says, "Now to him who is able to do immeasurably more than all we ask or imagine, according to his power that is at work within us . . ." The very real danger to most Christians is not asking extravagantly, but not asking at all.

[37]Each day Jesus was teaching at the temple, and each evening he went out to spend the night on the hill called the Mount of Olives, [38]and all the people came early in the morning to hear him at the temple.

Lk 21:37-38

Luke makes it sound like Jesus camped out on the Mt. of Olives each evening of the last week. While the warm weather of Palestine would certainly permit this, it is more likely that he made the trek across the Mt. of Olives back to Bethany where he was likely housed by Mary, Martha and Lazarus. Each day he returned to the temple courts early in the morning to teach. When he arrived the people gathered around him, eager to hear what he would say next.

**§ 132a**
**Jesus'**
**Authority**
**Questioned by**
**the Sanhedrin**
(Mt 21:23-27;
Mk 11:27-33;
Lk 20:1-8)

The last two days have been good for Jesus' popularity polls. The Triumphal Entry on Sunday and the cleansing of the temple on Monday have attracted a lot of attention. It is now early Tuesday morning in the temple. The people have already gathered around Jesus. The Jewish leaders must do something. What we have here is their attempt to discredit Jesus and win back their following.

[MK 11:]27They arrived again in Jerusalem, and while Jesus was walking in the temple courts {teaching the people and preaching the gospel,LK} the chief priests, the teachers of the law and the elders came to him. 28"{Tell usLK} By what authority are you doing these things?" they asked. "And who gave you authority to do this?"

29Jesus replied, "I will {alsoMT,LK} ask you one question. Answer me, and I will tell you by what authority I am doing these things. 30John's baptism — was it from heaven, or from men? Tell me!"

Right out of the blocks the Sanhedrin is in Jesus' face. You can already tell that this is going to be a full day, packed with questions and controversies. In fact, there are more details given about this day in the life of Jesus than any other. Matthew devotes nearly one sixth of his gospel to it.

Representatives from all three "branches" of the Sanhedrin are there: Chief priests (Sadducean), teachers of the law (Pharisaic), and elders ("lay" leaders). They come with what seems to be an innocent and fair question: "By what authority are you doing these things?" After all, Jesus had just cleared out the temple the day before. In other words, he intruded into the temple mount, the jurisdiction of the Sanhedrin. Part of their job would be to oversee the proceedings during the Passover at the temple. This is especially true since the Romans are looking on from the Tower of Antonia, eager to pounce on any potential Jewish revolt. Thus, it was their job to protect both the Jewish religion and the civic peace of their people.

Ostensibly their question was reasonable and fair. But Jesus saw through their motives. They were still looking for an opportunity to trap him in his words, accuse him of blasphemy, and turn public opinion away from him. So Jesus appropriately answers their question with a question. Now that may sound to us like Jesus is trying to evade their question. But it was common in Rabbinic debates to answer a question with a question. That would not sound to them like avoidance, but like leading. It was assumed that Jesus would answer their question but that he first wanted to lead the discussion in a certain direction. In addition, the answer they give to Jesus' question will become the answer to their own. By answering Jesus, they will get the answer they seek.

Because John the Baptist was the forerunner of Jesus, and because their message and purposes were the same, their authority would also be the same (Jn 1:19, 26-27; 3:25-30; Mt 11:7-10). So Jesus asks this counter question: Was John's baptism from heaven or from men. In other words, was John's authority from God or was he just out there "doing his own thing." Jesus concentrated on John's baptism because it epitomized his whole ministry and because it was at that point that the Jewish leaders refused to following his teaching (Lk 7:30).

<sup>25</sup>They discussed it among themselves and said, "If we say, 'From heaven,' he will ask, 'Then why didn't you believe him?' <sup>26</sup>But if we say, 'From men' — we are afraid of the people {[that they] will stone us,<sup>LK</sup>} for they all hold that John {really<sup>MK</sup>} was a prophet."
<sup>27</sup>So they answered Jesus, "We don't know."
Then he said, "Neither will I tell you by what authority I am doing these things."

Mt 21:25b-27 *with*
Lk 20:6; Mk 11:32

Suddenly the hunters become the hunted. Their private discussion/debate betrayed the fact that they were in a catch-22. No matter what they say, it will be turned against them. If they say, "John's authority was from heaven," then Jesus also gets his authority from the same place. What's worse, they refused to follow John. Thus this answer would betray their blatant hypocrisy. On the other hand, if they say, "John's authority was from men," they might very well get stoned on the spot. This pilgrim crowd[17] adamantly believes in John. They were still seething over his murder by Herod. Furthermore, just two days ago, they hailed Jesus, John's successor, king at the Triumphal Entry. If these Sanhedrin delegates turn on John (and Jesus), they might very well turn this precarious crowd against them.

So they cop out. "We don't know," they say. Jesus responds in kind. But notice, he didn't say, "I don't know" but "Neither will I tell you." Jesus knows they're not ignorant. They simply refuse to admit the truth. And if they refused the truth before, they are not likely to receive it now.

---

[17]In verse 1 Luke describes this crowd as "the people" [*laos*]. Liefeld notes (p. 1013) that in Luke this word always designates a crowd that is receptive to Jesus' teaching. In other words, they were his supporters.

So Jesus doesn't waste his words. They're not looking for an answer but an opportunity. The Master is not about to give it to them.

**§ 132b**
**Three Parables**
**on Accepting/**
**Rejecting**
**Jesus**
(Mt 21:28-22:14;
Mk 12:1-12;
Lk 20:9-19)

The Jewish leaders refuse to answer Jesus' question about John's authority (cf. § 132a). Jesus responds to their silence with three appropriate parables. Only Matthew includes all three; Mark and Luke only tell the parable of the vineyard.[18] Nonetheless, all three parables are designed to show how the Jews had rejected God's authority through Jesus.

With each parable both the rejection and punishment grow progressively worse. In the first parable, those who reject Jesus are like the wicked son who didn't do what the father asked. In the second, they are like the wicked servants who kill the son and will receive just recompense. In the third parable, they are like those who rejected the king's invitation and will thus be rejected from the Messianic banquet.

## PARABLE OF THE TWO SONS:

Mt 21:28-32

[28]"What do you think? There was a man who had two sons. He went to the first and said, 'Son, go and work today in the vineyard.'

[29]"'I will not,' he answered, but later he changed his mind and went.

[30]"Then the father went to the other son and said the same thing. He answered, 'I will, sir,' but he did not go.

[31]"Which of the two did what his father wanted?"

"The first," they answered.

Jesus said to them, "I tell you the truth, the tax collectors and the prostitutes are entering the kingdom of God ahead of you. [32]For John came to you to show you the way of righteousness, and you did not believe him, but the tax collectors and the prostitutes did. And even after you saw this, you did not repent and believe him."

This is a simple parable. Jesus says, "It's not those who talk the right talk that honor God, but those that walk the right walk." Even Jesus' opponents readily acknowledge this. This is the first time that Jesus openly applies one of his parables to the Jewish leaders (Carson, p. 449).

---

[18]An abbreviated version of this parable is also found in the Gospel of Thomas. Some suggest that it is the most "original" version (cf. J.D. Crossan, "The Parable of the Wicked Husbandmen," *JBL* 90 [1971]: 451-465 & J.A.T. Robinson, "The Parable of the Wicked Husbandmen: A Test of Synoptic Relationships," *NTS* 21 [1974-75]: 443-461). However, the editorial changes are better explained as Gnostic heresy, not earlier oral transmission (cf. W.R. Schoedel, "Parables in the Gospel of Thomas: Oral Tradition or Gnostic Exegesis," *CTM* 43 [1972]: 548-560; also K.R. Snodgrass, "The Parable of the Wicked Husbandmen: Is the Gospel of Thomas Version the Original?" *NTS* 20 [1974-75]: 142-144).

They are scandalized by it. Why would tax collectors and prostitutes enter the kingdom ahead[19] of religious folks? According to the story, they repented and did what God asked them to do. Now, the Pharisees would be shocked at Jesus' implication that they were not working for God. Their lives were devoted to his work . . . or so they thought.

The work God requires is not so much "church business," but trusting Christ. Jesus put it this way, "The work of God is this: to believe in the one he has sent" (Jn 6:29). At first the tax collectors and prostitutes rejected God's plan through their wicked lifestyles. But when they heard John, they repented and were baptized and subsequently followed Jesus. Their leaders, however, talk about doing God's will, but are not obedient to it. For when John came preaching a baptism of repentance, they refused to submit (Lk 7:30). And now that Jesus stands before them, they are trying to figure out a way to kill him.

## PARABLE OF THE VINEYARD:

[33]"Listen to another parable: There was a landowner who planted a vineyard. He put a wall around it, dug a winepress in it and built a watchtower. Then he rented the vineyard to some farmers and went away on a journey {for a long time.[LK]} [34]When the harvest time approached, he sent his servants to the tenants to collect {some of[MK]} his fruit {of the vineyard.[MK,LK]}

*Mt 21:33-39 with Lk 20:9-16; Mk 12:2-5*

[35]"The tenants seized his servants; they beat one {and sent him away empty-handed,[MK,LK]} killed another, and stoned a third. [36]Then he sent other servants to them, more than the first time, and the tenants treated them the same way. {He sent many others; some of them they beat, others they killed.[MK]} [37]{Then the owner of the vineyard said, 'What shall I do?[LK]} Last of all, he sent his son {whom I love[LK]} to them. 'They will respect my son,' he said.

[38]"But when the tenants saw the son, they said to each other {talked the matter over,[LK]} 'This is the heir. Come, let's kill him and take his inheritance.' [39]So they took him and threw him out of the vineyard and killed him. {When the people heard this, they said, "May this never be!"[LK]}

Vineyards were among the most common agricultural ventures of Jesus' day. Frequently a landowner would purchase and prepare the property and then lease it out to tenants. The tenants would then raise the crop and give a certain percentage of the product or proceeds to the owner (generally 25-30%). Furthermore, the vineyard was a frequent OT metaphor for Israel (Isa 5:1-7; Ps 80:6-16; see also Jer 2:21; 6:9; 8:13; 12:10; Ezek 15:1-8; 19:10-14; Hosea 10:1). No doubt these Pharisees are keenly aware that Jesus used the vineyard to represent their people.

---

[19]The word *proago* may indicate "taking precedence over," not merely "entering before." Thus, the implication *may* go so far as to say that sinners enter "instead" of the Pharisees.

Jesus describes a vineyard that is particularly well prepared with: (1) a wall, to protect the crop from wild animals and thieves; (2) a wine-press, so the grapes could be harvested and "stomped" into wine right there on the site; and (3) a tower, where a worker could watch for fires or robbers.

Once the vineyard had been prepared and its workers contracted, the owner was free to take an extended leave of absence. When the harvest rolled around, he sent his servants to collect his share of the crop (Mk 12:1-2). Blomberg (p. 323) notes that Jesus' language sounds much like John's at this point: "Fruit in keeping with repentance" (Mt 3:8; cf. 3:10; 7:16-20; 12:33; 13:8, 24-26; 21:19). This may even allude to Psalm 1:3.

The behavior of the tenants was scandalous! Instead of paying their bills, they beat (the word can also mean to flay or flog) and killed the collectors. This didn't just happen once, but repeatedly. The owner is at his "wit's end." What can he do? He decides to send his very own son![20] Surely in his presence they will repent and meet their obligations.

However, when they saw him coming up the road they discussed the matter among themselves. They reasoned that the owner must be dead and the son has come to collect his inheritance. So, if they kill the son, there will be no one else to demand the vineyard from them. The property and all its proceeds will be theirs. Thus, they killed the son and threw him out of the vineyard.[21] The people standing around Jesus gasp in shock. "May this never be!" they say. But it would be, and sooner than they could possibly imagine.

Mt 21:40-42

[40]"Therefore, when the owner of the vineyard comes, what will he do to those tenants?"

[41]"He will bring those wretches to a wretched end," they replied, "and he will rent the vineyard to other tenants, who will give him his share of the crop at harvest time."

[42]Jesus said to them, "Have you never read in the Scriptures:
"'The stone the builders rejected
    has become the capstone[a];

---

[20]The word "beloved" [*agapētos*] (Lk 20:13) is sometimes virtually synonymous with "only" [*monogenēs*] in the LXX (e.g., Gen 22:2). Therefore, we might see an allusion in this passage to Jn 3:16, Jesus' baptismal narrative (Mt 3:17; Lk 3:22), and his transfiguration experience (Mt 17:5).

[21]Matthew and Luke have the son thrown out of the vineyard first and then killed (Mt 21:39; Lk 20:15), whereas Mark has him killed inside the vineyard (Mk 12:8). There is virtually no difference in the meaning, unless one takes the vineyard as a metaphor for the city of Jerusalem rather than for Israel. In that case, Jesus was taken out of the city first and then killed. However, this interpretation probably reads more into the text than Mark intended.

the Lord has done this,
and it is marvelous in our eyes"ᵇ?"

ᵃ*42 Or cornerstone*   ᵇ*42 Psalm 118:22,23*

No landowner is going to put up with this kind of behavior. So when Jesus asks, "What will he do to those tenants?" the answer is obvious. He will destroy them and replace them with tenants who will respect the owner and pay their debts.

Just as with the previous parable, they know the correct interpretation but badly miss its application. They are the wicked tenants. God has sent prophets to them time and again whom they beat and killed (Jer 20:1-2; 26:20-23; 1 Kgs 18:4, 13; 2 Chr 24:20-21; Mt 23:34; Heb 11:37). Now God is sending them his very own Son.[22] But they are plotting to take his life in order to save their own positions and prestige (cf. Jn 11:45-54, § 119). They are about to fulfill Psalm 118:22. They will reject Jesus by killing him. With that act, Jesus will be placed by God as the cornerstone.

Jesus introduces Psalm 118:22 with this insulting retort, "Have you never read?" (Mt 12:3; 19:4; 21:16; Mk 12:10). It was a common Messianic psalm to which they had not paid much attention. You can understand why. A rejected cornerstone was a novel idea. This "cornerstone" could stand for three different construction stones. It may be a *cornerstone*. That was the first and most important stone laid in the foundation of a building. If it was laid correctly the whole building would be straight. Second, the *capstone* was the "roof" of a building and was the final stone which held all the pillars in place. Third, the *keystone* was the last stone put in the middle of an arch. Once it was in place, all the supporting beams could be removed. Now the idea of a cornerstone would best fit the first part of verse 44 — falling on this stone is detrimental to your health. However, the capstone or keystone would best fit the second part of verse 44 — if this stone falls on you it will crush you. Perhaps Jesus intends a dual metaphor here.

This metaphor comes from Psalm 118:22 and originally signified the Jewish nation. Other nations would mistreat them, but they were precious to God. Here, however, Jesus claims to be the representative or even the embodiment of the entire nation.[23] What is true for the nation of

---

[22]This may well be the first time Jesus publicly claimed to be the "Son of God." Caiaphas would remember this and bring it up against Jesus in just three days during the trial (Mt 26:63).

[23]F.F. Bruce, "New Wine in Old Wine Skins: III. The Corner Stone," *ExpT* 84 (1972-73): 231-235.

Israel is true of Jesus as an individual, as the Messiah. Surely we are correct in applying this Psalm messianically. The early church certainly did (Acts 4:11; Rom 9:33; 1 Pet 2:7). We read "salvation talk" in the verses that surround Psalm 118:22 (cf. 21, 25). We are called back to the Triumphal Entry (Mt 21:9) by v. 26, "Blessed is he who comes in the name of the Lord."[24]

One final note on Psalm 118:22. It is followed by these words in vv. 23-24, "The Lord has done this, and it is marvelous in our eyes. *This is the day the Lord has made; let us rejoice and be glad in it.*" Although the death of Jesus was a horrible injustice against God incarnate, it is also the source of our salvation. As ugly as it is, we cherish it. Indeed, its beauty is shrouded in blood.

Mt 21:43-46 *with* Mk 12:12

43"Therefore I tell you that the kingdom of God will be taken away from you and given to a people who will produce its fruit. 44He who falls on this stone will be broken to pieces, but he on whom it falls will be crushed."[a]

45When the chief priests and the Pharisees heard Jesus' parables, they knew he was talking about them. 46They looked for a way to arrest him, but they were afraid of the crowd because the people held that he was a prophet. {So they left him and went away.[MK]}

[a]44 Some manuscripts do not have verse 44.

The "vineyard" of God would be stripped from these wicked tenants and given to people who will give God his due. Initially we see these new tenants as tax collectors and prostitutes. But eventually they will include even the Gentiles.[25] There are great blessings in store for those who accept Jesus, but frightening consequences for those who don't. They will be crushed to dust by this very stone they attempted to cast out (cf. Isa 8:14; Dan 2:35, 44).

The implications of this parable are more than they can stand. They want to arrest Jesus in the worst way. But the crowds hang on every word he says. They were both insulted and impotent, which is a bad combination.

---

[24]Blomberg (p. 325) notes that "Matthew has not introduced so many scriptural quotations into one chapter since his infancy narratives (chaps. 1-2), and they continue to pervade the rest of his Gospel."

[25]A.A. Milavec, "Mark's Parable of the Wicked Husbandmen as Reaffirming God's Predilection for Israel," *JES* 26/2 (1989):289-312, based on a redactional comparison of Mk 12:1-12 and Isa 5:1-7, concludes that this parable is not about Jesus and the church but about God's continuing predilection for Israel. While his interpretation is untenable, Milavec does offer a valid warning against anti-Semitism based on this parable. The primary point of Mt 21:43 is not Gentile inclusion but faith in Jesus.

## PARABLE OF THE WEDDING BANQUET:

This parable has several similarities to one told in Luke 14:15-24. But they are told at different times, with different details and for different purposes. It simply does not seem reasonable to view them as stemming from the same "core" and being edited into their present form. Certainly Jesus was clever enough to create two entirely distinct parables from a single theme, especially one as common and rich as a "banquet."

¹Jesus spoke to them again in parables, saying: ²"The kingdom of heaven is like a king who prepared a wedding banquet for his son. ³He sent his servants to those who had been invited to the banquet to tell them to come, but they refused to come.

⁴"Then he sent some more servants and said, 'Tell those who have been invited that I have prepared my dinner: My oxen and fattened cattle have been butchered, and everything is ready. Come to the wedding banquet.'

⁵"But they paid no attention and went off — one to his field, another to his business. ⁶The rest seized his servants, mistreated them and killed them. ⁷The king was enraged. He sent his army and destroyed those murderers and burned their city."

Mt 22:1-7

The NIV leaves the first word of verse one untranslated. It says that Jesus "answered" [*apokritheis*]. It may be nothing more than a literary formula, which introduces a new discussion. Then again, it may suggest that Jesus is somehow responding to the Jewish leaders' desires, facial expressions, or even words which we are not privileged to know.

Wedding banquets often lasted for several days. Therefore preliminary messengers were sent out to alert the guests of the upcoming gala so that they could make plans to attend. When the day rolled around for this banquet to begin the king urgently sent out the messengers to tell the guests to come immediately since the morning meal [*ariston*] was on the table. The banquet was often used to symbolize the fellowship between the Messiah and his people (Mt 8:11; Lk 13:29; Rev 19:9). We should also keep in mind that the Messiah is often symbolized as a bridegroom (Mt 9:15; 25:1; Jn 3:29; Eph 5:25-32; Rev 21:2, 9).

Quite unexpectedly, those who were invited refused to come. In fact, they refused persistently (as is implied by the imperfect verb tense). So the king sent out even more messengers to try to entice them to come with descriptions of the sumptuous feast awaiting them. But they "blew them off." Some went to work in the field and others to business meetings. Still others didn't merely ignore the messengers but actually beat and killed them. The king's rage and response were predictable. The entire first guest list was wiped out by the king's militia and their city was burned. This is a pretty potent picture of judgment using OT imagery.

Mt 22:8-14

8"Then he said to his servants, 'The wedding banquet is ready, but those I invited did not deserve to come. 9Go to the street corners and invite to the banquet anyone you find.' 10So the servants went out into the streets and gathered all the people they could find, both good and bad, and the wedding hall was filled with guests.

11"But when the king came in to see the guests, he noticed a man there who was not wearing wedding clothes. 12'Friend,' he asked, 'how did you get in here without wedding clothes?' The man was speechless.

13"Then the king told the attendants, 'Tie him hand and foot, and throw him outside, into the darkness, where there will be weeping and gnashing of teeth.'

14"For many are invited, but few are chosen."

The king was not satisfied merely with vengeance; he had a banquet hall to fill. His son was getting married and he wanted a party fit for a king. Hence, the invitation went out to all the citizens of the kingdom, both great and small. The messengers were sent to every street corner and fork in the road [*tas diexodous ton hodon*] where people might be found. One of the guests, however, had not dressed appropriately for the banquet. Kings in ancient times would often provide wedding garments for their guests. Whether or not that is the case here, the man's silence betrays his guilt and disrespect by not adequately preparing to come to the king.

Even the king's address, "Friend," is a rebuke (cf. Mt 20:13). Such a man is cast out, not because he is unworthy to enter, for all the present guests were unworthy. He is cast out because he, like the first guests, refused to enter worthily.

Verse fourteen helps us understand much about the sovereignty of God. It says that many[26] are called (NIV "invited"), but few are chosen. How are they called? The messengers in the parable represent the prophets who were rejected and killed. Their preaching was the invitation — the calling. And how were they chosen? By their willingness to respond to the call of God (i.e., the preaching). According to this text, the call of God is not irresistible. God's election includes our response as well as his choice.

**§ 133**
**Question #1,**
**by Herodians:**
**Paying Tribute**
**to Caesar**
(Mt 22:15-22;
Mk 12:13-17;
Lk 20:20-26)

In the following passages we will read about four questions. The first three are asked by Jesus' opponents, representing the three major political/religious parties of the day: Herodians, Sadducees, and Pharisees. In turn, they each try to trap Jesus with a particularly difficult question.

---

[26]It was common for the word "many" to signify "all" or "most everyone" in Semitic usage.

Not only does Jesus answer their questions so well that they don't dare ask him another, but he perceives and exposes their true hypocritical and hostile motives in the process. Finally, Jesus asks his own difficult question which no one is able to answer. This will end the discourse between Jesus and his enemies. There is nothing left to talk about. Now their only recourse is assassination.

¹⁵Then the Pharisees went out and laid plans to trap him in his words {so that they might hand him over to the power and authority of the governor.ᴸᴷ} ¹⁶They sent their disciples to him along with the Herodians, {spies, who pretended to be honest.ᴸᴷ} "Teacher," they said, "we know you are a man of integrity and that you teach the way of God in accordance with the truth. You aren't swayed by men, because you pay no attention to who they are. ¹⁷Tell us then, what is your opinion? Is it right to pay taxes to Caesar or not? {Should we pay or shouldn't we?ᴹᴷ}"

Mt 22:15-17 *with* Lk 20:20; Mk 12:15

The first group to try their hand at outwitting Jesus is a tag-team of Pharisees and Herodians. Under normal circumstances, these two groups were enemies. The Pharisees represent the religious right-wing. The Herodians, on the other hand, believe the road to peace and prosperity in Palestine is alignment with Rome. Since no one did that better than the Herod family, they are supporters of the Herods in their various governmental positions.

Through their false flattery they act like they sincerely want an answer. They say to Jesus: (1) You are a man of integrity, therefore, we can follow your example in this. (2) You accurately teach the will of God, therefore we can trust your opinion on this. And (3) you are not swayed by men, therefore we can believe your answer will be unbiased.

No one is fooled by their false flattery. It is clear that their simple question, "Should we pay taxes to Caesar or not?" is designed to trap Jesus. If he says, "No," the crowds will be delighted, of course. They hate taxation. More than one third of their income goes to pay Roman taxes. In addition, the coin itself has an offensive inscription: "Tiberius Caesar, son of the divine Augustus" and on the flip side, *"pontifex maximus"* ("the most high priest"). While the crowds would have loved Jesus to ban taxation, the Herodians would have immediately arranged for his arrest and execution. On the other hand, if Jesus says "Yes, we should pay taxes to Caesar," the people, urged on by the Pharisees, will stop following him. After all, any Messiah who can't throw off the shackles of Roman domination (and especially taxation) is not worthy of support. Jesus is trapped!

¹⁸But Jesus, knowing their evil intent, said, "You hypocrites, why are you trying to trap me? ¹⁹Show me the coin used for payirj the tax." They brought him a

Mt 22:18-22

denarius, [20]and he asked them, "Whose portrait is this? And whose inscription?" [21]"Caesar's," they replied.

[22]Then he said to them, "Give to Caesar what is Caesar's, and to God what is God's."

Lk 20:26 *with* Mt 22:22

[26]They were unable to trap him in what he had said there in public. And astonished by his answer, they became silent. {So they left him and went away.[MT]}

Jesus knows what they are up to and calls them on the carpet. It must have hurt being identified publicly as a "hypocrite." But the big sting is yet to come. Jesus calls for a coin. The very fact that they have a Roman denarius in their possession indicates they accept Roman rule at some level. After all, you can't accept a government's right of coinage without also admitting its right of taxation.

Jesus simply holds up the coin and asks whose picture is on it. They must have seen where he was headed even as their answer slips from their tongues. The logic is so simple and yet so profound: Give to Caesar what belongs to Caesar and give to God what belongs to God. The word "give" is literally "give back." Thus, Jesus implies that our taxes are obligatory. That is, we owe them to the government as surely as we have financial obligations to God as part of our stewardship.

This has some ponderous implications. First, a government does have the right to taxation. If we cheat on our taxes, we are disobeying the ordained authority of God (Rom 13:1-7; 1 Pet 2:13-17). We don't obey a government because we like what it does, who's in charge, or how it spends its money. Indeed, there are appropriate occasions for civil disobedience (Acts 4:19; 5:29). However, these should only be reserved for times when the government asks us directly or individually to disobey what God has commanded us to do or not to do.[27]

Second, the image on the coin is Caesar (Tiberius). Obviously, if his picture is on it, then it belongs to him. But as Jesus looks around the audience, he sees men and women who are as clearly imprinted with the image of God. They have an obligation to give their lives to him. But even now, Jesus the Messiah stands before them. Instead of following him, as God intended, they are trying to trap him. They are, in this very moment, robbing God of his due.

The Pharisees and Herodians are stymied. They have laboriously contrived this "impenetrable" question. Their scheme was foolproof. Yet in less than fifteen seconds this uneducated Galilean dismantles their question, exposes their motives, and convicts their hypocrisy. All they can do is

---

[27]Cf. A. Stock, "Render to Caesar," *BibT* 62 (1972): 929-934.

walk away with their tail between their legs. Strike one — the Herodians are out. The Pharisees, however, will be back for a second beating.

[MK 12:][18]Then {that same day[MT]} the Sadducees, who say there is no resurrection, came to him with a question. [19]"Teacher," they said, "Moses wrote for us that if a man's brother dies and leaves a wife but no children, the man must marry the widow and have children for his brother. [20]Now there were seven brothers {among us.[MT]} The first one married and died without leaving any children. [21]The second one married the widow, but he also died, leaving no child. It was the same with the third. [22]In fact, none of the seven left any children. Last of all, the woman died too. [23]At the resurrection[a] whose wife will she be, since the seven were married to her?"

[a]23 Some manuscripts *resurrection, when men rise from the dead*

§ 134
Question #2,
by Sadducees:
**Marriage in the**
**Resurrection**
(Mt 22:23-33;
Mk 12:18-27;
Lk 20:27-40)

Here comes "round two": The Sadducees. This group died out with the destruction of the temple in A.D. 70. So the little we know of them comes from the Bible (only mentioned fourteen times in the Gospels), from Josephus, and early Christian writers. Since all of these sources were "enemies" of the Sadducees we should handle our information with care. Nevertheless, the Sadducees were apparently the religious "liberals," denying any kind of a resurrection, either in the form of angels or spirits (Acts 23:8; cf. Josephus, *Ant* 18.1.3-4; *Wars* 2.8.14). They also apparently prioritized the Pentateuch over the rest of the OT, and certainly denied the validity of the oral traditions of the Pharisees. It looks like they were the dominant force in the priesthood, hence they would also control the temple.

They, too, come to Jesus with a cool civility, philosophic "objectivity," and false flattery. Their question concerns Levirate marriage as it would apply to the resurrection. All three Synoptics clarify that the Sadducees do not believe in a resurrection. Thus their goal is not to trap Jesus with a false dilemma or to illicit any kind of real answer from him. Rather, they try to force him to deny the concept of resurrection by showing how ridiculous it would be with a "worst case scenario" of Levirate marriage (loosely citing Deut 25:5 and Gen 38:8).[28] In doing so they would not only defeat Jesus, but the Pharisees as well. Levirate

---

[28]Edersheim (II:399) gives a number of examples showing how ridiculous the Rabbinic extrapolations of resurrection had become. For instance some suggested that even if someone was buried naked that they would be raised clothed in likeness to a kernel of wheat. And another suggested that our resurrection bodies would look exactly as our present bodies based on the apparition of Samuel (1 Sam 28:14). Still another said that all Jews were to be raised from Palestinian soil. Hence, for those buried in foreign soil, there were cavities underneath the earth through which their corpses would roll until they reached the Holy Land.

marriage was not at all common in Jesus' day, if even practiced at all. In fact, the only two recorded examples of it in the OT are Tamar (Gen 38) and Ruth (1:11-13; 4:1-22).

Nonetheless, if all seven brothers had this woman as their wife, trying to fulfill their obligations to provide an heir for their brother(s), to whom would she belong if a literal bodily resurrection were true? Would that not necessitate a "heavenly incest?" They could have made the same point with just two brothers, but seven makes the point all the more vivid and ludicrous.[29]

Mk 12:24

²⁴Jesus replied, "Are you not in error because you do not know the Scriptures or the power of God?

Lk 20:34-36

³⁴"The people of this age marry and are given in marriage. ³⁵But those who are considered worthy of taking part in that age and in the resurrection from the dead will neither marry nor be given in marriage, ³⁶and they can no longer die; for they are like the angels. They are God's children, since they are children of the resurrection."

Jesus is going to give two answers to their question. The first relates to the power of God and the second relates to the Scriptures, both of which the Sadducees are ignorant. First, the Sadducees apparently believe the resurrection would necessitate a new body like this present one, including sexual attributes. But God can give us new bodies that are beyond the bounds of marriage.

Marriage is an excellent idea in our present world. It provides a resource for intimacy, procreation, and protection of the family unit. But in the resurrection, none of those things will be necessary. Procreation will be a thing of the past for the new earth will be filled already with saints of all ages. Nor will we have the need for intimacy provided through sex. In heaven, we will have the capacity for intimacy with many people without jealousy or competition. And the family unit will no longer be necessary because (1) there will be no need for protection, and (2) it will have already served its function in teaching us the structure of our relationship with God. The only value of sex, then, would be physical pleasure. Granted, that's no small thing. But is it not reasonable to believe that God, the giver of good gifts, could replace sexual pleasure with an even greater sensation in our new bodies? The bottom line is that sex will not be needed or missed.

---

²⁹This tale of seven brothers may have been inspired by the apocryphal story of Tobit (3:8-9; 6:13-15; 7:11). It tells of a certain woman named Sarah, whose seven husbands were killed on their wedding night by a demon that afflicted her (cf. P.G. Bolt, "What Were the Sadducees Reading? An Enquiry into the Literary Background of Mark 12:18-23," *TB* 45/2 [1994]: 369-394).

Now, when Jesus says that we will be "like the angels," he does not mean to imply that we will share each and every quality they have. In fact, the primary comparison is in the fact that we will no longer die, and also *perhaps* that angels do not engage in sexual intercourse. This mention of angels would also conflict with Sadducean beliefs since they denied not only the fact of resurrection, but the angelic nature of those resurrected bodies (Acts 23:8).

"{Have you not read in the book of Moses?ᴹᴷ} ³⁷But in the account of the bush, even Moses showed that the dead rise, for he calls the Lord 'the God of Abraham, and the God of Isaac, and the God of Jacob.' ³⁸He is not the God of the dead, but of the living, for to him all are alive. {You are badly mistaken"ᴹᴷ}

Lk 20:37-38 *with* Mk 12:26-27

³³When the crowds heard this, they were astonished at his teaching.

Mt 22:33

³⁹Some of the teachers of the law responded, "Well said, teacher!" ⁴⁰And no one dared to ask him any more questions.

Lk 20:39-40

Jesus' second answer concerned the interpretation of the Scriptures. His rhetorical question, "Have you not read . . . ?" was, no doubt, taken as it was intended — as an insult (cf. Mt 21:42). Now, there are a couple of passages in the OT that describe a resuscitation (1 Kgs 17:22; 2 Kgs 4:35; 13:21) and a few that speak of resurrection (Isa 26:19; Dan 12:2; Job 19:25-27; see also 2 Sam 12:23; Isa 53:10-12; Eccl 12:7). But admittedly they are not as clear or as many as we would like. What complicates the issue further is that the Sadducees prefer the Pentateuch above other portions of the OT. If Jesus is going to convince them, he will have to do so on their own ground.

Quoting from Exodus 3:6, Jesus uses typical and acceptable Jewish interpretation.[30] Arguing from the verb tense, Jesus asserts that the resurrection is a logical necessity. But more than this, God's immense greatness demands his servants be raised in his presence.[31] That is, God is the

---

[30]Rabbi D.M. Cohn-Sherbok argues that Jesus' logic is NOT acceptable Jewish hermeneutic. He goes so far as to say that Jesus' argument is "strikingly inadequate from a rabbinic point of view. The fact that Jesus could use such an argument should not surprise us, since it bears out the truth of the Gospel tradition in suggesting that Jesus was not a skilled casuist in the style of the Pharisees and Sadducees" ("Jesus' Defence of the Resurrection of the Dead," *JSNT* 11 [1981]: 64-73). Indeed, Jesus' argument was unique, but not because he was a bumpkin, rather because he was brilliant! True enough, the Sadducees would likely have rejected Jesus' conclusions, but the primary teachers of the law congratulated him on his answer which stymied the opposition (Lk 20:39-40)! Furthermore, F.G. Downing, "The Resurrection of the Dead: Jesus and Philo," *JSNT* 15 (1982): 42-50, notes a number of similarities between Jesus' and Philo's handling of Exodus 3:15. Therefore we can, in fact, conclude that Jesus' answer would have been acceptable hermeneutical logic to the Pharisees if not to the Sadducees.

[31]J.J. Kilgallen puts it this way, "Those judged worthy of life with Yahwah must rise, for

God of the living and not the dead. Strictly speaking, however, Jesus only logically argues for the immortality of the soul. Nevertheless, the Jews would not have considered the immortality of the soul apart from bodily resurrection.

Jesus then jibes them again by saying, "You are badly mistaken." One might get the impression that Jesus is just plain rude to these fellows. But they are mistaken about the final and greatest evidential miracle that Jesus is going to perform. If they miss this one there is no other hope for them to repent and find eternal life. Yes, Jesus' words are stern, perhaps even harsh, but they are fitting for such a critical topic and time.

Again, the crowds are duly impressed. The teachers of the law (Pharisees) are pleasantly surprised. They had frequently debated with the Sadducees over this very issue and could not, with their cumulative wisdom, come up with an argument as cogent and conclusive as Jesus'. The Sadducees are confounded. They had nothing to say in response and no more questions to ask. Strike two — the Sadducees are out.

**§ 135
Question #3,
by Pharisees:
Which is the
Greatest
Commandment
(Mt 22:34-40;
Mk 12:28-34;
cf. Lk 10:25-27)**

[MT 22:]34Hearing that Jesus had silenced the Sadducees, the Pharisees got together.

[MK 12:]28One of the teachers {expertsMT} of the law came and heard them debating. Noticing that Jesus had given them a good answer, he asked him, "Of all the commandments, which is the most important?"

In the first round the Pharisees sent their disciples along with the Herodians to try and trap Jesus. They were soundly defeated. They went out and regrouped, deciding to send one of their "hot-shot" legal professors rather than a novice this time.[32] He arrives in time to watch the Sadducees try their hand at outwitting Christ. They had no better luck than did the Herodians. This, of course, delighted the Pharisees.

Now this legal expert seems to be more amiable to Jesus than the others. (1) He notes that Jesus has given a good answer to the Sadducees. (2) He asks a more reasonable and more important question.

His love for them knows no other conclusion" ("The Sadducees and Resurrection from the Dead: Luke 20:27-40," *Biblica* 67 [1986]: 478-495). J.G. Jansen "Resurrection and Hermeneutics: On Exodus 3:6 in Mark 12:26," *JSNT* 23 (1985): 43-58, goes a step further. He speculates that Exod 3:6 and Mk 12:26 deal with the same problem, namely barrenness which is metaphorically a "living death" from which God rescued them through "generational resurrection." Thus the tripartate formula "Abraham, Isaac, and Jacob" is a statement of God's faithfulness and saving acts, especially in the context of Exod 3:6. If God saves his people by raising their dead seed (Rom 4:19; Heb 11:11-12), will he not also raise them from death?

[32]The term "lawyer" refers to an expert in the law of Moses and should not be anachronistically equated with modern lawyers.

(3) He acknowledges the beauty of Jesus' answer. So (4) Jesus affirms his integrity by saying that he, himself, is not far from the kingdom of God.

The lawyer's question was a common debate among the Pharisees. With six hundred and thirteen OT commands and innumerable oral traditions, the answer is not a simple one. We should also note that this is not the first time Jesus has been asked this question. One day a lawyer came to Jesus and asked him "What must I do to inherit eternal life?" Jesus turned the question back on him by asking, "What is written in the law? How do you read it?" The lawyer answered by citing these same two commands. This became the springboard into the parable of the Good Samaritan (Lk 10:25-37; § 103). Hence, neither the question nor Jesus' answer is new.[33]

²⁹"The most important one," answered Jesus, "is this: 'Hear, O Israel, the Lord our God, the Lord is one.ᵃ ³⁰Love the Lord your God with all your heart and with all your soul and with all your mind and with all your strength.'ᵇ                    Mk 12:29-30

ᵃ*29* Or *the Lord our God is one Lord*     ᵇ*30* Deut. 6:4,5

³⁸"This is the first and greatest commandment.                    Mt 22:38

³¹"The second is this {like it:ᴹᵀ} 'Love your neighbor as yourself.'ᶜ There is no commandment greater than these."                    Mk 12:31 *with* Mt 22:39

ᶜ*31* Lev. 19:18

⁴⁰"All the Law and the Prophets hang on these two commandments."                    Mt 22:40

[Mt 22:37-39 and Mk 12:29-31 = Lk 10:27, see comments on § 103]

The first command, from Deuteronomy 6:4-6, is called the *shema*, named after the first Hebrew word in the sentence, "Hear." Pious Jews recited it at the beginning and end of each day and it opened the synagogue services each Friday evening. It affirmed the unity of God and our obligation to love him with our entire being. For the Jew, there was no greater obligation and no greater theological tenet. Jesus chose wisely the greatest commandment.

The astute student will observe that while there are only three descriptors in Deuteronomy (heart, soul, strength), Mark uses four, adding *mind* to the list. The reason is that the third Hebrew word can indicate a couple of different things. Mark (12:30) and Luke (10:27),

---

[33]In fact, E.E. Lemcio, "Pirke 'Abot 1:2(3) and the Synoptic Redactions of the Commands to Love God and Neighbor," *ATJ* 43 (1988): 43-53, suggests that the combination of Deut 6:5 and Lev 19:18 is based on a statement by Simeon the Just (c. 350-200 B.C.E.): "On three things the world stands: On the Torah, on the [Temple] service, and on deeds of lovingkindness" (*Pirke 'Abot* 1:2 [3]).

both writing to a more Gentile audience, use two Greek words (*mind* and *strength*) to adequately translate that single Hebrew word. None of these four, however, are mutually exclusive. All of them are intertwined.

The second greatest command comes from Leviticus 19:18. Once we recognize that our greatest obligation is to love God, the obvious question is, "How does one express his love to God?" Certainly we can do so through liturgy and worship, that is, religious piety. But this is not so very helpful in the community.[34] God would rather us show our love to him by meeting the needs of our fellows (Mt 25:40, 45) which, according to Jesus, is anyone we come in contact with (Lk 10:25-37). If we keep these two commands we will, by necessity, fulfill all the crucial features of the entire Old Testament law (Rom 13:8, 10; Gal 5:14; James 2:8).

Mk 12:32-34

[32]"Well said, teacher," the man replied. "You are right in saying that God is one and there is no other but him. [33]To love him with all your heart, with all your understanding and with all your strength, and to love your neighbor as yourself is more important than all burnt offerings and sacrifices."
[34]When Jesus saw that he had answered wisely, he said to him, "You are not far from the kingdom of God." And from then on no one dared ask him any more questions.

This "lawyer" is impressed. Jesus strikes a chord in his Jewish heart. For the true Jew there is nothing more central than the love of the one true God and charity shown to our neighbor. These are more important than all the liturgical signs of piety such as offerings and sacrifices (1 Sam 15:22; Hos 6:6).

Not only is the "lawyer" impressed with Jesus, Jesus is impressed with the lawyer. He has approached Jesus respectfully and has asked him a serious and important question. Now he publicly acknowledges the beauty of Jesus' answer. So Jesus affirms him by saying, "You are not far from the kingdom." We're not told if he ever entered or not. This little tidbit reminds us that all of Jesus' opponents are not all bad. The Pharisees are not evil incarnate. They are religious leaders with a lot of pride and position to protect. Coming to Christ was a serious sacrifice for this group.

Well, that was strike three — the Pharisees are out. All three major religio-political parties have tried their hand at trapping Jesus, only to be

---

[34]A. Malamat shows that "love" used intransitively (only 4 times, Lev 19:18, 34; 1 Kgs 5:1; 2 Chr 19:2), is not about an emotion, but an action. He explains, "The Bible is not commanding us to *feel* something — love — but to *do* something — to be useful or beneficial, to help your neighbor. This understanding also eliminates from the passage what some have considered an inappropriate adoration of self-love" ("Love Your Neighbor as Yourself," *BAR* 16 [1990]: 50-51).

badly rebuffed. It is no small wonder that no one dared to ask him any more questions.

Jesus answered these three questions from the three major parties of the day. They have no more questions for him. So Jesus has a question for them. It was really the only question left to be answered — the only one that really matters: Who is Jesus?

**§ 136**
**Question #4,**
**by Jesus: How**
**Can the Christ**
**be David's**
**Son?**
(Mt 22:41-46;
Mk 12:35-37;
Lk 20:41-44)

[MT 22:]41While the Pharisees were gathered together, Jesus {was teaching in the temple courts [and]MK} asked them, 42"What do you think about the Christª? Whose son is he?"

"The son of David," they replied.

43He said to them, "{How is it that the teachers of the law say that the Christ is the son of David?MK} How is it then that David {himself,MK} speaking by the {HolyMK} Spirit, calls him 'Lord' {in the book of Psalms?LK} For he says,

44"'The Lord said to my Lord:

"Sit at my right hand until I put your enemies under your feet {make your enemies a footstool for your feet.LK}'"b

45If then David calls him 'Lord,' how can he be his son?" 46No one could say a word in reply, and from that day on no one dared to ask him any more questions. {The large crowd listened to him with delight.MK}

ª42 Or Messiah    b44 Psalm 110:1

By the end of this third round the Jewish leaders are thoroughly frustrated and the crowds are ecstatic. This is a major league spectacle! Now that Jesus has disarmed all their ambushes he turns the tables and they have to answer a question of his.

It was a simple question, "Who is the Christ?" Why that would be David's son (progenitor); everyone knew that (cf. 2 Sam 7:13-14; Isa 9:2-7; 11:1, 10; Jer 23:5; etc.). "All right," Jesus says, "that being the case, let's exegete Psalm 110, beginning at verse 1. How can the Christ be both the son of David and his Lord (*adonai*)?" Now that was a more difficult question for a couple of reasons. First, in their culture, the father was always greater than the son. There is simply no "natural" way that David would call one of his offspring his Lord. Second, this Psalm was understood as a Messianic Psalm, predicting the coming of the Christ. It is also the most often cited OT passage in the NT (cf. Acts 2:34-35; Heb 1:13; 5:6; 7:17, 21; 10:13). They couldn't dodge it or deny it. After all, it was Scripture inspired by the Holy Spirit, so says Jesus (cf. Jn 10:35; also Acts 4:25; Heb 3:7; 9:8; 10:15; 2 Pet 1:21). But neither could they explain it!

The implication is that this human Son of David (referring, of course to Jesus [Mt 1:1; Lk 3:23, 31]) was also the divine Son of God (Paul states this clearly in Rom 1:3-4). There were ample indications of this in the prophets (Isa 9:6; Jer 23:5-6; 33:15-16; Zech 12:10; 13:7). That being the case, their accusations of blasphemy are false and their resistance to Jesus as Messiah is resistance to the very God, himself.

They have not been able to explain the first half of the first verse of Psalm 110. Jesus does not even get into the second half of the verse: "Until I make your enemies a footstool for your feet!" That would have been a frightening proposition for these antagonistic questioners. Jesus could have further elaborated on verse 2: "The Lord will extend your mighty scepter from Zion." Or again, verse 4: "You are a priest forever in the order of Melchizedek." How does a king become a priest? The answer will come at Calvary.

This must have been a serious embarrassment and a shock to these "Bible scholars" to suddenly realize how little they know about the basics of their faith. They are stunned by this uneducated Galilean. Not only has he slipped through their theological nooses, but he has stumped them with a simple question from one of their favorite Bible verses. And he does all this in the midst of the temple courts, while they have home-field advantage! The leaders are stymied; the crowds are ecstatic.

**§ 137a**
**"Woe to You, Teachers of the Law and Pharisees"**
(Mt 23:1-36; Mk 12:38-40; Lk 20:45-47; cf. Lk 11:37-54)

This is the conclusion to Tuesday's teaching in the temple. The Jewish leaders have likely withdrawn in defeat (Mt 22:22, 34, 46). They go off to plot Jesus' assassination. The crowds, however, continue to grow in number and delight. Jesus turns to them with this surprisingly acrimonious rebuke of the Pharisees. It is so strong, in fact, that some have sensed a conflict between Matthew 23 and the Sermon on the Mount (Mt 5-7). However, even the Sermon on the Mount contained some frighteningly stern warnings (e.g., Mt 7:13-29). And this speech is concluded with some tender concern for the Jewish people (vv. 37-39).[35] Furthermore, Jesus has said this kind of thing before in a variety of places and situations (e.g., Lk 11:37-54). It is merely catalogued here more fully. Finally, we must remember that these Pharisees have just

---

[35]Any accusation that Jesus was anti-Semitic here fails to recognize that: (1) Both Jesus and his "biographer," Matthew, were Jews themselves and had a passion for Jewish evangelism. (2) Jesus does not rebuke all the Jews but merely one segment of their leadership. And this rebuke was for the "category" of Pharisees, but would not necessarily extend to each individual Pharisee. (3) This group had just tried to trap him and were presently plotting his assassination. (4) Jesus spoke the truth. He accurately described the character of this group. And (5) Jesus' words are no harsher than many of the Psalms and Prophets (e.g., Ps 58; Isa 5:8-23; Jer 23; Hab 2:6-20).

tried to trap him and are presently planning his death. Jesus' response, therefore, is both warranted and fair.

After an introductory warning to the disciples (vv. 1-12), Jesus delivers a series of seven "Woes." This word "Woe" [*ouai*] can contain pathos, anger, warning and derision; and may include a bit of all of them at the same time. The first six seem to come in pairs. One and two deal with the Pharisees' evangelism; three and four deal with their ritual; and five and six deal with their inner vs. outer purity. The grand finale, number seven, gets at the heart of the matter: their desire to murder Jesus.

¹Then Jesus said to the crowds and to his disciples: ²"The teachers of the law and the Pharisees sit in Moses' seat. ³So you must obey them and do everything they tell you. But do not do what they do, for they do not practice what they preach. ⁴They tie up heavy loads and put them on men's shoulders, but they themselves are not willing to lift a finger to move them."

Mt 23:1-4

Jesus' audience includes two groups: his disciples and the less committed crowds who are merely there for the show. It is a bit difficult, however, to determine how much difference there is between these two groups. On the other side of the fence, Jesus' target also contains two groups: The Pharisees and the Teachers of the Law. There is even less clear distinction between these two groups. The word "Pharisee" connotes a religio-political/theological group, whereas "teacher of the law" describes the scriptural/educational function of basically the same group of people with the same "leanings." The distinctions are few and subtle.

These men sit on Moses' seat. Now there was actually a seat in the synagogue which represented Moses' seat. Here sat the primary teacher of the synagogue. It was *the* prominent seat of position and power in the community. It represented the line of succession that extended clear back to Moses himself. This dominant teacher supposedly carried the mantle of Moses' leadership, the torch of faith from earlier generations. Our closest equivalent would be the pulpit as a symbol of authoritative teaching. Whoever "owns" the pulpit has the ears of the congregation. This position belonged to the Pharisees.

"So," Jesus says, "do everything they tell you." Now Jesus could not have meant that absolutely. The Pharisees had literally thousands of nitpicky rules laced throughout their oral traditions. And Jesus himself purposefully broke the foolish oral teachings of the Pharisees (Mt 9:10-13; Mk 2:18-19, 23-24; Lk 6:6-8; 11:38-39; Jn 5:8-10). Certainly he is not saying, "Follow all their nitpicky rules." What he means is, "To the extent that they teach what Moses taught, follow them" (cf. Deut 17:10).

But that, of course, requires adding to what Jesus actually said. So we might want to read a bit of sarcasm into what Jesus said. After all, sarcasm was not completely foreign to Jesus. Hence we might paraphrase Jesus words, "O sure, they occupy pretty important places of authority, therefore you are safe in following their words, but following their example will kill you!"

The OT law was hard enough to keep. But these guys added to it meticulous rules that only a lawyer could understand (or weasel out of). They could keep it themselves because of their superior devotion (not to mention they knew all the loopholes). But the average "Joe(seph)" doesn't have a chance. And they aren't about to help him. Instead, they beat him down with more rules and guilt. That is so different than what Jesus does with us (cf. Mt 11:28-30).

Mt 23:5-12

⁵"Everything they do is done for men to see: They make their phylacteriesᵃ wide and the tassels on their garments long; ⁶they love the place of honor at banquets and the most important seats in the synagogues; ⁷they love to be greeted in the marketplaces and to have men call them 'Rabbi.'

⁸"But you are not to be called 'Rabbi,' for you have only one Master and you are all brothers. ⁹And do not call anyone on earth 'father,' for you have one Father, and he is in heaven. ¹⁰Nor are you to be called 'teacher,' for you have one Teacher, the Christ.ᵇ ¹¹The greatest among you will be your servant. ¹²For whoever exalts himself will be humbled, and whoever humbles himself will be exalted."

ᵃ5 That is, boxes containing Scripture verses, worn on forehead and arm    ᵇ10 Or Messiah

The primary goal of a Pharisee was to get noticed. He did this through titles, position, and performance of religious duties. Jesus mentions two such religious duties here: Bible study (embodied in phylacteries) and prayer (embodied in tassels at the edges of their garments). These phylacteries were small boxes worn on the forehead and/or the left arm.[36] They held miniature scrolls which usually contained Exodus 13:2-16; Deuteronomy 6:4-9; and 11:13-21. This practice likely grew out of an overly literal interpretation of Deuteronomy 6:8 and 11:18: "Fix these words of mine in your hearts and minds; tie them on your hands and bind them on your foreheads." They had effectively become like the charms of the pagans. Apparently the Pharisees would make their phylacteries and/or their straps especially large so that they would be easily noticed.

---

[36]Cf. J.H. Tigay, "On the Term Phylacteries (Matt 23:5)," *HTR* 72 (1979): 45-53. He points out that the Greek word *phylakteria* referred to charms or amulets. Based on that, he suggests that using *phylakteria* (Gk) to translate *tefillin* (Heb) indicates that these boxes had degenerated into amulets for the Pharisees.

Likewise they enlarged their prayer tassels at the edges of their robes. This was a normal part of Jewish apparel (Num 15:37-41; Deut 22:12). Even Jesus wore tassels (Mt 9:21). They were used much like rosary beads which could be fingered and counted as one recited the obligatory liturgical prayers. But the Pharisees wanted theirs to be extra long so that they would be easily noticed and perhaps to demonstrate just how many more prayers they said than everybody else.

The Pharisees also sought to be recognized through position. We've already seen how they aspired to "Moses'" seat in the synagogue. And if they couldn't be the primary teacher of the synagogue, they at least wanted to sit up on the podium in front of everyone where they could be gawked at in their supercilious attainments. When they went to a dinner party, they were zealous to grab the seats of honor, closest to the host (cf. Lk 14:7-11; see comments on § 114).

They wanted to be recognized through titles such as "Rabbi" (lit., "my great one"), "Teacher," or even "Father" (which appears to have been reserved for the great Rabbis of the past). As we have seen before, Jesus' injunctions are not always to be taken absolutely (e.g., Mt 5:22, 29; 6:3, 6, 17). Such is the case here. For instance, there is nothing wrong with addressing your biological parent as "Father" or even a mentor (1 Cor 4:15; Acts 22:1; 1 Jn 2:13). Nor is it always wrong to address someone as "teacher" (Acts 13:1; 1 Tim 2:7; Eph 4:11; James 3:1). But we should studiously avoid titles which arrogantly promote an individual's accomplishments or divide brothers by rank. God alone deserves praise and honor. Pompous titles which detract from God by focusing on man are taboo for disciples of Jesus (cf. Jer 31:33-34). The kingdom economy is filled with paradox. The greatest is the least and the least the greatest. He who exalts himself will be humbled and the one who humbles himself will be exalted (cf. Mt 18:1-5; 20:26; Lk 14:11; 18:14).

## WOE #1: Turning People away from the Kingdom of Heaven

[13]"Woe to you, teachers of the law and Pharisees, you hypocrites! You shut the kingdom of heaven in men's faces. You yourselves do not enter, nor will you let those enter who are trying to."[a]

[a]*13 Some manuscripts to. [14]Woe to you, teachers of the law and Pharisees, you hypocrites! You devour widows' houses and for a show make lengthy prayers. Therefore you will be punished more severely.*

Mt 23:13

Jesus calls the Pharisees hypocrites. That's pretty strong language, straight from the Greek theater. A hypocrite, literally, was an actor who put on a mask to assume a false identity while he played for the audience.

This accusation would be particularly offensive to the Pharisees who hated all forms of Hellenization, including the Greek theater.[37] In essence, Jesus was calling them the very thing they hated.

Jesus' critique was right on. The Pharisees at that very moment were doing what Jesus accuses them of. Here he was, the king of this kingdom of heaven, in their very midst. Not only did the Pharisees not accept him, but they zealously tried to hinder anyone else from accepting him either (Mt 11:19; 12:23-24; 21:15). They opposed Jesus.[38] They threatened members of their own ranks who appeared amiable to him (Jn 7:45-52). And they excommunicated lay people who followed him (Jn 9:22, 34-35). Thus they frightened many people away from the kingdom of heaven.

Mk 12:40

[40]"They devour widows' houses and for a show make lengthy prayers. Such men will be punished most severely."

Not only were some Pharisees using their religious positions to corrupt new converts, they were using them to fleece widows financially. It may be that they were charging widows for the "services" of their prayers on the widows' behalf. More likely, however, this verse refers to the Pharisees' service as guardians of the widows' estates.[39] Such guardians could charge a healthy fee for legal arbitration, and on top of that, they could legally charge expenses to the estate. Obviously, there was a good bit of latitude for corruption. That's why long oaths and prayers were used to assure the widows of their honesty and to secure their "business."

## WOE #2: Turning Proselytes Toward Hell

Mt 23:15

[15]"Woe to you, teachers of the law and Pharisees, you hypocrites! You travel over land and sea to win a single convert, and when he becomes one, you make him twice as much a son of hell as you are."

There is considerable evidence in the first century of Pharisaic proselytizers (Carson, p. 478). But they were not "door to door" evangelists. Rather, when a pagan expressed interest in Judaism, the Pharisees would latch on to him and see that he adopted their particular brand of legalism.

---

[37]Jesus would be familiar with the Greek theater built by Herod Antipas at his headquarters in Sepphoris, less than a mile walk from Jesus' hometown. Furthermore, the fact that there is no functional equivalent of *hypocrites* in Hebrew or Aramaic indicates that Jesus knew at least a little Greek and threw in this foreign word to spice up his rebuke just a bit (cf. R.A. Batey, "Jesus and the Theater," *NTS* 30 [1984]: 463-574).

[38]For a full catalogue of Pharisaic opposition to Jesus, see notes on Lk 11:37, § 107.

[39]J.D.M. Derrett makes a strong case for this in "Eating up the Houses of Widows: Jesus's Comment on Lawyers?" *NovT* 14 (1972): 1-9.

As is often the case, their students became even more extreme and zealous than their teachers. It appears that both Peter and Paul fought this same phenomenon in the first century church (Acts 11:1-3; 15:1-2; 1 Cor 4:6, 9-10; Gal 1:7-8).

### WOE #3: Deceptive Oaths

<sup>16</sup>"Woe to you, blind guides! You say, 'If anyone swears by the temple, it means nothing; but if anyone swears by the gold of the temple, he is bound by his oath.' <sup>17</sup>You blind fools! Which is greater: the gold, or the temple that makes the gold sacred? <sup>18</sup>You also say, 'If anyone swears by the altar, it means nothing; but if anyone swears by the gift on it, he is bound by his oath.' <sup>19</sup>You blind men! Which is greater: the gift, or the altar that makes the gift sacred? <sup>20</sup>Therefore, he who swears by the altar swears by it and by everything on it. <sup>21</sup>And he who swears by the temple swears by it and by the one who dwells in it. <sup>22</sup>And he who swears by heaven swears by God's throne and by the one who sits on it."

Mt 23:16-22

Apparently, the Pharisees "ruled" that an oath could only be made with something you could use as collateral (Gundry, p. 463). That way, if someone lied, there could be financial repercussions. Therefore, oaths made by the temple or its altar were *not* valid, but oaths made by the gold of the temple or the offering on the altar were valid. But their motive behind this hair-splitting was deception. Their casuistry allowed them to rob people "religiously."

Jesus said that the purpose of oaths was not financial security but honesty. You keep your word, not because you might lose money by breaking it, but because you are answerable to a higher power, ultimately God. Hence, the greater the object of the oath, the more responsible one is to keep it. Therefore, oaths made to the temple and its altar are greater than those made to the gold of the temple or the offering on the altar.

Jesus took it even one step further. When you swear by either the temple or its altar, you swear by him who owns them both. Even if you swear by heaven or its throne, you swear by him who dwells therein. This logic could be extrapolated to all the earth and its contents. Hence, every oath is equally binding. For this very reason, in the Sermon on the Mount, Jesus said not to use oaths at all (Mt 5:33-37). But "simply let your yes be yes and your no, no. Anything beyond this comes from the evil one." The bottom line is that we are to be honest people. Any need for oaths, crossed fingers, or legal fine print betrays the influence in our lives of Satan, the Father of Lies (Jn 8:44).

### WOE #4: Deceptive Tithes

<sup>23</sup>"Woe to you, teachers of the law and Pharisees, you hypocrites! You give a tenth of your spices — mint, dill and cummin. But you have neglected the more

Mt 23:23-24

important matters of the law — justice, mercy and faithfulness. You should have practiced the latter, without neglecting the former. ²⁴You blind guides! You strain out a gnat but swallow a camel."

This is an expansion of what Jesus said in Luke 11:42. The Pharisees were truly impressive in their execution of religious duties. They even tithed the mint leaves and dill seeds from their herbal gardens (which borders on ludicrous). Yet somehow they "missed the forest for the trees." No doubt, God is pleased with tithing; it ought to be done. But it is not central to his heart as are justice, mercy and faithfulness, which these fellows missed by a mile.

Jesus excoriated them through this cynical proverb: "You strain out a gnat but swallow a camel." Both of them were unclean animals, and neither of them would you want in your soup. But if you had to choose betwixt the two, you ought to eliminate the camel . . . it's easier to choke on. This is humorous enough in English. But in Aramaic, the play on words (camel [*gamla*] and gnat [*galma*]) makes it even more delightful.

The modern church ought to pay particular attention to this proverb. The little things in the eyes of God are often the most visible to the world (dress, tithing, church attendance, etc.), while the weightier matters are often practiced in private (justice, mercy, and faithfulness). If we're not careful, we'll wind up playing for the wrong audience and neglecting God's priorities.

### WOE #5: Unwashed Insides

Mt 23:25-26

²⁵"Woe to you, teachers of the law and Pharisees, you hypocrites! You clean the outside of the cup and dish, but inside they are full of greed and self-indulgence. ²⁶Blind Pharisee! First clean the inside of the cup and dish, and then the outside also will be clean."

Christians today are not so much different than the Pharisees of yesterday. We are more concerned with what people see on the outside than what God sees on the inside. The inner life, which determines our motives and aspirations, demands our attention. It is easy to ignore the cry for inner cleansing as we frantically respond to the external expectations all around us. But once again, the bottom line is: "Who is your primary audience?" Are you playing for God, who looks on the inside, or for men (even religious men), who are only able to see externals?

Jesus identified their inner motives as greed and self-indulgence. That may sound like a description of a profligate, but those of us who are "professional clergy" know all too well that these desires can comfortably fit religious leaders. It is the desire to look good and to be honored by your peers and followers. They are religious desires, but not righteous ones. To be clean before God, we must go deep. The heart is not sanctified through haircuts and ties, attendance pins or titles. Cleansing simply must be from the inside out.

## WOE #6: Whitewashed Outsides

27"Woe to you, teachers of the law and Pharisees, you hypocrites! You are like whitewashed tombs, which look beautiful on the outside but on the inside are full of dead men's bones and everything unclean. 28In the same way, on the outside you appear to people as righteous but on the inside you are full of hypocrisy and wickedness."

Mt 23:27-28

Now Jesus takes this cleansing one step further. Not only must cleansing start from the inside out, but when it doesn't there are dire consequences. Religious leaders who are outwardly sterile but inwardly corrupt can have a contaminating effect on their followers.

The OT declared anyone unclean who touched a dead body (Num 19:16). The Jews extrapolated that to coffins and even tombs. Therefore, about a month before Passover, crews would go out to the area around Jerusalem and whitewash all the sepulchers so that an innocent pilgrim would not inadvertently step on one and be disqualified from participating in Passover. As Jesus made his way to the Holy City just two days ago, he would be reminded of this again by all the freshly painted graves. You were drawn to their beauty but defiled by their touch. So it was with the Pharisees.

There could hardly be a greater insult to a Pharisee than to call him a coffin. Jesus' words may be harsh, but they are not inaccurate. The Jewish populace was impressed with the Pharisees. They knew the Scriptures so well. And they were so meticulous with their piety. But their hearts were proud and self-seeking. As people followed the Pharisees, they too had their priorities skewed. They justified themselves for ritual keeping, without feeling obliged to love their neighbor or be merciful with the least and the lost. Thus, they were corrupted by "touching" the Pharisees.

## WOE #7: Finale — Murderous Desires

29"Woe to you, teachers of the law and Pharisees, you hypocrites! You build tombs for the prophets and decorate the graves of the righteous. 30And you say, 'If we had lived in the days of our forefathers, we would not have taken part with them in shedding the blood of the prophets.' 31So you testify against yourselves that you are the descendants of those who murdered the prophets. 32Fill up, then, the measure of the sin of your forefathers!"

Mt 23:29-32

Worse than all their flaws combined, the Pharisees were seeking to kill Jesus, the finale of all the prophets. They claimed that they disagreed with their forefathers for killing the prophets. They showed their disapproval by decorating the prophets' tombs. But Jesus says that all this decorating was a continuation of their forefathers' work, not a contrast to it.

[vv. 29-32 = Lk 11:47-48, see notes on § 107]

Mt 23:33-36     ³³"You snakes! You brood of vipers! [cf. 3:7; 12:34] How will you escape being condemned to hell? ³⁴Therefore I am sending you prophets and wise men and teachers. Some of them you will kill and crucify; others you will flog in your synagogues and pursue from town to town. ³⁵And so upon you will come all the righteous blood that has been shed on earth, from the blood of righteous Abel to the blood of Zechariah son of Berekiah, whom you murdered between the temple and the altar. ³⁶I tell you the truth, all this will come upon this generation.

God not only sent Jesus, but other prophets, wise men, teachers and apostles (Lk 11:49). These are probably not merely the martyrs who preceded Jesus, but those who followed him as well. In other words, those who die for the faith die in solidarity with the death of Jesus.

Jesus, the pinnacle of all the prophets, would be killed in just three days. Hence, this generation would become guilty of murdering all the prophets from Abel to Zechariah. We don't know for sure who this Zechariah was but there are at least three possibilities. (1) It might be Zechariah, son of Baris (or Baruch or Bariscaeus, depending on the manuscript one follows). He was killed in the temple precincts in A.D. 67-68 (Josephus, *War* 4. 334-344). Those who accept the inspiration of the Scriptures, or even the honesty of Matthew, must reject that option because it is too late for Jesus' time. (2) It might be the prophet Zechariah, the son of Berekiah (Zech 1:1). The only problem here is that there is no scriptural reference to the murder of Zechariah although there are some post-Christian Jewish references to his death. Or (3) it could be Zechariah the priest (2 Chr 24:20-25). Two difficulties arise with his identity. First, he was the son of Jehoiada, not the son of Berekiah, as Matthew says. However, the word "son" often meant "descendant." Hence, Zechariah may be identified as the descendant of a famous ancestor rather than his own father (cf. Carson, pp. 485-486). The second difficulty is that Zechariah, the son of Jehoiada appears to have been murdered in the Holy Place and not the outer court between the altar and the sanctuary (v. 35). However, that may be close enough for Matthew. If this is the right reference, Jesus is speaking of a canonical order (i.e., the order of the books of the OT) rather than a chronological order. Abel was the first person murdered (Gen 4:8-10), Zechariah was the last murdered according to the order of the books of the OT.

Notice, Jesus shifts from a rebuke of the Pharisees to their followers in v. 36. Because they refused to abandon their leaders after Jesus warned them, they too would be held responsible for Jesus' death. The murder of Jesus would bring the judgment of God on the Holy City. Far from pleasing Jesus, the fate of Jerusalem brings tears to his eyes.

Jesus got no pleasure from lambasting the Pharisees (Mt 23). Nor does he rejoice over Jerusalem's impending destruction (Mt 24). Here we see his heart, full of pathos, and his eyes full of tears for what he sees for this city's future.

**§ 137b**
**Jesus Weeps**
**Over Jerusalem**
(Mt 23:37-39)

[37]"O Jerusalem, Jerusalem, you who kill the prophets and stone those sent to you, how often I have longed to gather your children together, as a hen gathers her chicks under her wings, but you were not willing. [38]Look, your house is left to you desolate. [39]For I tell you, you will not see me again until you say, 'Blessed is he who comes in the name of the Lord.'"[a]

Mt 23:37-39

[a]*39* Psalm 118:26

This pericope forms a bridge between Jesus' warnings against the Pharisees (Mt 23) and against the city of Jerusalem (Mt 24). It prepares us to read the "Olivet Discourse" in the following chapter. Here Jesus spoke as God did. He uses an OT figure of God for his own desire to gather Israel under his wings (Deut 32:11; Ps 17:8; 36:7; 91:4; Isa 31:5).

These words are almost identical to those found in Luke 13:34-35 (see comments on § 113b), spoken three months earlier in Perea. Although the pericope functions differently in Luke's narrative than it does here, the meaning of the words are essentially the same.

Jesus praises this poor woman for her great sacrifice. That's clear enough. But there may be more here than meets the eye. The context of both Mark and Luke is significant. Jesus has just criticized the Pharisees because "they devour widow's houses" (Mk 12:40; Lk 20:47). And in the following verses Jesus predicts the destruction of the temple. Thus this passage may well illustrate how this bankrupt religion bankrupts widows.[40]

**§ 138**
**Widow's Mite**
(Mk 12:41-44;
Lk 21:1-4)

---

[40]A.G. Wright, "The Widow's Mites: Praise or Lament? — A Matter of Context," *CBQ* 44 (1982): 256-265 & R. S. Sugirtharajah, "The Widow's Mites Revalued," *ExpT* 103 (1991): 42-43.

Mk 12:41-44 *with*
Lk 21:1

[41]Jesus sat down opposite the place where the offerings were put and watched the crowd putting their money into the temple treasury. {As he looked up[LK]} Many rich people threw in large amounts. [42]But a poor widow came and put in two very small copper coins,[a] worth only a fraction of a penny.[b]

[43]Calling his disciples to him, Jesus said, "I tell you the truth, this poor widow has put more into the treasury than all the others. [44]They all gave out of their wealth; but she, out of her poverty, put in everything — all she had to live on."

[a]42 Greek *two lepta*    [b]42 Greek *kodrantes*

Jesus leaves the temple courts proper for the last time. He seats himself in the court of the women across from the 13 trumpet-shaped bronze receptacles. Each of these boxes were for different kinds of offerings, with labels telling what the money was for. Jesus watched deliberately and carefully as the rich proudly tossed in fistfuls of coins. As they slid down the bronze coffer and clanked against the metal, they made quite a clamor and no doubt attracted a great deal of desired attention.

In the midst of this spectacle, there came an unassuming widow. In fact, she probably wanted to go unnoticed, a bit embarrassed by her meager gift. You could barely hear her two puny coins in the coffer. They were so small, in fact, that their name *lepta*,[41] often called *mites*, was derived from the word "to peel." They were a mere shaving of metal. Together, they were only worth 1/64 of a day's wage. They would almost be more of a hassle to count than they were worth, kind of like pennies in our offering plates.

Jesus excitedly calls his disciples. They must have had great expectations as they ran to his side. With all the colossal events that have taken place that day, Jesus must have something for them that is immensely important to get so excited over it. How shocked they must have been to discover that all the hubbub was over two *lepta*. But to Jesus it is a big deal. You see, he doesn't measure gifts with a scale but with a thermometer. He looks at the size of the sacrifice, not the size of the denomination. People can see only that which is given, but God sees that which is kept (2 Cor 8:1-7, 12). This woman has given more than all the rich because she has kept nothing.

In those days people got paid daily. So she at least had to fast that day for her sacrifice to God. But considering that she was a widow, that may have been the end of her savings and not merely the end of her daily stipend. Like the widow at Zarephath, she gave the last little bit she had to the service of God (1 Kgs 17:12-16).

---

[41]"That Mark felt it necessary to explain the value of a *lepton* and that he does so by the use of a Latin coin (*quadrans*) only known in the west suggests strongly, in spite of contrary opinion, that he was writing to Romans" (Wessel, p. 741).

With her last two *lepta*, she could have barely bought a dinner roll. So perhaps she said, "Big deal, I'm going to go hungry anyway. What's the difference whether I get one last meal before I am totally dependent on the mercy of God to care for me?" That may be easier to do with a few pennies than with $1,000. Yet that is the place we need to come to in our faith with financial affairs. If we can't trust God with our pennies, then it is not likely that he will have control of our more substantial savings.

# PART ELEVEN
# PREPARATION FOR THE DEATH OF CHRIST

## THE OLIVET DISCOURSE

§ 139a
Setting the
Stage
(Mt 24:1-3;
Mk 13:1-4;
Lk 21:5-7)

In this section Jesus will describe two events: The destruction of Jerusalem (A.D. 70) and the Second Coming. Somewhere in the middle of this chapter we need to draw a line between these two events. But that is easier said than done, and there has been great diversity in where various scholars draw their lines. There are several reasons this simple task has been so hard.

First, some of this stuff we're about to read could easily describe *both* the destruction of Jerusalem and the Second Coming. That's not so uncommon with prophecy (e.g., Isa 7:14; Jer 31:15; Micah 5:2). The initial "fulfillment" may merely picture and/or point to a greater future fulfillment. Thus, it has a "now-but-not-yet" feel to it. In the same way, here in Matthew 24, words which are presently applied to the destruction of Jerusalem, may ultimately describe the Second Coming (vv. 23-31). For example, some of the trouble Jerusalem experienced in A.D. 70 may be expanded to a global scale at the "end of the age." In fact, Luke takes a picture that Matthew relates to the destruction of Jerusalem (Mt 24:17-20), and, in a different context, relates it to the Second Coming (Lk 17:31).[1]

Second, prophecy is often fulfilled figuratively. Somehow we feel sheepish about interpreting these things figuratively. It just feels less "faithful." But if we interpret something literally that was *intended* to be figurative we will miss the real meaning of the passage (cf. Jn 2:19-21; 3:3-4; 6:51-52; 11:11-12; etc.). This practice may make for good movies, but relies on poor exegesis. Furthermore, we assume that this passage moves along chronologically, but that may not be the case. Some have

---

[1] It is this author's opinion that Mt 24:4-35 deal primarily with A.D. 70. Mt 24:23-31 has dual reference to both A.D. 70 and the Second Coming. And the material after Mt 24:36 deals exclusively with the return of Christ.

suggested that Jesus moves back and forth, intertwining talk about the destruction of Jerusalem and the Second Coming.

Third, this is apocalyptic material. It might be called hyper-prophecy (like Daniel and Revelation). It is filled with prophetic imagery and vocabulary, much of which is non-literal. Although this sounds very odd to us in the 20th century, apocalyptic literature was not all that uncommon in the first century.[2] Even so, it clearly is a difficult genre to interpret. Part of the problem is that it was not written for the purpose of explanation as much as for exhortation. That is, apocalyptic literature is not designed to describe eschatological chronology[3] but to encourage suffering saints to remain faithful until the end.

Fourth, the millennial system with which we approach this passage will affect where we "draw our line." Some can rightly claim that they have adopted no millennial view (a-, pre-, or post-). But nearly everyone has some presuppositions about eschatology and prophetic literature whether aware of them or not. These will color our thinking and partially determine where we draw the line between A.D. 70 and the return of our Lord.

Mt 24:1-3 *with*
Mk 13:1-3;
Lk 21:5-6

[1]Jesus left the temple and was walking away when his disciples came up to him to call his attention to its buildings. {"Look, Teacher! What massive stones! What magnificent buildings!$^{MK}$} {adorned with beautiful stones and with gifts dedicated to God.$^{LK}$} [2]"Do you see all these things?" he asked. "I tell you the truth, {the time will come when$^{LK}$} not one stone here will be left on another; every one will be thrown down."

[3]As Jesus was sitting on the Mount of Olives {opposite the temple, Peter, James, John and Andrew,$^{MK}$} the disciples came to him privately. "Tell us," they said, "when will this happen, and what will be the sign of your coming and of the end of the age?"

It has been a wonderful day in the temple for the disciples. Their master has answered every question thrown at him and has stumped the Jewish leaders with questions of his own. Then Jesus denounced the Pharisees more harshly than ever before (Mt 23). Now it was time to return to Bethany for the evening.

The disciples are beside themselves. It has been a day of decisive victory for Jesus and consequently, for them. As they strut out of the

---

[2]B.S. Easton, "The Little Apocalypse," *BW* 40 (1912): 130-138, goes so far as to say that nothing in this passage is new; each image can all be paralleled in extant apocalyptic literature.

[3]We find in Matthew 24 a series of *thens*. This is a rather loose chronological marker in apocalyptic literature. It may mean, "right after this," or "the next in a series of events," or merely "therefore" (a logical rather than a chronological marker).

temple, they are soaking in the moment as deeply as one would sniff fresh spring blossoms. It is indeed a great day. They note, in particular, the grandeur of the temple. They have no thought of its destruction, only its occupancy. Very likely they think that Jesus is on the verge of taking over the very temple buildings for the establishment of his kingdom. Perhaps they are making "dibs" on their own personal office space. After all, they are the chief executives of this new kingdom.

The temple was a spectacular sight (Josephus, *Ant* 15. 391-402; *Wars* 5. 184-227; Tacitus, *Histories*, 5.8.12). Herod the Great began renovating it in 19 B.C. It would not be completed until about A.D. 60. But even now it was mostly finished and elaborately decorated.

Jesus lays a bombshell on them: "Do you see these buildings? They will be obliterated!" Then, without any further word of explanation, Jesus walks out of the eastern gate, across the Kidron Valley and up the Mt. of Olives[4] about three fifths of a mile away, overlooking the temple mount. There he sits down. A bewildered group of disciples catch up with him. Mark says that it is Peter, Andrew, James and John who ask the questions, but surely the other disciples followed along and are also privy to Jesus' answer.

The disciples ask three questions: (1) When will the temple be destroyed? (2) What will be the sign of your coming? And (3) what will be the sign of the end of the age? In their minds all three of these things will happen simultaneously. They cannot imagine the destruction of the temple before the "end of the age." From our vantage point we can see at least two distinct events: (1) The destruction of Jerusalem; and (2) the Second Coming. Jesus will describe both events in the following chapter. Unfortunately, he will make as little distinction between the two events in his answer as the disciples did in their questions. This has caused a great deal of difficulty in explaining this passage.

§ 139b
**Birth Pains**
(Mt 24:4-14;
Mk 13:5-13;
Lk 21:8-19)

These verses are often applied to the Second Coming of Jesus. But if they can be applied to A.D. 70, they probably ought to be. After all, you would expect Jesus to answer his disciples' first question first — about the temple. More importantly, verse 16 urges the disciples to flee to the Judean hills. That can hardly apply to Jesus' return. It will do no good to run when Jesus comes back, and his disciples certainly wouldn't want to.

---

[4]Hence this discourse is called "The Olivet Discourse." This mountain held special eschatological overtones for the disciples (cf. Zech 14:4).

Mt 24:4-8 *with*
Lk 21:8-11

⁴Jesus answered: "Watch out that no one deceives you. ⁵For many will come in my name, claiming, 'I am the Christ,ª' {and, 'The time is near.'ᴸᴷ} and will deceive many. {Do not follow them.ᴸᴷ} ⁶You will hear of wars and rumors of wars, but see to it that you are not alarmed. Such things must happen {first,ᴸᴷ} but the end is still to come. ⁷Nation will rise against nation, and kingdom against kingdom. There will be famines and earthquakes {and pestilences and fearful events and great signs from heavenᴸᴷ} in various places. ⁸All these are the beginning of birth pains."

ª5 Or *Messiah*; also in verse 23

There were a number of signals that pointed to the destruction of Jerusalem. Jesus called them "birth pains." That is an appropriate description since they were painful to endure, they signaled that something big was coming, and they made you think it was right around the corner when, in fact, it was yet a ways off. Jesus points out three birth pains in particular: False christs, wars and rumors of wars, natural disasters and diseases. All three can be located between A.D. 30-70.

*False christs:* Josephus testifies that this period was rife with false messiahs (*Wars* 2. 259-264). Even the book of Acts lists a few of them: Theudas and Judas (5:36-37), an Egyptian (21:38), and perhaps even Bar Jesus (13:6-8), and Simon Magus (8:9ff). There is no question that many such self-proclaimed messiahs took advantage of sociopolitical unrest and deceived many.

*Wars and rumors of wars:* The Jews were threatened during this period by three different emperors: Caligula, Claudius, and Nero (Meserve, p. 23). But far more dangerous to the Jewish nation were the internal factions which waged civil war among the Jewish people.

*Famines and earthquakes:* There were a number of documented earthquakes and famines during this period including the one predicted by Agabus in Acts 11:28 during the reign of Claudius (A.D. 44). Others include A.D. 46 or 47; 51; 60; 62 or 63 (Meserve, p. 25).

Luke's phrase "fearful events and great signs from heaven" probably represents prophetic vocabulary summarizing the three previous "birth pains." Even so, none of these indicates that the end is imminent. They only signal the coming of yet greater suffering.

Lk 21:12-18 *with*
Mark 13:9-11;
Mt 24:9

{You must be on your guard.ᴹᴷ} ¹²"But before all this, they will lay hands on you and persecute you {and put [you] to death.ᴹᵀ} They will deliver you to {the local councils and flogged in theᴹᴷ} synagogues and prisons, and you will be brought before kings and governors, and all on account of my name. ¹³This will result in your being witnesses to them. ¹⁴But make up your mind not to worry beforehand how you will defend yourselves. ¹⁵For I will give you words and wisdom that none of your adversaries will be able to resist or contradict. {For it is not you speaking, but the Holy Spirit.ᴹᴷ} ¹⁶You will be betrayed even by parents, brothers, relatives and friends, and they will put some of you to death. ¹⁷All men {all nations^MT} will hate you because of me. ¹⁸But not a hair of your head will perish."

[vv. 12-18 = Mt 10:17-22, see comments on § 70b]

It is appropriate that both Mark and Luke incorporate this passage into the Olivet Discourse. When Jesus first spoke these words he was sending out the 12 for their first "solo flight." But none of these things took place during the Apostles' first tour. Thus, we know that Jesus was prophesying about future events, many of which can be catalogued in the book of Acts. Therefore, these words are just as applicable here, if not more so, than in Matthew 10.

¹⁰"At that time many will turn away from the faith and will betray and hate each other, ¹¹and many false prophets will appear and deceive many people. ¹²Because of the increase of wickedness, the love of most will grow cold, ¹³but he who stands firm to the end will be saved {gain life.^LK} ¹⁴And this gospel of the kingdom will be preached in the whole world as a testimony to all nations, and then the end will come."

Mt 24:10-14 *with* Lk 21:19

Here are three more signs that come before the destruction of Jerusalem: Persecution, heresies, and preaching the gospel to the "whole world." These, too, merely presage the impending doom.

*Persecution:* The book of Acts catalogues sufficiently both civil, organized persecutions (7:54-60; 8:1-9:2; 23) and local, sporadic persecution (13:50-51; 14:18-19; 16:19-23; 17:5-10; 19:23-41). Tacitus speaks for much of the Roman world when he describes Christians as a "class hated for their abominations" (*Annals*, 15.44). In A.D. 64-68, Nero enacted the first official Roman persecution against the church.[5]

*Heresies:* The church constantly had to fight heresies, from the Judaizers of Acts 15 to the Gnostics of 1 John. Galatians, Colossians, 2 Corinthians, 2 Timothy, 2 Peter, 1 John and Jude were all written in part to counter the false doctrines prevalent in the early church. And it gets no better after the destruction of Jerusalem when John writes in Revelation against false apostles (2:2), the synagogue of Satan (2:9, 13; 3:9), Nicolaitans (2:6, 15), teachings of Balaam (2:14) and Jezebel (2:20).

*Preaching the gospel to the "whole world":* This verse is often used to "prove" that this section must refer to Jesus' Second Coming and cannot refer to the destruction of Jerusalem (e.g., Barclay, p. 336;

---

[5]For a more detailed list of first century persecution and animosity toward Christians, see W. Barclay, "Great Themes of the NT: VI Matthew 24," *ExpT* 70 (1959): 327-328.

Walvoord, p. 183). Armerding, in fact, says that Jesus' return cannot be imminent because the gospel has not been fully preached.[6] Using the same logic, Hendriksen comes to a totally different conclusion. He says, "A brief survey of the progress of missions from the earliest period until the present day will convince anyone that we are approaching the end."[7]

However, the phrase "whole world" [*oikoumenē*] signified "the inhabited known world" (cf. Mt 4:23; 9:35; Lk 2:1; Josephus, *Ant* 15.387; 19.193). This is quite different than what we think of — we would include South America, Hawaii, Russia, Japan, etc. The word *oikoumenē* did not indicate all this. It was essentially equivalent with the Roman Empire.

In other words, Jesus did not mean that every last person would hear the gospel, but that the gospel would reach to all *known* nations. "Nor does it seem probable or practicable that the gospel should be preached to every individual member of any one particular generation in all the world."[8] The bottom line is this: Paul claimed that the gospel *had* reached the *oikoumenē* (Rom 1:8; 10:18; 16:26; Col 1:6, 23; 1 Thess 1:8). It is therefore fair to say that this prophecy was fulfilled prior to A.D. 70.

One final note before moving on to the next section. Jesus said, "He who stands firm to the end will be saved," or as Luke puts it, "will gain life." This is not talking about steadfastness as a requirement for salvation, although that sentiment is expressed elsewhere (Mt 10:22; Heb 10:36-39; Rev 2:10-11; etc.). It refers to the destruction of Jerusalem. Those who continued in their belief in Jesus fled the city and were spared its horrible destruction. As Luke says, they "gained life." On the other hand, those who forsook Jesus were under the same doom as the rest of Jerusalem.

**§ 139c**
**Abomination of**
**Desolation**
(Mt 24:15-28;
Mk 13:14-23;
Lk 21:20-24)

[MT 24:]15"So when you see standing in the holy place {where it does not belong[MK]} 'the abomination that causes desolation,'[a] spoken of through the prophet Daniel — let the reader understand — {When you see Jerusalem being surrounded by armies,[LK]} 16then let those who are in Judea flee to the mountains. 17Let no one on the roof of his house go down to take anything out of the house. 18Let no one in the field go back to get his cloak. {Let those in the city get out, and let those in the country not enter the city. 22For this is the time of punishment in fulfillment of all that has been written.[LK]}"

[a]*15* Daniel 9:27; 11:31; 12:11

---

[6]C.E. Armerding, *Dreams, Visions, & Oracles* (Grand Rapids: Baker, 1977), p. 169.

[7]W. Hendriksen, *Lectures on the Last Things* (Grand Rapids: Baker, 1951), p. 19.

[8]T.T. Shields, "What is the Great Tribulation?" *GWPA*, (Jan 15, 1948): 3.

The "Abomination that Causes Desolation" is some action or entity which causes both sacrilege and destruction. Daniel predicted that this terrible thing would be in the holy place (i.e., the temple). The Jews of the intertestamental period applied this appropriately to Antiochus Epiphanes who entered the temple with his Syrian armies in 167 B.C. He murdered a number of worshipers, allowed his troops to fornicate in the temple, slaughtered a pig on the altar of God and then ransacked the edifice (1 Macc. 1:54-61; 6:7). That is a good example of the "abomination that causes desolation." Yet Jesus looks for a still future, greater fulfillment. Certainly the destruction of A.D. 70 fits that description. This is especially true considering that Luke describes this event as "Jerusalem being surrounded by armies" (21:20). Josephus (*Wars*) describes the horrors of that desolating sacrilege:

| | |
|---|---|
| 5.31 | People's cries were louder than the fighting. |
| 5.429-438 | Jewish soldiers tormented citizens for food. Children stole food from elderly parents and mothers stole food from their infants. |
| 5.446-451 | Thousands of crucifixions. |
| 6.1-2 | Horrid descriptions of the famine and piles of dead bodies. |
| 6.201-213 | Cannibalism within the city — a mother consumed her own baby. |
| 6.271-280 | Burning of Jerusalem. |
| 6.285-288 | False prophets said that God would save them. |
| 6.406 | Fire quenched by blood. |
| 6.420 | 1,100,000 died and 97,000 taken captives and sold into slavery. |
| 7.1-3 | Every stone torn down except for a few notable towers. |

These predictions surely must refer to A.D. 70. If they refer to the Second Coming, why were the people commanded to flee to the Judean hills? Are they really going to escape Jesus' coming? And why would Christians want to run from Jesus? Verses 16-18 have no relevance to the Second Coming in this context. But they have great relevance to the destruction of Jerusalem. During the siege that culminated in A.D. 70, Cestius Gallus made a mysterious retreat from the city in A.D. 68 (Josephus, *Wars* 2.538-539).

But the people of the church in Jerusalem had been commanded by a revelation, vouchsafed to approved men there before the war, to leave the city and to dwell in a certain town of Perea called Pella. And when those that believed in Christ had come thither from Jerusalem, then, as if

the royal city of the Jews and the whole land of Judea were entirely des-
titute of holy men . . . (Eusebius, *Ecclesiastical History*, 3.5.3)

Jesus was talking about a literal flight out of the city once the
Roman armies had surrounded it. It would be easier to escape if the
women were not pregnant, if the flight was not in winter, or on the
Sabbath when it would be more difficult to secure food and lodging (cf.
Mt 24:19-20). The Christians a generation later took Jesus at his word
and did, in fact, escape the massacre of Jerusalem, saving their lives and
their families.

Luke claims that all these sufferings were in fulfillment of that
which had been written. He is speaking, of course, of OT prophecies
such as Daniel 9:27; 11:31; 12:11. But Jesus himself predicted these
events on more than one occasion: Lk 13:35; 19:43-44; 23:28-31; Mt
23:35-38. These verses add important details about the specific sufferings during the siege of Jerusalem. They also clarify the fact that this
was not a result of poor politics or the natural cruelty of men. This was
God's divine judgment on the city for killing the Messiah, God's very
own Son.

But does this text *only* refer to A.D. 70? Many Bible students look
for another future fulfillment in connection with the "Man of Sin" standing in the Holy Place (2 Thess 2:1-9; Rev 13:3-10).[9] While that may be
true (time will certainly tell), the clear parallel of Luke 21:20 & 24
points to the armies surrounding Jerusalem in A.D. 70. These words
were literally and completely fulfilled in the fall of Jerusalem. A future
event is not needed to adequately fulfill this prophecy.

Lk 21:23b-24

"There will be great distress in the land and wrath against this people. [24]They
will fall by the sword and will be taken as prisoners to all the nations. Jerusalem
will be trampled on by the Gentiles until the times of the Gentiles are fulfilled.

Mt 24:19-22 *with*
Mk 13:19-20

[19]"How dreadful it will be in those days for pregnant women and nursing mothers! [20]Pray that your flight will not take place in winter or on the Sabbath. [21]For
then there will be great distress, unequaled from the beginning of {when God
created[MK]} the world until now — and never to be equaled again. [22]If those days
had not been cut short, no one would survive, but for the sake of the elect
{whom he has chosen[MK]} those days will be shortened."

There are two things that might point to a yet future fulfillment of
these verses. First, Luke 21:24 sounds like Romans 11:25 "until the full

---

[9]E.g., Lewis Chafer, *The Kingdom in History and Prophecy* (Philadelphia: Sunday
School Times, 1922) and John Walvoord, *Matthew — Thy Kingdom Come* (Chicago:
Moody Press, 1974).

number of the Gentiles has come in." Since Romans 11:25 is still future, some have wanted to make Luke 21:24 future as well. But just because two verses use similar words does not mean they are talking about the same thing. Indeed, Luke and Paul are dealing with two different topics. Luke is talking about the destruction of Jerusalem. Paul is talking about Gentile evangelism. They are not true parallels even though they sound similar. Thus, Romans 11:25 can't push Luke 21:24 into the future.

Second, Matthew says that this suffering was unparalleled since the beginning of time and will not be surpassed until the end of the world. It is pointed out that more Jews were killed in Nazi Germany than were killed in A.D. 70. Hence, it is said, A.D. 70 was not the worst persecution of the world. Therefore, these prophecies must point to the tribulation of the last days. However, the measure of this tribulation may not be in its sheer numbers but in its magnitude. As a punishment from God, as described by Josephus, A.D. 70 was unsurpassed in its spiritual and physical terror. In addition, during the fall of Jerusalem, they not only had to contend with the Romans but with the civil war inside the city as well. To make matters worse, the suffering of A.D. 70 was not merely the loss of human life, but the desecration of the Holy City and the temple of God. In that sense, A.D. 70 was the worst suffering ever experienced by the Jews.

In addition, placing this tribulation at the end of the world introduces a couple of difficulties into the text. First, there is this uncomfortable gap of at least 2,000 years between Matthew 24:20 and 21. Second, why would Jesus say that this suffering was "never to be equaled again"? If it is the final tribulation, it goes without saying that it would be unsurpassed.[10]

Matthew 24:22 also seems to point to A.D. 70 rather than the end of the world. Jesus said that this tribulation would be cut short so that the elect would survive. What would be the value of the physical survival of the elect at the end of the world? It seems more appropriately applied to the Jews of A.D. 70. By cutting short the time of tribulation, God preserved for himself a remnant of Jews. That is God's consistent promise for his people (Isa 6:13; Rom 9:27-29; 11:5, 29). The most straightforward reading of this passage seems to refer to A.D. 70, especially if we allow for a bit of apocalyptic hyperbole.

---

[10]Blomberg (p. 359), suggests that this tribulation period encompasses the entire period from the devastation of A.D. 70 through Christ's return. While that solves the problem of describing A.D. 70 as the worst suffering of all time, it creates another problem. These descriptions (vv. 15-25) are quite specific. To make a generic application of verse 21 seems out of character for this context.

Mt 24:23-28 *with*
Mk 13:23

²³"At that time if anyone says to you, 'Look, here is the Christ!' or, 'There he is!' do not believe it. ²⁴For false Christs and false prophets will appear and perform great signs and miracles to deceive even the elect — if that were possible. {So be on your guard.ᴹᴷ} ²⁵See, I have told you ahead of time.

²⁶"So if anyone tells you, 'There he is, out in the desert,' do not go out; or, 'Here he is, in the inner rooms,' do not believe it. ²⁷For as lightning that comes from the east is visible even in the west, so will be the coming of the Son of Man. ²⁸Wherever there is a carcass, there the vultures will gather."

[vv. 25-28 = Lk 17:23-24, 37, see comments on § 120b]

"At that time" [lit., "then," Gk. *tote*] is sometimes used as a chronological marker and sometimes as a logical marker. Here it seems to be the latter. It doesn't tell so much what will happen next, but the logical implication of false messiahs whenever they appear. We are anxious to see Jesus. We are fatigued by the trouble of this world. That makes us ripe for deception by false messiahs who claim to be Jesus. It's nothing new (cf. 2 Thess 2:1-2). Nor is it really complicated. When Jesus returns it will be as obvious as lightning. Therefore, if anyone claims to be Christ and calls you to follow him, don't. Christ will come get you; you don't have to chase after him to some desert or secret cult compound.

These guys will appear throughout history, until Jesus returns. Luke, for instance, uses these very words to describe Jesus' Second Coming (17:22-24, 37). But they have equal relevance to A.D. 70 (cf. Mt 24:5). The only difference is that Matthew adds that these false messiahs would also perform great signs. Although this sounds like "End Time Talk" (cf. Mt 7:21-23; 2 Thess 2:9-12; Rev 13:11-17), it can be fairly applied to both events.

With vv. 27-28 we now move clearly to the end.[11] When Jesus does return, there will be some pretty severe judgment. Verse 28 describes it with a picture, not from a courtroom but on the battlefield. Dead bodies are strewn across the land with vultures feasting on their carrion (cf. Rev 19:11-21). Judgment will be like that when Jesus returns. In other words, wherever there is sin there is sure to be judgment. Just as Jesus' return will be seen by all, so every sin will fall prey to his judgment.

**§ 139d**
**Coming of the**
**Son of Man**
(Mt 24:29-31;
Mk 13:24-27;
Lk 21:25-27)

Like verses 27-28, this passage is primarily pointed at the Second Coming. But when we read them against their OT background, they can

---

[11]Although J.A. O'Flynn would argue that even verse 27 could be viewed apocalyptically with Jesus' judgment at A.D. 70 ("The Eschatological Discourse," *ITQ* 18 [1951]: 277-281).

also describe the social and political upheaval of A.D. 70. In fact, in Luke these galactic disorders are connected with the fall of Jerusalem even more closely than in Matthew and Mark.

[29]"Immediately after the distress of those days
"'the sun will be darkened,
   and the moon will not give its light;
the stars will fall [Ezek 32:7; Joel 2:10,31; 3:15] from the sky,
   and the heavenly bodies will be shaken.'[a]

Mt 24:29

[a]29 Isaiah 13:10; 34:4

[25]"On the earth, nations will be in anguish and perplexity at the roaring and tossing of the sea. [26]Men will faint from terror, apprehensive of what is coming on the world for the heavenly bodies will be shaken.

Lk 21:25-26

[30]"At that time the sign of the Son of Man will appear in the sky, and all the nations of the earth will mourn. They will see the Son of Man coming on the clouds of the sky, with power and great glory. [31]And he will send his angels with a loud trumpet call, and they will gather his elect from the four winds, from one end of the heavens to the other."

Mt 24:30-31

"Immediately" after the tribulation period there will be "galactic" turmoil. When will that be? Well, the word "immediately" may indicate, using prophetic vocabulary, "the next in a series of events" which may, in fact, still be a long way off. It is like looking at a mountain range from a distance. Two peaks might appear to be close to each other. But when you actually travel from one peak to another, you realize just how far apart the two are. We are thus warned about trying to construct a chronology of end-time events.

At the same time, this word "immediately" is used eighty times in the NT and always means "without delay, on the spot, right then." There are only two exceptions to this. First, Mark 4:5, in the parable of the soil, says that the little plant sprang up "immediately" because it had no depth of soil. Here the word signifies a very short time, especially as compared to other plants. The other exception is 3 John 14, where John says, "I hope to see you immediately." Of course, it would take some travel time. Thus, the word could be understood as "a short time."[12] But a delay of 2,000 years is probably out of the question. And since "immediately" is an uncommon word for Matthew, it seems to have particular relevance for him here. Consequently, if Matthew 24:23-28 has any relevance to the destruction of Jerusalem, then the events of vv. 29-31, which follow

---

[12]It is certainly not correct to interpret *eutheōs* "immediately" merely as an indefinite period of time, contra Floyd Hamilton, *The Basis of Millennial Faith* (Grand Rapids: Baker, 1959), p. 68.

"immediately," must be applied figuratively to the events of A.D. 70.

So while these verses will be ultimately fulfilled when Jesus returns, these galactic events also picture the destruction of Jerusalem. That sounds odd to us. But the disciples, steeped in OT literature, would have no problem seeing the connection. For instance, this phrase, "the sun will be darkened and the moon will not give its light, and the stars will fall from heaven . . ." was used several times in the OT to describe the fall of a great nation. In Isaiah 13:10, 19 it refers to **Babylon**; in Isaiah 34:4 it refers to **Edom**; and in Ezekiel 32:7-8 it refers to **Egypt**. Borrowing language from the prophets, Jesus describes the fall of a great nation. "This language need not be the break up of the entire universe" (Lewis, p. 128).

Some, in fact, would even relate Matthew 24:30 to the fall of Jerusalem. The "Son of Man in the clouds" can be interpreted as a Jewish idiom for "the day of the Lord," when he comes in wrath and punishment (based on Dan 7:13-14). This agrees with a number of figurative OT references to the Lord coming in the clouds (Deut 33:26; Ps 68:4) and in judgment (Isa 30:27; Ezek 30:3; Nah 1:3). After all, this destruction was a result of God's punishment for the murder of Jesus (Lk 19:42-44; 23:28-31; Mt 23:35-39). Furthermore, "All nations of the earth mourning" can be literally translated "All the tribes of the land." Thus, this mourning of verse 30 could refer to the tears of the Jews. Some would mourn their own suffering, others would regret having killed Jesus (Zech 12:10-14; Jn 19:37). But ultimately this pictures the Second Coming of Jesus when all nations will mourn at their own judgment (1 Thess 4:17; Rev 1:7). That will be a day of divine harvest (v. 31; cf. Mt 13:24-30, 47-50).

§ 139e
**Lesson of the Fig Tree**
(Mt 24:32-41;
Mk 13:28-32;
Lk 21:28-33).

[MT 24:]32"Now learn this lesson {parable[LK]} from the fig tree: As soon as its twigs get tender and its leaves come out, you know that summer is near. 33Even so, when you see all these things {happening,[MK]} {stand up and lift up your heads, because[LK]} you know that it {your redemption[LK]} is near, right at the door. 34I tell you the truth, this generation[a] will certainly not pass away until all these things have happened. 35Heaven and earth will pass away, but my words will never pass away."

[a] 34 Or race

The parable of the fig tree is simple. When you see the shoots coming off the branch turn green and start to put out little leaves, you know that summer is right around the corner. In other words, there are certain signs in the natural world which foretell the coming season. So also, Jesus gives the disciples certain signs which allow them to recognize the impending destruction of Jerusalem (cf. Mt 16:28; Mk 9:1; Lk 9:27). They can bank on Jesus' words. In fact, Jesus' words are even more stable and enduring than the physical universe (Mt 24:35). That is just the kind of comfort needed in the kind of tribulation they are about to face.

Now many expositors will apply the parable of the fig tree to the Second Coming of Jesus.[13] Luke's "redemption" talk does sound an awful lot like Romans 8:23. And as we have noted, the previous verses (Mt 24:27-31; Mk 13:24-27; Lk 21:25-27) can be applied to the Second Coming as well as to the destruction of Jerusalem. However, this does not obligate us to press the present verses into the same "double service" as the previous pericope. Remember, Jesus is answering two questions without clearly differentiating between them. It would not be unnatural for him to mingle a double metaphor in with the material which speaks primarily of A.D. 70, and then to return to speak only of these initial events. And there are several reasons why this parable probably does not apply to the parousia.

First, the parable urges the disciples to look for and discern the season of this tribulation. While that is appropriate for the events of A.D. 70, it is not appropriate for the Second Coming. The whole point of Matthew 24:36-25:30 is that you *cannot* know when Jesus will come. Some find a way around this conundrum by saying that while we can't know the day or hour (Mt 24:36), we can know the month and year. Aside from the fact that all such prognostications presently have a batting average of 0%, they also fail to appreciate the simple language of Jesus. Whether it is a day, an hour, a month or a year, we simply cannot know when Jesus is coming back.

The words "day" and "hour" signify time in general and not specific chronological increments (Mt 7:22; 10:19; 24:42, 44, 50; 25:13; 26:45). The word "day" likely suggests "Day of the Lord," meaning, in prophetic vocabulary "the day God comes for judgment and salvation" (Joel 2:11; Amos 5:18, 20; Mal 4:5). In other words, "day" stands for the end of the age. We just can't know when that will be. Hence we are urged to be prepared. It is a strange paradox that such "date-setting" creates much excitement but does little to increase people's practical preparation for Jesus' coming. (It also seems strange that one would have the audacity to sell, for profit, a book which predicts the imminent rapture of the church.)

---

[13]For a comparison of these two interpretations, see A. McNicol, "The Lesson of the Fig Tree in Mark 13:28-32: A Comparison Between Two Exegetical Methodologies," *RestQ* 27 (1984): 193-207.

Second, verse 36 begins with a pair of particles *peri de* (= "but"). The NIV leaves them totally untranslated. That's surprising since this combination sets up a fairly strong contrast. It would be like capitalizing our word "**BUT**." In other words, verse 36 seems to indicate a distinct shift in emphasis. Hence, it is reasonable to read verse 36 as the dividing line of the chapter. Although there is some material in the first half of the chapter which has dual reference to A.D. 70 and Christ's return (i.e., vv. 23-31), it deals primarily with the events of the first century. The rest of Matthew 24 & 25, however, deals exclusively with the Second Coming.

Third, Jesus says that all these things would take place within a generation. His audience would be thinking in terms of about forty years and certainly would include themselves in that group. This, of course, fits perfectly with A.D. 70 but not well at all with "end-time" events. There are several proposed solutions. (1) Chalk it up to error either on the part of Jesus or of Matthew. We reject that because (a) there is a better explanation and (b) the Bible has demonstrated its accuracy. (2) Begin counting the generation (i.e., 40 years) not from Jesus' day but from the "budding of the fig tree" which, in our day, is almost invariably applied to the reestablishment of the Jewish nation in 1948 or the Six Day War of 1967. Although this is linguistically *possible*, it seems improbable in this context and in light of the other places Jesus uses this word *generation* (cf. Mt 16:28; 23:35-36; Mk 9:1; Lk 9:27). (3) Some have suggested that "generation" should be translated as "nation," with special reference to the Jewish nation. As Alford points out, "*genea*" has in Hellenistic Greek the meaning of 'a race or family of people' (cf. Jer 8:3 LXX, and Mt 23:36).[14] This has led some to think of it in terms of a continuing generation until the end of time (Ryle, p. 323). It is true that Matthew 12:45; 17:17; 23:36; Luke 16:8; 17:25 and Philippians 2:15 *may* be understood as referring to the whole nation of Israel. But it still meant the nation AT THAT TIME. The simplest and most straightforward understanding of "generation" would be the contemporaries of Jesus. Those standing before Jesus would see the fulfillment of everything written between verses 4 and 35 of Matthew 24, even if verses 27-31 also apply to the Second Coming.

**§ 139e (cont.)**
**No One Knows**
**the Time of His**
**Coming**
(Mt 24:36-41;
Mk 13:32)

[MT 24:]36"No one knows about that day or hour, not even the angels in heaven, nor the Son, but only the Father. 37As it was in the days of Noah, so it will be at the coming of the Son of Man. 38For in the days before the flood, people were eating and drinking, marrying and giving in marriage, up to the day Noah entered

---

[14]Henry Alford, *The Greek Testament, Vol. 1* (Chicago: Moody, 1958), p. 244.

the ark; ³⁹and they knew nothing about what would happen until the flood came and took them all away. That is how it will be at the coming of the Son of Man. ⁴⁰Two men will be in the field; one will be taken and the other left. ⁴¹Two women will be grinding with a hand mill; one will be taken and the other left."

[vv. 37-41 = Lk 17:26-27, 34-35, see comments on § 120b]

Everything from here on out refers to the Second Coming. Jesus lays out three important truths about his return. First, he tells us, in no uncertain terms, that we cannot know when it is. The angels don't even know when it is. In fact, Jesus, himself, did not know when he would return. And we think we will figure it out?!

Second, Jesus tells us that his coming will surprise a lot of people. He compares it to the days of Noah. Noah preached for decades that a flood was coming. But people ignored him, going about business as usual. When the flood came it caught them by surprise with catastrophic results. That is how it will be when Jesus comes back.

Third, the Second Coming will divide even the most intimate relationships. A couple of guys are farming a field together; they will be separated. Female coworkers, grinding at the mill, will be separated. Luke 17:34 adds that two people will be separated even from the same bed — husbands from wives and children from parents.

Because we don't know when Jesus is coming back, because his return will be a surprise to so many, and because it will sever so severely even the most intimate relationships, we had better be ready for Jesus to return at any moment. That's the thrust of the following four parables. In their own way, they each say the same thing: BE READY! These are parables of warning with the same choral refrain: BE READY!

§ 139f
**Four Parables to Urge Us to be Ready for Jesus**
(Mt 24:42-25:30; Mk 13:33-37; Lk 21:34-36)

[LK 21:]³⁴"Be careful, or your hearts will be weighed down with dissipation, drunkenness and the anxieties of life, and that day will close on you unexpectedly like a trap. ³⁵For it will come upon all those who live on the face of the whole earth. ³⁶Be always on the watch, and pray that you may be able to escape all that is about to happen, and that you may be able to stand before the Son of Man.

³⁴"It's like a man going away: He leaves his house and puts his servants in charge, each with his assigned task, and tells the one at the door to keep watch."

Mk 13:34

Mark and Luke both give summary statements prior to this first parable which warn the disciples to keep watch. It sounds most like Matthew's first parable but it is also similar to the fourth (Mt 25:14-30).

### #1: *Like a Thief in the Night: Jesus Comes Unexpectedly*

Mt 24:42-44

⁴²"Therefore keep watch, because you do not know on what day your Lord will come. ⁴³But understand this: If the owner of the house had known at what time of night the thief was coming, he would have kept watch and would not have let his house be broken into. ⁴⁴So you also must be ready, because the Son of Man will come at an hour when you do not expect him."

[vv. 42-44 = Lk 12:39-40, see comments on § 108c]

Thieves don't send you their itinerary with an expected time of arrival. If they did, they would likely find a pit bull or a shotgun waiting for them. Like a thief, Jesus will come with no advanced warning (Lk 12:39; 1 Thess 5:2, 4; 2 Pet 3:10; Rev 3:3; 16:15). This does not indicate a secret rapture anymore than it indicates that Jesus is a criminal. The single point of comparison is that Jesus comes without warning.

Jesus used a common prophetic phrase to describe his coming: "Day of the Lord" (Joel 2:11; Amos 5:18, 20; Mal 4:5). Even in the OT, it is often pictured as imminent (Isa 13:6, 9; Ezek 30:3; Joel 1:15; 2:1; 3:14; Obad 1:15; Zeph 1:7, 14). It signified, of course, the coming of God. And it had a two-pronged result. First, those who were faithful to God would receive his protection and rewards. Those who were not would be severely punished. In the OT "The Day of the Lord" often signified a temporal judgment on a particular nation. But in the NT it usually indicates the final judgment (cf. 1 Cor 5:5; 2 Pet 3:10). Hence, there is neither a distinction nor an interval here between Jesus' return and judgment day. In order to insert a millennial reign between the two events, one must import Revelation 20.

### #2: *Like a Faithful Servant: Jesus Comes Later than Expected*

Mt 24:45-51

⁴⁵"Who then is the faithful and wise servant, whom the master has put in charge of the servants in his household to give them their food at the proper time? ⁴⁶It will be good for that servant whose master finds him doing so when he returns. ⁴⁷I tell you the truth, he will put him in charge of all his possessions. ⁴⁸But suppose that servant is wicked and says to himself, 'My master is staying away a long time,' ⁴⁹and he then begins to beat his fellow servants and to eat and drink with drunkards. ⁵⁰The master of that servant will come on a day when he does not expect him and at an hour he is not aware of. ⁵¹He will cut him to pieces and assign him a place with the hypocrites, where there will be weeping and gnashing of teeth."

[vv. 45-51 = Lk 12:42-46, see comments on § 108c]

Matthew and Luke tell this same parable word for word,[15] but they

---

[15]Out of 102 words in the Greek text there are only 14 words that are not identical, letter

place them in different contexts. In Luke, Peter sparks this response by asking Jesus if his parable refers to everyone or only a special few. In other words, Peter is asking about special privileges. Jesus turns the tables and talks about Peter's special responsibilities. Here, however, the emphasis is not on responsibility so much as it is on preparedness.

As the weeks roll into months, and months into years, it is easy for a servant to be seduced into slacking off from his duties. The longer the master is away, the less likely, it seems, that he will return in the very next moment. But the opposite, in fact, is the case. He is coming back. And with each tick of the clock, his return is that much closer (Rom 13:11)!

### #3: *Like Foolish/Wise Virgins: Jesus Comes Sooner than Expected*

Mt 25:1-5

[1]"At that time the kingdom of heaven will be like ten virgins who took their lamps and went out to meet the bridegroom. [2]Five of them were foolish and five were wise. [3]The foolish ones took their lamps but did not take any oil with them. [4]The wise, however, took oil in jars along with their lamps. [5]The bridegroom was a long time in coming, and they all became drowsy and fell asleep."

It was not uncommon for the Messiah to be compared to a bridegroom (Isa 54:4-6; 62:4-5; Ezek 16:7-34; Hos 2:19; cf. Jn 3:27-30; Mt 9:15; Mk 2:19-20). This is a typical picture of a Palestinian wedding. After the wedding ceremony at the bride's home, there would be a parade through the streets which led to the home of the groom where there would be a big banquet. It was the job of the bridesmaids to wait for the groom and his procession. But one never knew just how long that would take. Since it was night, they took their handheld oil lamps with them. These lamps were nothing more than a clay bowl about three inches in diameter and pinched on one side so as to hold a wick. These lamps only held about a tablespoon of oil. Thus, it was important to carry extra oil with you if the groom was delayed.

WARNING: This parable has a number of details which are merely for rhetorical interest and should not be allegorized. (1) Five were wise and five were foolish. This does not mean that about 50% of the church will not go with Jesus when he returns. (2) The fact that they all fell asleep does not suggest that they were unfaithful or "backslidden." These maidens were expected to be prepared to escort the groom into the wedding gala, but they were not expected to stay awake as they waited. After all, they were not Roman soldiers, they were bridesmaids. (3) The bridesmaids were virgins. This is not intended to symbolize the purity of

---

for letter. Six of the words are synonyms, five of them are different verb tenses, and there are three words which one writer uses that the other does not.

the church. Single women of that era were not typically sexually active. Thus the term "virgin" is virtually equivalent to "young woman." (4) Five of them took a flask of oil. This does not likely represent the Holy Spirit. Some have used such an allegory to explain the apparent selfishness of the five wise women. If oil represents the Holy Spirit then of course they did not share their "Spirit" because that is not possible whereas oil they may have been able to share. But that is an over-interpretation of the parable. The point of the parable is simply this: You must be prepared for Jesus. If you are, then you are wise and get to go with Jesus. If you are not prepared, then you are foolish and excluded from the party.

Mt 25:6-13

⁶"At midnight the cry rang out: 'Here's the bridegroom! Come out to meet him!'

⁷"Then all the virgins woke up and trimmed their lamps. ⁸The foolish ones said to the wise, 'Give us some of your oil; our lamps are going out.'

⁹"'No,' they replied, 'there may not be enough for both us and you. Instead, go to those who sell oil and buy some for yourselves.'

¹⁰"But while they were on their way to buy the oil, the bridegroom arrived. The virgins who were ready went in with him to the wedding banquet. And the door was shut.

¹¹"Later the others also came. 'Sir! Sir!' they said. 'Open the door for us!'

¹²"But he replied, 'I tell you the truth, I don't know you.'

¹³"Therefore keep watch, because you do not know the day or the hour."

In the middle of the night the ten bridesmaids were awakened with a cry announcing that the groom was on his way (cf. Mt 24:31; 1 Cor 15:52; 1 Thess 4:16). As they wiped the sleep from their eyes and scurried to their feet, they fiddled with their wicks to kindle a decent flame. The "foolish five" pulled their wicks out so as to increase the flame. But it only sucked the last few drops of oil from their lamps. They begged the "flasked five" to share some of their oil. But that might jeopardize their own supply since the bridegroom was still a short distance away and still might have an unexpected delay. So the wise virgins refused. Instead they sent the "foolish five" off to the local merchant to purchase their own oil.

The foolish five scampered off to buy some oil. Normally the shops would be closed. But during a big wedding celebration in the community they would naturally open up their little shops to supply whatever needs the family might have. Remember, we are not talking about a department store here; it's a small family business.

By the time the foolish five returned, the groom had already arrived, entered the house and shut the door, taking the five wise maidens with him. The foolish five beat on the door and begged to come in. But the groom said, "Go away, I never knew you." That may sound calloused, especially since these poor gals ran to the store to get the oil. But this is the same reception Jesus promised the false prophets (Mt 7:23). Their lack of preparation betrays their lack of love.

### #4: *Like Servants Entrusted with Wealth*:

This parable is an awful lot like the one Jesus told about five days earlier while en route from Jericho to Bethany (Lk 19:11-27; § 127b). The main difference is that Jesus tells the parable in Luke to warn them that the kingdom of God was not imminent as they expected (Lk 19:1). In Matthew, however, this parable warns them to keep on the lookout for that kingdom.

There are other minor differences:

| Luke 19:11-27 | Matthew 25:14-30 |
|---|---|
| Nearing Jerusalem | Leaving Jerusalem |
| 10 Servants, given one "mina" each. | Three Servants, given 5, 2, and 1 talent respectively. |
| The citizens hated the would-be king. | No mention of other characters |
| King | Rich Man |
| Each servant given one city for each mina earned | No specific reward mentioned |
| The last servant hid the money in a "napkin." | The last servant hid the money in the ground. |

The similarities, however, outweigh the differences:
1.  The last servant hides the money rather than depositing it.
2.  "Well done, good and faithful servant! You have been faithful with a few things; I will put you in charge of many things . . ."
3.  The wicked servants give a similar evaluation of their master.
4.  The extra money is given to the servant who earned the most.
5.  "For everyone who has will be given more . . ."
6.  Both parables end in judgment.

These similarities do not necessarily indicate that Matthew and Luke were editors rather than reporters of Jesus' words. In fact, a more likely explanation is that Jesus told the parable twice, altering the details for rhetorical interest and variation for his audience.

---

[14]"Again, it will be like a man going on a journey, who called his servants and                Mt 25:14-18

entrusted his property to them. [15]To one he gave five talents[a] of money, to another two talents, and to another one talent, each according to his ability. Then he went on his journey. [16]The man who had received the five talents went at once and put his money to work and gained five more. [17]So also, the one with the two talents gained two more. [18]But the man who had received the one talent went off, dug a hole in the ground and hid his master's money."

[a]15 A talent was worth more than a thousand dollars

It is difficult to know for sure just how much money the master gave his servants. For one thing, a talent was a unit of weight, not a monetary value. The value of a talent would vary greatly depending on whether you have a talent of gold, silver, or bronze. All we can say for certain is that this is a huge amount of money to play with.

When Jesus used the word "talent" his audience thought about money. When we use the word "talent" our audiences think about skills and abilities, and to that extent we misread the parable. At the same time, the symbol of money in the parable represents all the resources we have been given by God including our money and our abilities, as well as our time, opportunities, etc.

Each servant was endowed according to his ability. The first two lived up to their reputation and past performance, earning 100% of what was entrusted to them. The last servant refused to even try. Instead he dug a hole in the backyard and hid the money.

Mt 25:19-23

[19]"After a long time the master of those servants returned and settled accounts with them. [20]The man who had received the five talents brought the other five. 'Master,' he said, 'you entrusted me with five talents. See, I have gained five more.'

[21]"His master replied, 'Well done, good and faithful servant! You have been faithful with a few things; I will put you in charge of many things. Come and share your master's happiness!'

[22]"The man with the two talents also came. 'Master,' he said, 'you entrusted me with two talents; see, I have gained two more.'

[23]"His master replied, 'Well done, good and faithful servant! You have been faithful with a few things; I will put you in charge of many things. Come and share your master's happiness!'"

[vv. 19-23 = Lk 19:15-18, see comments on § 127b]

As in the previous account of this parable, the master rewarded the faithful servants with multiplied wealth.

Mt 25:24-30

[24]"Then the man who had received the one talent came. 'Master,' he said, 'I knew that you are a hard man, harvesting where you have not sown and gathering where you have not scattered seed. [25]So I was afraid and went out and hid

your talent in the ground. See, here is what belongs to you.'

26"His master replied, 'You wicked, lazy servant! So you knew that I harvest where I have not sown and gather where I have not scattered seed? 27Well then, you should have put my money on deposit with the bankers, so that when I returned I would have received it back with interest.

28"Take the talent from him and give it to the one who has the ten talents. 29For everyone who has will be given more, and he will have an abundance. Whoever does not have, even what he has will be taken from him. 30And throw that worthless servant outside, into the darkness, where there will be weeping and gnashing of teeth.'"

[vv. 24-30 = Lk 19:20-27, see comments on § 127b].

This wicked servant obviously lied when he said he was afraid of the master. Had he actually been afraid of the master, he would have deposited the money for interest with a moneylender. The truth is, he was convinced that the master was not coming back. He hid the money so that he could dig it up later and use it for himself! This turned out to be a bad bet, for when the master returned the servant got what was coming to him (v. 30). Steinmetz says:

> The swift justice meted out to the lazy servant puts a merciful end to any notion that the disobedient and the dishonest will be able to blackmail their way into the Kingdom of heaven by manipulating the goodness of God or playing on divine pity. God's goodness is too clever to be taken in by such nursery tricks. Divine pity will forgive sins, but it will not condone them.[16]

Although Jesus' return has been delayed for a long time, he is coming back. And when he does, we will give an account to him of our stewardship of life. Those who prepared well for his coming will be delighted with their reward. Those who have counted on his continued delay will be shocked, judged and punished most severely.

This pericope concludes the series of parables about Jesus' return, and closes out the entire Olivet discourse. It shares the basic theme of the previous parables: Be ready . . . Jesus *IS* coming back! This scene, though, does not appear to be a parable itself. Rather it looks like a sketch of the judgment which comes with Christ's return. The sheep and the goats are metaphors for the righteous and the wicked. But the rest

**§ 139g**
**Judgment at**
**the Second**
**Coming**
**(Mt 25:31-46)**

---

[16]D.C. Steinmetz, "Mt 25:14-30," *Int* 34 (1980): 172-176.

seems to be a true description rather than a parabolic illustration of judgment.

Mt 25:31-33

³¹"When the Son of Man comes in his glory, and all the angels with him, he will sit on his throne in heavenly glory. ³²All the nations will be gathered before him, and he will separate the people one from another as a shepherd separates the sheep from the goats. ³³He will put the sheep on his right and the goats on his left."

This is a vivid picture of judgment using a shepherding analogy. It was common for several flocks of sheep and goats to be penned up together for the night or even to graze together during the day. But there were times when they had to be separated (for instance, when shearing the valuable wool from the sheep). Although these shaggy animals may look quite a bit alike, there is a great difference in their character and value. The divisions were clear. In the same way, the judgment will clarify who is for Jesus and who is not.[17]

Mt 25:34-40

³⁴"Then the King will say to those on his right, 'Come, you who are blessed by my Father; take your inheritance, the kingdom prepared for you since the creation of the world. ³⁵For I was hungry and you gave me something to eat, I was thirsty and you gave me something to drink, I was a stranger and you invited me in, ³⁶I needed clothes and you clothed me, I was sick and you looked after me, I was in prison and you came to visit me.'
³⁷"Then the righteous will answer him, 'Lord, when did we see you hungry and feed you, or thirsty and give you something to drink? ³⁸When did we see you a stranger and invite you in, or needing clothes and clothe you? ³⁹When did we see you sick or in prison and go to visit you?'
⁴⁰"The King will reply, 'I tell you the truth, whatever you did for one of the least of these brothers of mine, you did for me.'"

What determines whether someone is a sheep or a goat? Like every other judgment scene of the NT it is made on the basis of deeds (Mt 16:27; Jn 5:28-30; Rom 2:5-11; 2 Cor 5:10; 1 Pet 1:17; Rev 20:11-15). Does this grate against salvation by grace? How can one be saved by grace but judged by works? It is simply this: When we stand before the judgment seat of Christ, the only thing that will really matter is our

---

[17]Verse 31 reminds us of Rev 19:11-18; verse 32 reminds us of Rev 20:11-15. The difference is that Matthew says nothing about a thousand year gap that separates the Second Coming from judgment day (Rev 20:1-10). So should we incorporate a millennium here between Mt 25:31 & 32? Probably not. Both Matthew 25 and 2 Peter 3:10-13 (both of which are less figurative than Revelation) present a simple chronology for the end of time: Jesus comes, the earth is destroyed, judgment ensues (cf. Mt 16:27; Jn 5:28-30). While this does not satisfactorily answer all our questions, especially about the book of Revelation, it does seem to be the simplest reading of Jesus and Peter.

relationship to Jesus — have we trusted (i.e., placed our faith) in him? The answer to that question is not in our talk but in our walk. How we live our lives is the surest way to tell what we believe. Our good deeds don't save us. But they clearly demonstrate our primary commitments.

Jesus highlights six deeds that are typical of his followers. These aren't all the things they do but they are characteristic of the kinds of things they do. They aptly summarize the basic needs of humanity: Food, clothing, shelter, and acceptance. As we analyze these six behaviors, we find that they require large amounts of personal time and money, the two most precious commodities for most of us.

The sheep are shocked, not that they inherit the kingdom but that they had personally ministered to the King in his times of distress. They simply did not recognize him. Jesus explains why. They did not actually minister to him personally. But when they met the needs of the least and the lost, Jesus took it personally. There is some debate as to whether the "least of these brothers" are disciples or not. Likely Jesus intends for us to extend our kindness to all people, but especially to Christians (Gal 6:10).

Mt 25:41-46

[41]"Then he will say to those on his left, 'Depart from me, you who are cursed, into the eternal fire prepared for the devil and his angels. [42]For I was hungry and you gave me nothing to eat, I was thirsty and you gave me nothing to drink, [43]I was a stranger and you did not invite me in, I needed clothes and you did not clothe me, I was sick and in prison and you did not look after me.'

[44]"They also will answer, 'Lord, when did we see you hungry or thirsty or a stranger or needing clothes or sick or in prison, and did not help you?'

[45]"He will reply, 'I tell you the truth, whatever you did not do for one of the least of these, you did not do for me.'

[46]"Then they will go away to eternal punishment, but the righteous to eternal life."

The goats are sent to hell with Satan and his angels.[18] They are punished, not because of the evil they did, but the good they neglected to do. This is not because they didn't "pay their dues" to get into heaven, but because their behavior betrays their lack of commitment to Jesus, the only way into heaven.

Jesus said earlier that the wicked from Sodom and Gomorrah (Mt 10:15), Tyre and Sidon (Mt 11:22, 24; Lk 10:14), Nineveh (Mt 12:41; Lk 11:32), and the Queen of Sheba (Mt 12:42; Lk 11:31) would stand in

---

[18]Let's not be confused by this verse into thinking that God has his angels and his counterpart, Satan, also has his angels. God is ontologically different than his angels. That is, He is creator, they are created. But Satan is ontologically equal to his followers/angels. They are both created by God and will ultimately be in subjection to God.

judgment and testify against Israel for rejecting Jesus and demanding signs. Now that would sound scandalous to the Jews. This text retains that same element of shock. These goats can't believe what they are hearing because (1) they did not accept the truth that Jesus is judge (Jn 5:22, 30; 9:39), and (2) they underestimated the seriousness and thoroughness of that judgment (Mt 12:36, words; Rom 2:16, thoughts; and 1 Cor 4:3-5, motives).

**§ 140
Preparations
for Jesus'
Passion: Jesus
& the Priests
(Mt 26:1-5;
Mk 14:1-2;
Lk 22:1-2;
cf. Lk 21:37-38
in § 131)**

This is the beginning of the end. We watch as the various players move into position for this final act. In this section Jesus prepares for his part with one final passion prediction. The Jewish rulers prepared for their role by plotting Jesus' arrest and assassination. In the next two sections, Mary prepares by anointing Jesus as if for burial. Finally, Iscariot prepares by consulting with the Sanhedrin about betraying Jesus.

[MT 26:]¹When Jesus had finished saying all these things, he said to his disciples, ²"As you know, the Passover is two days away — and the Son of Man will be handed over to be crucified."

³Then the chief priests and the elders of the people assembled in the palace of the high priest, whose name was Caiaphas, ⁴and they plotted to arrest Jesus in some sly way and kill him. ⁵"But not during the Feast," they said, "or there may be a riot among the people."

We have just ended the fifth and final discourse of the book of Matthew, as indicated by the words "when Jesus had finished saying all these things" (cf. Mt 8:1; 11:1; 13:53; 19:1). These events may have taken place as Jesus' band left the city late Tuesday afternoon after a very full day in the temple. But more likely they took place on Wednesday. That, after all, would still be counted by the Jews as two (inclusive) days before the Passover, which would begin after sundown on Thursday. Of more importance is the fact that Jesus, in this fourth prediction, specifies the exact time of his trial.

While Jesus is tucked away in Bethany (cf. Lk 21:37-38), the Sanhedrin is busily working on this sticky little problem. Some two months ago, also under Caiaphas' direction,[19] they determined to kill Jesus (Jn 11:49-53). Now, under Caiaphas' own roof, they reiterate their purpose and redouble their efforts. Their very first assassination attempt goes back two years and two Passovers (Jn 5:18). Since that time,

---

[19]In November of 1990, the burial cave of a wealthy "Caiaphas" family was uncovered just south of Jerusalem. It contained ossuaries (which were most common between 30 B.C. and A.D. 70). This is very possibly the tomb of this same Caiaphas we read about in our text. Cf. Z. Greenhut, "Burial Cave of the Caiaphas Family," *BAR* (Sept/Oct, 1992): 29-36.

however, they have learned to watch out for the crowds because the common people just love Jesus (Mt 21:46; Mk 12:12). After the Triumphal Entry (Sunday), the cleansing of the temple (Monday) and the day of discussions (Tuesday), they will have to be especially careful to avoid arresting Jesus in the presence of his growing supporters. Indeed, if the people riot, Rome would be quick to squelch the riot and replace these rulers. They fear for their country and their own positions. They determine that "one man must die for the nation" (Jn 11:50).

In verse 2 Jesus says that he will be betrayed during the Passover feast. But in verse 5 the Sanhedrin wants to avoid any confrontation during the feast for fear of the people. What they don't count on is this golden opportunity named Iscariot. When he comes along and offers to hand Jesus over to them, they just can't pass that up, even though it would entail obvious risks. We are also reminded that the following events did not proceed based on the plans of men but on the sovereignty of God. These events are on the track of God's predetermined will and are not to be derailed.

---

**§ 141**
**Preparations for Jesus' Passion: Mary**
**(Mt 26:6-13; Mk 14:3-9; Jn 12:2-8)**

This event actually took place about five days ago. Chronologically it fits between the time Jesus arrived in Bethany and the Triumphal Entry (see § 128a). Matthew and Mark place it topically here, to show the ignorance of the apostles. John adds Iscariot to the mix, highlighting his greed.[20] The only clear motive we are given for Judas' betrayal is his lust for petty cash. But this event also shows how ignorant the Eleven were of Judas' true character. Because he held the purse strings, they fell in behind him in his condemnation of Mary's act of devotion.

---

**§ 142**
**Preparations for Jesus' Passion: Judas**
**(Mt 26:14-16; Mk 14:10-11; Lk 22:3-6)**

[LK 22:]3Then Satan entered Judas, called Iscariot, one of the Twelve. 4And Judas went to the chief priests and the officers of the temple guard and discussed with them how he might betray Jesus,

[MT 26:]15and asked, "What are you willing to give me if I hand him over to you?" {They were delighted to hear this andMK} counted out for him {promised himMK} thirty silver coins.

[LK 22:]6He consented, and watched for an opportunity to hand Jesus over to them when no crowd was present.

---

[20]Some have suggested that Judas just wanted to force Jesus' hand and push him into his role as Messiah. But what good would that have done Judas? Even if it worked, would Jesus have retained such a traitor as treasurer in the kingdom?! (cf. W.B. Smith, "Judas Iscariot," *HibJ* 9 [1911]: 529-544).

Luke tells us that Satan entered Judas (Lk 22:3), likely on Wednesday. Then again on Thursday evening, after Judas ate the bread that Jesus handed to him, John also says that Satan entered Judas (Jn 13:27). This sounds like Acts 5:3, when Peter said to Ananias, "How is it that Satan has so filled your heart that you have lied to the Holy Spirit?" Apparently Satan has the ability to plant ideas into people's minds and hearts that they then implement. We may never know the mechanics of how Satan influences people, but we are warned that he indeed does. All three Synoptics note that Judas was one of the twelve, as if to say, "If he was not above such deviance, you too be careful!" We must be vigilant in warding off Satanic influence. By resisting his suggestions and temptations we can send him scurrying away (James 4:7).

There have been numerous suggestions as to what motivated Judas to betray Jesus. Perhaps he was jealous of Jesus or disgruntled over the Mary incident. Perhaps he was impatient and wanted to force Jesus to institute the kingdom through a final conflict with the Sanhedrin. Perhaps he was disillusioned that Jesus did not turn out to be the political Messiah that Judas expected. Perhaps Judas was trying to turn a fast buck to replace the money he pilfered from the funds. Perhaps he was trying to save himself as he saw the inevitable and ugly conflict between Jesus and the religious hierarchy coming to a head. We will probably never know the motive, only the result, both for Jesus and Judas. We do know, however, that Judas was operating under the heavy hand of predestination (Ps 41:9; Zech 11:7-14). That is not to say that he had no control over what he did. But it is to say that he, like Jesus, worked out exactly what God had ordained from long ago.

He was promised thirty pieces of silver, the price of a common slave (Exod 21:32). In return, Judas promised to hand over Jesus at an opportune time, away from the crowds.

**§ 143
Preparation for
the Passover
Meal**
(Mt 26:17-19;
Mk 14:12-16;
Lk 22:7-13)

The Synoptics indicate that Jesus ate the actual Passover meal on Nisan 14 before he was crucified on Nisan 15 (roughly equivalent to our April). Some, however, have interpreted John 18:28 and 19:14 to say that Jesus died at the very time the Passover lambs were being slain on Nisan 14. If that is true then we have an obvious contradiction between John and the Synoptics.

One solution has been to suggest that either John or the Synoptics were mistaken or purposefully altered the text to make a theological point. Not only does this denigrate the integrity of the Scripture, it lacks substantial evidence. A second solution suggests that there were two actual dates of the Passover based on two different calendars. For example, Jaubert argues that Jesus followed the Essene solar calendar.[21] This would put the Passover on Tuesday for the disciples but on Friday for the Sadducees.[22] Hoehner argues that there was a difference in how the Galileans and Judeans reckoned their days (from sunrise or sunset).[23] Hence Jesus and the other Galileans ate the Passover a day before the Judeans did. Others have suggested that the discrepancy stemmed from an argument between the Pharisees and Sadducees. However, none of these arguments based on a calendar have strong documentary support.

There is a third solution that is much simpler. Jesus and his disciples celebrated the actual Passover. John knew that. After all, he was familiar with synoptic chronology. In fact, John 13 also describes the Passover Jesus celebrated. (1) It was in Jerusalem rather than Bethany, which had been their haunt the entire week. (2) They are pictured as reclining at the table at night, which is indicative of a festival meal. And (3) when the disciples saw Judas exit urgently they believed he was going out to get last minute supplies for the Passover meal or to give alms to the poor. These are indications of a Passover meal. Consequently, what John calls the Passover (18:28), is actually the *chagigah* (Num 28:18-19), which opened the Feast of Unleavened Bread. Was John confused about what it was actually called? No. In John's day, there was little distinction between the Passover (Nisan 14) and the Feast of Unleavened Bread (Nisan 15-21). Both terms were used interchangeably (Mt 26:17; Mk 14:1, 12; Lk 2:41; 22:1; Josephus, *Ant* 2.317; *Wars* 5.98). So it was perfectly acceptable for John to identify this special meal as the Passover. Besides, every other time John uses the term "Passover" he refers to the entire feast, not the single meal (Jn 2:13, 23; 6:4; 11:55; 12:1; 13:1). Therefore, we suggest that Jesus and the disciples ate the actual Passover meal, celebrated on Nisan 14. Furthermore, the Jews of John 18:12 refused to enter Pilate's praetorium so they would not be disqualified from the rest of the seven day Feast of Unleavened Bread, not the actual Passover meal.[24]

---

[21]Annie Jaubert, *The Date of the Last Supper* (New York: Alba House, 1965). One great weakness of her view is that her evidence for the Essene solar calendar comes from a third century document.

[22]N. Walker argues that the sixteen passion events recorded in the Gospels would have to occupy three days rather than a 24-hour period. Thus, he supports a Tuesday Last Supper in "Pauses in the Passion Story and Their Significance for Chronology," *NovT* 6 (1963): 16-19 and "Yet Another Look at the Passion Chronology," *NovT* 6 (1963): 286-289.

[23]H.W. Hoehner, *Chronological Aspects of the Life of Christ* (Grand Rapids: Zondervan, 1977).

[24]Cf. Carson, pp. 528-532; and B. Smith, "The Chronology of the Last Supper," *WTJ* 53 (1991): 29-45. F. Chenderlin, "Distributed Observance of the Passover: A Preliminary

Mk 14:12-16 *with*
Lk 22:8; Mt 26:18

[12]On the first day of the Feast of Unleavened Bread, when it was customary to sacrifice the Passover lamb, Jesus' disciples asked him, "Where do you want us to go and make preparations for you to eat the Passover?"

[13]So he sent two of his disciples, {Peter and John,[LK]} telling them, "Go into the city, and a man carrying a jar of water will meet you. Follow him. [14]Say to the owner of the house he enters, 'The Teacher asks: {My appointed time is near.[MT]} Where is my guest room, where I may eat the Passover with my disciples?' [15]He will show you a large upper room, furnished and ready. Make preparations for us there."

[16]The disciples left, went into the city and found things just as Jesus had told them. So they prepared the Passover.

It is now Thursday, the 14th of Nisan. The Passover was a seven day memorial to the Exodus (Exod 12:13-27; 23:15; 34:18; Deut 16:1-8; Jubilees 49:1-2, 10-12; Philo VI, 2.41.224 & 2.42.228), also called the Feast of Unleavened Bread (Josephus, *Ant* 2.317). Faithful Jewish worshipers gathered in Jerusalem from all over the empire. Some estimate as many as a million Jews packed the city, requiring some 100,000 sacrificial lambs (Butler, p. 524). The slaughter and stench of burning entrails and rivers of warm blood would be unimaginable.

Each home celebrated with a roasted lamb, bitter herbs (horseradish, bay, thyme, marjoram and basil [Butler, p. 524]), wine, and a dipping sauce for the lamb [*haroset*]. They would gather enough people to consume the entire lamb. During the meal four ceremonial cups of wine were passed around the table, separated by the singing of the "Hallel" Psalms (113-118). After the second cup of wine, the youngest in the house was instructed to ask the meaning of the Passover observances. The patriarch of the family then explained the story of how God delivered Israel from their bondage in Egypt.

The disciples know that it was for this purpose that they had come to the holy city, for the residents of Palestine were only allowed to eat the Passover in Jerusalem (Carson, p. 534). So they ask Jesus where they should prepare for the celebration. He sends Peter and John to look for a man carrying a water jar. This fellow would stick out like a sore thumb. After all, carrying water jars was typically "women's work." They are to follow him to his house and then tell its owner that Jesus is ready to use their upper room. This is quite possibly the home of Mary, the mother of

---

Test of the Hypothesis," *Biblica* 57 (1976): 1-24, adds a couple of additional keen points. First, there were probably too many Passover participants to have all the lambs killed and eaten in a single day. Hence, he argues for a "distributed observance" in which the Passover would be celebrated on successive days. Second, if that were the case, the Jewish leaders may have preferred to eat the Passover on the holy high Sabbath during Passover week rather than strictly on Nisan 14.

John Mark, where Jesus first appeared to the Eleven (Lk 24:33-36; Jn 20:19), where the early church met for prayer (Acts 1:13-14; 12:12), and where the Holy Spirit first descended on the disciples (Acts 2:1-4).

Apparently they had some kind of agreement already since the room is already prepared when the disciples arrive. Either that or the owner expects some other pilgrim group to request the use of his upper room, which was not uncommon. But Jesus has been in the area for the better part of a week and has had ample opportunity to make such arrangements. All of this allows the disciples to meet privately, if not secretly, away from the crowds. It also prevents Judas from "leaking" their location to the Sanhedrin.

[LK 22:]14When the hour came, Jesus and his apostles reclined at the table. 15And he said to them, "I have eagerly desired to eat this Passover with you before I suffer. 16For I tell you, I will not eat it again until it finds fulfillment in the kingdom of God."

§ 144
Opening
Conflict at the
Passover Meal
(Mt 26:20;
Mk 14:17;
Lk 22:14-16,
24-30)

After sundown on Thursday, Jesus and his men meet privately, perhaps even secretly, in the upper room of some unnamed home in Jerusalem. Like the other families who met in Jerusalem for this feast, this little band has bound together as a spiritual family for a sacred memorial (Mt 12:50). They take their places around a "U" shaped table which sits about six or eight inches off the ground. They lay on their left elbow on cushions around the perimeter of the table. For Jesus, this is much more than a festive meal. It is even much more than a Passover celebration. Jesus knows that he is the antitype of the exodus; he is the Passover lamb, slain for the deliverance of his people. This meal commemorates his imminent destiny (Jn 1:29). It is the last time he will participate in the Passover incarnationally. There will be another banquet . . . a wedding feast. But that will be another day. For now he expresses his intense longing to share this meal with his men with the Hebrew idiom, *"With desire, I have desired to eat this Passover with you."*

24Also a dispute arose among them as to which of them was considered to be greatest. 25Jesus said to them, "The kings of the Gentiles lord it over them; and those who exercise authority over them call themselves Benefactors. 26But you are not to be like that. Instead, the greatest among you should be like the youngest, and the one who rules like the one who serves. 27For who is greater, the one who is at the table or the one who serves? Is it not the one who is at the table? But I am among you as one who serves. 28You are those who have stood by me in my trials. 29And I confer on you a kingdom, just as my Father conferred one on me, 30so that you may eat and drink at my table in my kingdom and sit on thrones, judging the twelve tribes of Israel."

Lk 22:24-30

[vv. 25-27 = Mt 20:25-28 & Mk 10:42-45, see comments on § 125b].

As they enter the upper room, the Twelve rekindle an argument that has come up twice before: Which of them is the greatest? The first time they argued about this was over a year ago (Mt 18:1-5; Mk 9:33-37; Lk 9:46-48; § 90). The last time couldn't have been much more than a week ago (Mt 20:17-28; Mk 10:32-45; § 125b). All three times this argument followed on the heels of Jesus' passion prediction. And all three times Jesus rebuked them rather sternly. Surely they are a bit embarrassed when he again overhears their debate.

The Twelve have given up three years of their lives to follow Jesus and they have sacrificed much to do so. Jesus assures them that such sacrifice will not be in vain. They will be rewarded in a big way — leadership in the kingdom, special places at the Messianic banquet, and a judgment throne for each of them. However, all this is still a ways off. They are called now to continue to sacrifice and serve.

This concept is one of Jesus' most common themes. It runs counter to everything the world teaches: "Look out for #1," "Do your own thing," "Me first," etc. But Christians operate by a different set of rules.

**§ 145
Jesus Washes
the Apostles'
Feet
(Jn 13:1-20)**

As they enter the upper room, the disciples get into a little foray about their prospective positions. The argument is likely kindled over who is to sit closest to Jesus. Undoubtedly they neglected Jesus' six-month-old advice to the Pharisees about sitting in the lowest position rather than elbowing your way up the table (Lk 14:7-11).

Jesus has just given a verbal response to the disciples' debate about who was the greatest (Lk 22:24-30). He now gives a visual response. He said that he came as one who served and not as one who sits at the table (Lk 22:27). The astonished disciples are about to learn just how true that is. This foot washing is a prelude to the cross; both bring cleansing.

Jn 13:1-5

¹It was just before the Passover Feast. Jesus knew that the time had come for him to leave this world and go to the Father. Having loved his own who were in the world, he now showed them the full extent of his love.ᵃ

²The evening meal was being served, and the devil had already prompted Judas Iscariot, son of Simon, to betray Jesus. ³Jesus knew that the Father had put all things under his power, and that he had come from God and was returning to God; ⁴so he got up from the meal, took off his outer clothing, and wrapped a towel around his waist. ⁵After that, he poured water into a basin and began to wash his disciples' feet, drying them with the towel that was wrapped around him.

ᵃ1 Or he loved them to the last

John sets the theological stage for this event by noting several things. First (v. 1), the Passover is approaching. This feast symbolizes all that Jesus came to accomplish. This is the beginning of the final act. Second (vv. 1-2), Jesus loves his disciples thoroughly, to the "bitter end." Even so, Iscariot, whose heart is now submitted to Satan, plans to betray that consummate love. The contrast is colossal. Third (v. 3), Jesus is fully in control. There are no accidents here, no runaway trains. Jesus purposes, plans, and executes the will of God to whom he shall soon return.

While the disciples settle into their prospective cushions and the Passover meal is being served, Jesus unpretentiously rises from the table and wraps himself with a towel. It appears that he is wearing nothing but a loincloth in the fashion of a slave (cf. v. 12; 19:23-24; Phil 2:7). He undertakes the neglected task of washing the disciples' feet. They are appalled! It was, after all, the job of the lowest servant in the house to wash peoples' feet as they entered, before they ever started serving the meal. Foot washing saved the guests from the embarrassment of sullying the hosts' throw rugs. But the disciples neglected it in lieu of their own argument about their individual importance. One of them should have at least offered to wash Jesus' feet. But while they are busy arguing about seats, Jesus sets out to perform this humble task. How humiliating it must have been for the Twelve, knowing that Jesus was doing for them what they should have offered to do for him.

[6]He came to Simon Peter, who said to him, "Lord, are you going to wash my feet?"

Jn 13:6-11

[7]Jesus replied, "You do not realize now what I am doing, but later you will understand."

[8]"No," said Peter, "you shall never wash my feet."

Jesus answered, "Unless I wash you, you have no part with me."

[9]"Then, Lord," Simon Peter replied, "not just my feet but my hands and my head as well!"

[10]Jesus answered, "A person who has had a bath needs only to wash his feet; his whole body is clean. And you are clean, though not every one of you." [11]For he knew who was going to betray him, and that was why he said not every one was clean.

Peter objects strenuously. In fact, he goes overboard (which was not the first time either literally or figuratively). He orders Jesus to back off, saying, "You will never wash my feet 'forever,'" [*eis ton aiōna*]. Jesus replies, "If I don't wash your feet, you have no part with me." So Peter swings the pendulum clear to the other side and requests a complete sponge bath. You know, if a little is good a lot must be better. But since he has already taken a bath his feet are the only part that need washing.

Jesus is not merely talking about water and body parts. This is symbolic of a deeper cleansing. There is one in their presence whose avarice cannot be wiped away as easily as Palestinian dirt. John, in a parenthetical comment, explains that Jesus knows good and well what Judas plans to do. These words must burn deeply within Iscariot. One is also compelled to wonder what this foot washing did to him as the loving hands of the Master touched him tenderly.

Jn 13:12-17

[12]When he had finished washing their feet, he put on his clothes and returned to his place. "Do you understand what I have done for you?" he asked them. [13]"You call me 'Teacher' and 'Lord,' and rightly so, for that is what I am. [14]Now that I, your Lord and Teacher, have washed your feet, you also should wash one another's feet. [15]I have set you an example that you should do as I have done for you. [16]I tell you the truth, no servant is greater than his master, nor is a messenger greater than the one who sent him. [17]Now that you know these things, you will be blessed if you do them."

The lesson is simple. Jesus is the teacher. His students are not greater than he. Therefore, if he serves in such a lowly fashion, his disciples must be prepared to do the same. Now the act of washing feet certainly does not hold the same cultural significance for us as it did in the first century. So while foot washing may be a humbling gesture and a beautiful religious act, it lacks the same pragmatic significance as it had with the apostles. Jesus calls us, not to a single act but to a single attitude which may manifest itself in many different ways. In our day it might mean taking out the trash, cleaning bathrooms, or changing diapers. "Foot washing" translates into performing lowly tasks which everyone else avoids because of pride.[25] While that grates against our fallen instinct, Jesus promises a blessing to those who live this way (v. 20).

Jn 13:18-20

[18]"I am not referring to all of you; I know those I have chosen. But this is to fulfill the scripture: 'He who shares my bread has lifted up his heel against me.'[a]
[19]"I am telling you now before it happens, so that when it does happen you will believe that I am He. [20]I tell you the truth, whoever accepts anyone I send accepts me; and whoever accepts me accepts the one who sent me."

[a] 18 Psalm 41:9

Judas was predestined to fulfill Psalm 41:9 (cf. Zech 11:7-14; Ps 69:25; 109:8; Acts 1:20). Apparently God looked into the future and saw

---

[25]However, A. Edgington, "Foot washing as an ordinance," *GTJ* 6.2 (1985): 425-434, argues that it should be practiced as an ordinance. He suggests that foot washing in Jn 13:1-17 and 1 Tim 5:10 meet the three criterion of an ordinance: (1) A physical act which is ceremonial in nature. (2) A symbolic representation of a spiritual reality expressly taught in the NT. (3) A command to perpetuate it by Christ or his apostles. However, all three of these are questionable at some level.

what Judas was going to do and recorded it in Scripture before Judas was ever born (1 Pet 1:2). That does not necessarily mean, however, that God predestined Judas to damnation. There are a considerable number of men who were individually predestined by God in the Bible.[26] Not one of them was predestined to salvation or damnation but to a task God assigned for them to perform. No doubt, they would perform the task. But they could either do it God's way or their own way. For example, Pharaoh was going to let the Israelites go. He chose to do it his own way and God forced his hand. Jonah's biography tells a similar story. While we may not be able to solve the apparent paradox between the sovereignty of God and the free will of man, we assume that Judas Iscariot *chose* to betray Jesus and will be held personally accountable for his actions.

As interesting as such theological speculation might be, it misses the thrust of Jesus' words. He predicted Judas' betrayal so that when it came to pass, his faithful followers would know for certain that Jesus was indeed the Christ. That would be crucial in those dark days of his death when he looked like anything but a conquering Messiah. Not only that, in the days following his ascension, this prediction will serve as a reminder of their own predestined position with Jesus. Those who accept the Apostles accept Jesus; and those who accept Jesus accept God the Father.

---

[JN 13:]21After he had said this, {while they were reclining at the table eating,[MK]} Jesus was troubled in spirit and testified, "I tell you the truth, one of you is going to betray me {one who is eating with me."[MK]}

22His disciples stared at one another, at a loss to know which of them he meant.

[MT 26:]22They were very sad and began to say to him one after the other, "Surely not I, Lord?" 23Jesus replied, "The one who has dipped his hand into the bowl with me will betray me. 24The Son of Man will go just as it is written about him. But woe to that man who betrays the Son of Man! It would be better for him if he had not been born." 25Then Judas, the one who would betray him, said, "Surely not I, Rabbi?" Jesus answered, "Yes, it is you."a

a25 Or *"You yourself have said it"*

**§ 146**
**Identification**
**of the Betrayer**
(Mt 26:21-25;
Mk 14:18-21;
Lk 22:21-23;
Jn 13:21-30)

---

26Abraham (Neh 9:7); Jacob and Esau (Gen 25:19ff; Mal 1:2-3; Rom 9:10-13); Pharaoh (Exod 9:16; Rom 9:17); Saul and David (1 Sam 16:1-14); Josiah (1 Kgs 13:1-3); Cyrus (Isa 41:25; 44:28; 45:1-13; 2 Chr 36:22ff); John the Baptist (Mal 4:6; Isa 40:3; Lk 1:17ff); Jesus (Isa 42:1; Mt 12:18; Lk 9:35; Acts 2:23; 4:28); Iscariot (Ps 41:9; 69:25; 109:8; Mk 14:10; Acts 1:20); Apostles (Lk 6:13; Jn 6:70; 15:16); Paul (Acts 9:15; 13:2; Rom 1:1; Gal 1:15; Eph 3:7); Rufus (Rom 16:13); Jeremiah (Jer 1:5).

As the liturgy of the Passover meal progresses, Jesus becomes more and more disturbed. He lets loose this bombshell: One of you is going to betray me! Jesus has predicted his betrayal before (§ 88: Mt 17:22; Mk 9:31; Lk 9:44 and § 125a: Mt 20:18; Mk 10:33). But now he says it will be one cloaked in the garb of an intimate friend. He (a) is eating with Jesus (Mk 14:18), (b) is one of the twelve (Mk 14:20), and (c) will actually be given a morsel by the Master's own hand (Jn 13:26). In an Oriental culture such as this, to betray one with whom you have shared intimate table fellowship is the height of treachery.

The Apostles are shocked, saddened, confused, and a bit embarrassed (as the word *aporeō* ["at a loss"] implies). Predictably, the Twelve try to identify who Jesus is talking about. But as they look around the room they can't see a more likely candidate than themselves. With a healthy self-doubt, they each in turn ask, "Is it I, Lord?" Of course they all use a phrase that expects a negative answer. Even Judas takes his turn, using that identical line "Is it I?," perhaps so as not to give himself away. Unlike the rest, however, he doesn't call Jesus, "Lord," but merely "Rabbi." His hypocrisy knows no bounds. Jesus replies literally, "It is as you have said" (cf. Mt 26:64). This brief interaction appears to be kept between the two of them. But even if it has been overheard by the Eleven, Jesus' words are vague enough that they could be easily overlooked . . . except by Judas. Even though both Judas and Jesus know the score (cf. Jn 13:10-11, 18-19), the Eleven are still left in the dark.

Jesus was destined to be betrayed according to the Scriptures (cf. Zech 11:7-14; Ps 41:9). If Judas had not done it, another would have. But since he has accepted the role, he would be held responsible for his actions. He will be stripped of his office of Apostle (Ps 69:25; 109:8; Acts 1:20), die a gruesome death (Mt 27:3-10; Acts 1:18-19), and receive his proper place of punishment. Truly, when all is said and done, Iscariot, the son of perdition (Jn 17:12), will wish he had never been born.

Lk 22:23

[23]They began to question among themselves which of them it might be who would do this.

Jn 13:23-26 *with*
Mk 14:20

[23]One of them, the disciple whom Jesus loved, was reclining next to him. [24]Simon Peter motioned to this disciple and said, "Ask him which one he means." [25]Leaning back against Jesus, he asked him, "Lord, who is it?" [26]Jesus answered, "It is {one of the twelve,[MK]} the one to whom I will give this piece of bread when I have dipped it in the dish." Then, dipping the piece of bread, he gave it to Judas Iscariot, son of Simon.

The Apostles continue to question Jesus and each other. Peter, from across the table, motions with a nod [*neuō*] to John, the "Beloved Apostle" (Jn 19:26; 20:2; 21:7, 20). Peter wants John to ask Jesus,

personally, who it is. Edersheim's reconstruction of the seating arrangement can't be far off (II:494). He describes how cushions or couches
were placed on three sides of the table and food was served from the
open end. The table lay low to the ground and those around the table
were laying on these cushions on their left side forming a "U" around
the table. The host sat on one side of the "U" with his honored guests on
his right and left. The least honored spot was at the other end of the "U"
across the table. John lay in front of Jesus (i.e., to his right), John 13:23-
25. To his back, the position Edersheim identifies as the most honored
place, must have been Judas. After all, he and Jesus have, what appears
to be, a private conversation (Mt 26:25), and Jesus is close enough to
hand him the morsel of bread (Jn 13:26-27). Judas apparently has won
the argument about who is the greatest, or perhaps Jesus placed him in
this "chief seat" in a final attempt to win his love. Peter, on the other
hand, appears to have humbled himself by choosing one of the lowest
seats across the table. Perhaps he acted impetuously after the foot washing incident.

John leans back on the breast of Jesus and simply asks, "Lord, who
is it?" Jesus gives him a sign. He will dip a morsel of the bread into the
sop (made of mashed fruit, water and vinegar) and hand it to the
betrayer. This act is a sign of intimate friendship (cf. Ruth 2:14). Earlier
Jesus said that the betrayer would dip in the same bowl as Jesus. But by
the end of the evening, that could potentially describe all Twelve.
"Dipping in the bowl" was synonymous with "sharing a meal." But this
sign is more specific, more immediate. He takes a piece of bread, dips it
in the bowl and hands it back to Judas.

[27]As soon as Judas took the bread, Satan entered into him.                    Jn 13:27-30
"What you are about to do, do quickly," Jesus told him, [28]but no one at the
meal understood why Jesus said this to him. [29]Since Judas had charge of the
money, some thought Jesus was telling him to buy what was needed for the
Feast, or to give something to the poor. [30]As soon as Judas had taken the bread,
he went out. And it was night.

Satan enters Judas' heart even as the morsel enters his mouth. Jesus
orders him to expedite his deed, which the others interpret as the potential duties of the treasurer. As he leaves the room, the Apostles, with the
probable exception of Peter and John, are still in the dark about Judas.
Judas too is in the dark, not merely the cover of night, but the Satanic
veil of deception and treachery. John's four brief words, "And it was
night" serve as an appropriate description of the end of Judas' life. Now
that the cat is out of the bag with Peter and John, as well as with Jesus,
Judas must act quickly. He has to get while the gettin' is good.

**§ 147
Prediction of
Peter's Denial**
(Mt 26:31-35;
Mk 14:27-31;
Lk 22:31-38;
Jn 13:31-38)

The chronology at this point is somewhat difficult for two reasons. First, John did not choose to record the Lord's Supper (§ 148). Apparently he felt that it was adequately covered by the Synoptics and perhaps by his own allusion to it in John 6:53-54. Second, Matthew and Mark place the prediction of Peter's denial after Jesus left the house and headed toward Gethsemane (cf. § 152). John, however, places it before Jesus' farewell address (Jn 14-17), while they are still in the house. We agree with the Thomas and Gundry harmony that we should follow John at this point over Matthew and Mark. John, after all, devotes nearly a quarter of his book to this one evening. We disagree, however, that the prediction of Peter's denial precedes the Lord's Supper (§ 148). There is no reason to take all three Synoptics out of order at this point. Therefore, we will do two things. First, we will extract Matthew 26:30 and Mark 14:26 from their context here and place them with § 152 in order to follow John's chronology. Second, we will rearrange the Thomas and Gundry harmony by commenting on § 148 *before* § 147. A caution is in order here. When we begin shifting texts around for the purpose of chronology, we must be extra sensitive to the context of each pericope in its own gospel lest we lose the unique flavor of each in striving for a composite picture of all four.

**§ 148
The Lord's
Supper**
(Mt 26:26-29;
Mk 14:22-25;
Lk 22:17-20;
1 Cor. 11:23-26)

Four voices record this holy sacrament. Matthew and Mark are nearly identical while Luke and Paul overlap significantly. Even though we weren't there, every Christian is privileged to play a part.[27] For two thousand years now, the church of Jesus has reenacted and remembered his death. Strangely, divinely, this celebration draws us back in time. It allows us to relive all the events which follow: Peter's denial and Jesus' death; the joy of the resurrection and the hope of Peter's restitution. This

---

[27]B.B. Thurston, "'Do This': A Study on the Institution of the Lord's Supper," *RestQ* 30 (1988): 207-217. She argues that the primary importance of the eucharist is in its actions, not the elements. In other words, it is a dramatic reenactment of the atonement. Furthermore, it has evangelistic overtones in that it proclaims the Lord's death until he comes. N. A. Beck, "The Last Supper as an Efficacious Symbolic Act," *JBL* 89 (1970): 192-198, even suggests that Jesus' original institution of the supper was somewhat like an enacted parable. As the prophets of the OT taught through dramatic demonstrations, so Jesus does here with the eucharist. Going a step further, B. Cooke defends the Catholic position of Jesus' continuing presence in the eucharist as a logical necessity if Jesus continues as our covenental mediator. In other words, this is not merely a symbol which we reenact, it is a sacrament in which Jesus participates (cf. B. Cooke, "Synoptic Presentation of the Eucharist as Covenant Sacrifice," *TS* 21 [1960]: 1-44).

is the Lord's Supper; it is the Christian's celebration. As the church consumes his body, his body is united in the church.[28]

[17]After taking the cup, he gave thanks and said, "Take this and divide it among you. [18]For I tell you I will not drink again of the fruit of the vine until the kingdom of God comes."

Lk 22:17-18

[26]While they were eating, Jesus took bread, gave thanks and broke it, and gave it to his disciples, saying, "Take and eat; this is my body {given for you; do this in remembrance of me."[LK]}
[27]{In the same way, after the supper[LK]} he took the cup, gave thanks and offered it to them, saying, "Drink from it, all of you {in remembrance of me.[1COR]} {And they all drank from it.[MK]} [28]This is my blood of the {new[LK]} covenant, which is poured out for many for the forgiveness of sins. [29]I tell you, I will not drink of this fruit of the vine from now on until that day when I drink it anew with you in my Father's kingdom."

Mt 26:26-29 *with* Lk 22:19-20; Mk 14:23; 1 Cor 11:24

[26]For whenever you eat this bread and drink this cup, you proclaim the Lord's death until he comes.

1 Cor 11:26

Jesus sits down with his closest friends for one last meal. For the Jews, eating together was a sacred event. In fact, Jeremias points out five implications of Jewish/Christian meals:[29] (1) Jewish meals demonstrated deep affinity between the participants. It was a declaration of kinship. (2) Jewish meals were sacred events because God's presence was invoked through the blessing. They were not merely thanking God for the food; they were inviting him to be present at the table. (3) Table fellowship with Jesus most often indicated that you were part of his new family. Furthermore, the least and the lost were uniquely welcomed to eat with him. (4) Meals with Jesus were celebration feasts. They declared the inauguration of the kingdom — redemption and forgiveness. (5) After Jesus' ascension, the communal meals of the church remembered Jesus.

---

[28]Sadly, the eucharist has been the center of much controversy. The dismal fact is that a great percentage of the Christians killed, as recorded in *Foxe's Book of Martyrs*, were killed by other believers because of their differences over Communion. There are no less than ten debates over this simple memorial which have divided the Lord's church: (1) Wine or grape juice? (2) Leavened or unleavened bread? (3) How often? (4) Symbol or Sacrament: Metaphor, transubstantiation, consubstantiation? (5) Is a priest, pontiff, or elder required to pray for and/or distribute the emblems? (6) Are the emblems essential for perpetuating the blood atonement from week to week? (Some believe that if one does not partake of the Lord's Supper on a particular Sunday and then dies that week that their salvation would be in jeopardy). (7) One cup or many? (8) Could other emblems (such as rice cakes in the Orient) be substituted? (9) Can those who are not members of a certain church or denomination participate? Or can unbaptized children or nonbelievers participate? (10) What shall this be called: Eucharist, Lord's Supper, Communion?

[29]J. Jeremias, "'This is My Body . . .'" *ExpT* 83 (1972): 196-203.

As a result these meals were used as opportunities for benevolence. All of this is the backdrop of Jesus' last supper.

Of all Jewish meals, the annual Passover is the most sacred. But this year it gets a new twist. The *Seder* is finally fulfilled in the Lord's Supper.[30] It's been waiting for nearly 1,500 years.

The table is set. Before us we see the bread and the wine and a dish of *haroset*, a sauce made from pureed fruit and bitter herbs. The host brings out the roasted lamb. But before we eat, a young boy is to ask, "Father, what does this mean?" The patriarch of the house then recounts the history of Exodus and the glorious liberation of God's people. As near as we can tell, there is no young boy in the upper room. Nevertheless, it was likely at this point of the supper that Jesus picked up the first cup of wine and explained to his "family" the true meaning of the Exodus.

Matthew and Mark only mention one cup of wine while Luke mentions two.[31] In actuality, the Passover meal included four cups, each of which stood for one line from Exodus 6:6-7a.

Cup #1: "I am the Lord, and I will bring you out from under the yoke of the Egyptians."

Cup #2: "I will free you from being slaves to them."

Cup #3: "I will redeem you with an outstretched arm and with mighty acts of judgment."

Cup #4: "I will take you as my own people, and I will be your God."

If G.J. Bahr is correct, cup #1 would be served with the hors d'oeuvres in the main house before they ever got to the upper room.[32] Thus, the two

---

[30]For regulations on the Passover celebration see Exod 12; Lev 23:4-8; Num 9:1-14; Deut 16:1-8; also Rabbi D. Cohn-Sherbok, "A Jewish Note on *TO POTĒRION TĒS EULO-GIAS," NTS* 27 (1980-81): 704-709 and G. J. Bahr, "The Seder of Passover and the Eucharistic Words," *NovT* 12 (1970): 181-202. However, B.M. Bosker warns that the Passover meal was altered after A.D. 70 (the destruction of the temple) and more so after A.D. 135 (the second Jewish revolt against Rome) to meet the changing needs of the Jewish worshipers ("Was the Last Supper a Passover Seder?" *BR* [Summer, 1987]: 24-33). F.C. Senn goes further, stating that there are no Seder texts earlier than the Middle Ages. Hence, the modern Jewish Seder celebrations, so intriguing to some Christians, may be quite different than what Jesus and his Apostles experienced. Furthermore, he suggests that the meaning of the Last Supper for the Christian is not in historical reenactment of a Jewish Seder, but the symbolic remembrance of Christ's redemptive work through the Eucharistic elements (cf. F.C. Senn, "The Lord's Supper, Not the Passover Seder," *Worship* 60 [1986]: 362-368).

[31]The phrase "fruit of the vine" was Jewish prayer terminology for "wine." It was, indeed, fermented, and not merely grape juice. However, Palestinian wine was typically diluted with 2-3 times the amount of water to wine.

[32]G.J. Bahr, "The Seder of Passover and the Eucharistic Words," *NovT* 12 (1970): 181-202, gives a superlative outline of Jewish festival meals based on ancient descriptions.

cups Luke mentions would be the second and third cups mentioned above, served on either side of the Passover meal. Both of these cups were attached to some pretty strong "salvation talk." This makes for a pretty rich institution of the Lord's Supper. The fourth cup represented God's presence. Carson speculates that Jesus, in fact, abstained from this fourth cup (Mt 26:29; Mk 14:25), preparing for his passion. He will not celebrate the presence of God with the disciples again until the Messianic Banquet (Lk 22:16, 18; Mt 26:29).

Jesus then takes the unleavened loaf and prays a prayer of thanksgiving (*eucharisteō*, "give thanks," from which we get the word "Eucharist"). This represents his body. It is no more literal here than it was in John 6:53-58, and no less picturesque.

With these two simple elements, Jesus explains what this Exodus is really all about. (1) The bread and the wine, representing Jesus' body and blood, point to his vicarious death (e.g., Isa 53; Mt 20:28). It is now not more than twelve hours away. (2) Jesus' death will establish a new covenant. We remember the words of Jeremiah 31:31-34, especially 34b: "For I will forgive their wickedness and will remember their sins no more." The two words "blood" and "covenant" are used together only two other times (Exod 24:8; Zech 9:11). Exodus 24:8, in fact, told how the Mosaic covenant was ratified by the shedding of blood. "The Mishnah (*Pesahim* 10:6), which in this instance may well preserve traditions alive in Jesus' day, uses Exodus 24:8 to interpret the Passover wine as a metaphor for blood that seals a covenant between God and his people" (Carson, p. 537). Likewise, the new covenant was ratified by the shedding of blood. Hebrews 9:22 explains why: "In fact, the law requires that nearly everything be cleansed with blood, and without the shedding of blood there is no forgiveness." (3) The words "poured out for many" ("many" meaning "all") would kindle, in the minds of the Eleven, the massive bloodletting of the Passover lambs, which Jesus typifies (Jn 1:29). Perhaps they even connected it with Isaiah 53:12, "Because he poured out his life unto death . . ."

What Jesus is doing is clear. He memorializes his death — not his life, his miracles, or his teaching! Jesus' primary purpose in coming to earth was to die for the sins of the world (Mk 10:45). So the Eucharist is for the purpose of remembering the cross (1 Cor 11:26). But it also looks forward to Jesus' return. As Carl puts it, "We remember forward."[33] The final cup of wine, the symbol of God's presence, is still awaiting the consummation of the wedding supper of the lamb (Mt 22:1-14; Rev

---

[33]W.J. Carl, "Mark 14:22-25," *Int* 39 (1985): 296-301.

19:6-9; see also Isa 25:6; 1 Enoch 72:14; Mt 8:11; Lk 22:29-30). Beyond this **forward** and **backward** glance, the Lord's Supper urges us to look **inward**, to examine ourselves (1 Cor 11:27-32), and **outward**, to proclaim the unity of Christ's body (1 Cor 10:17; 11:17-19). It is indeed a wondrous mystery that such a fragile memorial, comprised of such common and transitory elements, has endured so tenaciously the ravages of time.

§ 147
Prediction of
Peter's Denial
(Mt 26:31-35;
Mk 14:27-31;
Lk 22:31-38;
Jn 13:31-38)[34]

[JN 13:]31When he was gone, Jesus said, "Now is the Son of Man glorified and God is glorified in him. 32If God is glorified in him, God will glorify the Son in himself, and will glorify him at once.

33"My children, I will be with you only a little longer. You will look for me, and just as I told the Jews, so I tell you now: Where I am going, you cannot come.

34"A new command I give you: Love one another. As I have loved you, so you must love one another. 35By this all men will know that you are my disciples, if you love one another."

36Simon Peter asked him, "Lord, where are you going?"

Jesus replied, "Where I am going, you cannot follow now, but you will follow later."

John picks up as Judas leaves the upper room. In response to Judas' departure, Jesus says, "Now is the Son of Man glorified." That includes lifting Jesus up not only in praise, but also in the crucifixion, resurrection and ascension (Jn 7:39; 12:16, 23). The world viewed the crucifixion as Jesus' demise, but Jesus views it as his defining deed. Now that Judas has left the room, this final "lifting up" can begin. The cross will be the beginning of Jesus' journey to "glorification."

God, himself, is glorified in Jesus' death, burial and resurrection. For in these, Jesus' demonstrates obedience to the Father, and accomplishes the plans which the Father willed from the beginning.

Jesus addresses his band tenderly, "My children." John will later borrow that same language to address his own flock (1 John 2:1, 12, 28; 3:7, 18; 4:4; 5:21). Jesus tries to prepare the Apostles for his imminent absence. This is not new information. Six months ago, at the Feast of

---

[34]We note here that Mt 26:30 & Mk 14:26 are included with § 152. These verses say that Jesus left the upper room and went to the Mt. of Olives. Thus, Matthew and Mark place this prediction in the night air *en route* to the Mt. of Olives while Luke and John keep it in the upper room. There is really no problem with two of the evangelists placing this account thematically rather than chronologically. However, Thomas & Gundry (p. 202, note b) suggest that perhaps Jesus made two predictions rather than one, Luke and John recording the former and Matthew and Mark recording the latter. If that is true, then the remarks here by Matthew and Mark should be reserved for when they leave the room.

Tabernacles, he warned the Jews of the same thing (Jn 7:33; 8:21; see also 12:35; 14:19; 16:16-20). But bad news is often hard to hear.

Jesus moves now to a new topic — a new command. There is nothing new in the command to love one another. It was imbedded in the old law (Lev 19:18). Furthermore, twice now Jesus has discussed the greatest command and verified this verse (§ 103 & 135). But the *way* in which Jesus loves is something entirely new. Paul puts it this way in Romans 5:7-8: "Very rarely will anyone die for a righteous man, though for a good man someone might possibly dare to die. But God demonstrates his own love for us in this: While we were still sinners, Christ died for us." And 1 John 3:16 (perhaps the greatest commentary on John 3:16) says: "This is how we know what love is: Jesus Christ laid down his life for us. And we ought to lay down our lives for our brothers." Indeed, Jesus declared that this is to be the definitive mark of believers, that they love others with selfless sacrifice.

Peter is still stuck back on the "going away" thing. He has been faithfully following Jesus now for three years. And they have come so close to the inauguration of the kingdom. He is not about to let it slip away now! "Where are you going, Lord?" he asks. How is Jesus going to answer that one?! It is too much for poor Peter to grasp. What will he say? "Well Pete, my first stop after crucifixion will be Hades where I'll preach to disobedient departed souls for a couple of days (1 Pet 3:19-20). Then I'll come back and hang out with you guys for another 40 days (Acts 1:3). After that, I'll just kind of float up to the throne room of my Father (Mk 16:19), where I'll sit at his right hand for an indeterminate period of time before returning to earth on a white stallion (Rev 19:11)." There is no way Peter can understand. It is enough that Jesus says, "You cannot follow me now." Peter will, however, follow Jesus to martyrdom. According to tradition he was crucified by Nero in A.D. 68. Peter did not feel worthy to die in the same manner as his Lord and so asked to be crucified upside down. His request was granted. Peter then followed Jesus to the throne room of God with the other martyrs (Rev 6:9-11).

[31]Then Jesus told them, "This very night you will all fall away on account of me, for it is written:

"'I will strike the shepherd,
    and the sheep of the flock will be scattered.'[a]
[32]But after I have risen, I will go ahead of you into Galilee."
[33]Peter replied, "Even if all fall away on account of you, I never will."

[a]*31* Zech. 13:7

Mt 26:31-33

Everything is happening so quickly. Each element of this age-old plan is falling into place with frightening speed and precision. Like

Judas, the Eleven also have roles to play, barely more flattering than his. Based on Zechariah 13:7, Jesus predicts the flight of the Eleven in Gethsemane (Mt 26:56; Mk 14:50). There are some significant differences in the text of Zechariah 13:7 (between the MT, LXX, and NT). There is also some question as to the meaning of the original context of Zechariah 13:7 (it appears to have primary references to Israel's evil rulers/shepherds who are smitten in punishment, which does not look a lot like Jesus). Yet these difficulties seem to be answered well enough by viewing this prophecy as typology. In other words, Jesus is the antitype of all Jewish leaders; the Eleven likewise represent Israel. When Israel lost their leaders, they were scattered. Likewise, when the Apostles lose Jesus, they are scattered. Not all the contextual details of Zechariah 13 apply to the present situation.

Peter, as one might suspect, objects strenuously. He claims that he will remain true even if all these other scalawags defect. Peter's little self-defense speech hardly endears him to his comrades. But when all is said and done, his denial will be much more blatant than theirs.

Lk 22:31-33

[31]"Simon, Simon, Satan has asked to sift you[a] as wheat. [32]But I have prayed for you, Simon, that your faith may not fail. And when you have turned back, strengthen your brothers." [33]But he replied, "Lord, I am ready to go with you to prison and to death."

[a]*31* The Greek is plural

Mk 14:30-31

[30]"I tell you the truth," Jesus answered, "today — yes, tonight — before the rooster crows twice[b] you yourself will disown me three times." [31]But Peter insisted emphatically, "Even if I have to die with you, I will never disown you." And all the others said the same.

[b]*30* Some early manuscripts do not have *twice*

Jesus no doubt gets Peter's attention by using his old name and using it twice. It's a good thing too; Peter needs to hear what Jesus is about to say, not so much for the present moment, but for his future ministry. The word Luke uses for "asked" (v. 31) indicates that Satan had gotten what he asked for. In other words, Peter is in the hands of the enemy. This scene is intended to contrast that of Iscariot. While their actions are not totally dissimilar, their love for Jesus is at opposite ends of the spectrum. Hence the nature of their repentance and the results thereof are polar opposites.

Satan has control of Peter only through God's permission. God will allow Peter to be sifted, but not destroyed (Jn 10:29). Like many of Satan's schemes in which he intends to harm the individual, God uses Peter's failure for purifying and perfecting him. Thus, God answers

Jesus' prayer in behalf of Peter. Although Peter fails, his faith does not. His faith leads him to repentance, his repentance leads him to strength, his strength spreads throughout the Christian community and continues to this day. Peter models for most of us the hope of forgiveness, reconciliation, personal improvement through faith, love, and perseverance. We see in Peter our own pilgrimage.[35]

But Peter still objects. In essence, he says, "Jesus, you are wrong!" He claims that he will go to prison or even die for Jesus. Indeed, he is willing to. Who could deny the devotion and courage (albeit misplaced and reckless) of a man who challenges an entire Roman cohort with two swords (Lk 22:38, 50)? How could such a devoted disciple deny Jesus? It is simple really. He is willing to stake his life on a miracle working, power wielding Messiah. But when Jesus orders him to put away the sword (Mt 26:52), he took away the only resource that Peter really knew and trusted. Peter is willing to fight for his life; he is not willing to lay it down.

Jesus' prediction gets more pointed: You will deny me three times tonight, between 12 and 3 a.m. In Palestine the cocks crowed during what the Romans designated the 3rd watch (12-3 a.m.). In fact, they even nicknamed that watch "cock-crow." Peter doesn't believe it and denies Jesus' words as vehemenently as he will deny his person in just a few hours. The other ten side with Peter against Jesus. They can't believe it either! But all too soon they will need no one to convince them just how accurate Jesus' prediction is. The rooster will literally crow a second time at the very instant that Peter denies Jesus for the third time, and the eyes of the two will meet at that decisive moment (Lk 22:60-61).

---

[35]Then Jesus asked them, "When I sent you without purse, bag or sandals, did you lack anything?"

"Nothing," they answered.

[36]He said to them, "But now if you have a purse, take it, and also a bag; and if you don't have a sword, sell your cloak and buy one. [37]It is written: 'And he was numbered with the transgressors'[a]; and I tell you that this must be fulfilled in me. Yes, what is written about me is reaching its fulfillment."

[38]The disciples said, "See, Lord, here are two swords."

"That is enough," he replied.

[a]*37* Isaiah 53:12

*Lk 22:35-38*

Jesus sent out the Twelve (Mt 10), as well as the seventy-two (Lk 10), without extra money, changes of clothes, or weapons of defense. But times have changed. We are no longer talking about local evangelistic tours with familiar neighbors. We are talking about global conquest in

---

[35]J. Thompson, "The Odyssey of a Disciple," *RestQ* 23 (1980): 77-81.

an atmosphere of opposition and often physical persecution. As predicted in Isaiah 53:12, Jesus will be considered an outlaw.[36] Thus his followers will also be considered renegades. These extra provisions will be essential under these new conditions.

The swords Jesus told them to bring have caused some concern. Are we talking about "holy" crusades here? No! Jesus makes it clear these swords are not to be used for aggression (cf. Jn 18:10-11). In fact, when Peter pulls his out and attacks Malchus, Jesus makes him put it away (Mt 26:52). Nor are these swords to be used to fight our way out of a pickle. The example in Acts is of non-retaliation (cf. Mt 5:39) and submission to governing authorities (cf. Rom 13:1-5). For example, Peter and John could have hailed the crowds to halt the temple guards, but they chose rather to go along quietly (cf. Acts 4:1-4 and 5:26-27). So what are these swords for? They are simply used to avert unnecessary persecution and dissuade would-be rabble rousers.

The disciples pick up on this "revolutionary" talk immediately. They inform Jesus that there are only two swords in their arsenal. Jesus quells their militant exuberance simply by saying "That's all you need."

## UPPER ROOM DISCOURSE

This is Jesus' farewell discourse. In the next four chapters (Jn 14-17), Jesus must drive home three critical facts:[37] (1) He is leaving (Jn 13:1, 31-33, 36; 14:1-4, 18, 25, 27-29; 16:5, 11-19, 28; 17:11). (2) The Apostles will continue Jesus' mission with opposition from the world (Jn 13:13-17, 20, 34-35; 14:12-14, 18-21; 15:1-21, 27; 16:1-4, 23-24; 17:12-22). (3) The Holy Spirit will assist them in their mission (Jn 14:15-18, 26; 15:26-27; 16:6-11, 13-14). This is one of those "good news/bad news" scenarios. What lies ahead is difficult. But Jesus' promises are simply out of this world!

**§ 149**
**Jesus Goes to**
**the Father and**
**Sends the Holy**
**Spirit**
**(Jn 14)**

[1]"Do not let your hearts be troubled. Trust in God[a]; trust also in me. [2]In my Father's house are many rooms; if it were not so, I would have told you. I am going there to prepare a place for you. [3]And if I go and prepare a place for you, I will come back and take you to be with me that you also may be where I am. [4]You know the way to the place where I am going."

[a]1 Or *You trust in God*

---

[36]For other NT quotations of Isaiah 53 cf. Mt 8:17; Jn 12:38; Acts 8:32-33; Rom 10:16; 1 Pet 2:22.

[37]G.D. Fee, "John 14:8-17," *Int* 43 (1989): 170-174.

This has been unlike any other meal the disciples shared with Jesus. He seemed so grave, so solemn. An ominous finality lingered over the Passover "celebration" and the words "one of you will betray me" kept echoing in their minds. Jesus has just told Peter that he would deny him three times and the other ten would scarcely fare any better. They are visibly shaken. So Jesus tells them to stop being troubled.[38] With two more imperatives,[39] Jesus gives the solution: Trust in God; trust also in me!

While the crucifixion and ascension will be devastating losses for the disciples, their faith can be sustained in the midst of this present suffering by the assurance of three glorious realities: (1) The enduring presence of the Holy Spirit, (2) Jesus' return and (3) the hope of a heavenly home. This "dwelling place" represented one of the rooms surrounding the courtyard of a large Palestinian home. The room may have been quite modest even though the house was huge. Hence, the KJV translation "mansion" today conjures up the wrong idea. The glory of our future dwelling is not in its size or prestige but in the presence of Christ.

[5]Thomas said to him, "Lord, we don't know where you are going, so how can we know the way?"

[6]Jesus answered, "I am the way and the truth and the life. No one comes to the Father except through me. [7]If you really knew me, you would know[a] my Father as well. From now on, you do know him and have seen him."

[a]7 Some early manuscripts *If you really have known me, you will know*

Jn 14:5-7

Thomas is determined to follow Jesus wherever he goes. In fact, earlier he urged the other Apostles to join Jesus as he returned to Judea even if it meant dying with him (Jn 11:16). But he can't follow Jesus if he doesn't know where he is going or the way he is going to get there. So when Jesus declares that the Apostles know the way, Thomas feels obligated to correct him.

Where are we going to go to "find" God? He is an omnipresent Spirit. There is no certain place that one can travel to increase the odds of encountering him. However, God will manifest himself more visibly in the New Jerusalem (Rev 21:3). Even now Jesus is returning to the throne room where God's "manifestation" is surrounded by angels and elders (Rev 4-5). While Jesus can "travel" there now, the rest of us will have to wait. But we will, indeed, find ourselves standing before that

---

[38]The syntax of this imperative verb [*mē* with the present imperative] indicates to cease what you are presently doing.

[39]It is possible that "Believe in God" is indicative, "You are believing in God." But the NIV main text seems to make more sense, translating both as imperatives.

throne, turned judgment seat. Getting there is not the problem; it is where we stand when we get there that is in question. The way to the Father is not a road but a relationship. Only through Jesus will we be able to stand before the Father on that day. Once Jesus has explained to Thomas his unity with the Father, and demonstrated it through his resurrection and ascension, there will be no more question for Thomas.

Let there be no mistake, while Christianity is open to all people, heaven is not! Call it narrow-minded, call it intolerant, call it what you like as long as you call it truth from the lips of Jesus. He said, "I am the way and the truth and the life. No one comes to the Father except through me." If someone guides a lost child out of the forest, or a drifting ship back to shore they are considered a hero, not a bigot. Jesus, who proved his divinity through the resurrection, makes an unprecedented, exclusive claim that we dare not ignore.

This is the sixth of seven "I AM" statements in John (6:48; 8:12; 10:9; 10:11; 11:25; 15:1). The first description of Jesus, "The Way," became one of the names of the early church (Acts 9:2; 19:9, 23; 22:4; 24:22). The second and third descriptions of Jesus (truth and life) are found in a number of other places in John:

| Jesus is the **TRUTH** | Jesus is the **LIFE** |
|---|---|
| Jn 1:14, 17; 5:33; 7:18; 8:32, 40, 44-46; 18:23, 37-38 | Jn 1:4; 3:15-16, 36; 5:21-26, 39-40; 6:40; 10:10, 28; 17:2; 20:31 |
| The Holy Spirit is TRUTH (14:17; 15:26; 16:13) | The Holy Spirit is LIFE (6:63) |
| God's Word is TRUTH (17:17) | God's Word is LIFE (6:68) |
| "I Tell you the Truth" (24 times in John alone) | "I lay down my life" (10:11, 15-17; 15:13) |
| | Other references to Life: Bread of (6:33-35, 47-54), Water of (4:14), Light of (8:12) |

Jn 14:8-14

⁸Philip said, "Lord, show us the Father and that will be enough for us."

⁹Jesus answered: "Don't you know me, Philip, even after I have been among you such a long time? Anyone who has seen me has seen the Father. How can you say, 'Show us the Father'? ¹⁰Don't you believe that I am in the Father, and that the Father is in me? The words I say to you are not just my own. Rather, it is the Father, living in me, who is doing his work. ¹¹Believe me when I say that I am in the Father and the Father is in me; or at least believe on the evidence of the miracles themselves. ¹²I tell you the truth, anyone who has faith in me will do what I have been doing. He will do even greater things than these, because I am

going to the Father. [13]And I will do whatever you ask in my name, so that the Son may bring glory to the Father. [14]You may ask me for anything in my name, and I will do it."

Next we find Philip questioning Jesus.[40] We get three glimpses of Philip in John. He was one of the first to follow Jesus clear back in the days of John the Baptist (Jn 1:43-46). His first act of devotion to Jesus was to lead him to Nathanael. A couple of years later it was Philip whom Jesus tested at the feeding of the five thousand by asking how they would feed all these people (Jn 6:5-7). Finally, in John 12:21, the Greeks who wanted to see Jesus petitioned Philip to take them to him.

Philip wants a visual glimpse of God. He is probably thinking in terms of a vision like Ezekiel's (1-2) or Isaiah's (6) or even Moses' (Exod 33:18-23). But Jesus gives him nothing more than he needs and nothing less than himself. To see Jesus is to see the Father (Heb 1:3). Granted, Jesus' incarnational form is not nearly as striking as these visions of God. Then again, his incarnational form was not nearly as striking as his own non-incarnational visions (Isa 11:3-5; Ezek 40:3; Dan 10:6; Rev 1:12-16). Nevertheless, what is needed here is not a striking vision but an accurate revelation of the character, purpose and acts of God. These are represented with striking clarity in Jesus' incarnational ministry through his words (v. 10) and his works (v. 11), both of which come directly from the Father (Jn 5:18-23, 36-39; 8:41-42; 10:30-32, 37-38; 12:49-50). Throughout John, the miracles of Jesus are portrayed as evidence for his claims (Jn 9:31-33; 10:37-38; 11:39-43; 20:30-31; cf. Acts 2:22; 2 Cor 12:12).

Jesus' unity with the Father is a wondrous thing (Jn 1:18; 10:38; 14:10, 20; 17:21). But even more wondrous is his solidarity with his followers. As Jesus performed his Father's will, his Father empowered him supernaturally. Likewise, when we carry out Jesus' marching orders, the power of the Father flows through him to us. In fact, Jesus said that the works of the disciples would even be greater than his own works. Now, part of Jesus' work was performing miracles (v. 11). And there is as strong a connection in the book of Acts between prayer and miracles as there is here (cf. Acts 4:31; 6:6-7; 8:15; 9:11, 40-41; 10:4; 11:5; 12:5; 13:3; 16:25-34; 28:8). But it is unlikely that Jesus only has miracles in mind when he says the Apostles will do greater works than he himself

---

[40]J.M. Reese points out that there is a consistent three-part pattern in John 13-16 where Jesus gives a revelation, a disciple superficially questions what he means and then Jesus clarifies the statement ("Literary Structure of John 13:31-14:31; 16:5-6, 16-33," *CBQ* 34 [1972]: 321-331).

has done. After all, what greater miracle could there be than raising a person from the dead? And Jesus did three of these (excluding his own), while the "greatest" Apostles, Peter and Paul, only had one each (Acts 9:40-41; 20:10). Certainly, the greatness of Jesus' followers would not be in the number or character of their miracles but in the number and character of their converts. How great indeed are the works of those who break the barriers of geography and ethnicity to bring to Christ people from every tongue and tribe.

In order to accomplish this great work, Jesus promises that he, himself, would answer our prayers no matter how great the request. This is not a blank check to satisfy our whimsical desires. There are some parameters around Jesus' promise from parallel passages. We must ask in faith (Mt 21:22), in agreement with other believers (Mt 18:19), in Jesus' name (Jn 14:13-16; 16:23-26), according to his will (1 John 5:14-15), while obeying his Word (Jn 15:7; 1 John 3:22) and bearing fruit for him (Jn 15:16). The promise does not apply where we ask selfishly or with the wrong motives (Mk 10:35; James 4:2-3). But certainly God will grant our requests when we pray for things he told us to ask for. So what shall we request? Jesus told us to ask for at least three things: The Holy Spirit (Lk 11:13), workers in the harvest (Mt 9:38), and wisdom (James 1:5). Our greatest error is not that we ask inappropriately or that we ask for the wrong things, but that we don't ask at all (Lk 11:9; Eph 3:20; James 4:2).

Jn 14:15-21

[15]"If you love me, you will obey what I command. [16]And I will ask the Father, and he will give you another Counselor to be with you forever — [17]the Spirit of truth. The world cannot accept him, because it neither sees him nor knows him. But you know him, for he lives with you and will be[a] in you. [18]I will not leave you as orphans; I will come to you. [19]Before long, the world will not see me anymore, but you will see me. Because I live, you also will live. [20]On that day you will realize that I am in my Father, and you are in me, and I am in you. [21]Whoever has my commands and obeys them, he is the one who loves me. He who loves me will be loved by my Father, and I too will love him and show myself to him."

[a]17 Some early manuscripts *and is*

A Christian, in essence, is one who loves Jesus. We have used our religious exercises (such as offerings, church attendance, and dress), as a barometer of love for Christ. While religious devotion *may* fulfill the greatest commandment, it hardly touches the second greatest — to love our neighbor as ourself. If Jesus is correct, this second command will have primary emphasis on Judgment Day (Mt 25:31-46). After all, the best barometer of our love for God is our love for his children.

Those whose love for Christ is validated by their obedience are granted a most precious gift, the Holy Spirit (Acts 5:32). He is called the Counselor [lit., *paraklētos* — one called alongside to assist or succor]. The indwelling of the Holy Spirit was reserved for Christians (Jn 7:39-40). He actually enters our bodies (Rom 8:9-11; 1 Cor 6:19), and marks us as God's possession (2 Cor 1:22; Eph 1:13; 4:30). Through him we are sanctified (Rom 15:16; 2 Thess 2:13), taught (1 Cor 2:10-16; Eph 1:17-18; 1 Jn 2:27), guided (Rom 8:14; Gal 5:18), and strengthened (Jn 14:26). Through him we receive adoption (Rom 8:12-17), gifts with which we serve the church (Rom 12:6-8; 1 Cor 12:7-11; Eph 4:11-13), and fruit for the glory of God (Gal 5:22-23). He intercedes for us when we don't know how to pray (Rom 8:26), and refreshes us when we are downcast (Acts 3:19 [cf. Acts 2:38]; John 7:38-39; Isa 40:1-2; 41:17-20; 44:1-5; 54:11-17; 55:1-5; Heb 4:1-11). Even this brief job description of the Holy Spirit makes one want to shout with thankful praise! The Christian community must be cautious not to allow contention over miraculous gifts to overshadow the beauty and necessity of the Holy Spirit in the life of every believer.

The Apostles are going to lose Jesus in a "little while" (cf. Jn 7:33; 12:35; 13:33; 16:16-19). This will be a devastating blow. They will lose their teacher, their guide, their empowerment. However, all they lose when Jesus leaves will be replaced when the Spirit comes. In fact, the book of Acts, the continuing story of Jesus (Acts 1:1), is not so much the Acts of the Apostles as it is the Acts of the Holy Spirit. He is "another" [*allon*] helper of the same nature and ability as Jesus. It is clear in Acts that the world knows nothing of this marvelous gift (cf. Acts 2:6ff) because it operates on the earthly plane. Because the Holy Spirit can't be dissected or marketed he is rejected by the worldly person (1 Cor 2:14). Yet verses 19-20 make it clear that we, in our bodies, participate in the unity of the Trinity through the indwelling of the Spirit. We are, indeed, partakers of the divine nature (2 Pet 1:4).

²²Then Judas (not Judas Iscariot) said, "But, Lord, why do you intend to show yourself to us and not to the world?"

²³Jesus replied, "If anyone loves me, he will obey my teaching. My Father will love him, and we will come to him and make our home with him. ²⁴He who does not love me will not obey my teaching. These words you hear are not my own; they belong to the Father who sent me.

²⁵"All this I have spoken while still with you. ²⁶But the Counselor, the Holy Spirit, whom the Father will send in my name, will teach you all things and will remind you of everything I have said to you. ²⁷Peace I leave with you; my peace I give you. I do not give to you as the world gives. Do not let your hearts be troubled and do not be afraid."

Jn 14:22-27

A third question springs from the table by a third relatively obscure Apostle — the *other* Judas, also known as Thaddaeus (Mt 10:3; Mk 3:18) or Lebbaeus. Still thinking about a political kingdom, he can't understand why Jesus wouldn't manifest himself to the entire country. Wouldn't a king, after all, want a wildly publicized coronation?! Jesus scarcely acknowledges that Judas even spoke. Instead of answering his question, Jesus reiterates the points that Judas obviously missed:

1. Love is shown by obedience.
2. Those that love Jesus have a home with God. However, the home Jesus described to Thomas was a future "heavenly" one. The home promised to Judas is a present earthly one through the indwelling of the Holy Spirit.
3. The Father, the Son and the Holy Spirit are essentially one in character, quality and purpose.
4. The Holy Spirit will continue the ministry of Jesus after he leaves.

Part of the Holy Spirit's continued ministry is to establish Apostolic doctrine (Acts 2:42). In order to accomplish that, the Apostles will need "divine recall" of the words and acts of Jesus (cf. Jn 16:13). Even more, the Holy Spirit will interpret and apply those words and actions for the Apostles, especially when they stand to preach (Mt 10:19-20). Eventually this Apostolic doctrine was written down, through the inspiration of the Holy Spirit, for successive generations of Christians. Although the process was a bit more complex than we have time to describe here, we basically believe that the twenty-seven books of the NT comprise that Apostolic doctrine. It is the core message of the faith. While it is not all Jesus said or did, or even all that the Apostles taught about him, it is all that is needed for the church to exist, grow, and endure until Christ returns for his bride.

With verse 27 Jesus returns to verse one: "Let not your hearts be troubled." The next couple of days will be fairly traumatic for the Twelve. They will run from Jesus in his crucible hour and then watch from a distance as he is beaten and crucified. Then their joy at the resurrection will turn again to consternation at the ascension. Their road ahead leads to rejection, mocking, beatings, and for all but John, martyrdom. Yet Jesus offers them peace. Not peace without tribulation, but in the midst of it. That offer continues to extend to each of his followers. Because we have the Holy Spirit in us, because we have the hope of a home with God, and because we are confident in the return of Christ, these brief and momentary afflictions are palatable, almost pleasurable, for what they promise to bring (Rom 8:18, 22-23).

[28]"You heard me say, 'I am going away and I am coming back to you.' If you loved me, you would be glad that I am going to the Father, for the Father is greater than I. [29]I have told you now before it happens, so that when it does happen you will believe. [30]I will not speak with you much longer, for the prince of this world is coming. He has no hold on me, [31]but the world must learn that I love the Father and that I do exactly what my Father has commanded me.

"Come now; let us leave."

Jn 14:28-31

Jesus has already twice described his imminent exodus and return (14:2-3, 18-19). The disciples should be happy for Jesus' "homecoming." But they are too overwhelmed with their own loss to rejoice in Jesus' gain. Even so, Jesus doesn't tell them all this so they can rejoice with him, but so they can be assured that Jesus knows what he is talking about.[41]

Satan's onslaught is only hours away. He will conquer Judas Iscariot, defeat Peter and the other Apostles, and have his way with the body of Jesus. Even though it looks pretty bad, the truth is that Satan has no power over Jesus. He was unable to tempt him in the wilderness, and he will be unable to defeat him on the cross or hold him in the tomb. Satan doesn't have the power to influence Jesus and he has no accusation to make against him. Jesus dies, not because of Satan's power, but because of God's will.

Having said this, it is now time to leave. But we still have three chapters of this upper room discourse left! The remaining three chapters only take about ten minutes to read. Even though this is likely only a summary of what Jesus said, we are probably not looking at an extended discourse. Jesus apparently continues to talk as they linger a few minutes in the upper room to sweep up after supper, collect their things, and put on their tunics before going out into the night air. Jesus will continue talking as they march through the streets of Jerusalem to the Kidron Valley (Jn 18:1). That gives him ample time to get all this in before his private prayer in the garden.

This chapter can be divided into three parts: (a) Unity with Jesus (allegory of the Vine), vv. 1-8; (b) Unity with other believers, vv. 9-17; and (c) Opposition from the World, vv. 18-27. Our unity with Jesus is, in fact, the basis of both our unity with other believers and the opposition we get from the world.

**§ 150a**
**The Vine and**
**the Branches**
**(Jn 15:1-17)**

---

[41]Tenney (p. 149) says, "Throughout the Gospel the necessity of believing is emphasized (Jn 1:50; 3:12, 15; 4:21, 41; 5:24, 44, 46; 6:29, 35, 47, 64; 7:38; 8:24, 45; 9:35; 10:38; 11:25, 40; 12:37, 44; 13:19; 14:1, 11; 16:31; 17:20; 20:27)."

This opening paragraph is an allegory based on common horticultural practices in Palestine. Vineyards were one of their major cash crops. Therefore, the lessons drawn from the vine would be obvious and picturesque to the Eleven. As we interpret such an allegory, distanced as we are by time and culture, we must concentrate on its key components: The vine, the branches and the gardener. The job of the vine is to provide the necessary "juice" to the branches so that they can bear fruit (vv. 4-5, 7). The job of the branch is to stay connected to the vine through which it naturally bears fruit (vv. 4-5, 8). The job of the gardener (lit., "farmer") is to cut off fruitless branches and prune fruitful branches (vv. 1-2, 6). Coming on the heels of Judas' desertion, this allegory has powerful implications for the Twelve.

This passage is a real warning to the Eleven. They must take care that neither they nor their converts become "dead wood." Any explanation of this text which minimizes Jesus' warning because of his previous promise of a believer's security (Jn 10:28) is misleading and potentially dangerous. Paul also offers a horticultural allegory which is quite similar to this one (Rom 11:11-24). He says that the branches, ingrafted by faith, could, in fact, be lopped off if they fell into unbelief (Rom 11:20-22).[42] Christians must take seriously Jesus' warning.

Jn 15:1-8

¹"I am the true vine, and my Father is the gardener. ²He cuts off every branch in me that bears no fruit, while every branch that does bear fruit he prunes[a] so that it will be even more fruitful. ³You are already clean because of the word I have spoken to you. ⁴Remain in me, and I will remain in you. No branch can bear fruit by itself; it must remain in the vine. Neither can you bear fruit unless you remain in me.

⁵"I am the vine; you are the branches. If a man remains in me and I in him, he will bear much fruit; apart from me you can do nothing. ⁶If anyone does not remain in me, he is like a branch that is thrown away and withers; such branches are picked up, thrown into the fire and burned. ⁷If you remain in me and my words remain in you, ask whatever you wish, and it will be given you. ⁸This is to my Father's glory, that you bear much fruit, showing yourselves to be my disciples."

ᵃ2 The Greek for *prunes* also means *cleans*

The vine was a common symbol of Israel (Ps 80:8-9, 14; Isa 5:1-7; Ezek 17:8). In fact, the Maccabeans of c. 150 B.C. inscribed it on their

---

[42]R.A. Peterson, "The Perseverance of the Saints," *Pres* 17/2 (1991): 95-112, argues that the branches that were cut off were never believers, that is, they were not actually "in" Christ (contra v. 2). He suggests that anyone who professes faith in Christ but either does not produce fruit or does not persevere in Christ was never a real believer. At this point, however, the distinction between Calvinism and Arminianism is merely a definition of terms.

coins to represent their nation. And Herod the Great, restoring the Jerusalem temple in 19 B.C., had a large vine of gold hung around the entrance to the Holy Place. Jesus has just instituted the Lord's Supper, complete with the "fruit of the vine." All this adds to the powerful picture that Jesus is about to paint for his disciples. This eucharistic celebration will be one of the most meaningful ways that believers can commemorate and consecrate their connection with the Vine.

It was important that the vines be pruned. Grapes only grow on the new branches, not on the woody stocks. Hence, every year the excess stock was cut off so that the vine could spend its strength on growing fruit rather than useless wood. Now some of these stocks could put out great vines, but the vines put out no fruit. These branches were completely cut off and thrown in a pile. Unfortunately, this "wood" was of such poor quality that nothing could be made from it except a good bonfire.

Like a good gardener, God refuses to allow "dead wood" in his vineyard. Those who by external appearances look like Christians, but bear no fruit, will be cut off. The combination of the words "cut off," "thrown" and "fire" is a pretty good picture of judgment (Mt 3:10; 7:19; Rev 20:14-15).[43] The word "clean" reminds us of John 13:10, "And you are clean, though not every one of you." Judas still looms in the background.

Even those who do bear fruit, however, are subject to the painful but essential process of pruning. Sometimes pruning takes place through difficult trials that one is forced to face. But verse 3 seems to indicate that this pruning, which Jesus now calls a cleansing, takes place through Jesus' words. For the Apostles, they were oral. For us, they are written. But the result is the same. The words of Jesus cut away all that is unfruitful in our lives (cf. Heb 4:12).

One question remains: How do we "abide in Jesus?" The two part answer is given in verse 7. We hang onto the words of Jesus and we pray. Although this is easier said than done, the concept is really very

---

[43]J.C. Dillow, "Abiding is Remaining in Fellowship: Another Look at John 15:1-6," *BibSac* 147 (1990): 44-53, cogently argues that the branches "in" Jesus (v. 2) are indeed Christians. After all, each of the 16 uses of "in me" in John's gospel refer to intimate fellowship with Jesus or Jesus' fellowship with the Father. He goes on to argue, however, that the separation from the vine is not damnation, but temporal discipline of a wandering child. He goes further to posit that in v. 2, the verb *airō* does not indicate separation from Christ but tender care by God, who "lifts up" struggling branches so they can bear fruit. This interpretation, however, fits neither the language of the allegory (cf. Mt 3:12; 5:22; 18:8-9; 25:41; 2 Thess 1:7-8; Rev 20:15) nor its historic background.

simple. Through Bible study, memorization and preaching/teaching, we fill our minds with the Word of Christ. Through faithful petitions to God we are granted the faith and endurance we need to cling to the Vine. [For comments on v. 7, cf. 14:13, § 149, p. 234]. In his first letter, John adds a third step: Obeying God's commands (1 Jn 2:3-6, 27; 5:1-4). While there may be other ways which help us cling to Christ, these three remain the God-given staples of our spiritual sustenance. Thus, in this context, the words "faith," "love," and "obedience" are practical synonyms.

By clinging to Christ we will bear fruit. It is not automatic but it is inevitable. That is to say, although it will require effort on our part, there is no question that all true disciples are fruitful. Just as branches connected to a vine produce grapes, so a Christian connected to Jesus bears fruit. This fruit includes such things as Christian character (Gal 5:22), righteous living and deeds of kindness (Eph 5:9), converts (Rom 1:13), and praise offered up to God (Heb 13:15), (cf. Mt 7:16-20; 12:33; 13:8, 23; Rom 7:4; 2 Cor 9:10; Eph 5:9; Col 1:6; Heb 12:11; James 3:18).

Jn 15:9-17

⁹"As the Father has loved me, so have I loved you. Now remain in my love. ¹⁰If you obey my commands, you will remain in my love, just as I have obeyed my Father's commands and remain in his love. ¹¹I have told you this so that my joy may be in you and that your joy may be complete. ¹²My command is this: Love each other as I have loved you. ¹³Greater love has no one than this, that he lay down his life for his friends. ¹⁴You are my friends if you do what I command. ¹⁵I no longer call you servants, because a servant does not know his master's business. Instead, I have called you friends, for everything that I learned from my Father I have made known to you. ¹⁶You did not choose me, but I chose you and appointed you to go and bear fruit — fruit that will last. Then the Father will give you whatever you ask in my name. ¹⁷This is my command: Love each other."

Perhaps the key word for Christianity is love. We're not talking about mere sentimentality, but self-sacrificing commitment for the good of another. It is the mark by which Christians will be recognized (Jn 13:34-35). If we don't love our brothers, it is a sure sign that we really don't love God either (1 Jn 4:20-21). Of course, Jesus was the perfect example of love; we are instructed to imitate him. His love was characterized by two things: (1) Absolute obedience to God (v. 10), and (2) laying down his life (v. 13).

If we seriously strive to imitate Jesus' love we must do two things. First, we must obey his commands implicitly. That doesn't mean we will flawlessly carry out every injunction he ever gave. However, we certainly cannot afford to be negligent in this primary command to love one another (cf. 13:34). This makes church squabbles and competition between preachers frightening breaches of the Christian ethic. Second, we will lay down our lives for others (1 Jn 3:16). Most of us gladly say that we would lay down our lives (especially for Jesus and our family) since we know that it is only a remote possibility. But we are not called to die as Jesus died.[44] Rather, we are called to live as he lived (1 Jn 3:17). That includes things like paying medical bills of those who will never repay us, visiting widows, adopting children, housing those who are traveling or who have been evicted, etc. Indeed, living for others is much more difficult than dying for them.

This kind of self-sacrificing love comes at a price. It also comes with a reward. Jesus promised three things for those who obey his command of love. (1) They would be filled with Jesus' joy (v. 11). Right now, Jesus is headed to the cross. You wouldn't expect him to be particularly jovial. But he *is* filled with a deep sense of satisfaction and peace. He knows that he is in the center of his Father's will and will soon be at his side. That reward is worth the cost. (2) Jesus is now a friend of the disciples, not merely their Master (vv. 14-15). He has shared with them his intimate feelings and plans. This kind of openness characterizes friendship. When we do what Jesus commands, we too enter his circle of friends. We have fellowship with Jesus that is deep and rich and full. The reward is worth the cost. (3) Jesus answers our prayers (v. 16b, cf. v. 7 & 14:13). We have influence with the Creator of the universe. Again, the reward is worth the cost!

Lest we feel particularly proud of ourselves for attaining such rewards, we are reminded in v. 16 that all our goodness is based in God's graciousness. He is the one that called us in the first place (Jn 6:44). He is the one that sustains us in our faith (Jn 10:28). He is the one that empowers us to bear fruit (Jn 15:5). All our goodness and all our product is merely a testimony to the wondrous grace of God (Jn 15:8)!

---

[18]"If the world hates you, keep in mind that it hated me first. [19]If you belonged to the world, it would love you as its own. As it is, you do not belong to the world, but I have chosen you out of the world. That is why the world hates you."

**§ 150b**
**Opposition**
**from the World**
**(Jn 15:18-16:4)**

Fellowship with Jesus (vv. 1-8) will inevitably lead to three things: (1) bearing fruit (vv. 2, 4, 5, 8); (2) loving people (vv. 9-17); and (3) persecution (vv. 18-25; cf. Mk 13:9; Lk 21:12). We like the idea of bearing fruit. We put up with the responsibility of loving others. But we generally loathe the prospect of persecution, although it comes with the territory. If

---

[44]Jesus' vicarious death seems to be alluded to here in verse thirteen by the preposition *hyper*, meaning "in place of" or "instead of."

you follow Jesus, you will be persecuted. It is really very simple. If you are affiliated with Jesus, the world will treat you the same way it treated him (cf. 13:16; 15:20). On the other hand, if you are affiliated with the world, you will be treated as an "insider." The Apostles had been hand-chosen by Jesus.[45] Indeed, all Christians have been "picked" by God and plucked from the world. Thus, we can expect persecution.

If this is true, then why is the church (of America) not persecuted? There are at least three valid answers. First, Jesus explained that perse-cution was not only physical (Mt 5:11-12), but may include slander, ridicule, rejection or ostracization. While few Christians in America are being beaten for their faith, the church is often verbally abused because it follows Jesus. In T.V. sitcoms, courts of law, talk-shows and Capitol Hill, the church frequently bears the brunt of the world's animosity toward Christ. On the other hand, the church often escapes persecution by adorning itself in acceptably secular garb and by concealing or even stripping the sting from its salt and light. To put it bluntly, the church "wimps out!" Instead of preaching "righteousness, self-control, and coming judgment" (Acts 24:25), it preaches a social(istic) gospel. Instead of confronting people with their sin, it "extends the right hand of fellowship" to a number of quality clubs.

Third, one of the major causes of persecution is the guilt a righteous life brings to those who surround it. Without saying a word, a righteous person shames a sinner. His purity testifies against the wicked man's evil ways. Such a righteous (wo)man must either be imitated or silenced. Unfortunately, it is often easier to do the latter. And even more unfortu-nate is the fact that most Christians lack the level of righteousness that galls the watching world. Their lives pose no threat to Satan's hosts nor any indictment against the secular man. In fact, it is difficult, if not impossible to distinguish between many Christians and non-Christians. That is just what Jesus deals with in v. 19 and again in 1 John 4:4-6. The world is adept at recognizing "its own." And if the world can't identify a Christian, it may be that Jesus won't either (Mt 10:32-33).

Jn 15:20-25

[20]"Remember the words I spoke to you: 'No servant is greater than his master.'[a] If they persecuted me, they will persecute you also. If they obeyed my teaching, they will obey yours also. [21]They will treat you this way because of my

---

[45]This "choosing" has special reference to the Apostles (cf. Lk 6:13; Jn 6:70; 13:18; 15:16; Acts 1:2, 24; 9:15; 22:14). But a number of references also describe God's prede-termined choosing of Christians (Rom 8:29-30; 11:5; Eph 1:4-5; 1:11; 2 Thess 2:13; 1 Pet 1:2; 2:9; Rev 17:14). See comments on Matthew 22:14 for how that "selection process" takes place.

name, for they do not know the One who sent me. [22]If I had not come and spoken to them, they would not be guilty of sin. Now, however, they have no excuse for their sin. [23]He who hates me hates my Father as well. [24]If I had not done among them what no one else did, they would not be guilty of sin. But now they have seen these miracles, and yet they have hated both me and my Father. [25]But this is to fulfill what is written in their Law: 'They hated me without reason.'"[b]

[a]20 John 13:16    [b]25 Psalms 35:19; 69:4

Persecution is never pleasant, but there are several things that make it palatable. First, as Jesus reminds his disciples, he went through persecution before we ever did (v. 20). What happens to Jesus in the next twenty-four hours is far worse than what we will ever go through. Because of what he went through, he can sympathize with our sufferings. Jesus truly does understand! What's more, as we share in his sufferings we also share in his power (Phil 3:10-11) and his inheritance (Rom 8:17). Second, there is a reward at the end of the road. Even now we have a personal relationship with God and forgiveness of our sins that the world lacks (vv. 21-25). But Jesus is coming, and with him judgment (as is implied in this passage). At that time our relationship with God and forgiveness of sins will be all the more sweet, and the world's lack of it will be all the more terrible. Third, our present suffering develops character and righteousness in our lives (2 Cor 4:17-18; Phil 3:10; James 1:2-4; 1 Pet 4:12-16). Persecution often comes with a high price. But what we gain from it, and become through it, is well worth the cost (Rom 8:18).

Besides all this, our options are no better on the "other side." Should we avoid persecution by rejecting Christ, there are several serious consequences: (1) Not only do we not know God but we wind up hating him. We hate God, because we reject what is precious to him (vv. 21-23). Consequently we fall under his frightful judgment. (2) We are guilty of sin (vv. 22, 24). Not merely the sin of sensual gratification or selfish ambitions, but of rejecting his own Son — the sin of unbelief. Such a sin carries with it the strictest of penalties. (3) We have no excuse and no defense (vv. 22-24). This is true in three ways. First, Jesus told us the truth so that we cannot claim ignorance (v. 22). Second, he verified his claims with unprecedented miracles (v. 24, e.g., Mk 2:12; Jn 9:32). Third, Jesus never did anything worthy of the kind of persecution he received (v. 25). This quotation borrows the sentiments of both Psalm 35:19 and 69:4. The violent attack of the Jews just a few hours from now will go well beyond any reasonable complaint against Jesus.

[26]"When the Counselor comes, whom I will send to you from the Father, the Spirit of truth who goes out from the Father, he will testify about me. [27]And you also must testify, for you have been with me from the beginning."

Jn 15:26-27

The preaching of the gospel is one of the major causes of persecution. This was illustrated over and over again in the book of Acts. It was true with Peter and John (Acts 4:1ff); all twelve Apostles (Acts 5:17ff); Stephen (Acts 6:8ff); and Paul (Acts 9:20ff; 13:6-9, 44-45; 14:1-2, 19-20, etc.).

Jesus prophesied such persecution (Mt 10:17-20), but with it came a promise — the Holy Spirit! He too would be partners with the disciples in their proclamation of Jesus. Indeed, the primary job of the Holy Spirit has always been to speak for God. He was the impetus behind every OT prophecy (2 Pet 1:20-21). He continues to teach (Jn 14:26; 15:26; 16:13, 15) and testify (Jn 15:26; 1 Tim 4:1; Rev 2:7) to Christians. In addition, he convicts the world of sin, righteousness, and judgment (Jn 16:8-11). We are not independent of God nor abandoned by him in our efforts to win the world for Christ.

Yet, the Holy Spirit will not do our job for us. We all have the responsibility of speaking out for Jesus (Rom 10:10). This was especially true of the Apostles who were the primary delegates for Christ. This special position required them to be followers of Jesus since the beginning of his ministry, even as far back as the days of John the Baptist (v. 27; Acts 1:21-22; 4:19).

Jn 16:1-4

¹"All this I have told you so that you will not go astray. ²They will put you out of the synagogue; in fact, a time is coming when anyone who kills you will think he is offering a service to God. ³They will do such things because they have not known the Father or me. ⁴I have told you this, so that when the time comes you will remember that I warned you. I did not tell you this at first because I was with you."

Jesus doesn't want the Eleven to be blindsided by this coming persecution, so he warns them to prepare for it. There was no need to warn them earlier because he was with them. Now that he is leaving, however, they need to have their eyes wide open. There will be a serious assault against them. It will be compounded by the fact that those persecuting the Apostles will imagine themselves to be doing God a favor. That will be especially true of Saul who carries on his own "holy war" of sorts (Acts 7:60-8:3; 9:1-3; 23:1; Gal 1:13). But it is also typical of Jewish persecution in the first century (cf. Acts 14:19; 17:5-9, 13-14; 18:12; 20:3; 21:27-32; 23:12-16). By the mid-nineties, Christians will no longer be welcome in the Jewish synagogues (cf. Rev 2:9; 3:9). In fact, the grandson of Gamaliel added an 18th benediction to their Sabbath liturgy which said, in effect, "May Nazarenes (i.e., Christians) and heretics die as in an instant!"

[5]"Now I am going to him who sent me, yet none of you asks me, 'Where are you going?' [6]Because I have said these things, you are filled with grief. [7]But I tell you the truth: It is for your good that I am going away. Unless I go away, the Counselor will not come to you; but if I go, I will send him to you."

It is simply not true that the disciples never asked where Jesus was going. Peter asked that very evening (Jn 13:36). And Thomas, moments later, asked "Lord, we don't know where you are going, so how can we know the way?" (Jn 14:5). The problem is not that they haven't asked, but that they've dropped the discussion before Jesus was finished talking about it. This is his "Farewell Address." Instead of considering where Jesus is going, they are wallowing in their own sorrow. They should be rejoicing with Jesus and investigating his plans.

Not only should they rejoice with Jesus, they should be happy for themselves. When Jesus leaves, they will receive the Holy Spirit. Granted, goodbyes are never easy, especially one of such magnitude. Granted, it is too much to expect the Apostles to appreciate what a colossal gift the Holy Spirit is. Nevertheless, from Jesus' perspective, both he and the Eleven are getting a pretty good deal, even if it is prefaced with a cross.

Jesus never explains why the Holy Spirit cannot come before he leaves. Surely it is not that heaven requires the presence of two members of the Godhead! The omnipresent Spirit (Ps 139:7-10) can be at both places at once, and did, in fact, come to earth in bodily form during Jesus' baptism (Jn 1:32-33). Therefore, we assume that the job the Holy Spirit comes to do is based upon the work that Jesus is about to accomplish in his "exodus." Jesus will leave the earth through the cross. The Holy Spirit comes to complete the work of the cross through conviction (vv. 8-11), regeneration (Jn 3:3-7; Titus 3:5), sanctification (2 Thess 2:13; Rom 15:16), intercession (Rom 8:26), guidance (Acts 16:6-7), and strengthening (Jn 14:26). The book of Luke is all about what Jesus *began* to do and to teach (Acts 1:1). The book of Acts continues the saga of Jesus' words and deeds as orchestrated by the Holy Spirit. Virtually all of the Spirit's work is to amplify, clarify and apply the death, resurrection and ascension of Jesus. Thus, one might paraphrase v. 7 this way, "If I don't do my job (which is to leave via the cross), then the Holy Spirit can't come and do his job."

[8]"When he comes, he will convict the world of guilt[a] in regard to sin and righteousness and judgment: [9]in regard to sin, because men do not believe in me; [10]in regard to righteousness, because I am going to the Father, where you can see me no longer; [11]and in regard to judgment, because the prince of this world now stands condemned."

Jn 16:8-11

[a]*8 Or will expose the guilt of the world*

The Holy Spirit will work on behalf of non-Christians (vv. 8-11), Christians (vv. 12-13), and Jesus (vv. 14-15). His job in relation to non-believers is to convict them of sin. Many will not appreciate his efforts and will vigilantly attempt to undo his work. For those that reject the work of the Spirit, his conviction actually becomes a legal indictment which will stand on judgment day. But for those who repent, the Spirit's conviction becomes a welcome call to the cross.[46]

He will convict concerning three things. First, in regard to sin, particularly the sin of unbelief. Although God is displeased with sins of the flesh, he is absolutely dismayed by a person's rejection of Jesus and takes it personally. There will be no excuse for that come judgment day. Second, in regard to righteousness, which Jesus connects with his own return to the Father. How is a pagan convicted of righteousness because Jesus returned to the Father? Likely it has to do with the fact that Jesus' life was vindicated through his resurrection and ascension. He *is* the Righteous One (Acts 3:14-15; 2 Cor 5:21; 1 Pet 3:18; 1 Jn 2:1; 3:7). Therefore he becomes the standard by which our own righteousness is measured. Unless he becomes our righteousness (2 Cor 5:21), we have no hope to measure up. Through Jesus, we see how anemic our best efforts are. Third, in regard to judgment. Satan has already been conquered, convicted and sentenced (Lk 10:18; Rom 16:20; Rev 12:12; 20:7-10). He merely has a temporary stay of execution by God's sovereign will. By tomorrow morning the world's judgment will fall on Jesus. But in that very act, God's judgment will fall against Satan. The world will see just how wrong its judgments are.[47]

Jn 16:12-15

[12]"I have much more to say to you, more than you can now bear. [13]But when he, the Spirit of truth, comes, he will guide you into all truth. He will not speak on his own; he will speak only what he hears, and he will tell you what is yet to come. [14]He will bring glory to me by taking from what is mine and making it known to you. [15]All that belongs to the Father is mine. That is why I said the Spirit will take from what is mine and make it known to you."

There are many things that the Apostles could not understand this night. Part of it is that their minds are shadowed by sorrow; part of it is that certain things will just have to be seen to be believed. But after the death, resurrection and ascension of Jesus, they will be in a much better

---

[46]The Greek word "convict" [*elenchō*], has a fairly wide range of meaning. It can mean (1) "to verbally admonish," (2) "to expose to the light," (3) "to refute or confute," (4) or "to convict and punish." Which of these definitions applies to a particular individual depends on that person's response to the Holy Spirit's conviction.

[47]D.A. Carson, "The Function of the Paraclete in John 16:7-11," *JBL* 98/4 (1979): 547-566.

position to understand. The problem is that Jesus will no longer be available to explain it to them. The solution will be, once again, the presence of the Holy Spirit (Jn 14:26; 15:26; 16:7).

It is particularly important for the Apostles to receive such divine and clear guidance. As has been said [see comments on 14:26], the Apostles will be responsible for the establishment of Apostolic doctrine and the production of canonical Scripture. Therefore, this promise of objective/doctrinal teaching is directed most specifically to the Apostles. That does not mean that the Holy Spirit does not guide, direct, and teach Christians today. He indeed does! But we are taught more subjective and personal aspects of our faith, such as knowing God personally (Heb 8:11), how to remain in him (1 Jn 2:27), and how to love one another (1 Thess 4:8-9). The Spirit will teach the spiritual (1 Cor 2:10-16). This education is specifically about God's plan of salvation (1 Cor 2:6-9) and will not contradict what has been written in the Scriptures (1 Cor 4:6). "All truth" (v. 13) should be understood as "all truth necessary for the salvation message." It is not a blanket promise to the Apostles. While certain principles of this passage apply to us today, the promise is probably not one we can claim for ourselves with absolute certainty. There is a great deal of difference between the Apostles and the average Christian today. Those Christians who walk about flippantly claiming, "The Spirit told me . . ." are probably doing a disservice both to the church and to the Holy Spirit.

The Holy Spirit's task is to promote Jesus. He is not a maverick, he is not interested in making a name for himself. Just as Jesus was in constant submission to the Father, the Holy Spirit is in submission to the will and purposes of the Son (vv. 14-15). As Jesus' sole objective was to glorify the Father and carry out his marching orders, so too the Spirit desires to glorify the Son.

[16]"In a little while you will see me no more, and then after a little while you will see me."

[17]Some of his disciples said to one another, "What does he mean by saying, 'In a little while you will see me no more, and then after a little while you will see me,' and 'Because I am going to the Father'?" [18]They kept asking, "What does he mean by 'a little while'? We don't understand what he is saying."

**§ 150d**
**Prediction of**
**Joy at Jesus'**
**Resurrection**
(Jn 16:16-22)

This veiled prophecy puzzled the Apostles. How long was a little while? Why could they not see him? When and how would he come back? These questions are much easier to answer from our vantage point. Jesus is going to be crucified the next day and buried in a cave for three days. Afterward he will rise and appear to the Apostles for a period of forty days before his ascension. They will see it clearly soon enough.

Jn 16:19-22

¹⁹Jesus saw that they wanted to ask him about this, so he said to them, "Are you asking one another what I meant when I said, 'In a little while you will see me no more, and then after a little while you will see me'? ²⁰I tell you the truth, you will weep and mourn while the world rejoices. You will grieve, but your grief will turn to joy. ²¹A woman giving birth to a child has pain because her time has come; but when her baby is born she forgets the anguish because of her joy that a child is born into the world. ²²So with you: Now is your time of grief, but I will see you again and you will rejoice, and no one will take away your joy."

The Apostles are so shocked by this prediction that they continue to discuss it amongst themselves around the table. But they are too afraid or embarrassed to ask Jesus what it means. Now, Jesus realizes they are talking about it. While we do not doubt Jesus' prescience, he needs no divine insight to know what these guys are whispering about in their little huddles. Almost with a tone of humor Jesus asks, "Were you discussing what I meant when I said, 'In a little while you will see me no more . . .'"? They know they have been caught and that Jesus already knows the answer to his own question.

Jesus lets them off the hook by describing, in detail, the first, and perhaps the primary, fulfillment to this prediction — his death and resurrection. During Jesus' death and burial the Jewish leaders and Roman executioners will rejoice. The Apostles, of course, will be crushed (Mk 16:10; Lk 24:38; Jn 20:11, 15). But their sorrow will soon turn to joy when Jesus rose on Sunday. Jesus illustrates it with childbirth. A woman may suffer terribly during the delivery, but such intense pain is soon swallowed up by joy after the baby is born.

Furthermore, the resurrection is going to grant a joy to the Apostles that was impenetrable. They will be called to face many terrible mockings, beatings, and executions. Through all their travels and trials the joy of the resurrection is to sustain them because it is the promise and security of their own resurrection and reward. While we can't share with the eyewitnesses the surprise of the resurrection, we do share its joy. It is as significant and real today as it was in A.D. 30. Because Jesus rose from the dead, we too are granted the gift of the Holy Spirit, new bodies, a heavenly home and eternal life with our Lord and God. Such hope sustains our joy even through the greatest difficulties of life.

§ 150e
Promise of
Answered
Prayer and
Peace
(Jn 16:23-33)

²³"In that day you will no longer ask me anything. I tell you the truth, my Father will give you whatever you ask in my name. ²⁴Until now you have not asked for anything in my name. Ask and you will receive, and your joy will be complete.

²⁵"Though I have been speaking figuratively, a time is coming when I will no longer use this kind of language but will tell you plainly about my Father. ²⁶In that day you will ask in my name. I am not saying that I will ask the Father on your

behalf. [27]No, the Father himself loves you because you have loved me and have believed that I came from God. [28]I came from the Father and entered the world; now I am leaving the world and going back to the Father."

Jesus now describes the second fulfillment to his prediction, "After a little while you will see me." When Jesus returns to the Apostles through his delegate, the Holy Spirit, they will no longer need to ask Jesus questions. That does not mean that the Apostles will never ask Jesus to reveal his will (cf. Acts 1:24-26). What it means is that the Holy Spirit will guide their memories and teach them all truth necessary for establishing Apostolic doctrine through preaching and writing Scripture (Jn 14:26; 15:26; 16:13). In fact, the teaching of the Holy Spirit will be even clearer than the teaching of Jesus. Jesus often had to use figurative language to reveal that which was to come (e.g., 15:1-8; 16:17-21) and to conceal that which unbelievers would not accept (Mt 13:10-15). The Holy Spirit, however, will not need to use figurative language. He will tell them plainly about the Father (Heb 8:11). This clearer revelation will lead to a more open relationship.

Furthermore, because we have a more open relationship with the Father, we can be more free to petition him. It is not as though Jesus will have to make the request for us (vv. 26-27). No, we make the request, in Jesus' name, and that will move the Father to respond. As followers of Jesus we actually have influence with the God of the universe!

Now, asking in Jesus' name is not a magical formula appended to the back end of a prayer to make it "work." To the Jews, a person's name represented their character and authority. Thus, to ask in Jesus name, is to approach the Father with Jesus' authority based on our friendship with him (Jn 15:14-15). If we are truly affiliated with Jesus and our request aligns with his character and purposes, the Father is sure to respond. Up to now, the Apostles, as Jews, have prayed like Jews. Jesus now calls them to begin to pray like Christians through Jesus.

[29]Then Jesus' disciples said, "Now you are speaking clearly and without figures of speech. [30]Now we can see that you know all things and that you do not even need to have anyone ask you questions. This makes us believe that you came from God."

[31]"You believe at last!"[a] Jesus answered. [32]"But a time is coming, and has come, when you will be scattered, each to his own home. You will leave me all alone. Yet I am not alone, for my Father is with me. [33]"I have told you these things, so that in me you may have peace. In this world you will have trouble. But take heart! I have overcome the world."

[a]31 Or *"Do you now believe?"*

Jn 16:29-33

When Jesus says that he came from the Father and is returning to him, it somehow strikes a note of clarity with the Eleven. They are impressed that he understands their question before they ever ask it. In response, they affirm his divine ability to read people's minds.

While this is a glimmer of light from the otherwise obtuse disciples, they understand less than they think they do. First, they seem to believe that Jesus has already begun to speak clearly to them when that probably awaits the coming of the Spirit (vv. 25-26). Second, they seem to think the time has already come when no one would need to question Jesus (v. 23). This too likely awaits the coming of the Spirit. Perhaps this is a convenient way for the Apostles to close this uncomfortable conversation. After all, every question they ask seems to be misguided (14:5, 8, 22). Then they are chided for not asking the right question (16:5).

Jesus congratulates them, perhaps sarcastically, for this modest insight. Then, returning to the initial topic of this discourse, he warns them once again that they would be scattered (Mt 26:31). He says they would each go to their own home. Had they done that literally they would have fled to Galilee. But they stick around Jerusalem for at least another ten days before returning to Galilee to meet Jesus as he had commanded (Mt 26:32). When they do return to Galilee, they are not actually scattered. Thus we must interpret the phrase "each to his own home" as "each going his separate way." This accurately pictures the scene in Gethsemane, just hours away.

Jesus predicts this terrible abandonment in order to grant peace to the Apostles. How can such a painful prediction bring peace? Well, it wouldn't at the time. But after the dust settles, these specific predictions would demonstrate that Jesus was God's Son, that he and the Father were one, and that he was at the right hand of God. It would show that what Jesus suffered was not out of his control. He, indeed, conquered through what he suffered. This confidence will sustain the disciples as they in turn encounter persecution from a hostile world. Thus, these terrible predictions will *eventually* bring great peace to the Apostles (Jn 14:27). So the conclusion to this somewhat troubling discourse is: "Take heart![48] I have overcome the world."

**§ 151
The Lord's
Prayer
(Jn 17)**

What is normally thought of as the Lord's Prayer (Mt 6:9-12; Lk 11:2-4) is really what Jesus gave the disciples to pray. John 17 is truly Jesus' prayer. Cadier points out that the Gospels seldom record the actual

---

[48]With only one exception (Mk 10:49), this verb "take heart" [*tharsei*] is used only by Jesus (Mt 9:2, 22; 14:27; Mk 6:50; Jn 16:33; Acts 23:11).

prayers of Jesus (cf. Mt 11:25-26; Mk 14:36; Lk 10:21; 23:34, 46; Jn 11:41). His conclusion: We are treading here on holy ground.[49]

In this prayer, Jesus prays for himself (vv. 1-5), his disciples (vv. 6-19), and for the future church (vv. 20-26). Although this is John's vocabulary (i.e., "glory," "eternal life," "believe," "love," "word," "world"), it displays the heart of Jesus. In this final public prayer, he shows his concern for the Father's glory (vv. 1, 4-5), his own relationship to the Father (vv. 7-8, 10, 24-26), salvation of the disciples (vv. 2-3, 12), and the unity of all three (vv. 11, 21-23). This prayer is a fitting conclusion to this Passover meal and a fitting summary of Jesus' incarnational ministry.[50]

[1]After Jesus said this, he looked toward heaven and prayed: "Father, the time has come. Glorify your Son, that your Son may glorify you. [2]For you granted him authority over all people that he might give eternal life to all those you have given him. [3]Now this is eternal life: that they may know you, the only true God, and Jesus Christ, whom you have sent. [4]I have brought you glory on earth by completing the work you gave me to do. [5]And now, Father, glorify me in your presence with the glory I had with you before the world began."

Jesus likely utters this prayer in the upper room. However, it is possible that he and his men have already left the house and are en route to the brook Kidron (Mt 26:30; Jn 18:1). Jesus assumes the typical Jewish posture for prayer: Eyes looking toward heaven and probably hands outstretched in the same direction. He begins his prayer with an intimate address "Father," and a personal request, "Glorify your Son." That sounds a bit selfish at first. But Jesus only asks for glory in order to return glory to the Father. Furthermore, Jesus' glorification would come via the cross. He notes that "the time has [finally] come" (cf. 2:4; 7:8, 30; 8:20; 12:23; 13:1). That refers to the hour of his death. Through his obedience in death (v. 4), Jesus honors the Father and through his resurrection and ascension, the Father honors Jesus. That's hardly selfish. In addition, the word "glorify" [*doxazō*] means "to give honor" or "to bestow splendor." But it also carries a hint of representing one's character. In other words, Jesus came in order to represent the Father (v. 6, cf. Jn 1:18; Heb 1:3). He now calls on God to assist him in that task, by raising him from the tomb and later into heaven. This would show the disciples the glory of God through the person of Jesus.

Jesus did not come to earth merely to introduce people to God but to reconcile them to God. It is what we call "salvation." In short, Jesus has the authority to grant eternal life, not to all, but to all the Father has

---

[49]J. Cadier, "The Unity of the Church," *Int* 11 (1957): 166-176.

[50]Cf. D.A. Black, "On the Style and Significance of John 17," *CTR* 3 (1988): 141-159.

given him. Does this mean that God arbitrarily elects some to be saved and others he leaves to be damned? No doubt, no one can come to God unless God draws him (Jn 6:44). And God does predestine some to be saved (Mt 24:22; Rom 8:29-30; Eph 1:5, 11). But the Scriptures seem to indicate that God's predestination is based on three things (in addition to his sovereign will): (1) His foreknowledge (Rom 8:29; 1 Pet 1:2). Because God knows a person's heart before (s)he is born, he is able to make a fair judgment of one's destiny. (2) In Christ (Eph 1:4, 11). Anyone in Christ is predestined to be saved; anyone who rejects him is predestined to be lost. (3) Man's response (Mt 22:14; 2 Pet 1:10). The parable of Matthew 22:1-14 suggests that those who respond to God's invitation are chosen by him for the banquet. And Peter says that by living godly lives we can make our election even more secure. It would appear then that God, in his sovereign decree, declared that all who accept Jesus are predestined to be saved and all who don't are predestined to be lost. Furthermore, God knows before a person is born which choice (s)he will make.

Therefore, we conclude that God's election is neither arbitrary nor limited by his own will, but by human response. Indeed, God desires for all people to be saved (2 Pet 3:9), and Jesus' sacrifice is powerful enough to do just that (1 Jn 2:2).

We're talking about eternal life (v. 3). This is not a duration of time but a relationship with God. Eternal life is knowing God personally and intimately. He is known, not through mystic meditation but through a person, Jesus. It is through Jesus' death and resurrection that we have access to God. Oddly enough, Jesus talks like it's already done (vv. 4-5). He can do this because of his determination to complete the task God has assigned him. Since Jesus is determined to do his part, he asks God to do God's part, that is, glorifying Jesus through the resurrection and ascension (v. 5). We can only guess what kind of glory Jesus had before he came to earth. We do know that he was in the form of God (Jn 1:1-4; Phil 2:6; Col 1:15, 19). He worked with God (e.g., Gen 1:26), appeared as God (Isa 11:3-5; Ezek 40:3; Dan 10:6) and is now, again, worshiped as God (Rev 5).

Jn 17:6-12

⁶"I have revealed you[a] to those whom you gave me out of the world. They were yours; you gave them to me and they have obeyed your word. ⁷Now they know that everything you have given me comes from you. ⁸For I gave them the words you gave me and they accepted them. They knew with certainty that I came from you, and they believed that you sent me. ⁹I pray for them. I am not praying for the world, but for those you have given me, for they are yours. ¹⁰All I have is yours, and all you have is mine. And glory has come to me through them. ¹¹I will remain

in the world no longer, but they are still in the world, and I am coming to you. Holy Father, protect them by the power of your name — the name you gave me — so that they may be one as we are one. ¹²While I was with them, I protected them and kept them safe by that name you gave me. None has been lost except the one doomed to destruction so that Scripture would be fulfilled."

ª6 Greek *your name*; also in verse 26

All believers are gifts to Jesus from the Father (v. 2). Among these gifts were certain special people Jesus considered friends. These he designated as Apostles and these were allowed to eavesdrop on his conversation with the Father. Prior to following Jesus, the Apostles already belonged to God (v. 6). That is, they already had a heart bent on following God. In fact, at least half of them had been disciples of John the Baptist (Jn 1:35-51, see comments § 28).

Jesus appreciated his Father's gifts, and in appreciation essentially gave them back to God. He did this in two ways. First, Jesus filled them with his Father's words (vv. 6, 8). He refused to speak on his own or promote himself (Jn 7:17; 8:28; 12:49). Second, Jesus clarified for his followers that he was merely a delegate, acting on another's authority (4:34; 5:30; 6:38). The Apostles have now come to understand just how fully Jesus represents the Father (v. 7-8).

Jesus is leaving the world. He can no longer personally train and care for his disciples. So he asks his Father to intervene on their behalf. This is only the beginning of Jesus' work of intercession for his disciples (Rom 8:34; Heb 7:25; 9:24; 1 Jn 2:1). This is a special favor for the disciples that is not extended to unbelievers (v. 9). When God answers Jesus' prayer, the disciples will know, without a doubt, that Jesus and the Father think and act as one.

Jesus successfully protected the Twelve while he was with them, he now calls on the Father to successfully protect the Eleven. Judas, as prophesied, left Jesus (Jn 13:18; Ps 41:9; 69:25; 109:6-8). For such treachery, he earned the title "Son of Perdition" or as the NIV translates it, "One doomed to destruction." This phrase is also used to describe the Man of Lawlessness (2 Thess 2:3).

¹³"I am coming to you now, but I say these things while I am still in the world, so that they may have the full measure of my joy within them. ¹⁴I have given them your word and the world has hated them, for they are not of the world any more than I am of the world. ¹⁵My prayer is not that you take them out of the world but that you protect them from the evil one. ¹⁶They are not of the world, even as I am not of it. ¹⁷Sanctifyª them by the truth; your word is truth. ¹⁸As you sent me into the world, I have sent them into the world. ¹⁹For them I sanctify myself, that they too may be truly sanctified."

ª17 Greek *hagiazo (set apart for sacred use* or *make holy)*; also in verse 19

Jn 17:13-19

For the Apostles, this is a farewell address. For Jesus, it is a homecoming. After a long ordeal he is about to be reunited with his Father and even his own divine nature. But in his own joy, Jesus doesn't lose sight of the disciples' sorrow. They need to have confidence, once he is gone, that Jesus did come from the Father and has indeed returned to the Father to make intercession for them. Such confidence allows the disciples of Jesus to share his joy even in the midst of persecution.

For the Christian, persecution is inevitable (Jn 15:18-25, see comments there). We don't live like the world or condone its practices. In fact, we are salt and light (Mt 5:13-16). That is, our message may preserve and purify but not without pain. The Word of God threatens the philosophy and practices of the pagan world with all its arrogance, self-reliance, and self-indulgence. That is precisely why Jesus identifies the word of God as the dividing agent between Christians and the world twice in this passage. Twice he states that Christians do not belong to the world even as he does not belong to it.

The solution to persecution is not removal from the world but sanctification in the world. Jesus doesn't pray that Christians be exempt from suffering. Rather, he prays that we be protected from the evil one. This is not a prayer for our bodies but for our souls. Through both Jewish and Roman authorities, Satan had his way with the bodies of thousands of Christians. But Jesus is the guardian of our souls.

The goal of the Christian is to be like Jesus in every way. As he suffered so we will suffer. As he was sanctified (i.e., set apart — different, holy) in the world so are we to be also.

Jn 17:20-23

[20]"My prayer is not for them alone. I pray also for those who will believe in me through their message, [21]that all of them may be one, Father, just as you are in me and I am in you. May they also be in us so that the world may believe that you have sent me. [22]I have given them the glory that you gave me, that they may be one as we are one: [23]I in them and you in me. May they be brought to complete unity to let the world know that you sent me and have loved them even as you have loved me."

Jesus has thus far prayed for himself (vv. 1-5), and for his disciples (vv. 6-19). He now turns his attention to those who will become Christians through the Apostles' preaching. His primary concern is for the unity of all believers. Surely a fragmented church is a colossal embarrassment to Jesus. In North America and Canada alone there are over 300 different denominational groups. That doesn't even count all the unnamed factions within those denominations. Jesus pays no attention to denominational names or headquarters; he recognizes only one body (Eph 4:4-6).

Those who seek organizational unity through church mergers or doctrinal forums are perhaps naively optimistic.[51] Denominations are built around human personalities and philosophies. Because we have confused loyalty to a denomination or doctrinal position with loyalty to the Lord, it is not likely that we will soon drop our divisive labels or doctrinal distinctions. To merely be a Christian would be "unfaithful." We feel like we need a clearer description of God's *true* people (e.g., Catholic, Baptist, Methodist, Lutheran, Pentecostal, etc.).

We have been bamboozled into believing that affiliation is equivalent to approval. That is, if we march in a pro-life parade with Catholics then we must approve of the Pope. Or if we participate in an ecumenical Thanksgiving service then we deny the inspiration of the Scriptures. Or if we operate a food-bank with Methodists then we must all approve of the World Council of Churches. We must be warned here about two things. (1) We are saved by Jesus, not by adhering to a long list of doctrinal particulars. There are a few things that are non-negotiable: Blood atonement of Jesus, bodily resurrection, deity of Christ, etc. But most often what divides us are incidentals: methods of communion, leadership styles, millennial systems, vestments, music, etc. There are times to reject fellowship of a person who is not a part of Jesus' body. But we are never to sever the body of Christ for our own pet platforms. (2) World missions are severely hampered by our schisms. We divide our resources into thousands of tiny fractions and then try to outdo, or re-do, each other's efforts. It is painfully ludicrous. If only the evangelical church would unite its efforts, we could go a long way to reducing world hunger and suffering, translating the Bible into all known languages, determining family and religious policy in our own nation, eliminating homelessness in our cities, clothing and housing unwed mothers, evangelizing foreign students, etc. All this is neglected because we believe that if we work together someone might think that we believe the same incidental things.

In addition, organizations (such as church denominations) can never truly merge. Either one is swallowed up by the other or both lose their corporate identity to create a brand new organization with combined resources. Organizations are based on a founding personality and perpetuated by people of power within those organizations. Therefore, in order

---

[51]T.E. Pollard, "'That They All May Be One' (John 17:21) — and the Unity of the Church," *ExpT* 70 (1958-59): 149-150, argues that the unity Jesus envisions is not organizational or denominational unity. Rather, it is a unity in the midst of diversity since it is a unity patterned after Jesus and his Father (John 17:11, 21, 22-23), and they were certainly different. This much is correct in his argument, that the unity Jesus desires is individuals who are aligned in spirit and purpose, not organizations under the same roof.

for denominations to merge into one corporate body, the founding personality must be abandoned and positions of power must be abdicated with no promise of them being replaced in the new organization. Unfortunately that is not likely to happen because we generally don't believe Jesus is capable to heading up his church. Certainly he must need our help! He can do a much better job if certain prominent personalities take charge of various pockets of the kingdom!

As a result, we are probably stuck with these embarrassing and debilitating denominational divisions. But does that mean that Jesus' prayer was not answered? Is the church really not one? If by "church" we mean "denominations," then no, Jesus' prayer could not have been answered. However, if we used a Scriptural definition of "church" as "kingdom," then his prayer most certainly was answered. True Christians, of all brands, make up the kingdom of God on this earth. While denominations, with all good intent, attempt to organize and orchestrate the kingdom of God, our human efforts have been found wanting. This does not mean that organized churches are totally ineffective or should be abandoned. Likely this would eventually lead to new denominations! But it does mean this: (1) Christians need to accept one another and work together in both personal (employment, neighborhoods, schools) and public arenas (demonstrations, publications, crusades). We can only afford the luxury of fighting other Christians when we have lost sight of the true enemy. (2) Without abandoning our devotion to the Word of God and our commitment to correct doctrine, we must be clear about what is essential doctrine for salvation and what is not. We must learn to dialogue about our opinions without dividing over them (Rom 14:1-8). (3) Church officials need to be reminded that they neither own nor rule the church.

The unity of the church was critical to Jesus. We have already noted that unity is essential for effective missions and benevolence. Jesus gives three additional reasons for unity. (1) GLORY — Unity is based on the glory Jesus bestowed on his body (v. 22). Through Jesus' glory we are not only one with each other but we become partakers of his divine nature (2 Cor 3:18; Heb 12:10; 1 Jn 3:2; 2 Pet 1:4). One might suggest, therefore, that divisions arise when we lose sight of Jesus. Furthermore, our unity brings God glory. When the world sees a divided body they mock the head as being schizophrenic. (2) APOLOGETICS — Jesus said that the unity of the church would prove to the world that Jesus came from God (v. 23; cf. Jn 3:17, 34; 5:36-37; 8:18, 27, 29; 9:7). (3) LOVE — Through a united church, the world realizes that God loves his people (v. 23). For the cause of Christ, for the glory of the Father, the church must be unified.

[24]"Father, I want those you have given me to be with me where I am, and to see my glory, the glory you have given me because you loved me before the creation of the world.

[25]"Righteous Father, though the world does not know you, I know you, and they know that you have sent me. [26]I have made you known to them, and will continue to make you known in order that the love you have for me may be in them and that I myself may be in them."

Jn 17:24-26

This tender conclusion recaptures the major points of the prayer: The glory and revelation of God, the love God had for Jesus which he passed on to the Apostles, and Jesus' return to his Father.

This is Jesus' crucible hour. Here he makes his final decision. Will he go to the cross or not? We know what Jesus is going to do; he always obeys his Father. But that doesn't make it one bit easier. Not since the wilderness temptations has Jesus wrestled so strenuously with the evil one.[53] Nor has he been so alone since then. Yet, as in the wilderness, in his deepest pain, God sent an angel to minister to him (Lk 22:43). And as in the wilderness, Jesus resolves to carry out his mission. From here on out, there will be no vacillation, no more questions, no turning back.

**§ 152
Jesus' Prayer
in Gethsemane**
(Mt 26:30,[52] 36-
46; Mk 14:26,
32-42; Lk 22:39-
46; Jn 18:1)

[30]When {he had finished praying [and][JN]} they had sung a hymn, they went out {and crossed the Kidron Valley[JN]} to the Mount of Olives {as usual.[LK]}

Mt 26:30 *with*
Jn 18:1; Lk 22:39

[36]Then Jesus went with his disciples to {an olive grove,[JN]} a place called Gethsemane, and he said to them, "Sit here while I go over there and pray. {[You p]ray that you will not fall into temptation.[LK]}" [37]He took Peter and the two sons of Zebedee {James and John,[MK]} along with him, and he began to be sorrowful and troubled. [38]Then he said to them, "My soul is overwhelmed with sorrow to the point of death. Stay here and keep watch with me."

Mt 26:36-38 *with*
Jn 18:1; Lk 22:40;
Mk 14:33

The Passover meal concludes with Jesus' "High Priestly" prayer and the traditional singing of one of the Hallel Psalms (likely Ps 136 or else Ps 115-118 after the third cup). The Jesus band makes their way through the streets of Jerusalem deep into the night. But there is still much activity in the city. Many homes send out couriers to gather needed supplies for the meal. Many go out to offer gifts to the poor. Some head to the

---

[52]We are reminded again that there may, in fact, be two predictions of Peter's denial, Luke and John recording the first in the upper room and Matthew and Mark recording the second en route to Gethsemane. Nevertheless, we have placed all four evangelists together in § 147. Thus there is a gap of 5 verses in Matthew and Mark here.

[53]R.S. Barbour, "Gethsemane in the Tradition of the Passion," *NTS* 16 (1969-70): 231-251, argues persuasively that to Jesus, Gethsemane was a temptation experience like unto his wilderness experience.

temple, which is reopened at midnight to prepare for the massive number of sacrifices on the following holy day. Jesus leads his disciples out of the city through the eastern temple gate. They cross over the brook Kidron. As they ascend the Mt. of Olives they come upon an enclosed wooded area called Gethsemane (meaning "oil-press"). It was apparently a private olive grove that Jesus has permission to frequent.

He leaves eight of the Apostles at the gate of the garden.[54] He tells them to pray so they will not fall into temptation (Lk 22:40). Then he and the inner three (Peter, James and John) go to the interior of the grove. With his closest friends, and a keen awareness of his impending passion, Jesus is stricken with grief. The English translation hardly does justice to the seriousness of his suffering. Between Matthew and Mark there are three different words used to describe Jesus' inner turmoil.[55] His sorrow is so strong he feels like he's about to die. Jesus' suffering begins in Gethsemane, not Golgotha. Two days ago Jesus mentioned how grief-stricken he was (Jn 12:27-36). Yet it is here that he begins to realize the weight of guilt from the sins of the world and the imminent absence of his Father (2 Cor 5:21). These are new feelings. From time eternal, Jesus has never felt guilt or abandonment. He asks his three best friends to keep watch. They are not a military sentry to warn Jesus when the enemy is coming. They are to watch by praying, guarding themselves (Lk 22:40; Mt 26:40-41), and joining Jesus in spiritual warfare (Eph 6:17-18).

Mk 14:35-36 *with* Lk 22:41; Mt 26:39

[35]Going a little farther {about a stone's throw beyond them,[LK]} he {knelt down and[LK]} fell {with his face[MT]} to the ground and prayed that if possible the hour might pass from him. [36]"*Abba*,[a] Father," he said, "everything is possible for you. Take this cup from me. Yet not what I will but what you will."

[a]*36* Aramaic for *Father*

Lk 22:43-44

[43]An angel from heaven appeared to him and strengthened him. [44]And being in anguish, he prayed more earnestly, and his sweat was like drops of blood falling to the ground.[b]

[b]*44* Some early manuscripts do not have verses 43 and 44.

---

[54]There were apparently a few disciples with Jesus other than the Apostles. Luke's use of "disciples" (22:39) seems to distinguish them from the Twelve (cf. 6:13), according to M. L. Soards, "On Understanding Luke 22:39," *BT* 36 (1985): 336-337. This conclusion seems to be confirmed by Mark's mention of a young unnamed disciple in the garden (Mk 14:51-52).

[55]*Lypeō* is "to grieve." *Ademoneō* is only used here and in Phil 2:26. It speaks of an anguish which disturbs one's soul. And *ekthambeō* means "to be thrown into amazement or terror." Perhaps these words were intended to mirror the kind of language we find in Ps 42:5-6 or 43:5.

After Jesus exhorts the inner three to pray, he walks about a "stone's throw away." How far that is, exactly, depends on the size of the stone and one's biceps. This much seems clear, it is out of earshot yet still within eyesight. There Jesus drops to his knees (Luke) and then falls on his face (Matthew) under the full moon of Passover. In his pain, Jesus addresses his Father with intimacy. The word "Abba" is an Aramaic term of endearment that the Jews generally felt too "familiar" to use in reference to God. He then prays these words: "Take this cup from me." Look out! If Jesus doesn't drink this cup of suffering, our eternal destinies are left hanging precariously in the balance. Woe to us had Jesus not finished the prayer: "Yet not what I will but what you will." Jesus doesn't have to die — there is no moral imperative calling for his execution. Furthermore, there was no earthly power forcing him to do it (Jn 10:18). He dies by choice.

Why does Jesus ask to avoid the cross? Does that not make him weaker than other martyrs who marched resiliently to their executions with never so much as a grimace? This question has led some to say that the cup which Jesus was speaking of was not the cross but a premature death in Gethsemane. He was, after all, "sorrowful unto death" (Mt 26:38). Furthermore, his suffering led to some kind of bloody sweat (Lk 22:44), which could have been life-threatening. So it is suggested that Jesus prays for God to spare his life for another fifteen hours or so.[56]

A better explanation seems to follow this line of reasoning: First, it is not cowardice to want to avoid death or to look for another way out. Bravery is defined by a person's actions, not his emotions. Second, it is not fair to compare Jesus' death with martyrdom. Martyrs die for a cause; Jesus died for the sins of the world. He *became* sin on the cross

---

[56]H.R. Cowles, "'This Cup': What Did Jesus Mean," *AL* 128 (Apr 1993): 6ff., offers a second suggestion. He argues that Jesus asks not to be *abandoned* in death but to be resurrected. Both of these solutions free Jesus from nearly "wimping out," asking to be released from the cross. And both solutions allow God to grant Jesus' request. But neither of them comfortably account for the second half of the prayer, "Nevertheless not my will," and neither take seriously enough the magnitude of Jesus' suffering in Gethsemane. A third explanation is that the "cup" in the OT was a metaphor for God's wrath, hence Jesus is praying to avert God's personal anger against him (C.E.B. Cranfield, "The Cup Metaphor in Mark 14:36 and Parallels," *ExpT* 59 [1947-48]: 137-138). C.A. Blaising, "Gethsemane: A Prayer of Faith," *JETS* 22 (1979): 333-343, combines both of these views and suggests that when Jesus asked the Father to remove the cup he was not trying to avoid the cross but asking that God would raise him from death and not allow his cup of wrath to remain on him. Be that as it may, the cup metaphor also signifies "my portion." And in Mark 10:39, Jesus has already used this cup metaphor to describe his portion as one of suffering and martyrdom. Therefore, that is the understanding we will adopt here.

(2 Cor 5:21) and took in his own body the sins of the world (1 Pet 2:24). What troubled Jesus was not the physical torture of a martyr, but the spiritual torment of the God-man experiencing for the first time both the guilt of humanity and separation from the Father. There is no way that we can understand how far Jesus had to condescend in order to do that. Consequently we are unable to measure the depths of his spiritual torture. Carson (p. 543) says, "The pericope must be interpreted in light of Mt 1:21 and 20:28 . . . Small wonder that the NT writers make much of Jesus' unique and redemptive death (Rom 3:21-26; 4:25; 5:6, 9; 1 Cor 1:23; 2 Cor 5:21; Heb 2:18; 4:15; 5:7-9; 1 Pet 2:24)." Furthermore, the "cup" was not merely suffering. It was a common OT symbol of the wrath of God (Ps 75:8; Isa 51:22; Jer 25:15-16; Lam 4:21; Hab 2:16). Jesus is not merely looking back to Matthew 20:22-23, but looking forward to Matthew 27:46 when God's anger against sin would fall full-force on him. Finally, had Jesus marched like a stoic through the passion we could have little hope of him understanding our human frailty. It is, paradoxically, his humanity that draws us to his divinity. The writer of Hebrews recalls the weight of this prayer to Jesus (Heb 5:7).

A second question arises from Jesus' prayer: "Was there another way?" Jesus uses a first class conditional clause in Matthew "If it is possible . . ." This speaks of a real possibility, at least in Jesus' mind (although cf. Mt 26:42). In Mark it is even more bold — "Everything is possible with you." Theoretically there may have been another way to save humanity without a vicarious death. But that is mere speculation. God's sovereign will had determined that his own Son would die for the sins of the world. Therefore, in reality, there was no other choice. Jesus was determined to carry out his Father's will no matter how unpleasant or painful the consequences.

While it is not unnatural for Dr. Luke to mention either the angel or the physical condition of Jesus (bloody-sweat), the text of Luke 22:43-44 has weak textual support. In other words, it is not found in the oldest and best manuscripts. Since it is more likely that this information would be later added than purposefully dropped, we conclude that it was probably not penned by Luke but added later, based on a reliable oral tradition.[57] So we accept it as true, but not as a part of the original text. It tells

---

[57]B.D. Ehrman & M.A. Plunkett, "The Angel and the Agony: The Textual Problem of Luke 22:43-44," *CBQ* 45 (1983): 401-416, analyzes this textual variant in detail. They come to this conclusion: "An omission must be dated c. 200-300 and an interpolation before A.D. 160" (p. 403). They agree that it was an interpolation, but point out that it had to have been *extremely* early, which increases its chances of historic reliability. T. Baarda, "Luke 22:42-47a: The Emperor Julian as a Witness to the Text of Luke," *NovT* 30/4 (1988): 289-296, lists Emperor Julian "the apostate's" (c. 331-63) objections to this

us that in the midst of Jesus' suffering an angel came and ministered to him. That would be the first time since his wilderness temptation three years earlier (Mt 4:11). As a result of his suffering, Jesus experienced what Luke describes as "sweat like drops of blood." The most likely medical explanation for this is hematidrosis. It is a condition where the capillaries of the forehead actually burst due to stress.[58] This certainly describes accurately Jesus' condition.

[40]Then {[w]hen he rose from prayer[LK]} he returned to his disciples and found them sleeping, {exhausted from sorrow.[LK]} "{Why are you sleeping?[LK]} Could you men not keep watch with me for one hour?" he asked Peter. [41]"Watch and pray so that you will not fall into temptation. The spirit is willing, but the body is weak."
    [42]He went away a second time and prayed, "My Father, if it is not possible for this cup to be taken away unless I drink it, may your will be done."
    [43]When he came back, he again found them sleeping, because their eyes were heavy. {They did not know what to say to him.[MK]} [44]So he left them and went away once more and prayed the third time, saying the same thing.
    [45]Then he returned {the third time[MK]} to the disciples and said to them, "Are you still sleeping and resting? {Enough![MK]} Look, the hour is near, and the Son of Man is betrayed into the hands of sinners. [46]Rise, let us go! Here comes my betrayer!"

Mt 26:40-46 *with*
Lk 22:45-46;
Mk 14:40-41

Three times Jesus prays, "Father, let this cup pass from me." Three times God answers his prayer, "No." God could send Jesus an angel in this hour, he could promise him a resurrection, he could restore him to the heavenly throne room. But it is not in his will to release Jesus from this task. Neither our prayers nor our faith are weak merely because God says, "No" to our requests. Although this passage is not directly about prayer, we learn much from it.[59] We are called to pray like Jesus but typically wind up praying like Peter.

Three times Jesus returns to the inner three; and three times finds them sleeping. He singles out Peter, asking, "Could you not watch with me for one hour?" (Although an hour is not an exact sixty minutes it gives us a general impression of the length of Jesus' first prayer.) Likely

---

text as well as Theodore Mopsuestia's (c. 350-428) responses. Regardless of their arguments, the two become early witnesses to the widespread acceptance of this passage.

[58]Cf. W.D. Edwards, W.J. Gabel, & F.E. Hosmer, "On the Physical Death of Jesus Christ," *JAMA* 255/11 (March 21, 1986): 1455-1463.

[59]Here are some of the lessons we learn about prayer from this passage: (1) Corporate prayer is powerful. Jesus even called on the three to pray with/for him! (Mt 26:38, 40). (2) You are not unspiritual if God does not grant your request. In fact, that may indicate that you are presently in the center of God's will and he refuses to move you. (3) Often we neglect prayer for physical needs (like sleep). It is a mistake to let our bodies direct our affairs rather than our spirits. (4) Prayer gives us the power to avoid succumbing to temptation.

he picks on Peter because just a few hours earlier he had boasted that he would even die with him. And just a few minutes from now he will draw his sword and bear down on Malchus. Conclusion: He is willing to fight with a physical sword for Jesus but too sleepy to fight with spiritual weapons of war.

Try as they might, they just can't stay awake! They are fatigued with sorrow. It had been an exhausting week of great emotional peaks and valleys. On Sunday was the Triumphal Entry. Monday was the cleansing of the temple. Tuesday was the great day of discussions and controversies with the great leaders of Israel. And each evening they walked several miles back to Bethany where they stayed. Wednesday and Thursday were spent in preparation of the Passover when Jesus said things like: "I'm leaving you," "You will be persecuted," "One of you will betray me and the rest of you will abandon me." All the while they are arguing over seats and putting up with Peter's boasting. To make matters worse Jesus rebuked them for asking stupid questions (Jn 14:7, 9) and for not asking the right ones (Jn 16:5). They are simply wrung out. But now is when they need prayer the most! They are about to undergo an unparalleled spiritual trial which physical rest won't help. They need prayer to empower them to resist the temptation of abandoning Jesus. Jesus is right. Their spirits are willing, but their flesh is weak. As the following narrative will show, they made the wrong choice. They followed the prompting of their bodies rather than their spirits.

The second time Jesus prays to the Father, he changes his request a little bit. He says, "If it is not possible . . ." It sounds as if he is resigning himself to the task. Again he finds the three sleeping; again they are speechless — caught and embarrassed. After finding them sleeping for the third time Jesus says, "Enough!" The word means "to restrain or refrain from a certain activity" (cf. Acts 15:29). Some interpret this to mean, "I'm done praying, I've settled my affairs, let's go." But it could also mean, "You've slept long enough, let's go." Either way, they are moving on to the next step toward the cross. Judas had completed his preparations as had Jesus. The two are about to meet at the gate of the garden.

**§ 153**
**Betrayal &**
**Arrest in**
**Gethsemane**
(Mt 26:47-56;
Mk 14:43-52;
Lk 22:47-53;
Jn 18:1-12)

[JN 18:]¹When he had finished praying, Jesus left with his disciples and crossed the Kidron Valley. On the other side there was an olive grove, and he and his disciples went into it.

²Now Judas, who betrayed him, knew the place, because Jesus had often met there with his disciples. ³So Judas {one of the twelve^MT,MK,LK} came to the grove, guiding a detachment of soldiers and some officials from the chief priests {the teachers of the law,^MK} {and the elders of the people^MT,MK} and Pharisees

{while [Jesus] was still speaking.<sup>MT,MK,LK</sup>} They were carrying torches, lanterns and weapons {swords and clubs.<sup>MT,MK</sup>}

⁴Jesus, knowing all that was going to happen to him, went out and asked them, "Who is it you want?"

⁵"Jesus of Nazareth," they replied.

"I am he," Jesus said. (And Judas the traitor was standing there with them.) ⁶When Jesus said, "I am he," they drew back and fell to the ground.

⁷Again he asked them, "Who is it you want?"

And they said, "Jesus of Nazareth."

⁸"I told you that I am he," Jesus answered. "If you are looking for me, then let these men go." ⁹This happened so that the words he had spoken would be fulfilled: "I have not lost one of those you gave me."

John takes us back to when the disciples entered Gethsemane. He chooses not to record Jesus' prayer in the garden which must have taken upwards of two hours.[60] Instead, John moves right into Judas' betrayal which followed Jesus' prayers. It is possible that Judas first led the mob to the upper room, the location of which had been kept secret until the meal began. That would be a good place for them to arrest Jesus. It was private, so a riot was unlikely. And it was enclosed, so it would be difficult for Jesus to escape. When they found the place empty, Judas knew to look in Gethsemane, one of Jesus' favorite haunts (Lk 22:39). Jesus comes down the mountain to meet Judas at the gate of the garden. The other eight Apostles must be dumbfounded! Only Judas and Jesus know what is about to transpire.

There has been some debate about the composition of the crowd which followed Judas out to Gethsemane. Some suggest that the soldiers were Jewish temple guards. However, John says that there was a cohort (NIV "detachment"). This would normally indicate a militia unit of six hundred men. It is questionable whether the Jews could muster that many temple guards. So some have concluded that they were a motley mob of patriots following their beloved leaders. The word "crowd," used by the Synoptics (Mt 26:47; Mk 14:43), seems to support that conclusion. However, a more likely suggestion is that they were Roman soldiers dispatched by Pilate himself. Why would Pilate get involved in such a thing? To squelch a potential revolt. Jesus had already stirred up quite a bit of excitement on Sunday with the Triumphal Entry and on Monday with the cleansing of the temple. The Romans would be on edge, looking for an uprising during this high and holy feast. If the chief priests promised Pilate they could take Jesus without incident, then both political parties would be pleased. And if Pilate was aware of Jesus'

---

[60]John, writing about A.D. 95 saw little need to repeat what the Synoptics had told in such detail, especially after he had just recorded Jesus' long prayer in chapter 17.

arrest, that would explain why they were able to bring Jesus to him so early in the morning and why the Sanhedrin worked through the night (illegally) to trump up appropriate charges against Jesus. Furthermore, it would explain why Pilate's wife had a bad dream about Jesus while all these events transpire.

At the gate of the garden Jesus makes the first move by asking who they were looking for. They replied, "Jesus of Nazareth." When Jesus said, "I am he," he foiled Judas' scheme. There is now no need to kiss Jesus. The entire mob falls to the ground. Are they blown over by a miraculous blast from Jesus' nostrils? Probably not. A more natural explanation might be that Judas is so shocked that he takes a step backward, tripping over Annas and Caiaphas, who then trip over the chief priests who trip over the elders . . . and on back it goes through the Pharisees, Roman centurions, commanders and soldiers, like tumbling dominoes. Well, whatever happened, you can be sure that they rise quickly, brush themselves off and try to regain their composure. But they are tongue-tied. What do they do now? Jesus breaks the silence by repeating his question, "Who are you looking for?" Their answer hasn't changed. So Jesus says, "If I am the one you are looking for, then let these men go." It is truly amazing that even in his crucible hour Jesus looks after those who are his own, even when he knows they are about to desert him. This not only fulfills Jesus' compassion for the Eleven but his promise to them (Jn 6:39; 17:12).

| | |
|---|---|
| Mk 14:44-45 *with* Mt 26:49 | [44]Now the betrayer had arranged a signal with them: "The one I kiss is the man; arrest him and lead him away under guard." [45]Going at once to Jesus, Judas said "{Greetings,[MT]} Rabbi!" and kissed him. |
| Mt 26:50 *with* Lk 22:48 | [50]Jesus replied, "{Judas, are you betraying the Son of Man with a kiss?[LK]} Friend, do what you came for."[a] Then the men stepped forward, seized Jesus and arrested him. |
| | [a]50 Or *"Friend, why have you come?"* |
| Lk 22:49 | [49]When Jesus' followers saw what was going to happen, they said, "Lord, should we strike with our swords?" |
| Mt 26:51-54 *with* Jn 18:10-11; Lk 22:51 | [51]With that, one of Jesus' companions {Simon Peter,[JN]} reached for his sword, drew it out and struck the servant of the high priest, cutting off his ear. {The servant's name was Malchus.[JN]} |
| | "{No more of this![LK]} [52]Put your sword back in its place," Jesus said to him, "for all who draw the sword will die by the sword. {Shall I not drink the cup the Father has given me?[JN]} [53]Do you think I cannot call on my Father, and he will at once put at my disposal more than twelve legions of angels? [54]But how then would the Scriptures be fulfilled that say it must happen in this way?" {And he touched the man's ear and healed him.[LK]} |

Judas has arranged to betray Jesus with a kiss, a customary greeting, especially from a disciple to his teacher. But since Jesus identifies himself, Judas doesn't need to kiss him. But he does anyway! That fact betrays a heart completely controlled by Satan. He greets Jesus respectfully, but certainly not lovingly. Jesus responds by calling him "friend," a word that has previously been used as a warning or a rebuke (Mt 20:13; 22:12). He then asks Judas, "Are you really going to do this? Well, then come on, get it over with." And Judas does. In fact, Matthew and Mark indicate that Judas kissed him profusely [*katephilēsen*], perhaps multiple times on each cheek or holding him tightly. It is the height of hypocrisy and treachery. Indeed, this was a colossal affront to God. In many ways it epitomizes humanity's rejection of Jesus — trying to rid ourselves of him by gestures of feigned kindness.

The soldiers now move into place. They grab Jesus' arms and bind him as a common criminal. The disciples are ready to fight. They are badly outnumbered (about sixty to one). But hey, they've seen Jesus calm storms and cleanse the temple. He could fight for them and win. Before Jesus can answer their question about whether or not to pull out their swords, Peter whips out the butcher knife[61] they used to carve the Passover lamb and takes a shot at Malchus, *THE* servant of the high priest. Malchus is apparently the right hand man of the High Priest. Peter swings. Malchus ducks. Peter catches his ear, but his intent was to give him a haircut at the collarbone. Jesus stops it before it goes any further.[62] Peter is likely not arrested because (1) Jesus stopped the situation from escalating, (2) they can't prove the charge since Jesus snapped his ear back on, and (3) it is a lot easier to haul in one calm prisoner than thirteen frightened and furious prisoners.

He tells Peter to put the sword away because that is not how his kingdom fights. Indeed, Jesus could have called down 72,000 angels (each able to slay 185,000 men, cf. Isa 37:36). If it came to a physical fray, there would be no contest, Jesus would win. But that is not the nature of Jesus' kingdom. All kingdoms and individuals who stake their claim with violence will eventually be destroyed by similar physical force. Besides, God's will for Jesus, as prophesied (Isa 53), is that he die for the sins of the world. Tenney (p. 170) suggests that John's mention of the word "cup" (18:11) connects the arrest with Jesus' prayer in the garden (Mt 26:42; Mk 14:36; Lk 22:42). Paradoxically, the next twelve hours will be driven by both human travesty and divine destiny.

---

[61]Perhaps he was taking Jesus' earlier command too literally (cf. Lk 22:36).

[62]"No more of this" (NIV), might also be rendered "Permit me this." It might be a request to the guards to release him long enough to pick up Malchus' ear.

| | |
|---|---|
| Lk 22:52 *with* Mt 26:55; Mk 14:49 | [52]Then Jesus said to the chief priests, the officers of the temple guard, and the elders, who had come for him, "Am I leading a rebellion, that you have come with swords and clubs {to capture me?[MT]} Every day I was with you in the temple courts {teaching,[MT,MK]} and you did not lay a hand on me. But this is your hour — when darkness reigns. |
| Mt 26:56 | [56]"But this has all taken place that the writings of the prophets might be fulfilled." Then all the disciples deserted him and fled. |
| Mk 14:51-52 | [51]A young man wearing nothing but a linen garment, was following Jesus. When they seized him, [52]he fled naked leaving his garment behind. |
| Jn 18:12-13a | [12]Then the detachment of soldiers with its commander and the Jewish officials arrested Jesus. They bound him [13]and brought him first to Annas . . . |

Jesus showed Iscariot that he knew exactly what was going on. Then he clarified for the Eleven that he knew exactly what was going on and it was under control. Now he turns to the Jewish leaders and again says, "I know what is going on here — you are operating under the power of darkness." They had ample opportunity to arrest Jesus in the temple but did not have either the guts (cf. Jn 7:32, 45-47), or sufficient support to get the job done. This was not because Jesus was an evil rebel but because he had the truth on his side. As a result the Sanhedrin, driven by circumstances and constrained by prophecy, has to operate under the cover of darkness.

When the disciples realize, perhaps for the first time, that Jesus' kingdom is spiritual and therefore not established through swords and shields, they flee. It is not so much that they are ashamed of Jesus or afraid to die for him. They just don't know how to fight spiritual battles. Once Jesus takes away their swords, they have nothing left with which to fight, and so they run.

Mark records a rather odd incident. Among the fleeing disciples is a young man wearing nothing but a linen garment. "Ordinarily men wore an undergarment called a *chiton*. This young man had only a *sindon*, an outer garment. Usually this garment was made of wool. His, however, was linen, an expensive material worn only by the rich" (Wessel, pp. 766-767). When they all scatter one of the guards grabs his cloak and he slips right out of it and runs home naked. Most scholars speculate that the young man was John Mark, the author of the Gospel. It is, after all, a rather insignificant detail unless, of course, it happened to you! Perhaps the Last Supper was in John Mark's home. When Judas came looking for Jesus, the young man got out of bed and ran to the garden to warn him or at least to see what would happen. There he got caught in a rather compromising situation.

Jesus is left alone with his enemies. Captured as a criminal, his trials begin.

# PART TWELVE
# THE DEATH OF CHRIST

## THE TRIALS

Jesus underwent six trials. The first three were Jewish, before Annas, Caiphas and the Sanhedrin. The second three were civil, before Pilate, Herod, and then back to Pilate again. It is hardly fair to call these trials, such a mockery was made of both Jewish and Roman law.[1] As for the Jewish verdict, it was already decided, not on the basis of truth or justice, but on the basis of jealousy and expediency. As for the Roman verdict, Jesus was never found guilty of any crime. Rather, Pilate handed him over to avoid another nasty confrontation with the Jewish leaders which surely would have ended his political career.

The following points catalogue the major breaches of justice in regard to Jesus' trials (especially according to the Mishnaic tractate *Sanhedrin*):[2]

1. He was arrested through a bribe (i.e., blood money).
2. He was arrested without a clear charge.
3. Trials could not be held at night or on feast days.
4. They used physical force to try to intimidate Jesus during the trial.
5. False witnesses offered conflicting testimony against him.
6. Witnesses were not supposed to testify in the presence of each other.
7. Jesus was asked to incriminate himself, which he really didn't do!

---

[1]The Jewish leaders clearly broke the law. Pilate, on the other hand, acted immorally, but was still within his legal jurisdiction according to R. L. Overstreet, "Roman Law and the Trial of Christ," *BibSac* 135 (1978): 323-332.

[2]Cf. D. Foreman, *Crucify Him: A Lawyer Looks at the Trial of Jesus* (Grand Rapids: Zondervan, 1990), pp. 116-120.

8. Jesus was not given the opportunity to cross-examine the witnesses.

9. The high priest never asked for a vote from the Sanhedrin, which should have started with the youngest and gone to the oldest.

10. He was charged with blasphemy and temple violation at his Jewish trial but the charges were changed at his civil trial to claiming to be king, causing disturbances, and refusing to pay taxes.

11. He was convicted and executed the same day as his trial.

Some people doubt the credibility of the Gospel accounts of Jesus' trial because they have a hard time believing that these respectable religious leaders would have allowed so many illegalities.[3] What complicates the issue further is these accounts have served as a platform for anti-Semitism on more than one occasion.[4] Because the Jewish leaders were the perpetrators of this crime against Jesus, their descendants have been brutalized throughout church history. That is repulsive and illogical, especially since Jesus died as a result of every person's sin, not as a result of Jewish schemes. We are all culpable. Furthermore, Matthew, Mark and John (not to mention Jesus and later Paul), were Jews and could hardly be accused of anti-Semitism (Carson, pp. 549-552).

While it is illogical to persecute Jewish people for what a few Jewish leaders did centuries ago, it is also illogical to rewrite history so as to exculpate those Jewish leaders who perpetrated this crime.[5] They were guilty, along with the Romans, for a heinous crime and radical breaches of justice. God has already judged this act (Mt 23:37-39; Lk 13:34-35; 23:27-30). "Christians" don't need to add to God's judgment nor execute it.

---

[3]For example, S.G.F. Brandon's work, *The Trial of Jesus of Nazareth* (New York: Stein and Day, 1968), purports that Mark (and the other Gospels after him) misrepresented the facts of the trial in order to save face with the Romans. He boldly asserts that Jesus died as a rebel against Rome when he, along with Barabbas, attempted to take over the temple as a zealot revolutionary and oust Caiaphas, Rome's appointed high priest (cf. M.S. Enslin, "The Trial of Jesus," *JQR* 60 [1970]: 353-355).

[4]Cf. A.T. Davies, "The Jews and the Death of Jesus," *Int* 23 (1969): 207-217.

[5]E.g., J.T. Pawlikowski, "The Trial and Death of Jesus: Reflections in Light of a New Understanding of Judaism," *ChicSt* 55 (1986): 79-94, after offering a number of explanations extricating Jews from involvement in Jesus' execution, he comes to this conclusion, quoting Robert Grant: "In the light of history any attempt to assign the crucifixion of Jesus to 'the Jews' is absolutely absurd" ("The Trial of Jesus in the Light of History," *Judaism,* 20:1, [Winter 1971]: 42).

As for these illegalities, they may not be as radical as they first appear. (1) The Mishnaic regulations may have had more relevance to the local courts (*Beth Din*) than to the Sanhedrin. (2) There may have been exceptions made for special cases held on feast days due to their exceptional nature and the constraints of time. (3) These regulations may not have all been extant during the time of Jesus' trial. (4) It seems clear that the Sanhedrin here acted out of expediency (i.e., to avoid a riot among the people). Because of time constraints of the coming Sabbath and the fact that Pilate, as a Roman governor, probably only entertained new cases early in the morning, the Jewish council had to act quickly.

The bottom line is this: There were significant breaches of justice which are understandable considering the pressures the Jewish leaders felt and the volatile nature of these events. There is nothing here that is historically unreasonable. Furthermore, while we are horrified by this judicial travesty allowed by both the Jewish and Roman leaders involved, we all must accept our own role in the death of Jesus. Ours is not to place blame, but to proclaim the wonderful news that Jesus died for our sins and freed us from the guilt and punishment deserved by all.

---

They bound him [13]and brought him first to Annas, who was the father-in-law of Caiaphas, the high priest that year. [14]Caiaphas was the one who had advised the Jews that it would be good if one man died for the people.

**§ 154**
**Phase #1:**
**Annas**
(Jn 18:12b-14,
[15-18][6] 19-23)

Jesus is escorted from Gethsemane to the palace of the high priest. Annas served as high priest from A.D. 7-14. Since the Jews accepted a high priest for life, Annas still holds sway over the people in spite of the fact that the Romans have installed another high priest in his place. He is an immensely wealthy and powerful man. He is the one who controls the buying and selling in the temple court. Hence, Jesus' two cleansings of the temple have been particularly irksome to Annas. His vicious greed and political clout are a deadly combination for anyone who stands in his way.

Annas uses his wealth and influence to get his way with the Romans as well as with the Jews. Five of his sons, his son-in-law, Caiaphas, and one grandson are installed by Rome as high priests. This allows Annas to

---

[6]John 18:15-18, following the Thomas and Gundry harmony, will be taken out of sequence here and placed in § 156 with Peter's other denials. The Synoptics record all three denials of Peter together at Caiaphas' house. John, however, places the first of his three denials at the house of Annas. Either the Synoptics compress their narratives, by placing all three denials at Caiaphas' house, or there were actually at least four denials (which would still appropriately fulfill Jesus' prediction).

manipulate their decisions without the constraints of the office (a very lucrative position, indeed). Thus, it is no surprise that Jesus is first brought to Annas even before his son-in-law, Caiaphas, the current "Roman" high priest (A.D. 18-36).

This preliminary investigation takes place in Annas' palace. It is likely that Caiaphas also lives in one wing of the palace.[7] Thus, it will not take long to "transfer" Jesus from Annas to Caiaphas. Both men are in agreement that Jesus must die. Caiaphas has explicitly stated so much a month or two earlier (Jn 11:49-50). If Annas and Caiaphas both live in the same palace, this would also explain how Peter's denial takes place in both the house of Annas and later in the house of Caiaphas (Cf. Mt 26:57-58 & Jn 18:13, 15, 24). All three denials take place in the same courtyard, which is surrounded by wings of rooms.

Jn 18:19-23

[19]Meanwhile, the high priest questioned Jesus about his disciples and his teaching.

[20]"I have spoken openly to the world," Jesus replied. "I always taught in synagogues or at the temple, where all the Jews come together. I said nothing in secret. [21]Why question me? Ask those who heard me. Surely they know what I said."

[22]When Jesus said this, one of the officials nearby struck him in the face. "Is this the way you answer the high priest?" he demanded. [23]"If I said something wrong," Jesus replied, "testify as to what is wrong. But if I spoke the truth, why did you strike me?"

Annas opens the investigation with some rather inane questions about Jesus' disciples and teachings. Jesus points out how senseless his questions are since his ministry has been public. One doesn't need a special investigation to ascertain what Jesus did and said. It is a matter of public record. Annas is, at best, buying time, and at worst, attempting to get Jesus to incriminate himself.

One of Annas' bruisers takes offense at Jesus' response and slaps him in the face (cf. Acts 23:1-5). Jesus may have been impudent, but nothing in his response was illegal or illogical. Jesus demands an explanation from the guard, which he has yet to receive.

---

[7]Rupprecht supports this conclusion. In fact, he has investigated the remains of a large Jewish palace which was discovered in the Jewish quarter of Jerusalem. He has determined that this was the high priestly palace in A.D. 66 and very likely a generation earlier as well. It conforms to all the descriptions of the palace of Annas/Caiaphas in the Gospels. If this wasn't Caiaphas' house, it was like it in size, structure and status (cf. A. Rupprecht, "The House of Annas-Caiaphas," *ABW* 1/1 [1991]: 1-17).

While Annas is investigating Jesus, Caiaphas is rounding up the troops. He has gathered certain members of the Sanhedrin, likely those privy to the plot. He has also subpoenaed a number of "friendly" but false witnesses. They are eager to testify against Jesus; they just aren't qualified.

**§ 155**
**Phase #2:**
**Caiaphas**
(Mt 26:57, 59-68;
Mk 14:53, 55-65;
Lk 22:54a, 63-65;
Jn 18:24)

[JN 18:]24Then Annas sent him, still bound, to Caiaphas the high priest.[a]

[a]24 Or *(Now Annas had sent him, still bound, to Caiaphas the high priest.)*

55The chief priests and the whole Sanhedrin were looking for {false[MT]} evidence against Jesus so that they could put him to death, but they did not find any. 56Many testified falsely against him, but their statements did not agree.

57Then some {two[MT]} stood up and gave this false testimony against him: 58"We heard him say, 'I will {am able to[MT]} destroy this man-made temple {of God[MT]} and in three days will build another, not made by man.'" 59Yet even then their testimony did not agree.

Mk 14:55-59 *with*
Mt 26:59-60

When Annas' interview comes to a sudden dead end, Jesus is transferred to another wing of the palace where Caiaphas resides. He bolsters himself with other members of the Sanhedrin. They are looking for evidence against Jesus. A number of antagonists volunteer to testify against Jesus but none of the them get their stories straight.

Finally a couple of stories gel. They remember a three-year-old incident. It took place at the beginning of Jesus' ministry when he claimed that he could rebuild the temple (Jn 2:19).[8] Both witnesses, however, misrepresent what Jesus said. They accuse him of threatening to destroy the temple of Jerusalem. But that is not what Jesus said. He said, "If *YOU* destroy this temple, I will rebuild it." In addition, he was talking about his own body, not the mortar and bricks of the building.

62Then the high priest stood up and said to Jesus, "Are you not going to answer? What is this testimony that these men are bringing against you?" 63But Jesus remained silent.

The high priest said to him, "I charge you under oath by the living God: Tell us if you are the Christ,[a] the Son of God {The Blessed One.[MK]}"

64"Yes {I am,[MK]} it is as you say," Jesus replied. "But I say to all of you: In the

Mt 26:62-64 *with*
Mk 14:61-62

---

[8]This can't refer to Mt 24:2 since only the apostles were privy to that discussion and not Jesus' accusers, and two days is not enough time for a private lecture of Jesus to become common knowledge. Jesus did cleanse the temple just 3 days ago and may have said something similar to what he said in John 2. In addition, some have suggested that John 2 records the same cleansing as the Synoptics but John "misplaced" it at the beginning of Jesus' ministry for theological emphasis. However, each of these suggestions require our own presuppositions to be read into the text rather than a straightforward reading of what the Evangelists say.

future you will see the Son of Man sitting at the right hand of the Mighty One and coming on the clouds of heaven."

ª*63* Or *Messiah*; also in verse 68

Jesus doesn't answer this foolish accusation about him threatening the temple. Why should he? Since their testimony doesn't agree, it is not admissible as evidence. In addition, Jesus has not come to defend himself but to die for the sins of the world. Therefore, he remains silent as prophesied (Isa 53:7).

Illegally, the high priest places Jesus under oath to testify against himself: "Are you the Messiah, the Son of God?" (Obviously Caiaphas used those two titles synonymously). Jesus' response in Matthew's rendition is somewhat ambiguous.[9] It might be interpreted as "Well, that's what *you* say," or "If that's what you want to think, then sure." In Mark, however, Jesus is all too clear, "I am." The time for veiled references and subtle suggestions is over. Caiaphas asks a straightforward question and gets a straightforward reply right between the eyes.

Caiaphas gets more than he has bargained for. Not only does Jesus claim to be the Messiah; he applies messianic prophesy to himself. "In the future [lit., "from now on"] you will see the Son of Man sitting at the right hand of God . . ." is a clear reference to Daniel 7:13 and Psalm 110:1, two of the most obviously messianic texts of the OT. These verses will be fulfilled literally when Jesus comes back to earth. But from the day that Jesus is crucified, he will not reveal himself to the Jewish leaders incarnationally anymore. Any glimpse they get of Jesus after that day will be the majestic, nonincarnational Christ.

Mt 26:65-68 *with*
Mk 14:64-65;
Lk 22:63-64

[65]Then the high priest tore his clothes and said, "He has spoken blasphemy! Why do we need any more witnesses? Look, now you have heard the blasphemy. [66]What do you think?" {They all condemned him.ᴹᴷ}
"He is worthy of death," they answered.
[67]Then they {[t]he men who were guarding Jesus,ᴸᴷ} spit in his face, {blindfolded himᴹᴷ} and struck him with their fists. Others slapped him [68]and said {demanded,ᴸᴷ} "Prophesy to us, Christ. Who hit you?" {The guards took him and beat him.ᴹᴷ}

Lk 22:65

[65]And they said many other insulting things to him.

This kind of talk sends Caiaphas into orbit. His fury at such "blasphemy" is fueled by delight — he finally has an excuse to kill Jesus. He tears his robe (a typical Jewish gesture of consternation either of sadness or anger: Gen 37:29; 2 Kgs 18:37; Judg 14:19; Acts 14:14). He shouts to

[9]D.R. Catchpole, "The Answer of Jesus to Caiaphas (Matt. 26:64)," *NTS* 17 (1970-71): 213-226.

his peers that Jesus had blasphemed. In Caiaphas' mind, such blatant blasphemy overrides any need for proper jurisprudence. They need no more witnesses, no more formalities, no more legalities. They gave Jesus enough rope and he hung himself. All that's left for them to do is kick the stool out from under his feet. The other counsel members present agree with Caiaphas.

Literally, blasphemy is reviling God. This can be done by bringing God down to the human level by criticism or accusations. Or it can be done by elevating yourself to God's level, thus making a human equal to God. This is what they accuse Jesus of doing. In their minds Jesus has scandalized God by making himself equal to God.[10] Now, if Jesus is not who he claims to be, he deserves to die as a blasphemer according to the OT (Lev 24:10-23). But if Jesus is who he claims to be, these men are about to make a galactic mistake.

Convinced of Jesus' guilt, they feel perfectly justified in roughing him up a bit. The guards surrounding Jesus spit in his face and begin to slap him around and perhaps even beat him with billy-clubs.[11] Then they blindfold him and punch him in the face. It is kind of a game they played which might be called "Pop the Prophet."[12] Mocking him, they demand that he reveal which one of them hit him.[13] Beyond the beating and the extended ridicule, Peter adds to Jesus' suffering by denying him.

Trying to harmonize this event is a mess! All four Gospels represent different people talking to Peter. And all four evangelists intermix the

**§ 156**
**Peter's Denials**
(Mt 26:58, 69-75;
Mk 14:54, 66-72;
Lk 22:54b-62;
Jn 18:15-18,
25-27)

---

[10]Jesus was not convicted of blasphemy because he claimed to be the Messiah, but because he made himself equal to God (cf. Mk 2:7; Jn 10:33, 36). By claiming to be the exclusive fulfillment of Psalm 110, Jesus was trespassing into God's terrain. O'Linton explains it this way: "If the sitting at the right hand of God is a poetical expression, emphasizing that God is someone's champion, the words of Ps 110 can be applied to more than one person without any contradiction. . . . If, however, the sitting at the right hand of God is thought of as a sitting on the right hand of God in heaven, the case is otherwise. Then it is a privilege for only one person, then it is a session intruding into God's exclusiveness . . . an attack on the confession of the one God, besides whom there is none else" ("The Trial of Jesus and the Interpretation of Psalm 110," *NTS* 7 [1960-61]: 258-262).

[11]The word *rapizō* has as its primary definition, "to beat with a rod" (Thayers, *A Greek/English Lexicon*, p. 561).

[12]D.L. Miller, "*Empaizein*: Playing the Mock Game (Luke 22:63-64), *JBL* 90 (1971): 309-313, suggests that it was a game called *kollabismos* or *chalkē muia*. These games are described by Pollux (*Onomasticon* 9.113). They are a sort of "blind-man's bluff." The details of the game are vague but this much is certain, these guards are toying with Jesus.

[13]This may have been based on a misinterpretation of Isaiah 11:2-4 which stated that the Messiah could judge by smell without sight (cf. Lane, p. 540).

narrative of Jesus' trial inside the palace and Peter's trial in the courtyard. As a result many of the verses describing Peter's denial are separated from each other.[14] This does not mean, however, that this story is
merely a literary product nor does it mean that all four evangelists do not
represent the events accurately. Consider these things: (1) There are two
major events taking place here at the same time, one with Jesus and one
with Peter. Thus one might expect a "soap-opera effect" when retelling
the story. That is, they switch from one scene to another and then back
again. (2) Out in the courtyard there was little light. Aside from the
Passover moon all you had was the dim light of a charcoal fire with perhaps a few torches off to the side. It was difficult for the servants to see
Peter. In fact, they finally identify him clearly not by sight but by his
Galilean accent. If they find it difficult to see Peter surely he and John
would find it difficult to clearly identify who exactly was speaking.
(3) Furthermore, there were likely several people speaking at once.
Thus, two evangelists might identify two different speakers and both be
right.[15] For instance, Luke says a man made the second accusation while
Matthew and Mark identify a slave girl. And Mark says it was the same
girl who made the second accusation while Matthew says it was a different one. John identifies a relative of Malchus who made the third accusation while Matthew and Mark say the whole group charged him. It is
entirely possible that they are all correct. (4) This incident was an
embarrassment to Peter and his friend John. It is not the kind of thing
they would want to talk about in great detail. Perhaps their reticence to
talk about it resulted in the paucity of details we now have.

We do have divergent (but not contradictory) details. The fact that
this event was an embarrassment to Peter, and thus the church at large,
lends credibility to its historicity. In other words, who is going to invent
a story like this?! Furthermore, the confusion of detail is just what one
would expect from an event on such a night as this, filled with tragedy,
veiled in darkness and bathed in tears.

---

[14]C.A. Evans, "'Peter Warming Himself': The Problem of an Editorial 'Seam,'" *JBL*
101/2 (1982) 245-249, shows how this literary device of swapping between scenes is
also used by ancient Greek writers. Consequently, we don't need to assume literary
dependence among the Gospels because they share this method of reporting Peter's
denials.

[15]N.J. McEleney, "Peter's Denials — How Many? To Whom?" *CBQ* 52 (1990): 467-472,
lists six different groups or individuals to whom Peter denied knowing Jesus.
Furthermore, he suggests that each of the evangelists describe three denials in terms that
are characteristic of their own particular style. Thus, each of the evangelists show their
own emphasis in reporting Peter's denials.

Yet we must not overlook the details that are consistent through each of the four Gospels. First, the confrontation with Peter began with a slave girl. The great Apostle, the manly fisherman, fell prey to fear, intimidated by a teeny-bopper doorkeeper. Second, there is Jesus. While he is on trial inside, getting beat up by diabolical men, Peter, out in the courtyard, is being sifted by Satan. Both trials are going badly but for very different reasons. Third, there is the fire. Specifically it was a heap of burning charcoal. Hence, it gave little light. There were dark shadows cast across the courtyard of the high priest that night. It was quite symbolic of the spiritual condition shrouding that palace. Finally, there is the rooster, a clarion reminder that Jesus is still in control. Although his crows were a horrific sound for Peter, they echo the sovereignty of God.

[15]Simon Peter and another disciple were following Jesus {at a distance.[MT,MK,LK]} Because this disciple was known to the high priest, he went with Jesus into the high priest's courtyard, [16]but Peter had to wait outside at the door. The other disciple, who was known to the high priest, came back, spoke to the girl on duty there and brought Peter in.
[17]"You are not one of his disciples, are you?" the girl at the door asked Peter. He replied, "I am not."

Jn 18:15-17 *with* Mt 26:58; Mk 14:54; Lk 22:54

Although Peter flees from Gethsemane he doesn't go far. Ducking behind buildings and shrubs, Peter follows at a distance with another disciple. It is almost certainly John. (1) Peter and John were known to spend a lot of time together (Jn 13:23-24; 20:2-3; Acts 3:1-2; 8:14). (2) John characteristically doesn't mention himself in his Gospel. Surely he is the "disciple whom Jesus loved" (Jn 13:23; 19:26; 20:2-3; 21:20, 24). (3) There were likely priestly ties in his family which may have allowed him access to the high priest's house.[16]

While John is able to march right in, Peter is held up outside the gate. John goes out, talks to the girl at the door and then ushers Peter in. On his way inside she gets a good, up-close look at him and asks if he was one of Jesus' disciples. She thinks she recognizes him; besides, he is with John. That's a dead giveaway. The NIV has translated her question well. This English phrase (v. 17), like the Greek original, expects a negative answer. Although the question calls for Peter to say "No," she knows better and refuses to let it go. At this point, Peter's motives may not be to save his own skin but to gain access to the palace in order to be near Jesus or perhaps even to effect his escape.

---

[16]"Salome, the mother of John, was a sister of Mary, Jesus' mother (cf. Jn 19:25 with Mk 15:40), and would have been equally related to Elizabeth, whose husband, Zechariah, was a priest (Lk 1:36). The evidence is tenuous, but the author does exhibit a considerable knowledge of Jerusalem and the events that took place there" (Tenney, p. 172).

Jn 18:18 *with*
Mt 26:58,69;
Mk 14:54,66;
Lk 22:55

Mk 14:66-68 *with*
Lk 22:56-57;
Mt 26:70

[18]It was cold, and the servants and officials stood {sat[MT,MK,LK]} around a fire they had made to keep warm. Peter also was standing {sitting[MT]/seated[LK]} with them, warming himself.

[66]While Peter was below in the courtyard, one of the servant girls of the high priest came by. [67]When she saw Peter {in the firelight[LK]} warming himself, she looked closely at him.

"{This man was with him.[LK]} You also were with that Nazarene, Jesus," she said.

[68]But he denied it {before them all.[MT]} "{Woman, I don't know him.[LK]} I don't know or understand what you're talking about," he said, and went out into the entryway.[a]

[a]68 Some early manuscripts *entryway and the rooster crowed*

The spring air in Jerusalem, at 2,600' above sea level, can get pretty chilly at night. So the servants and officials stoke up a charcoal fire [*anthrakian*] and sit around narrating their "heroic capture" of this villain. There must have been much speculation flipped around the fire as to what would come of all this. Perhaps they even mention the eleven fugitives that they allowed to escape. Peter gets close enough to the fire to absorb the heat but is surely careful not to allow the glowing embers to illuminate his face. Some of them sit near the coals, others stand around the perimeter. They alternate positions as they get too warm or if their knees get tired from crouching.[17]

While Peter huddles among the crowd around the fire, a slave girl approaches him again. It is likely the same girl who has been watching the gate. After thinking about it for a while and then watching Peter from a distance she can't let it go. She comes over to him and gets a better look at his face, orange with the glow of the embers. He squirms as she stares at him. Finally she blurts it out: "This man was with him!" You know she is no friend of the Jesus band by the way she refers to the Lord, "That Nazarene, Jesus" (Mk 14:67). Now the little twit is raising the suspicion of all the servants and officials in the courtyard. The situation around the fire is too hot to handle so Peter categorically and repeatedly[18] denies knowing Jesus, pleads total ignorance, and then excuses himself. He will feel a bit more comfortable at the gate of the courtyard. It's not so well lit, it's away from the gawking group of servants, and it's near the easiest escape route from the palace just in case things get out of hand.

---

[17]This explains why John says they were standing and why the Synoptics say they were sitting.

[18]The imperfect verb tense of Mk 14:68, 70 and 72 indicated that Peter's denials were repeated several times each.

[69]When the {another[MT]} servant girl saw him there {a little later,[LK]} she said again to those standing around, "This fellow is one of them {with Jesus of Nazareth.[MT]}"

Mk 14:69 with<br>Mt 26:71; Lk 22:58

[72]He denied it again, with an oath: "I don't know the man!"

Mt 26:72

[59]About an hour later another {those standing near went up to Peter and[MT]} asserted, "Certainly this fellow was with him, for he is a Galilean. {Your accent gives you away.[MT]}"

Lk 22:59 with<br>Mt 26:73

[26]One of the high priest's servants, a relative of the man whose ear Peter had cut off, challenged him, "Didn't I see you with him in the olive grove?"

Jn 18:26

[71]He began to call down curses on himself, and he swore to them, "I don't know this man you're talking about."
[72]Immediately the rooster crowed the second time.[a]

Mk 14:71-72

[61]The Lord turned and looked straight at Peter. Then Peter remembered the word the Lord had spoken to him: "Before the rooster crows today {twice[b],[MK]} you will disown me three times." [62]And he went outside, {broke down[MK]} and wept bitterly.

Lk 22:61-62 with<br>Mk 14:72

[a][Mk 14:]72 Some early manuscripts do not have <i>the second time</i>     [b]72 Some early manuscripts do not have <i>twice</i>

Apparently Peter had a reprieve at the gate, but it was short lived. Another servant girl notices him and she too calls attention to the whole group, "Hey look what I found! It's one of Jesus' disciples." This time Peter denies it more vehemently, even swearing with an oath that he doesn't know Jesus.[19]

The crowd around the fire isn't all that intent on pursuing Peter. But after about an hour, when they had talked it over, and after getting a good long look at him in the shadows, several of the men decide to go have a chat with this fellow. That pretty much settled the issue in their minds. Their questions (expecting a negative answer) now become bold assertions: "You are a disciple of Jesus!" After all, they could tell by his accent that he was a hillbilly from the northern country.[20] Then one of Malchus' relatives confirmed it as an eyewitness, "Yes, I do know you! I saw you in the garden when you took a swipe at Malchus."

Things are now looking rather desperate. His cover is blown. This calls for drastic measures. Peter calls down curses on himself [<i>anathematizō</i>]![21] Essentially he swears on the penalty of hell that he doesn't know

---

[19]Lane (p. 542), says that Peter used a common Rabbinic legal oath form (e.g., M. <i>Shebuoth</i> VIII.3).

[20]Galileans tended to swallow their guttural sounds. To the Jews of Judea this made Galileans sound like uneducated buffoons and they were often treated as such.

[21]Grammatically it is also possible that Peter called down curses on Jesus. But this is a less attractive option.

Jesus. But he is interrupted by a rooster . . . just two crows.[22] It snaps Peter out of his hypnotic desertion. At that moment he glances inside the room where Jesus is being tried. Their eyes lock. He sees Jesus' swollen and bloodied face. But by the look in his eyes, Peter knows that none of those blows hurt quite so deeply as what Peter has just done to him. Then, like a cannon blast, the words of Jesus ring inside his head, "Before the rooster crows today, you will disown me three times." He has denied his Lord! He has fallen, and is a broken man. He runs out into the darkness, breaks down and weeps bitterly.[23] This marks the end for Peter. In a way, it is. He will never again be the same.

**§ 157**
**Phase #3: The**
**Sanhedrin**
**(Mt 27:1;**
**Mk 15:1a;**
**Lk 22:66-71)**

Luke is the only Gospel to record this third phase in detail. In fact, Matthew 27:1 and Mark 15:1 could easily be seen as the conclusion to phase two. Furthermore, Luke does not record the first two phases of the trial at all. This has led some to say that phase 2 (Matthew & Mark) and phase 3 (Luke) are one and the same (compare Lk 22:67-71 & Mt 26:63-66), and that there are only five phases rather than six. While this is possible, it still appears that Jesus was led before the whole council at daybreak, probably in their official meeting place, the hall of Gazith.[24] They wanted to try and make this whole messy business look as kosher as possible before they led Jesus to Pilate.

---

[22]Mark 14:72 says this was the second time the rooster crowed. It seems strange that Peter would not have remembered Jesus' words after the first crowing of the rooster and abandon ship before it was too late. This oddity has led to some interesting explanations of this passage. For example, J.W. Wenham argues that each mention of the second crowing is an interpolation into the text and should be removed ("How Many Cock-Crowings? The Problem of Harmonistic Text-Variants," *NTS* 25 [1978-79]: 523-525). J.D.M. Derrett, on the other hand, looks for a cultural explanation. He suggests that the Jews believed that evil spirits stayed out at night until the third cock-crowing. Since Peter's third denial (full and final according to Deut 17:6; 19:15) took place between the first and second cock-crow, the demons have not yet fully left the scene. In other words, the gospel presentation of Peter's denial would suggest demonic involvement to the Jewish mind (cf. "The Reason for the Cock-crowings," *NTS* 29 [1983]: 142-144).

[23]The meaning of Mark's phrase [*epibalon eklaien*] is unclear. Wessel (p. 772) offers several possible translations: "He began to cry," "He burst into tears," "He thought on it and wept," "He covered his head and wept," "He threw himself on the ground," "He dashed out." Perhaps the NIV's "broke down" leaves as much leeway for the English reader as did the original Greek phrase.

[24]Luke hints at this by placing Jesus' beating *before* being led to the Sanhedrin (Lk 22:63-65). From the other Gospels we realize that the beating was part of phase #2 and the Sanhedrin verdict was part of phase three.

[66]At daybreak the council of the elders of the people, both the chief priests and teachers of the law, {the whole Sanhedrin,[MK]} met together, and Jesus was led before them. {[They] came to the decision to put Jesus to death.[MT]} [67]"If you are the Christ,[a]" they said, "tell us."

Jesus answered, "If I tell you, you will not believe me, [68]and if I asked you, you would not answer. [69]But from now on, the Son of Man will be seated at the right hand of the mighty God."

[70]They all asked, "Are you then the Son of God?"

He replied, "You are right in saying I am."

[71]Then they said, "Why do we need any more testimony? We have heard it from his own lips."

[a]67 Or *Messiah*

It must have been about 5:30-6:00 a.m. Jesus is led to the Sanhedrin. Most of its members have been involved in the arrest and preliminary hearings (Mt 26:59; Mk 14:55). There still may have been a few members, especially those with "pro-Jesus" leanings, who missed the "goings on" of the previous evening. They will now have to be brought into the loop for this "rubber-stamp" conviction to make it official. Even if a few vote "nay" or withhold their verdict, there is no doubt the majority will support the foregone conclusion that Jesus must die. Caiaphas and his cronies have this one all but in the bag.

The Sanhedrin was the high court of the land, much like the Supreme Court of America. There were seventy members who sat in three semicircles with the defendant in the middle. They had the right to proclaim a death sentence but were not allowed to execute capital punishment (except in matters of temple violation).[25] Any verdict of execution will have to be passed on to the Roman Governor, Pilate. Since Roman governors generally entertained new cases only early in the morning, this decision to kill Jesus must be reached "posthaste." This trial will be short and sweet. Perhaps this can account for the brevity of our narrative on this third phase. It could also explain why the Sanhedrin covers the same ground as Caiaphas. After all, this is what solicited Jesus' "blasphemous" confession the first time. If it worked once, surely it would work again.[26]

Jesus is again asked to incriminate himself (cf. Mt 26:63-66; Mk 14:61-64). Jesus answers in much the same way he did before. He points out what a farce this hearing was. Their questions are not designed to

---

[25]Cf. R.A. Stewart, "Judicial Procedure in New Testament Times," *EvQ* 47 (1975): 94-109.

[26]According to J. Plevnik, Luke's rendition makes it even more clear that Jesus is being condemned for claiming to be God's Son than Matthew's and Mark's ("Son of Man Seated at the Right Hand of God: Luke 22:69 in Lucan Christology" *Biblica* 72 [1991]: 331-347). He goes on to say that Jesus' claim to be God's Son was connected with his

discern the truth but to trap Jesus. Furthermore, if Jesus were to ask any questions of them, they will refuse to answer. Therefore, the examination is bogus and the cross-examination impossible. The trial is a sham!

Unlike Caiaphas' earlier question (Mt 26:63), the Sanhedrin asks separately if Jesus believes he is the Messiah and if he believes he is the Son of God. Instead of just coming right out and saying "Yes," Jesus says, "You'll see." When the Christ comes in the clouds with all his angels, there will be no doubt that he is who he claims to be. From this point on (v. 69) Jesus' enemies will no longer see the incarnate Christ. Any glimpse they get of him, whether in visions (Acts 9:1-5; Rev 1:12-16) or in vindication (Lk 21:27), will be of the glorified Christ. This is a bold assertion.

This leads to their second question: "Are you the Son of God?" Jesus responds boldly and clearly: "It is as you say." Their response is predictable; we've already seen it in Caiaphas. They all decide to have Jesus put to death. What an irony! The Sanhedrin finally procures the evidence needed to condemn Jesus. Yet this is also the evidence needed to believe in him. By condemning Jesus to death, the Sanhedrin condemns itself to ultimate unbelief.[27]

Jesus must now be handed over to Pilate. The problem is that Pilate is uninterested in their accusation of blasphemy. That is not enough to get Jesus executed by the Romans. So the last bit of business for the Sanhedrin is to trump up some Roman charges that are serious enough to get Pilate's attention. They come up with three: (1) He subverts the nation (i.e., causes riots), (2) refuses to pay taxes, and (3) claims to be a king (Lk 23:2).

**§ 158
Suicide of
Judas Iscariot
(Mt 27:3-10;
Ac 1:18-19)**

Matthew and Luke are the only two evangelists to record Judas' suicide. Luke reserves it for his second volume. In Acts this pericope proves the need for an apostolic "replacement" for one who abandoned his role. In Matthew, it serves to contrast the terrible end of Judas with the righteous suffering of Jesus. It also serves as a warning of the terrible consequences of rejecting Jesus. Just as Peter's denial "interrupts" the

---

claim to exaltation. This allusion to Ps 110:1,4 not only gave support to Jesus' claim, but served as a prophetic warning against his enemies. Luke continues the theme of exaltation through the ascension (Lk 24; Acts 1), a variety of sermons (e.g., Acts 2:14-42; 3:12-26; 5:29-32), and especially at Stephen's trial (Acts 7:56), as evidence that Jesus was vindicated by God.

[27]J.P. Heil, "Reader-Response and the Irony of Jesus before the Sanhedrin in Luke 22:66-71," *CBQ* 51 (1989): 271-284.

narrative of Jesus' trial before Caiaphas, so Judas' suicide "interrupts" Jesus' trial before the Sanhedrin. Again Matthew uses this "soap-opera" style for these simultaneous scenes.

There are two significant differences between Matthew and Luke's accounts: (1) How Judas died, and (2) who actually purchased the field. Some have asserted that they are irreconcilable. Such conclusions are irresponsible. You see, the problem is not so much that the accounts contradict each other but that they are only brief sketches. There are several good possibilities which could explain the variants between the accounts. However, with the information we have, we don't know which suggestion is best. But that is very different from saying that the two accounts are mutually exclusive.

<sup>3</sup>When Judas, who had betrayed him, saw that Jesus was condemned, he was seized with remorse and returned the thirty silver coins to the chief priests and the elders. <sup>4</sup>"I have sinned," he said, "for I have betrayed innocent blood."

"What is that to us?" they replied. "That's your responsibility."

<sup>5</sup>So Judas threw the money into the temple and left. Then he went away and hanged himself. {There he fell headlong, his body burst open and all his intestines spilled out.<sup>AC</sup>}

<sup>6</sup>The chief priests picked up the coins and said, "It is against the law to put this into the treasury, since it is blood money." <sup>7</sup>So they decided to use the money to buy the potter's field as a burial place for foreigners. <sup>8</sup>{Everyone in Jerusalem heard about this<sup>AC</sup>} That is why it has been called {in their language Akeldama, that is<sup>AC</sup>} the Field of Blood to this day.

Mt 27:3-8 *with*
Ac 1:18-19

The inevitable verdict of the Sanhedrin has finally and officially been announced. We're not told how or why Judas is privy to this announcement. But we do know that it breaks his spirit. He feels terrible about what happened [*metamelomai*]. Perhaps he never expected Jesus to actually be condemned. He may have thought that Jesus would overpower them as he had done before or that the people would rise to his rescue. Perhaps Judas didn't think at all about what the consequences might be and is now overwhelmed by the result of his actions. He would not be the first (or last) person to be blinded by greed. It is good and right for him to feel bad, but that is a far cry from biblical repentance.

When Judas tries to "undo" his deed by returning the money, it is too little too late. This is a significant gesture for a man who loves money as much as Judas did. The chief priests show how little they cared about Judas or about the truth. Try as he might, Judas couldn't stop what he has started.

So, in one last spiteful gesture, he throws the money into the temple. Now the temple is a big place so it may be difficult to pinpoint just where the coins landed. One good possibility is that he threw it back into the treasury [*korbanas*, a cognate of the word *korban* (see comments on Mt 15:5)], where the chief priests said blood money could not go. A more colorful possibility is that he threw it into the holy place [*naos*]. Of course no one but the priests were allowed in there. But Judas considers himself a dead man already, damned by God (Deut 21:23; Acts 1:20), so he would have few qualms about defiling the holy place, especially after how he was just treated by the chief priests. This supposition also respects Matthew's distinction between the temple compound [*hieron*] and the temple proper [*naos*].

Judas runs out of the temple to the potter's field where he commits suicide. Afterward the field is used as a burial plot and renamed "The Field of Blood" ("Akeldama" in Aramaic). Whether that was because it was a cemetery, because Judas died there, or because it was purchased with blood money makes little difference since all three of them are related. According to tradition, this field was on the south side of the city, on the steep hill overlooking the valley of Hinnom (i.e., Gehenna). It was a useless piece of ground where the potters of the city would come gather their clay.

We must now settle two discrepancies. First, why does Matthew say that chief priests purchased the field when Luke says that Iscariot purchased it? Answer: Luke is using "shorthand." Since the field was purchased with Judas' money, the sale is credited to him (posthumously) even though the chief priests actually did the paperwork. Second, why does Matthew say he hanged himself when Luke says that he fell and burst open?[28] Is it not possible that both are true? The potter's field is on the side of a steep hill. When Judas hanged himself, if the knot failed or if the branch broke (perhaps as a result of the earthquake), he could have fallen to a grisly death. A second more gruesome option is that he hanged himself on Friday morning and wasn't found until after the Sabbath. In the hot Palestinian sun he could have bloated and subsequently fallen with gruesome results.

Mt 27:9-10

[9]Then what was spoken by Jeremiah the prophet was fulfilled: "They took the thirty silver coins, the price set on him by the people of Israel, [10]and they used them to buy the potter's field, as the Lord commanded me."[a]

[a]*10* See Zech. 11:12,13; Jer. 19:1-13; 32:6-9

This prophecy presents some difficulty. The words most closely resemble Zechariah 11:12-13. But Matthew attributes the prophecy to

---

[28]The word Luke uses is quite graphic. It not only describes the action (something bursting open), but the sound which accompanies it ("pop").

Jeremiah. Now, there are some verbal similarities to Jeremiah 32:6-16 and 18:2-3, but these passages aren't talking about the same thing. So how are we to understand this prophetic fulfillment? A number of "solutions" have been proposed (cf. Carson, pp. 562-566). (1) Matthew made a mistake. (2) Matthew is citing the OT *section* which is headed by Jeremiah rather than the specific book from which the prophecy comes. (3) There is a textual variant, with weak support, which uses "Zechariah" rather than "Jeremiah." (4) Some have gone so far as to say that Matthew followed a lost portion of Jeremiah or that Jeremiah was actually the author of Zechariah 9-11. None of these solutions, most of which stem from source criticism, are satisfying.

Carson presents a more reasonable solution.[29] Instead of looking for verbal correspondence (word by word), we should look for correspondence of ideas (thought by thought).[30] Furthermore, we should analyze Matthew's use of these ideas through typological exegesis so common in Matthew's work. Here's what we find. The thoughts of Matthew 27:9-10 correspond to Jeremiah 19:1-13. Here Jeremiah is ordered by the Lord to purchase a clay jar from the potter. He is to take it, along with the priests and elders, to the valley of Hinnom. There he is to smash the jar on the ground as a symbol of what God was about to do to Jerusalem because of its idolatry and disobedience. Furthermore, Matthew not only uses the ideas of Jeremiah 19:1-13 but the words of Zechariah 11:12-13. When he combines the two passages he only gives credit to the more prominent one (cf. Mk 1:2 citing Isa 40:3 & Mal 3:1). This comes as no great surprise.

Now for the meaning of the prophecy. When we take the ideas from Jeremiah 19, couched in the words from Zechariah 11, and apply them typologically in Matthew 27, we come up with something like this: The shepherds of God's people were corrupt. In fact, they devalued God's true shepherd to thirty pieces of silver, the price of a slave (Exod 21:32). Instead of purchasing independence, their "dirty money" purchased punishment and death. What's worse, not only did the leaders of Israel reject God, so did the people. Instead of following the ones God sent to them (Jeremiah, Zechariah, and Jesus), they followed corrupt leaders and paid dearly for that mistake.

---

[29]See also D.J. Moo, "Tradition and Old Testament in Matt 27:3-10," in *Gospel Perspectives,* vol. 3, ed. R.T. France and D. Wenham (Sheffield: JSOT, 1983), 157-175; and J. A. Upton, "The Potter's Field and the Death of Judas," *CJ* 8 (1982): 213-219.

[30]Blomberg (p. 409) catalogues a number of parallel thoughts here: "Blood of the innocent" (v. 4), the "potter" (vv. 1, 11), the renaming of a place in the Valley of Hinnom (v. 6), violence (v. 11), and the judgment and burial by God of the Jewish leaders (v. 11).

§ 159
Phase #4:
Pilate
(Mt 27:2, 11-14;
Mk 15:1b-5;
Lk 23:1-5;
Jn 18:28-38)

The Sanhedrin has rubber-stamped Jesus' death sentence. They've trumped up several charges acceptable to a Roman tribunal. They are now ready to lead him to Pilate. Normally Pilate resided in Caesarea. But during the feasts he would often come to Jerusalem to keep a close eye on the explosive Jewish population.

[JN 18:28]Then the Jews {the whole assembly rose and[LK]} {bound [him and][MT,MK]} led Jesus from Caiaphas to the palace of the Roman governor, {Pilate.[MT,MK,LK]} By now it was early morning, and to avoid ceremonial uncleanness the Jews did not enter the palace; they wanted to be able to eat the Passover.

Jesus is tied up and led from the Hall of Gazith to the governor's palace. We're not exactly sure where that was. It could have been in the Tower of Antonia on the northwest corner of the temple compound where the Roman garrison was stationed. A more likely spot, however, is Herod the Great's old palace on the west side of the city. Pilate often stayed there when he came to town. If Pilate is in Herod's palace, that would explain why Jesus is transferred so quickly to and from Herod. After all, Herod, no doubt, would also stay in this same palace when he visited Jerusalem.

Our ancient sources are even less flattering to Pilate than the Gospels. He was a self-seeking political opportunist who disdained the Jews. He was procurator of Palestine which gave him absolute power of life and death. The only court higher would be Caesar, and appeal to the emperor was reserved for Roman citizens. Upon entering office, he wanted to flatter Emperor Tiberius by hanging shields in the temple compound which had the emperor's picture on them. The Jews were appalled. When they arrived at Pilate's palace in Caesarea (several hundred strong) and asked him to remove the shields, not only did Pilate refuse, but he threatened to have them killed if they didn't leave. Far from being intimidated, the Jews laid on the ground and exposed their necks for slaughter. Fortunately, Pilate realized that such a massacre would end his political career (if not his life) and granted the Jews' request. Later, Pilate wanted to build an aqueduct in Jerusalem. He confiscated money from the temple treasury for the project. This infuriated the Jews to riot. But this time Pilate refused to back down. Obviously the emperor was well aware of these incidents and the tension between the Jews and Pilate. To make matters worse, there were rumors floating around Rome that Pilate was an accomplice in some of the uprisings against the emperor.[31] Now, the rumors were likely not true. But Pilate

---

[31]Pilate's political troubles with Rome reached a peak after Sejanus was executed on October 18, A.D. 31. Based on this and other arguments, some have made a fairly strong

was, nonetheless, being carefully watched by Rome. All this resulted in undue leverage for the Sanhedrin to coerce Pilate into executing an innocent man.

The Jewish leaders escort Jesus to the Praetorium but refuse to enter themselves lest they be defiled. If they came in contact with a Gentile, idolater, unclean foods, or any number of other such items which abounded in a pagan's household, they would not be able to celebrate the Passover. Now, according to the chronology outlined in § 143, the Passover meal was eaten on Thursday evening. It is now Friday morning. Is there a discrepancy between the Synoptics? We think not! The Passover/Feast of Unleavened Bread lasted for seven days. On Friday there was another important meal called the *Chagigah*, "the leaders." These Sanhedrinites would not want to miss it.[32] What is striking about this verse is that these men are so scrupulous about the religious observances and so corrupt in their judicial practices at the same time (Mt 12:9-14; 15:1-9; 23:23; 28:12-13).

[29]So Pilate came out to them and asked, "What charges are you bringing against this man?"

[30]"If he were not a criminal," they replied, "we would not have handed him over to you."

[31]Pilate said, "Take him yourselves and judge him by your own law."

"But we have no right to execute anyone," the Jews objected. [32]This happened so that the words Jesus had spoken indicating the kind of death he was going to die would be fulfilled.

Jn 18:29-32

[2]And they began to accuse him, saying, "We have found this man subverting our nation. He opposes payment of taxes to Caesar and claims to be Christ,[a] a king.

Lk 23:2

[a]2 Or *Messiah*; also in verses 35 and 39

This scene is incredible! These men are asking Pilate to condemn Jesus without so much as raising a charge against him. They want Pilate to rely on their own Jewish judicial process. He is not about to fall for it.

Surely Pilate is aware that a major arrest has taken place the night before. It was likely that Pilate's own troops apprehended Jesus in

---

case for Jesus' death taking place in A.D. 33 (cf. P.L. Maier, "Sejanus, Pilate, and the Date of the Crucifixion," *ChHist* 37 [1968]: 3-13; and H.W. Hoehner, "Chronological Aspects of the Life of Christ," *BibSac* 131 [1974]: 332-348).

[32]The phrase, "to eat the Passover" has so far referred exclusively to the Passover proper (Mt 26:17; Mk 14:12, 14; Lk 22:8, 11, 15). Hence, it is possible that the Jewish leaders ate it later than the rest of the populace either because they were preoccupied with "business" last night or because there were too many sacrifices to get them all in on one day and they chose to eat their Passover on the high Sabbath.

Gethsemane. What Pilate is not aware of is that the Sanhedrin wants an execution. So when Pilate says, "Take him yourself," they respond, "We can't! Rome has stripped us of our authority for capital punishment." That must have stopped Pilate's pulse for just a second.

The Sanhedrin may feel that they have been constricted by Rome. The truth is, this whole scenario has been designed by God. It was he who said that the Messiah was to be crucified (Ps 22), as a cursed sin offering (Deut 21:23, Gal 3:13). Jesus knew that and predicted it (Mt 20:19; 26:2; Jn 12:32-33). Had he been executed by the Jews, he would have been stoned.[33] However, the Roman method of execution for foreigners and traitors was crucifixion.[34]

The Jews bring three specific charges against Jesus. (1) He subverts the nation. Now, if they could show that Jesus caused riots then Pilate would take this charge seriously. The Roman empire was so huge that they were constantly stamping out little rebellions. Consequently, they took a no-nonsense approach to rebel leaders. Furthermore, Palestine was one of the most difficult pockets to govern. Hence, this charge alone could have gotten Jesus killed. However, when Pilate sees the mild disposition of Jesus, resigned to his inevitable suffering, and contrasts that with the boisterous, demanding leaders, it is clear who is the cause of the riots. (2) They say Jesus opposes paying taxes to Caesar. That is such an obvious lie that Pilate doesn't even touch it. Just three days earlier in the temple, in front of hundreds of witnesses, Jesus commanded the payment of taxes to Caesar (Mt 22:21). (3) Jesus claims to be the Christ, a King. That is the most serious charge, for there is only one king allowed in this empire and that was the emperor. Anyone else who makes such a claim would be executed for sedition. While it is true that Jesus claimed to be king, it doesn't take Pilate very long to discover that Jesus' kingdom poses no political threat to Rome.

---

[33]Otto Betz, however, points out that the Jews would not necessarily be opposed to execution by crucifixion based on Deut. 21:22. "King Alexander Jannaeus (103-76 B.C.) hung 800 of his Jewish enemies on trees . . . The famous teacher Shimeon ben Shetach, a Pharisee living during the first half of the first century B.C. hanged up eighty witches at Ashqelon." This very issue was debated in the Temple Scroll (11 Q Miqdash 64:6-13), as to the mode by which one could be hanged on a tree ("The Temple Scroll and the Trial of Jesus," *SwJT* 30 [1988]: 5-8). Cf. D.J. Halperin, "Crucifixion, the Nahum Pesher, and the Rabbinic Penalty of Strangulation," *JJS* 32 (1981): 32-46 and J.A. Fitzmyer, "Crucifixion in Ancient Palestine, Qumran Literature, and the New Testament," *CBQ* 40 (1978): 493-513. However, J.M. Baumgarten, "Does *tlh* in the Temple Scroll Refer to Crucifixion?" *JBL* 91 (1972): 472-481, argues against this conclusion.

[34]R.A. Stewart, "Judicial Procedures in New Testament Times," *EvQ* 47 (1975): 94-109.

³³Pilate then went back inside the palace, summoned Jesus and asked him, "Are you the king of the Jews?"

³⁴"Is that your own idea," Jesus asked, "or did others talk to you about me?"

³⁵"Am I a Jew?" Pilate replied. "It was your people and your chief priests who handed you over to me. What is it you have done?

³⁶Jesus said, "My kingdom is not of this world. If it were, my servants would fight to prevent my arrest by the Jews. But now my kingdom is from another place."

³⁷"You are a king, then!" said Pilate.

Jesus answered, "You are right in saying I am a king. In fact, for this reason I was born, and for this I came into the world, to testify to the truth. Everyone on the side of truth listens to me."

³⁸"What is truth?" Pilate asked.

Jn 18:33-38a

Pilate, in typical Roman judicial form, interviews the defendant. He begins with the most serious charge. (It turns out to be the *only* serious charge.) Jesus' response (v. 34) is not flippant. The verdict will hinge on the definition of the term "king" and Jesus must determine whose definition Pilate is using. While Pilate was wanting a "yes" or "no" answer, either one would have been incomplete and therefore deceptive.

Pilate appears to be a little edgy from the "get-go." And why shouldn't he be? He has had nothing but trouble from the Jews. His response is basically this: "Now look, your own people delivered you to me. Now work with me on this! Tell me what you've done to upset them." So Jesus does. He answers both questions Pilate has asked up to this point: "Are you a king?" and "What have you done?" Answer: "I've established a spiritual kingdom."

Now that Jesus and Pilate are on the same page, Jesus freely admits, "Yes, I am that kind of a king!" Here the trial turns evangelistic! Jesus, as he has done so many times before, testifies to who he is and where he came from and attempts to get Pilate to listen to truth. But he is too sophisticated and cynical for any of that! He shuts Jesus off by asking a critical question which he doesn't even allow Jesus to answer. How different this trial could have been had Pilate listened. How different his own life could have been; how different his mark on history.

With this he went out again to the Jews {chief priests and the crowd<sup>LK</sup>} and said, "I find no basis for a charge against him."

Jn 18:38b *with*<br>Lk 23:4

¹²When he was accused by the chief priests and the elders, he gave no answer. ¹³Then Pilate asked him, "Don't you hear the testimony they are bringing against you? {Aren't you going to answer? See how many things they are accusing you of."<sup>MK</sup>} ¹⁴But Jesus made no reply, not even to a single charge — to the great amazement of the governor.

Mt 27:12-14 *with*<br>Mk 15:4

Lk 23:5

⁵But they insisted, "He stirs up the people all over Judeaᵃ by his teaching. He started in Galilee and has come all the way here."

ᵃ5 Or *over the land of the Jews*

John 18:38 records Pilate's second of ten attempts to release Jesus.[35] When he goes out to the courtyard where the Jews are awaiting a verdict, he plainly tells them, "The man is innocent!" That isn't what they want to hear and they throw a fit [*epischyon*]. They pester, demand, and threaten Pilate until he finally gives in.

They begin by laying one accusation after another against Jesus. He is as silent then as he had been before Caiaphas. This amazes Pilate. But what can Jesus say to change their minds? He has already addressed their major accusations. There is no reason to waste his breath, and it was predicted that he wouldn't (Isa 53:7).

**§ 160**
**Phase #5:**
**Herod**
**(Lk 23:6-12)**

Only Luke mentions this incident. We are not surprised for he shows more interest in politics than the other evangelists. Furthermore, Luke has already mentioned Herod on several different occasions (Lk 3:1; 9:7-9; 13:31). It is an interesting and unusual encounter when the king of the Jews meets the King of Kings.

Lk 23:6-12

⁶On hearing this, Pilate asked if the man was a Galilean. ⁷When he learned that Jesus was under Herod's jurisdiction, he sent him to Herod, who was also in Jerusalem at that time.

⁸When Herod saw Jesus, he was greatly pleased, because for a long time he had been wanting to see him. From what he had heard about him, he hoped to see him perform some miracle. ⁹He plied him with many questions, but Jesus gave him no answer. ¹⁰The chief priests and the teachers of the law were standing there, vehemently accusing him. ¹¹Then Herod and his soldiers ridiculed and mocked him. Dressing him in an elegant robe, they sent him back to Pilate. ¹²That day Herod and Pilate became friends — before this they had been enemies.

---

[35](1) "Judge him yourselves" (Jn 18:31); (2) "I find no basis for a charge against him" (Jn 18:38); (3) Pilate sent Jesus to Herod (Lk 23:7); (4) "I found no basis for your charges against him" (Lk 23:14); (5) "Which one do you want me to release to you: Barabbas or Jesus?" (Mt 27:17); (6) "What crime has this man committed? I have found in him no grounds for the death penalty. Therefore I will have him punished and then release him" (Lk 23:22). (7) "Look, I am bringing him out to you to let you know that I find no basis for a charge against him . . . Here is the man!" (Jn 19:4-5); (8) "You take him and crucify him. As for me, I find no basis for a charge against him." (Jn 19:6); (9) "From then on, Pilate tried to set Jesus free" (Jn 19:12); (10) "He took water and washed his hands in front of the crowd. 'I am innocent of this man's blood'" (Mt 27:24).

While the chief priests are shouting venomous accusations at Jesus, one of them says, "He started all this in *Galilee* and it has slithered all the way down here!" Bells and whistles go off in Pilate's mind. Galilee was not his jurisdiction. That area is governed by Herod Antipas who just happens to be in Jerusalem for the Passover.

How fortunate all this is for Pilate! Herod is a convert to Judaism and appointed by Rome as a ruler of the Jews. He would be more familiar with Jewish legalities and more accepted by the Jewish populace to try this case. Here's Pilate's chance to rid himself of this political hot potato. In addition, he and Herod have been political rivals up to this point (perhaps vying for power with Rome). This conciliatory move by Pilate seals their friendship afterwards.

Jesus is escorted by the guards to Herod. They don't have too far to go if Pilate and Herod are both staying in the palace of Herod the Great. Herod Antipas is eager to see Jesus for several reasons. First, he had attracted much attention in Galilee and Perea, some of which had been misconstrued as political aspirations. Herod is eager to ask him about his intentions but he hasn't been able to catch up with this traveling evangelist (Lk 13:32). Especially in these last twelve months, Jesus has moved quickly and laid low much of the time. Second, Herod had murdered Jesus' relative and forerunner, John the Baptist. Being superstitious, he assumed that John's spirit had empowered Jesus to perform miracles (Mt 14:2; 16:14). Third, out of crass curiosity, he wants to watch one of Jesus' miracles to see if they are as impressive as people say they are.

Not only does Jesus refuse to entertain Herod with a miracle, he won't even talk to the man! Oddly enough, this "Jewish" Edomite is the only person in the Gospels that Jesus refuses to talk to. His silence continues (Isa 53:7), even before Herod. Herod's last chance to repent had been at the preaching of John the Baptist, which he himself cut short.

The chief priests follow Jesus, spewing charges as they go. Herod grills Jesus who just stands there in stoic silence. Such a response (or lack of it) infuriates Herod. So he delivers Jesus to his guards to "toy" with him. Herod himself joins in the abuse and mockery. Such behavior is well beneath a king and betrays his lowly character. In fact, it is likely Herod's own expensive garment which is placed on Jesus' back. Perhaps he says something like "Well, if you are the king of the Jews, you ought to dress like one. Here, let me help." When they have exhausted the entertainment afforded by such derision, they send Jesus back to Pilate, much to Pilate's chagrin.

**§ 161 & 162**[36]
**Phase #6:**
**Pilate**
(Mt 27:15-30;
Mk 15:6-20a;
Lk 23:13-25;
Jn 18:39–19:16a)

[LK 23:]13Pilate called together the chief priests, the rulers and the people, 14and said to them, "You brought me this man as one who was inciting the people to rebellion. I have examined him in your presence and have found no basis for your charges against him. 15Neither has Herod, for he sent him back to us; as you can see, he has done nothing to deserve death. 16Therefore, I will punish him and then release him.ᵃ"

ᵃ16 Some manuscripts *him.*" 17*Now he was obliged to release one man to them at the Feast.*

Pilate's heart surely sinks when he sees Jesus returning from Herod. He wears a royal robe of mockery, but there is no guilty verdict. There are only accusations from the chief priests who continue to trail Jesus through these trials. Pilate assembles these leaders and says, "Now look, you have accused him of sedition. You've watched and listened as we interrogated him. But neither Herod nor I have found any substance to your allegations."

Pilate knows that the Jews will never for a minute allow Jesus off "scot-free." So he attempts to take the middle ground — beat him up real good and then let him go.[37] Pilate is attempting to gain clemency through pity.

Mk 15:6-10 *with*
Mt 27:15-17

6Now it was the {governor'sᴹᵀ} custom at the Feast to release a prisoner whom the people requested. 7{At that time they had a notorious prisoner,ᴹᵀ} A man called Barabbas was in prison with the insurrectionists who had committed murder in the uprising. 8The crowd came up and asked Pilate to do for them what he usually did.

9"Do you want me to release to you {Barabbas, orᴹᵀ} the king of the Jews, {Jesus who is called Christᴹᵀ}?" asked Pilate, 10knowing it was out of envy that the chief priests had handed Jesus over to him.

Up to this point, the primary movers and shakers of this trial have been the Jewish leaders of the Sanhedrin. It now appears that another crowd has shown up on Pilate's doorstep. They are Jewish citizens, probably most of whom live in Jerusalem. They've not come specifically for Jesus' trial. In fact, very few know about it outside the Apostles and

---

[36]"These two incidents are combined because we believe they happened at the same time. John pictures Jesus being flogged *before* Pilate hands him over to be crucified as another attempt to get Jesus released. The Synoptics, on the other hand, picture his flogging as part of the death sentence. It is very unlikely that Jesus was twice flogged. Hence we accept this variance between John and the Synoptics as one of rhetorical emphasis rather than two separate events. Luke 23:16 & 22 hint at John's arrangement. John, the closest eyewitness of this event, is likely the most chronologically accurate.

[37]The word "punish" [*paideuō*] can mean merely "to chastise" or to "castigate." According to John, however, this intermediate punishment was flogging, as Luke describes later in the trial.

the Sanhedrin. This group comes to ask Pilate to release a prisoner in celebration of the Passover. It is a mystery just when and how this custom developed.[38] Nonetheless, it would certainly endear Pilate to the Jews (which he badly needed). It also affords Pilate yet another opportunity to try to release Jesus.

Pilate is well aware, through his informants, that Jesus is an immensely popular man. Surely Jesus did not escape his notice at the Feast of Tabernacles six months ago or the Feast of Dedication three months ago. Surely Pilate is acutely aware of the Triumphal Entry, cleansing of the temple and the day of discussions on Sunday, Monday, and Tuesday of this week. The bottom line is this: The crowds love Jesus. Pilate knows this and is now going to attempt to turn the populace against their leaders.

Pilate gives them a choice: Jesus or Barabbas. That's not a choice between good and bad. To many in this crowd, Barabbas would be a hero as an insurrectionist against Rome. Although the NIV says he was "notorious," the word could also be understood as "noted" or "famous" (cf. Rom 16:7). It describes a person who was well-known whether it was for good or bad. He is called an insurrectionist (Lk 23:19), a murderer (Lk 23:19) and a robber (Jn 18:40). Most likely what we have here is someone who opposed Rome by plundering and even killing Roman soldiers and collaborators. It is interesting that the two other criminals crucified with Jesus are also described as "robbers" [lēstēs] like Barabbas. It is entirely possible that they are partners with Barabbas and that the three of them were already scheduled for crucifixion that day. If this is the case, then Jesus took Barabbas' place. Now that would be an odd turn of events. Jesus, the Son of God, takes the place of Barabbas, whose name means, "the son of a father."

While most of the crowd will be pleased with either option, Pilate is sure they will choose Jesus over Barabbas. After all, the people love Jesus; it's the Jewish leaders who hate him. Pilate sees through the veneer of their false accusations to the deep envy which motivates their castigation of the Christ.

---

[38]We have no solid historical documentation of this custom. However, there were a number of parallels in the ancient times from Babylon, Assyria, Greece and Rome of prisoners being pardoned during certain festivals (cf. R.L. Merritt, "Jesus Barabbas and the Paschal Pardon," *JBL* 104 [1985]: 57-68). Therefore, it is inappropriate to accuse the Evangelists of flagrant error or imaginative invention (e.g., H.Z. Maccoby, "Jesus and Barabbas," *NTS* 16 [1969-70]: 55-60).

Mt 27:19-21 *with*
Mk 15:11

[19]While Pilate was sitting on the judge's seat, his wife sent him this message: "Don't have anything to do with that innocent man, for I have suffered a great deal today in a dream because of him."

[20]But the chief priests and the elders persuaded {stirred up[MK]} the crowd to ask for Barabbas and to have Jesus executed. [21]"Which of the two do you want me to release to you?" asked the governor.

Lk 23:18

[18]With one voice they cried out, "Away with this man! Release Barabbas to us!"

The trial is interrupted by an urgent message from Pilate's wife. She warns him not to get tangled up with Jesus because he is innocent. The night before she had a nightmare about him. Perhaps it was prompted by hearing that her husband dispatched a cohort to arrest Jesus at the request of the Jews. Whatever prompted it, the Romans interpreted dreams as messages from the gods. Pilate, as a superstitious man, must be deeply moved by this communique which confirms what he has already unequivocally stated several times: Jesus is innocent. The dream would also start Pilate thinking that this execution involved more than the affairs of men.

The crowds, stirred by their leaders, begin to shout: "Away with this man!" That must have taken Pilate aback. They were shouting for him on Sunday and against him on Friday. How could this fickle crowd turn so quickly? First, the two crowds were not entirely the same. The majority of this crowd would have been Jerusalemites while the crowd on Sunday was primarily pilgrims coming up to Jerusalem. We have already seen at the Feast of Dedication (Jn 7) that the majority of the Jerusalemites were against Jesus while the majority of the pilgrims were for him. Second, the crowds supported Jesus as a political Messiah. Right now he doesn't look too much like a triumphant king, vanquishing the oppressive Roman empire. That may have quickly turned them off. Third, most commoners would buckle under the face-to-face pressure of these prominent leaders. These were desperate times, charged with emotion. These reactionary people were easily moved to action, whether right or wrong.

Lk 23:20-22 *with*
Mt 27:22-23;
Mk 15:12-14

[20]Wanting to release Jesus, Pilate appealed to them again. {"What shall I do, then, with Jesus who is called Christ, king of the Jews?"[MT,MK]} [21]But they kept shouting, "Crucify him! Crucify him!"

[22]For the third time he spoke to them: "Why? What crime has this man committed? I have found in him no grounds for the death penalty. Therefore I will have him punished and then release him." {But they shouted all the louder, "Crucify him!"[MT,MK]}

The judicial process has long since broken down. Reason is out the window. Pilate's attempts to release Jesus through Herod and through

Barabbas have failed. The leaders are more fervent than ever, and now the crowds have jumped on their bandwagon. Yet Pilate is more convinced than ever that Jesus is innocent and may even suspect that "the gods" are involved in this contest. Pilate wants, in the worst way, to let Jesus go. But things look pretty grim.

He now returns to his earlier plan (Lk 23:16), to beat Jesus soundly and hope for pity from the people. When he announces this to the crowd, they object all the louder. With one voice they chant: "Crucify him!"

| | |
|---|---|
| ¹Then Pilate took Jesus and had him flogged. | Jn 19:1 |

²⁷Then the governor's soldiers took Jesus into the Praetorium {palace^MK} and gathered the whole company of soldiers around.

Mt 27:27 *with* Mk 15:16

²The soldiers twisted together a crown of thorns and put it on his head. They {stripped him and^MT} clothed him in a purple {scarlet^MT} robe ³and went up to him again and again, {and knelt in front of him and mocked him^MT} saying, "Hail, king of the Jews!" And they struck him in the face.

Jn 19:2-3 *with* Mt 27:28-29

¹⁹Again and again they struck him on the head with a staff and spit on him. Falling on their knees, they paid homage to him.

Mk 15:19

⁴Once more Pilate came out and said to the Jews, "Look, I am bringing him out to you to let you know that I find no basis for a charge against him." ⁵When Jesus came out wearing the crown of thorns and the purple robe, Pilate said to them, "Here is the man!"

Jn 19:4-5

²⁰And when they had mocked him, they took off the purple robe and put his own clothes on him.

Mk 15:20a

Jesus is whisked back inside the Praetorium under guard. All the soldiers on duty from that cohort join in the attack.[39] Flogging was a gruesome punishment which these soldiers seemed to enjoy. Their inhumane and indecent treatment of Jesus springs not so much from anger at him personally, but at his people who had caused so much trouble for the Romans. To these soldiers, who are merely peace-keeping forces in an occupied territory, all this was mere sport. Like a cat who has caught a mouse, the joy is not in the kill but in the torture of its victim.

Flogging was such a horrible punishment that it was illegal to flog Roman citizens without a direct edict from the Caesar. The victim was tied to a post or hung from a wall. Either method drew the muscles taut across the victim's back. The soldier would then use a flagellum, also

---

[39]A cohort was a tenth of a legion, generally around 600 men. It is not likely that all 600 could have participated in Jesus' flogging and mockery. But it appears that most everyone on duty jeered this peasant from a hated race of people who were so troublesome to the Romans.

called a "cat of nine tails."[40] It was a short wooden stick with (often) nine thong strands attached to it. At the end of each strand was tied something sharp (e.g., bone, metal, glass), or metal balls. The purpose was not to lash out quickly so as to inflict welts. Rather, the soldier would attempt to rake the victim's back with the sharp objects, literally shredding the muscles of the back, buttocks and legs. The Jews limited the lashes to thirty-nine. The Romans, however, were hindered only by their animosity and endurance. So much muscle was left shredded and hanging that the victim's vertebrae were exposed and sometimes even his intestines. Often the "tails" would whip around the victim's face, gouging out his eyes. It is not surprising then, that flogging alone was lethal about six out of ten times. Those that survived were usually carried out on a stretcher with permanent mutilation.

Even after all this, the soldiers' thirst for blood is not satisfied. They find a thorny branch and weave it into a mock crown, imitating the coronation wreath of Roman leaders.[41] They place it on his head, then press it down on his brow. The pain from this would be minimal compared to what he has already suffered. There are not an abundance of nerve endings in the forehead, but there are many capillaries. The result would be a bloody mess which would mat Jesus' hair, fill his ears, and cloud his vision.

The mock coronation continues. Jesus is stripped (a shameful experience for a modest Jew), and dressed in a purple robe, most likely an old faded military cape.[42] They put a rod in his hand to imitate a ruler's staff. Then the soldiers come up one at a time to pay their homage to him. They kneel before him and mockingly say, "Hail, king of the Jews!" They rise, spit in his face, slap him upside the head, grab the rod from his hand and used it to drive the crown of thorns deeper into his brow.

When the soldiers are finished with him, Jesus is returned to the governor. Pilate goes out to the clamoring crowd and again affirms Jesus' innocence. Then with a dramatic flair he calls for the bloody spectacle. Surely this is enough to solicit their pity. . . . But it isn't. Against all humanity and sensibility, as if controlled by a Satanic spell of hatred, they shout all the more, "Crucify him!"

---

[40]For a physiological description of flogging see W.D. Edwards; W.J. Gabel; & F.E. Hosmer, "On the Physical Death of Jesus Christ," *JAMA* 255/11 (1986): 1455-1463.

[41]Palestine abounds with thorny bushes and vines. There is no way to guess which particular variety was used here.

[42]Mark and John say the robe was purple while Matthew says it was scarlet. But people back then did not differentiate colors as carefully as we do. Besides, this was undoubtedly an old faded cloth that they didn't mind staining with blood. Therefore its colors would no longer be distinct.

The blood from Jesus' back begins to coagulate in the fiber of the purple cloak. When they bring Jesus back inside, the soldiers callously rip the robe from his back, opening afresh the gaping wounds of the flogging. They return to him his simple garb, the cloak and tunic of a Palestinian peasant.

But Pilate answered, "You take him and crucify him. As for me, I find no basis for a charge against him."

[7]The Jews insisted, "We have a law, and according to that law he must die, because he claimed to be the Son of God."

[8]When Pilate heard this, he was even more afraid, [9]and he went back inside the palace. "Where do you come from?" he asked Jesus, but Jesus gave him no answer. [10]"Do you refuse to speak to me?" Pilate said. "Don't you realize I have power either to free you or to crucify you?"

[11]Jesus answered, "You would have no power over me if it were not given to you from above. Therefore the one who handed me over to you is guilty of a greater sin."

Jn 19:6b-11

Pilate is frustrated and wants no part of this messy business. Snidely he says, "You take him and crucify him." The fact is, they cannot legally do that. That's Pilate's point: "This is nothing more than a lynching, and I want no part of it." There is no evidence to support their charge of sedition against Jesus.

*Now* the truth comes out. The Jews want Jesus executed, not for sedition, but for blasphemy. Jesus has claimed to be the Son of God. That is true. Blasphemy, according to the OT, held the penalty of death. That was true. But what if Jesus really is the Son of God? That is the question racing through Pilate's mind now. His superstitious nature, his wife's dream and the Sanhedrin's new accusation all clash together in Pilate's mind in a single question: What if Jesus is who he claims to be?! This was a frightening thought (cf. v. 8).

Pilate is now at square one — interrogating Jesus again. Well, that makes sense; he has just received a new charge against him which must be investigated. The problem is, Jesus won't talk with him this time! Why? Because Pilate asks a stupid question. Pilate knows that Jesus is from Galilee; that's why he sent him over to Herod. Pilate knows that Jesus' kingdom is not from this world; that is the first thing they talked about (Jn 18:36). So why should he ask where Jesus is from? The problem is that Pilate is merely at a loss as to how to investigate this new charge. He is a Roman, not a Jew. He neither understands nor cares about this theological debate about blasphemy.

Jesus' silence adds to Pilate's frustration and fear. He lashes out at Jesus saying, "Don't you know that I have the power of life and death over you?" That is true; and Jesus doesn't deny it. But Jesus reminds Pilate that any power he has was bestowed to him as a trust. They may disagree on its origin. Jesus says it is from his Father, God. Pilate would claim that it was from Tiberius, the Roman emperor. Nonetheless, they agree that Pilate has an obligation to wield his power for justice, not for political expedience. Jesus' claim that God is indeed his Father again opens the floodgate in Pilate's mind to that single ominous question, "What if . . ." This discussion so moves Pilate, in fact, that he tries all the more earnestly to release Jesus from this moment on.

Jesus also points out another truth in his brief reply (v. 11). While Pilate has an obligation to execute justice and will be held liable if he does not, the Jewish leaders who arrested Jesus and press for his execution will be even more liable. Neither the Jews nor the Romans can be exonerated for this crime. In fact, the crowds will call for Jesus' blood to be on them and on their children (Mt 27:25). We have no way to know if God honored their request, but it would be a gross misinterpretation and a horrific injustice against humanity to use Matthew 27:25 to support anti-Semitism. At the same time it would be irresponsible exegesis and inaccurate history to say that the Jewish leaders were not the primary force behind the death of Jesus of Nazareth.[43]

Jn 19:12

[12]From then on, Pilate tried to set Jesus free, but the Jews kept shouting, "If you let this man go, you are no friend of Caesar. Anyone who claims to be a king opposes Caesar."

Lk 23:23

[23]But with loud shouts they insistently demanded that he be crucified.

Jn 19:13-15 *with* Lk 23:23

[13]When Pilate heard this, he brought Jesus out and sat down on the judge's seat at a place known as the Stone Pavement (which in Aramaic is Gabbatha). [14]It was the day of Preparation of Passover Week, about the sixth hour.

"Here is your king," Pilate said to the Jews.

[15]But they shouted, "Take him away! Take him away! Crucify him!"

"Shall I crucify your king?" Pilate asked.

"We have no king but Caesar," the chief priests answered. {And their shouts prevailed.[LK]}

Mt 27:24-25

[24]When Pilate saw that he was getting nowhere, but that instead an uproar was starting, he took water and washed his hands in front of the crowd. "I am innocent of this man's blood," he said. "It is your responsibility!"

[25]All the people answered, "Let his blood be on us and on our children!"

Lk 23:24

[24]So Pilate decided to grant their demand.

---

[43]Cf. R.E. Brown, "The Narratives of Jesus' Passion and Anti-Judaism," *America* 172/11 (1995): 8-12.

{Finally$^{JN}$} $^{15}$Wanting to satisfy the crowd, Pilate released Barabbas to them. He had Jesus flogged, and handed him over to be crucified {and surrendered Jesus to their will.$^{LK}$}

Mk 15:15 *with* Jn 19:16; Lk 23:25

Pilate knows that Jesus is right. He has to execute justice! He marches out to this clamoring mob with a new resolve to release Jesus. But now they start playing dirty. They say that if Pilate releases Jesus, he is no friend of Caesar because Jesus opposes Caesar when he claims to be a king. Translation: "If you don't kill Jesus for us, we will accuse you before Tiberius as a seditionist along with Jesus and your political career (if not your life), will be over!" That was a hit below the belt. Pilate begins to crack. He will not give Jesus over merely for the avarice and envy of the high priests. But he will give him over to save his petty political career which would end in a mere six years anyway. (He will be banished by the emperor.) As feeble as that sounds, many have betrayed Jesus for much less.

Pilate brings Jesus out before the mob once again. Now he stands on the stone pavement (Gabbatha) where he will hear his sentence. All is now mockery: the Sanhedrin pretends to be loyal to Caesar; Pilate pretends to absolve himself of Jesus' murder;[44] and both parties pretend to practice judicial proceedings. All that remains of justice is a veneer of formality. All senses are dulled by the incessant chant, "Crucify him!" When Pilate mocks the crowd saying, "Here is your king," they nearly riot in response. He knows he has lost and will cave in to their demands. He washes his hands. This too is a mockery of the Jews. The practice was probably Jewish, not Roman (cf. Deut 21:6; Ps 26:6). With a visual demonstration that his antagonistic audience would understand, Pilate says one last time, "I want no part of this!"

So Barabbas is released. Jesus is prepared for execution. We are horrified by the scene; repulsed by each player. Yet we strangely feel a part of the plot. Somehow we are there, on the wrong side of justice. As we survey the hordes we have come to loathe, we realize that we are among them.

John looks at his watch and marks the hour. It was approaching noon on Friday, the day of preparation.[45] However, Mark 15:25 says that Jesus was crucified about 9:00 a.m. It would appear that we have a contradiction on our hands. How can Jesus be crucified at nine if Pilate gives his

---

[44]Pilate's words are similar to those of the chief priests' (Mt 27:4) when they tried to absolve themselves of guilt from Judas' betrayal. Both parties are equally unsuccessful.

[45]The "day of preparation" was the day that preparations were made for the Sabbath. In other words, this was the official name of the day we call Friday (cf. Lk 23:54; Mk 15:42).

sentence at noon? In an attempt to solve this apparent discrepancy, some scholars propose that John uses a Roman-civil timing which begins counting the hours of a day from midnight and noon as we do today (cf. Hendriksen, pp. 104-105; B. F. Westcott, 2:324-326). Their main support is Pliny (*Natural History*, 2.79.188), who says that the Roman priests reckoned a civil day as lasting from midnight to midnight for the purposes of legal leases. However, in the previous sentence he said that "the common people everywhere" count the *hours of a day* from dawn until dark. In fact, the Roman sundials reflect this practice. The middle of the day is "VI" not "XII."[46]

How then do we solve this apparent discrepancy? A number of suggestions have been offered (cf. Brown, pp. 882-883; & Morris; pp. 649-650).[47] The most likely solution, however, is simply this: Neither Mark nor John can be expected to speak with chronological precision. Neither of them had a Timex. Nor is it likely there were sundials on every street corner. When each of them look into the sky and see the sun, they roughly estimate how late in the morning it is. The fact that their estimates differ by three hours is uncomfortable but certainly not an insurmountable difficulty. Furthermore, both of them likely record the time for rhetorical emphasis rather than chronological precision. John may be trying to emphasize how the trial drug on through the morning. Mark, on the other hand, divides the crucifixion into three segments, each three hours long. For both of them, the mention of time is not about punching a clock, but painting a picture.[48]

---

[46]In Jewish circles the hours of a day were sometimes counted from dawn and sometimes from dusk. But there is no example of the hours of a day ever being counted from midnight (R.T. Beckwith, "The Day, Its Divisions and Its Limits, In Biblical Thought," *EvQ* 43 [1971]: 218-227).

[47]Some of the less likely solutions are these: (1) By slightly altering the punctuation of Mark 15:25, we could understand the third hour to refer to the soldiers casting lots for Jesus' clothing. If we place this event in Pilate's praetorium and not on Golgotha, then there is no more contradiction. (2) It may have been a transcriptional error. The letter used for the third hour is "Γ" while the sixth hour is "F." Mark's original, therefore, may have read "sixth" hour and later it was inadvertently mistaken for "third" hour. While that is possible, there is no solid manuscript evidence for it. (3) Some have suggested that Mark meant the third watch. Counting in three-hour increments, that would represent 9:00 to 12:00 a.m. Again, the evidence is shaky.

[48]G.R. Osborne, "Redactional Trajectories in the Crucifixion Narrative," *EvQ* 51 (1979): 80-96.

## CRUCIFIXION

[MK 15:]20And when they {the soldiers[JN]} had mocked him, they took off the purple robe and put his own clothes on him. Then they led him out {carrying his own cross,[JN]} to crucify him.

21A certain man from Cyrene, Simon, the father of Alexander and Rufus, was passing by on his way in from the country, and they forced him to carry the cross {behind Jesus.[LK]}

**§ 163**
**En Route to**
**Golgotha**
(Mt 27:31-34;
Mk 15:20-23;
Lk 23:26-33a;
Jn 19:16b-17)

After the cohort toys with Jesus, they callously rip the purple robe from his back, taking with it shreds of flesh that have been "glued" to its fibers with coagulated blood. He is handed over to the execution squad which normally consisted of one centurion and four legionnaires (Jn 19:23 seems to support this). They put Jesus' clothes back on him before they parade him through the streets of Jerusalem. This is perhaps the only kind thing they did to Jesus all day. Normally a victim of crucifixion was marched naked to his place of execution, being scourged along the way. This would serve as a stern warning to others involved in illicit activity. But Jesus has already been scourged so there was no need for that. He is spared this particularly humiliating experience.

Like most victims of crucifixion, Jesus is forced to carry the *patibulum*, the horizontal beam of the cross (perhaps reminiscent of Gen 22:6). Estimates vary, but it weighed a minimum of about seventy-five pounds. A raw beam of this size would cause excruciating pain on Jesus' open wounds, especially as he staggers and gets jostled along the Via Dolorosa ("the Way of Suffering"). We are not surprised that Jesus falls beneath its weight, unable to carry it all the way to Golgotha. Simon, from Cyrene, on the North Shore of Africa, is coming into the city while the procession makes its way to the site of the execution. He is pressed into service, forced to carry Jesus' cross.

The centurion in charge of the execution marches ahead of the victim. An "assistant" marches next to him, carrying a placard which states the crimes of the victim (called a *titulus*).[49] Jesus' sign, which would later be nailed to the cross above his head, simply reads, "This is Jesus of Nazareth, King of the Jews"; no charge, no crime, simply a statement of fact.

Simon's two sons, Alexander and Rufus, were apparently well known to Mark's audience. This strongly suggests that they became Christians, perhaps under the influence of their father who was likely a Diaspora Jew. While Rufus was a common name, Romans 16:13 may refer to this

---

49V. Tzaferis, "Crucifixion — The Archaeological Evidence," *BAR* 11 (1985): 44-53.

son of Simon. Carson (p. 575) cites an excavation of 1941 which uncovered a burial cave on the southwest slope of Kidron which belonged to a Cyrenian Jew. The ossuary, dating pre-A.D. 70 was inscribed two times with the title, "Alexander son of Simon." Of course, we can't be certain that this is the same man, but there is a striking similarity.

Lk 23:27-32

²⁷A large number of people followed him, including women who mourned and wailed for him. ²⁸Jesus turned and said to them, "Daughters of Jerusalem, do not weep for me; weep for yourselves and for your children. ²⁹For the time will come when you will say, 'Blessed are the barren women, the wombs that never bore and the breasts that never nursed!' ³⁰Then

"'they will say to the mountains, "Fall on us!"
and to the hills, "Cover us!"'ᵃ

³¹For if men do these things when the tree is green, what will happen when it is dry?"

³²Two other men, both criminals, were also led out with him to be executed.

ᵃ*30* Hosea 10:8

Luke alone mentions the weeping of these woman along the route of this bloody entourage. Out of sheer compassion these Jerusalemite women mourn this spectacle. Freed from the burden of the cross, Jesus is able to turn to them and speak a word of warning. Reflective of Luke 19:41-44 and 21:3-32, Jesus forewarns of the impending doom of the city. The villainy they are about to commit is not without consequence; it is not without divine retribution.

Normally a Jewish woman considered it a curse to be barren (Hos 9:14). But in A.D. 70, the siege and suffering will be so terrible that childless women will be seen as the lucky ones. They won't have to worry about feeding kids during the famine or carrying kids when they try to escape the city. They won't have the horror of watching their children ripped from their arms and sold into slavery or prostitution. Nor will they have the temptation, which some women will reportedly succumb to, of cannibalism, which spared both mother and child the suffering of the famine (Josephus, *War* 6.205-208).

In those days they will cry out in vain for the hills themselves to hide them. But there will be no protection from the coming onslaught. Jesus is able to see the future of the city with divine clarity. In verse 31 he suggests that if the men of the city act with such cruel, unjust avarice during days of relative peace, there will be no limit to their cruelties during the war of A.D. 70. Just look at how they are treating Jesus now, a man of healing, kindness, peace and truth. How then will they treat true opposition leaders in these days of distress? Dark days are looming over the city.

Jesus isn't alone as he walks the Via Dolorosa. Two other criminals are executed alongside him. The crime they are charged with is "robbery," hardly a crime worthy of capital punishment, especially the extreme execution of crucifixion. However, Barabbas is also called a robber [*lēstēs*], which is understood to mean "an insurrectionist." Therefore, we see these men as Jewish rebels against Rome. Furthermore, it is possible that they are partners of Barabbas and scheduled already, along with Barabbas, to die this day. Now they find their leader free and this famed peasant standing in his place. They are probably unaware, however, that this has been ordained for centuries (Isa 53:12). It is part of Jesus' shame to be numbered with transgressors.

[33]They came to a place called Golgotha {in Aramaic[JN]} (which means The Place of the Skull). [34]There they offered Jesus wine to drink, mixed with gall {myrrh[MK]} but after tasting it, he refused to drink it.

*Mt 27:33-34 with Jn 19:17; Mk 15:23*

The place of execution is called Golgotha in Hebrew.[50] From the Latin translation we get the word "Calvary." Both mean "The Place of the Skull." We don't know how it got its name. Certainly it is not because skulls were lying around. The Jews of Jerusalem would never allow such a place anywhere near their city. It probably got its name from its appearance. Perhaps the site looked like a giant skull. We can't be certain.

There are two suggested sites of Golgotha. The one commonly shown to tourists is "Gordon's Calvary" just outside the Damascus Gate on the north side of the city. It is a hill that indeed looks like a skull. It is outside the present city walls, which would be a necessity for a kosher killing (Lev 24:14; Num 15:36; Deut 17:5; 1 Kgs 21:13; Acts 7:58; Heb 13:12). A second suggestion, which appears to have stronger ancient tradition, is a site very near the Church of the Holy Sepulchre. It is inside the present city, but outside the supposed city walls of the first century. There is no way to be certain of the exact location of Jesus' death. Both suggestions are reasonable, and it probably makes little difference since both sites are within a third of a mile of each other.

Once they arrive at the site, they offer Jesus wine to drink. Matthew stresses the taste of the wine by saying it is mixed with gall. Mark, on the other hand, focuses on the actual content which causes the wine to be bitter — myrrh. Some have suggested that the wine is offered by the women as an analgesic to deaden the pain. Such a gesture would be

---

[50]NIV translates *Hebraisti* interpretively as "Aramaic," assuming that Aramaic was the primary spoken language of Jesus' day.

based on Proverbs 31:6-7 (cf. *b. Sanh.* 43a). In that case, Jesus refuses the potion so as to experience the full extent of the suffering. It is also possible that the soldiers are the ones who offered the drink as yet another from of mockery in fulfillment of Psalm 69:21. It may have some analgesic effect, but the reason Jesus refuses it is because it is too bitter to drink. Such a "trick" would have entertained the soldiers.

The language here speaks of a curse. Jesus is cursed in Roman eyes by crucifixion, the most demeaning execution available. He is cursed in Jewish eyes by being hanged on a tree (Deut 21:23; cf. Gal 3:13; 1 Pet 2:24) and by being taken outside the city to die (Lev 24:14; Heb 13:12-13). He is cursed to be hung between two criminals (Isa 53:12). All this because he accepted in his body the sins of humanity (Isa 53:5; 1 Pet 2:24; 3:18).

**§ 164**
**The First Three Hours of the Crucifixion**
(Mt 27:35-44;
Mk 15:24-32;
Lk 23:33b-43;
Jn 19:18-27)

[JN 19:]18Here they crucified him, and with him two others {robbers[MT,MK]} — one on each side and Jesus in the middle.

[MK 15:]25It was the third hour when they crucified him.

[LK 23:]34Jesus said, "Father, forgive them, for they do not know what they are doing."

It is surprising how restrained the Gospels are in describing the crucifixion. All four simply state the fact with sober brevity: "They crucified him." Granted, the Christians of the first century needed no gruesome descriptions of the horrors of crucifixion. They were all too familiar with the details. But could it also be that the early church was more interested in the resurrection than the death of Christ? Could it be that the gruesome details could overshadow the theological significance of this event (2 Cor 5:21; Rom 3:21-26; Heb 9:26-28; see also 1 Cor 1:23)? With that in mind, we offer the following comments to help the reader understand and relive this horrible event. But we don't want to lose sight of the fact that all of this was designed and controlled by God's sovereign plan of saving a lost world.

Jesus arrives at Golgotha mid-morning (Mk 15:25). Three crosses are prepared. The Romans used four "styles" of crosses. The least common was the *crux decussata*, which was shaped like an "X." The simplest was the *crux simplex*, which was nothing more than a large stake in the ground. More common was the *crux commissa*, in the shape of the capital "T." But likely the cross that Jesus died on was the traditional image, the *crux immissa*.[51] This type of cross would allow room for the *titulus* to be nailed above his head (Mt 27:37).

---

[51]Justin Martyr, Irenaeus and others testify that Jesus was crucified on the *crux immissa*.

First Jesus is laid out across the horizontal cross beam (*patibulum*) and his hands nailed with square iron spikes. Some have suggested that his arms were tied to the cross rather than nailed[52] since the hands could not support the full weight of a man without tearing.[53] Perhaps the arms were tied to the *patibulum* while the victim was carrying it to the site of execution but the evidence indicates that the hands were indeed nailed in place, not tied. The word "hand" [*cheir*] includes most of the forearm. Hence, the nail could go through the complex of wrist bones or more likely, between the radius and ulna of the forearm just behind the wrist. Such a position of the nail would provide ample support for the body especially since the feet were also nailed and often the cross was equipped with a peg or small block of wood on which the victim could "sit."[54] But of equal importance to the Romans, a nail through the "wrist" would sever the median nerve, sending searing pain through the arms and shoulders of the victim.

Next, the *patibulum* was attached to the *stipes* (the vertical beam of the cross), and the victim's feet affixed. There are a number of possibilities as to how this was done. Likely the Romans used all of them at one time or another. (They were quite creative in their methods of crucifixion.) The traditional view has Jesus' feet hanging straight below him, the nail piercing both feet straight through the metatarsals. However, that doesn't match the only known skeletal remains of a crucifixion victim.[55]

---

[52]H. Shanks, "New Analysis of the Crucified Man," *BAR* 11 (Nov-Dec, 1985): 20-21.

[53]This research was originally done by medical doctor Pierre Barbet. He experimented with freshly amputated limbs. He determined that a hand with a nail in the middle of it would only support about eighty-eight pounds. During a crucifixion, with the convulsions and angle of the body, each hand would have to support much more weight than that (cf. P. Barbet, *A Doctor at Calvary* [New York: P.J. Kennedy, 1953]).

[54]Medical doctor, Frederick Zugibe, however, has demonstrated that a nail precisely positioned on the thenar furrow (at the thick base of the hand), pointing toward the thumb at 10-15 degrees and passing between the metacarpals of the index finger and the second finger and the wrist bones, could in fact support the weight of a man. Furthermore, a nail in this position would not break any bones (cf. F. Zugibe, *The Cross and the Shroud: A Medical Examiner Investigates the Crucifixion* [New York: Paragon House Publishers, 1988]).

[55]N. Haas, "Anthropological Observations on the Skeletal Remains from Giv'at ha-Mivtar," *IEJ* 20 (1970): 38-59; and J. Zias & E. Sekeles, "The Crucified Man from Giv'at ha-Mivtar: A Reappraisal," *IEJ* 35 (1985): 22-27. The fact that we have only identified one skeleton of a crucifixion victim does not mean that there were not thousands of crucifixions. Part of the problem is that deteriorated skeletal remains are nearly impossible to identify as victims of crucifixion. What further complicates the matter is that Romans often burned their dead or left crucifixion victims for the birds and beasts of prey to dispatch. Furthermore, considering the fact that Roman executioners were versatile in their methods of crucifixion, we should probably be cautious about making the remains of Jehohanan normative for all other crucifixion victims, including Jesus.

In a 1968 excavation of Giv'at ha-Mivtar, near the old Damascus gate in Jerusalem, the body of one Jehohanan (John) was found buried with his wife, Martha, and two children. His right calcaneum (heel bone) still held the nail. Apparently when they nailed Jehohanan the nail struck a knot in the wood which bent back its tip. Hence, they were not able to extract the nail from his foot before they buried him. Had it not been for this freak accident, we would not have known Jehohanan was a victim of crucifixion. But the nail did not go through the top of his foot but the side of his heel. Haas assumes that both feet were held side by side with a one inch thick board and then nailed with the toes pointing to the side of the cross. This would contort the lower torso at a ninety degree angle and cause excruciating cramps. The only problem is that this would require a nail approximately seventeen or eighteen centimeters (about seven inches). But the nail actually found imbedded in the victim was only eleven and a half centimeters (or about four and a half inches). Thus, Jehohanan must have had each heel nailed separately, either to the front of the cross (contorting the lower torso), or to the sides of the cross, spreading his legs to straddle the *stipes*. Either of these methods would send a shock of pain up through the pelvic area which matched that of the upper torso.

The cross is now lifted to display its spectacle. The victims hang helplessly, welcoming death to deliver them from this agony. Dr. Pierre Barbet popularized the idea that victims of crucifixion died of asphixiation.[56] His conclusions were drawn from World War II prisoners in Austro-Germany who were strung up by their hands. From this position, the victim is unable to exhale. Carbon dioxide builds up in the lungs. The blood becomes thick and sluggish. This sends the contorted muscles into severe cramps and intermittent convulsions. Eventually the pericardium fills with serum resulting in intense pressure on the heart and lungs causing deep chest pains for the victim. Finally, when all strength is gone, the victim can't exhale the carbon dioxide in his lungs and he dies of asphyxiation. Zugibe, however, disagrees. He is also a medical doctor who did experiments of his own. Instead of hanging subjects with their hands straight above their head, he created a device that simulated the position of a crucifixion victim. He found little or no evidence to suggest that a person hung by their arms at a sixty to seventy degree angle would suffer asphixiation.[57] Rather, he suggests that crucifixion

---

[56]P. Barbet, *A Doctor at Calvary* (New York: P.J. Kennedy, 1953).

[57]F.T. Zugibe, "Two Questions About Crucifixion," *BR* 5 (1989): 34-43. D.J. Halperin, however, based on linguistic evidence, asserts that crucifixion was considered a form of strangulation in Jewish jurisprudence, "Crucifixion, the Nahum Pesher, and the Rabbinic

victims died of shock. Jesus, in particular, died of shock resulting from multiple abuses which ultimately led to coronary failure.[58]

As Jesus hangs about two feet off the ground (Mt 27:48; Jn 19:29), he surveys the crowd. The Sanhedrinists make their presence known with ostentatious mockery. The soldiers follow suit. Passersby gawk as they travel in and out of the city with busy preparations for Passover. And the women wail at the awful spectacle. They are accompanied by only one of Jesus' Apostles, the beloved John. As Jesus takes it all in, he grapples for the breath to speak the first of seven sayings from the cross[59]: "Father, forgive them for they do not know what they are doing."[60] While this can hardly be understood as a king's pardon, it stresses two critical features of this event. First, those who participated were ignorant of just what they were doing (Acts 3:17; 1 Cor 2:8). To that extent their judgment will be lighter. Second, the cross is all about forgiveness. It is through this substitutionary sacrifice that our debt is paid. We are free because Jesus took on himself our punishment (Isa 53:5; Jn 3:17; Rom 4:25; 6:23; 1 Cor 15:3; Heb 9:28; 1 Pet 2:24; 1 Jn 2:2). In light of Jesus' first words from the cross, we find no justification for personal grudges, slander, or gossip in the church. Those with their noses bent out of shape should remember the contorted body of Christ and his initial response to his persecutors.

[19]Pilate had a notice prepared and fastened to the cross {above his head.[MT]} It read: {THIS IS[MT,LK]} JESUS OF NAZARETH, THE KING OF THE JEWS. [20]Many of the Jews read this sign, for the place where Jesus was crucified was near the city, and the sign was written in Aramaic, Latin and Greek. [21]The chief priests of the Jews protested to Pilate, "Do not write 'The King of the Jews,' but that this man claimed to be king of the Jews."

[22]Pilate answered, "What I have written, I have written."

Jn 19:19-22 *with* Mt 27:37; Lk 23:38

This placard accompanies Jesus to Golgotha. It is now affixed to the top of the cross above his head. It is his official sentence and paradoxically

---

Penalty of Strangulation," *JJS* 32 (1981): 32-46. **IF** his analysis is correct, it might demonstrate that crucifixion victims had difficulty breathing even if that was not the primary cause of death.

[58]G. Bare, "A Doctor Looks at the Crucifixion," *The Lookout* (April 4, 1982): 2-3, 6.

[59]The seven sayings of the cross are as follows: (1) "Father, forgive them for they do not know what they are doing" (Lk 23:34); (2) "I tell you the truth, today you will be with me in paradise" (Lk 23:43); (3) "Dear woman, here is your son." "Here is your mother." (Jn 19:26-27); (4) "My God, My God, why have you forsaken me? (Mt 27:46; Mk 15:34); (5) "I am thirsty" (Jn 19:28); (6) "It is finished" (Jn 19:30); (7) "Father, into your hands I commit my spirit" (Lk 23:46).

[60]Cf. J. Reid's masterful sermon on this saying, "'Father Forgive them' Lk 23:34," *ExpT* 41 (1929-30): 103-107.

a profound statement of truth. According to this accusation, Jesus is guilty as charged. Pilate, while attempting to irk the Jews with this statement, actually answered his own question: "What is truth?"

While all four Gospels record the sentence in a slightly different way, each of them accurately record the essence of the sentence without recording it verbatim. Part of this variance may be accounted for by the differences in translation. The sentence was written in three languages: Aramaic (the spoken language of Palestine), Greek (the universal language of the day), and Latin (the official language of Rome). How fitting that the savior of the *world* would be sentenced in such a way that all people of the Roman empire could have understood.

The chief priests are furious with the sign. They demand that Pilate change the wording to read, "This man claimed to be the king of the Jews." They want no misunderstandings. They don't want any of the passersby to mistakenly think that the Romans are executing a potential ruler of the Sanhedrin. No, this is a Jewish execution of an "impostor," not a Roman execution of a rebel. But Pilate has backed down for the last time. The sign stands as written.

Jn 19:23-24

[23]When the soldiers crucified Jesus, they took his clothes, dividing them into four shares, one for each of them, with the undergarment remaining. This garment was seamless, woven in one piece from top to bottom.

[24]"Let's not tear it," they said to one another. "Let's decide by lot who will get it."
This happened that the scripture might be fulfilled which said,
"They divided my garments among them
and cast lots for my clothing."[a]
So this is what the soldiers did.

[a]24 Psalm 22:18

Mt 27:36

[36]And sitting down, they kept watch over him there.

It was common for the executioners to confiscate the clothes of their victims for personal profit. The soldiers apparently divide up Jesus' sandals, head-gear, sash and cloak between the four of them. But that leaves the valuable seamless tunic. If they cut it up it will depreciate in value. So they decide to gamble for it (one of the favorite pastimes of Roman soldiers). Likely they draw straws or cast dice to determine who will get it. They think this is just sport, part of the mundane duties of peace-keeping forces. But their little game was recorded by God a thousand years earlier in Psalm 22:18. The soldiers imagine they are in charge of this execution. So they sit there and watch Jesus die, making sure that no rebels attempt to rescue him. But this prophecy reminds us that God is really in control. He too sits and watches from the heavens as his own Son dies.

³⁹Those who passed by hurled insults at him, shaking their heads ⁴⁰and saying, "You who are going to destroy the temple and build it in three days, save yourself! Come down from the cross {and save yourself,^MK} if you are the Son of God!"

⁴¹In the same way the chief priests, the teachers of the law and the elders mocked him {among themselves.^MK} ⁴²"He saved others," they said, "but he can't save himself! He's the King of Israel, {the Christ of God, the Chosen One!^LK} Let him come down now from the cross {that we may see,^MK} and we will believe in him. ⁴³He trusts in God. Let God rescue him now if he wants him, for he said, 'I am the Son of God.'"

Mt 27:39-43 *with* Mk 15:30-32; Lk 23:35

³⁶The soldiers also came up and mocked him. They offered him wine vinegar ³⁷and said, "If you are the king of the Jews, save yourself."

Lk 23:36-37

⁴⁴In the same way the robbers who were crucified with him also heaped insults on him.

Mt 27:44

Four groups join in the verbal assault against Jesus. First, there are the crowds. Jesus is apparently crucified next to a major road leading into the city. As crowds go in and out of the city, the gossip spreads about arrest and trials of the night before. Like puppets and parrots the ignorant populace repeats the accusations of their leaders. Recalling Jesus' promise to rebuild the temple they shout, "How do you expect to destroy the temple if you can't even get yourself down off the cross?! Some Son of God you are!" Little do they know that Jesus is in the act of fulfilling that very prophecy that they so badly misinterpret.

Next come the members of the Sanhedrin: Sadducean chief priests, Pharisaic lawyers, and the elderly delegates from the people. Apparently in a cluster (i.e., "among themselves"), they pat each other on the back and assure themselves that they have done the right thing. "True, his miracles of healing were impressive, but the fact that he cannot now deliver himself 'proves' that he was a fraud." "After all," they say, "if Jesus is some kind of God-sent messiah, he would be able to save himself. Furthermore, surely God would rescue his own son!" But that is NOT what the Scriptures predict. Isaiah 53:10 says, "Yet it was the Lord's will to crush him and cause him to suffer, and though the Lord makes his life a guilt offering, he will see his offspring and prolong his days and the will of the Lord will prosper in his hand." As if to justify their blatant unbelief they say, "Now if he were to come down off the cross, **THEN** we would believe him." But they aren't fooling anyone. If they tried to kill Lazarus after Jesus raised him from the dead, they would try to nail Jesus back on the cross if he came down.

The soldiers are the third group to join in the mockery, again offering Jesus wine vinegar to drink. They parrot the taunts of the crowds and the Sanhedrin, "Save yourself!" Finally, even the criminals on either side of Jesus are drawn into the mockery. As we will soon see from Luke, one of the criminals actually defends Jesus. Perhaps Matthew speaks of both men mocking Jesus when only one actually did. Or perhaps the second man repented after seeing Jesus' righteous response to unjust ridicule. We can't be sure. But this much we know, not only was God overseeing this scene, but he had predicted it a millennium earlier. Through David's pen God describes what took place at the foot of the cross: "All who see me mock me; they hurl insults, shaking their heads: 'He trusts in the Lord; let the Lord rescue him. Let him deliver him since he delights in him.' . . . Dogs have surrounded me; a band of evil men has encircled me, they have pierced my hands and my feet" (Ps 22:7-8, 16).

All four groups taunt Jesus saying, "He saved others, let him save himself." In a paradoxical way, they speak the truth. Jesus could not at the same time save himself and save others. He voluntarily gave up his life so that we could find true life in him (2 Cor 5:21; Rom 3:21-26; Heb 9:26-28).

Lk 23:39-43

[39]One of the criminals who hung there hurled insults at him: "Aren't you the Christ? Save yourself and us!"

[40]But the other criminal rebuked him. "Don't you fear God," he said, "since you are under the same sentence? [41]We are punished justly, for we are getting what our deeds deserve. But this man has done nothing wrong."

[42]Then he said, "Jesus, remember me when you come into your kingdom.[a]"

[43]Jesus answered him, "I tell you the truth, today you will be with me in paradise."

[a]42 Some manuscripts *come with your kingly power*

One of the insurrectionists ridicules (*blasphemeō*) Jesus as a false Messiah. Of course he is operating under the common misconception of a political, militaristic messiah who would throw off the shackles of Rome. Indeed, by that definition, Jesus is a miserable failure. To this guerrilla zealot, Jesus' passivity is offensive in the highest degree. How dare this pseudo-do-gooder claim to be Israel's deliverer!

While the first criminal speaks with impressive passion, it is his comrade on the other side that speaks with impressive reason and faith. Looking beyond Jesus, he rebukes his friend. While his first statement is a bit ambiguous, we can still determine at least three things from his comments: (1) The two of them are sinners and deserve to die. (2) Jesus is righteous and doesn't deserve to die. (3) God's hand is involved in the sentence they shared with Jesus — he is the key figure and the two of them are merely along for the ride. This calls for fear of God shown by respecting Jesus rather than ridiculing him.

With his head still turned toward his comrade, he speaks directly to

Jesus, "Remember me when you come into your kingdom." Considering the fact that Jesus is obviously about to die, this statement shows impressive faith. The man must believe in some kind of resurrection and spiritual kingdom. He has fought zealously for a political kingdom. Now, in the final moments of his life he meets the true king that he has been looking for. His request is simple and it is prompted by faith. Jesus' response must have soothed the man's suffering on the cross: "Today you will be with me in paradise." The word "paradise" indicates a place of beauty and happiness (cf. Isa 51:3; 2 Cor 12:4; Rev 2:7). It is used to describe the garden of Eden (Gen 2:8, LXX). But the beauty of this promise is not "paradise" (whatever that entails), but being with Jesus. The man responds to Jesus with repentance and faith. Jesus responds to him by promising him salvation. While we can't know how much this thief really understands about Jesus, nor can we be certain about the dynamics of his "deathbed" conversion, we can be certain that someday we will have the opportunity to ask him personally . . . if we are still so inclined.[61]

Jn 19:25-27

[25]Near the cross of Jesus stood his mother, his mother's sister, Mary the wife of Clopas, and Mary Magdalene. [26]When Jesus saw his mother there, and the disciple whom he loved standing nearby, he said to his mother, "Dear woman, here is your son," [27]and to the disciple, "Here is your mother." From that time on, this disciple took her into his home.

There is a glaring absence of Jesus' men at the cross. To our knowledge, John was the only one who showed up. He stands in the midst of a group of women. John mentions four of them while Mark and Matthew mention only three.[62] Of course Mark and Matthew list the women who were there when Jesus died and John lists the women present when Jesus was first crucified. It may be that John and Mary leave right after Jesus speaks to them.

In Jesus' second recorded statement from the cross, he commits his mother into the care of John, his beloved friend. This makes sense when you understand that Jesus' "family" consists of faithful believers and Jesus' half-brothers don't fit that category until after his resurrection.

---

[61]This little vignette is a beautiful paradigm of repentance and conversion. It shows that (1) Jesus does for us what he asked God to do — forgive, and (2) "Today" is the operative word for Christianity. God's kingdom has broken in, it is **here**! (cf. G.W. MacRae, "With Me In Paradise," *Worship* 35 [1961]: 235-240).

[62]Lenski believes that there were only three women described by John (Mary, the wife of Clopas, being described as Mary's sister). But if that is true then you would have two sisters, both named Mary. That is unlikely.

Furthermore, John is likely Jesus' cousin (see chart below). Therefore, he is the closest believing relative. John takes her home and gently cares for this dear saint who had a "sword wound" in her soul (Lk 2:35).[63]

| John 19:25 | Mark 15:40 | Matthew 27:56 |
|---|---|---|
| Mary, Jesus' mother | | |
| Mary's sister | Salome | Mother of Zebedee's sons (i.e., James and John) |
| Mary, wife of Clopas | Mary, mother of James the younger & Joses[64] | Mary, mother of James and Joses |
| Mary Magdalene | Mary Magdalene | Mary Magdalene |

**§ 165**
**Jesus' Death**
(Mt 27:45-50;
Mk 15:33-37;
Lk 23:44-46;
Jn 19:28-30)

[MK 15:]33At the sixth hour darkness came over the whole land until the ninth hour.

[LK 23:]45For the sun stopped shining.

[MK 15:]34And at the ninth hour Jesus cried out in a loud voice, *"Eloi, Eloi, lama sabachthani?"* — which means, "My God, my God, why have you forsaken me?"[a]
    35When some of those standing near heard this, they said, "Listen, he's calling Elijah."

[a]*34* Psalm 22:1

Between noon and 3 p.m. darkness covers Judea. This is the first of three phenomena that accompany Jesus' death. It is a supernatural sign of judgment (cf. Amos 8:9-10) which cannot adequately be explained naturalistically. For example, an eclipse doesn't last for three hours nor does it occur during the full moon of Passover. A sirocco (a desert windstorm) would hardly cover the land in complete darkness as if "the sun stopped shining."[65] No, the hand of God shrouded the land.

---

[63]John 19:27 may indicate that John had some kind of residence in Jerusalem. If so, that may explain how he was family friends with the high priest and had access to his home.

[64]There was an ancient tradition which states that Clopas (i.e., Alphaeus) was the brother of Joseph (*Hegesippus* in *Eusebius, H.E.* 3.11 and 4.22). This would make James the less Jesus' step-cousin. Edersheim (II:602-3) also suggests that Judas (Thaddeus) and Simon the zealot were sons of Clopas but not of Mary, based on their position in the list of Apostles (Mt 10:3-4; Acts 1:13, etc.) and on statements of Hegesippus. Hence they too would be step-cousins of Jesus.

[65]Another example is J. Sawyer's explanation which suggests that Luke anachronistically applies the solar eclipse of November, A.D. 29 to Jesus' death. While that eclipse only lasted 1½ minutes, Luke exaggerates it to 3 hours (cf. J. Sawyer "Why is a Solar Eclipse Mentioned in the Passion Narrative (Luke 23:44-45)," *JTS* 23 [1972]: 124-128). But this inappropriately impugns the veracity of the evangelists.

After only six hours on the cross, Jesus dies. He cries out in a loud voice, "Eloi, Eloi . . ."[66] This fourth saying from the cross is perhaps the most theologically significant and perhaps too deep for us to fully appreciate. But it seems to point in at least two directions. First, Jesus is calling us back to Psalm 22:1 by quoting it verbatim. This passage is an incredibly clear prediction of Jesus' crucifixion. It serves as a poignant reminder that this is God's plan and it is still under his control no matter what it looks like on the surface. What is most striking about this Psalm, however, is that it was written about 1000 B.C., a full 600 years before crucifixion was in vogue. We are also impressed that the Psalm of the Good Shepherd (Ps 23) is prefaced by the Psalm of God's Sacrificial Lamb (Ps 22).

Secondly, Jesus is not merely quoting Psalm 22:1; he is describing his present and insufferable separation from his Heavenly Father. From eternity past, Jesus has never known what it was like to be alienated from God's presence. While we want to studiously avoid the error of the Gnostics and docetics who believed that Jesus ceased to be God in this moment, we do affirm that the Father, at some level, turns his back on Jesus as he becomes the embodiment of sin (2 Cor 5:21; cf. Rom 3:26; Gal 3:13). Jesus is forsaken by God, that is, he is abandoned, left without God's resources or intervention, to suffer and die alone.[67] But this word pops up again in Acts 2:27, 31 to describe how God did NOT abandon Jesus in the grave. God's abandonment may be harsh, but it is only temporary. Even Psalm 22 ends with a note of victory. After all, behind the cross is an empty tomb.

[28]Later, knowing that all was now completed, and so that the Scripture would be fulfilled, Jesus said, "I am thirsty." [29]A jar of wine vinegar was there, so {immediately[MT]} they {one man[MK]} soaked a sponge in it, put the sponge on a stalk of the hyssop plant, and lifted it to Jesus' lips.

Jn 19:28 *with* Mt 27:48; Mk 15:36

[49]The rest said {he said,[MK]} "Now leave him alone. Let's see if Elijah comes to take him down."

Mt 27:49 *with* Mk 15:36

---

[66]There is some question about what language Jesus spoke when he said this. The second half ("Why have you forsaken me?") is clearly in Aramaic. But in Matthew, the first part *"Eli, Eli"* looks like Hebrew while Mark's *"Eloi, Eloi"* is Aramaic. If Jesus originally spoke in Hebrew that would more easily account for the crowd confusing *Eli* with Elijah. This would also mean that Mark placed Jesus' words in Aramaic rather than Hebrew for cultural reasons. But the textual evidence favors an Aramaic original. Furthermore, Matthew's *Eli* may reflect the Aramaic Targum of Psalm 22:1. "Apparently some Aramaic speakers preserved the Hebrew name for God in the same way some English speakers sometimes refer to him as Yahweh" (Carson, p. 578). The crowd's mishearing of "Elijah" may be accounted for by Jesus' strained speech.

[67]Paul uses this word to describe how his comrades had deserted him (2 Tim 4:10, 16).

Jn 19:30     [30]When he had received the drink, Jesus said, "It is finished."

Lk 23:46 *with*     [46]{With that, he[JN]} called out with a loud voice, "Father, into your hands I
Jn 19:30     commit my spirit." When he had said this he breathed his last, {bowed his head, and gave up his spirit.[JN]}

John interprets Jesus' fifth statement from the cross as a prophetic fulfillment, probably alluding to Psalm 69:21. Jesus asks for a drink and one of the men standing there responds immediately. He is likely a soldier who dips a sponge into his own stash. This wine vinegar is a poor-man's brew. It is a bit sour but a great thirst quencher. This time they apparently don't mix it with myrrh. He puts the sponge on a stick and lifts it to Jesus' lips before anyone really knew what was happening.[68] The crowd says, "Hey, leave him alone. We want to see if Elijah is going to come and save him." Because they misheard "Eloi" for "Elijah" this provides one last opportunity to mock Jesus. Since Elijah never actually died, the Jews expected him to return literally as a precursor to the Messiah based on Malachi 4:5. Now that Jesus is "praying to Elijah" this would provide one last point of ridicule.

Their derision is cut short. As soon as Jesus receives the drink he said, "It is finished" and then shouted, "Father, into your hands I commit my spirit." With that he takes one last breath, bows his head and releases his spirit. But what exactly was finished? His life? NO! . . . Easter's on its way! His work on earth was done (Heb 9:26; 10:12-14). The perfect verb tense [*tetelestai*] highlights the total completion of his task. He had accomplished what he had come here to do (Mt 20:28; Mk 10:45). In addition, some have speculated that Jesus is again alluding to Psalm 22, this time to the very last line, where God completes *his* task.

Even with his last breath he was alluding to Scripture. "Father, into your hands I commit my spirit" is likely taken from Psalm 31:5. Liefeld says that it was part of the Jews' evening prayer (p. 1045). In turning to the Psalm itself, there is much there that would be relevant to Jesus at this very moment:

> Turn your ear to me, come quickly to my rescue; be my rock of refuge, a strong fortress to save me. Free me from the trap that is set for me, for you are my refuge. Into your hands I commit my spirit; redeem me, O LORD,

---

[68]John says it was a hyssop plant. True hyssop is an herb which probably couldn't hold a sponge full of wine. Therefore, some have suggested an emendation of the text from "hyssop" [*hyssōpō*] to "javelin" [*hyssō*], based on a single late manuscript (MS 1242). That is not necessary. The word "hyssop" may refer to a number of small plant varieties. Besides, the stock on which the sponge was placed would likely only need to reach about two feet. Such a stick could easily have been available in the immediate vicinity.

the God of truth. I will be glad and rejoice in your love, for you saw my affliction and knew the anguish of my soul. Because of all my enemies, I am the utter contempt of my neighbors; I am a dread to my friends — those who see me on the street flee from me. I am forgotten by them as though I were dead; I have become like broken pottery. For I hear the slander of many; there is terror on every side; they conspire against me and plot to take my life. But I trust in you, O LORD; I say, "You are my God." In my alarm I said, "I am cut off from your sight!" Yet you heard my cry for mercy when I called to you for help. Be strong and take heart, all you who hope in the LORD (Ps 31:2, 4-5, 7, 11-14, 22, 24).

[MT 27:]51At that moment the curtain of the temple was torn in two from top to bottom. The earth shook and the rocks split. 52The tombs broke open and the bodies of many holy people who had died were raised to life. 53They came out of the tombs, and after Jesus' resurrection they went into the holy city and appeared to many people.

**§ 166**
**Responses to Jesus' Death**
(Mt 27:51-56; Mk 15:38-41; Lk 23:47-49)

At the moment Jesus dies, the curtain of the temple is torn in two. It would have been more public if the torn curtain was the one between the temple courts and holy place.[69] But Hebrews 4:16; 6:19-20; 9:11-28; 10:19-22 seems to indicate that the torn curtain was between the holy place and the holy of holies.[70] Even though this would not have been seen by the general populace, it could hardly be kept a secret, especially by the priests who were later converted to Christianity (Acts 6:7). Edersheim says this curtain was sixty feet wide, thirty feet high, and as thick as the breadth of the palm of a hand (II:611). The fact that it was torn from top to bottom indicates that it was rent by the hand of God rather than human sabotage. Furthermore, while this tear probably happened simultaneously with the earthquake, we would be mistaken to think that the earthquake caused the tear. The entire building would collapse from an earthquake sooner than that curtain could be torn in two. No, this is a supernatural event which probably points in two directions. First, it symbolizes the impending destruction of the temple and the obliteration of all other sacrifices. Second, it marks the open access of God's people to his holy presence.

---

[69]D. Ulansey, "The Heavenly Veil Torn: Mark's Cosmic *Inclusio*," *JBL* 110 (1991): 123-125, notes that Josephus describes the outer veil (*War*, 5.212-214). It was decorated to look like "a panorama of the entire heavens." This tapestry, which looked like the sky, was torn in two (Mk 15:38). Ulansey suggests that this would call Mark's readers back to 1:10. This would create an inclusio of the beginning and ending points of Jesus' ministry.

[70]See M. de Jonge, "Matthew 27:51 in Early Christian Exegesis," *HTR* 79 (1986): 67-79 & D.D. Sylva, "The Temple Curtain and Jesus' Death in the Gospel of Luke," *JBL* 105/2 (1986): 239-250.

More noticeable to those on Golgotha is the earthquake which shakes the city, also a sign of God's displeasure (Isa 29:6; Jer 10:10; Ezek 26:18).[71] The tombs of the city are torn open and the saints raised as if to preview 1 Corinthians 15:20-23. But exactly when are they raised? Verse 53 seems to indicate that they do not appear in the city until Sunday. Were they alive, hiding in their tombs for two days? Three simple changes in the NIV's translation will clarify this verse.[72] First, we place a period after "open" in v. 52. Next we eliminate the comma and the word "and" after "tombs" in v. 53. Third, we translate "they came out" (v. 53) [*exelthontes*] as a participle "having come out." It now reads, "The tombs broke open. And the bodies of many holy people who had died were raised to life, and *having come out* of the tombs after Jesus' resurrection, they went into the holy city." Hence, the tombs were broken open on Friday but the resurrection took place along with Jesus' on Sunday.

Because this account is so wondrously miraculous, some have questioned its historicity. But it is no more difficult to believe this account than 1 Corinthians 15, our own hope for resurrection. With this account, Matthew pulls together the death of Jesus and his resurrection and shows us the implications of both: The veil between us and God is torn apart by his death and the tombs which hold us in death are torn apart by his resurrection.

Mt 27:54 *with*
Mk 15:39;
Lk 23:47

[54]When the centurion and those with him who were guarding Jesus {heard his cry and saw how he died [and]MK} saw the earthquake and all that had happened, they were terrified, and {praised God andLK} exclaimed, "Surely he {this manMK} was the Son[a] of God! {a righteous man.LK}"

[a]54 Or *a son*

Lk 23:48

[48]When all the people who had gathered to witness this sight saw what took place, they beat their breasts and went away.

Mt 27:55-56 *with*
Lk 23:49;
Mk 15:40-41

[55]Many women {who knew himLK} were there, watching from a distance. They had followed Jesus from Galilee {to JerusalemMK} to care for his needs. [56]Among them were Mary Magdalene, Mary the mother of James and Joses, and {Salome,MK} the mother of Zebedee's sons.

This earthquake shakes the foundations of Jerusalem as well as this centurion's soul. There is something majestic, even divine, about the

---

[71]Cf. R.J. Bauckham, "The Eschatological Earthquake in Apocalypse of John," *NovT* 19 (1977): 224-233.

[72]Cf. J.W. Wenham, "When Were the Saints Raised?" *JTS* 32 (1981): 150-152; and D. Senior, "The Death of Jesus and the Resurrection of the Holy Ones (Mt 27:51-53)," *CBQ* 38 (1976): 312-329.

way Jesus dies. It is accompanied by this mysterious darkness, the earthquake, the rent veil and the opened tombs. All of this cascades upon his soul. In holy fear he worships God, affirming that Jesus was who he claimed to be — God's Son. A short time ago the crowds mocked Jesus for that very claim; now the centurion honors him with it.

Being a Roman, he may not understand all the implications of being God's Son. After all, the Romans often deified men upon their deaths. Furthermore, the definite article "the" is lacking in the Greek text. Hence, he may be saying nothing more than that Jesus was *a* Son of God.[73] Luke's version of "a righteous man" rather than "Son of God" may support this milder acclamation as well. But the centurion is a resident of Palestine and surely aware that this title was used by the Jews for their Messianic hope. Hence, he is at least saying this: "Jesus didn't deserve this. He was the Jewish Messiah he claimed to be."

The centurion isn't the only one shaken by Jesus' death. The crowds also go away in mourning in fulfillment of Zechariah 12:10 (cf. Jn 19:37). His faithful female followers stand there paralyzed with grief. They have come all the way from Galilee to care for his needs as they had done throughout his ministry (Mk 15:41; Lk 8:2-3). But here and now there is nothing to do but stand idly by and watch their master die. Their dreams are shattered. The man and the movement are dead.

---

[JN 19:]31Now it was the day of Preparation, and the next day was to be a special Sabbath. Because the Jews did not want the bodies left on the crosses during the Sabbath, they asked Pilate to have the legs broken and the bodies taken down. 32The soldiers therefore came and broke the legs of the first man who had been crucified with Jesus, and then those of the other. 33But when they came to Jesus and found that he was already dead, they did not break his legs. 34Instead, one of the soldiers pierced Jesus' side with a spear, bringing a sudden flow of blood and water. 35The man who saw it has given testimony, and his testimony is true. He knows that he tells the truth, and he testifies so that you also may believe. 36These things happened so that the scripture would be fulfilled: "Not one of his bones will be broken,"a 37and, as another scripture says, "They will look on the one they have pierced."b

a36 Exodus 12:46; Num. 9:12; Psalm 34:20    b37 Zech. 12:10

**§ 167a**
**Joseph Asks**
**Pilate for**
**Jesus' Body**
(Mt 27:57-58;
Mk 15:42-45;
Lk 23:50-52;
Jn 19:31-38)

It is now Friday afternoon. The sun has come out again after Jesus died about 3 p.m. and is quickly making its way to the western horizon.

---

[73]R. Bratcher points out that the lack of a definite article in a predicate construction such as this does not necessitate translating it in English with an indefinite article ("A Note on *Huios Theou* (Mk 15:39)," *ExpT* 68 [1956-57]: 27-28). Furthermore, this allows Mark to end his Gospel with a full confession of a Gentile as Luke does.

The setting sun (about 6 p.m. at this time of the year), marks the beginning of the next day for the Jews. In this case it is a very special day. Not only is it a Sabbath day, but the Sabbath during the week-long high holiday of Passover. According to the law (Deut 21:22-23), the Jews could not allow a body to hang on a tree overnight, especially on the holy Sabbath day. So they send a delegation to Pilate to ask him to dispatch the rebels quickly by breaking their legs. Romans often left their victims on their crosses until they were disposed of by scavengers. This would serve as a visual deterrent to other would-be criminals. But such an action offended the sensibilities of the Jews. In deference to his "subjects," Pilate agrees to "finish them off" and take them down from the crosses before the Sabbath.

One of the four soldiers of the execution squad was assigned the gruesome task of breaking the victim's legs (called *crurifragium*). It was done with a swift blow with an iron mallet. It sent the victim once again into writhing agony and sudden shock. Convulsed with pain, and weakened, he dies within minutes. The two insurrectionists are thus dispatched. But Jesus was already dead. Normally the soldier would have carried out the governor's orders anyway. But for some reason he doesn't. Perhaps his commanding officer, the centurion, moved by Jesus' death, hinders him.

Instead of breaking Jesus' legs, the soldier assures his death by piercing his side. He slips his sword up through (or under) his ribs. Out comes a copious flow of both blood and water. There is some debate about whether this indicates a coronary rupture.[74] But this much we can say: (1) The blood came either from the heart itself when it was punctured by the spear or from the lungs which may have filled with blood, indicating a coronary rupture. A punctured organ or even a severed artery probably wouldn't produce much blood since Jesus' heart had stopped beating. (2) The water most likely came from the pericardium, also indicating a coronary rupture. (3) No matter what explanation you use, the bottom line is that Jesus was dead. John devotes no less than four verses to this eyewitness evidence. There is no way to support the docetist claim that Jesus didn't really die, without denying John's veracity.

According to John, this strange turn of events fulfills two Messianic prophecies. First, Psalm 34:20, "Not one of his bones will be broken." This describes how God protected David when he had to pretend to be

----

[74]For a detailed analysis see J. Wilkinson, "The Incident of the Blood and Water in John 19:34," *SJT* 28 (1975): 149-172 and P. Barbet, *A Doctor at Calvary* (New York: Doubleday, 1963), esp. pp. 129-147.

insane before Abimelech in order to save his life. Although David was cast out, God spared him. Thus David serves as a "prototype" of the Messiah who is now cast out and yet eventually saved by God. In addition, Exodus 12:46 commands that the Passover Lamb be roasted whole without breaking a single bone. It too serves as a type of the Messiah, the Lamb of God who takes away the sins of the world (Jn 1:29). The second prophecy fulfilled here is Zechariah 12:10, predicting that the Messiah would be pierced and that the Jews would eventually mourn this wicked deed.

So as evening approached, [43]Joseph of Arimathea, a prominent member of the Council, {a good and upright man, [51]who had not consented to their decision and action,[LK]} who was himself waiting for the kingdom of God, went boldly to Pilate and asked for Jesus' body. {Now Joseph was a disciple of Jesus, but secretly because he feared the Jews.[JN]} [44]Pilate was surprised to hear that he was already dead. Summoning the centurion, he asked him if Jesus had already died. When he learned from the centurion that it was so, he gave the body to Joseph. {With Pilate's permission, he came and took the body away.[JN]}

Mk 15:42b-44 *with* Lk 23:50-51; Jn 19:38

There were less than three hours between the time the soldier pierced Jesus' side and the setting of the sun. Joseph must move fast. He is introduced into the narrative for the first time here with an impressive resume. He was a Sanhedrinist but did not agree with the council's decision. Either he is a dissenting voice during the trials or he is not even invited due to his pro-Jesus leanings. He is a secret disciple, fearing excommunication, but surely some knew of his hidden commitments to Jesus and his open passion for the coming of God's kingdom. The fact that he is a wealthy man and offers such a fine tomb fulfills Isaiah 53:9.

He now boldly asks Pilate for Jesus' body. Why the sudden surge of courage? Perhaps the death of Jesus drew him "out of the closet." Perhaps he hopes that the other Sanhedrin members will now be distracted with preparations for their own Passover meal or simply won't care since their demands have been satisfied. But for whatever reasons Joseph of Arimathea marches boldly into Pilate's palace and asks for Jesus' body.

Pilate is a bit surprised that Jesus is dead after only six hours on the cross. But why should he be surprised after he gave orders to have Jesus' legs broken? John is the one who records the breaking of the legs. Mark is the one who records Pilate's surprise. It could be that Pilate asks the centurion if he broke Jesus' legs and watched him die. But the centurion would say, "I didn't have to break his legs. The man was already dead. But we did verify it by lancing his heart." Thus, Pilate is surprised that Jesus died so soon.

Having verified the completion of the execution, Pilate releases Jesus' body to Joseph for burial. Joseph's and Pilate's actions here are further evidence that Jesus was not condemned for high treason. Had he been, Pilate would not have allowed a Jew to offer him a dignified burial, nor would Joseph have offered it. Instead, Jesus would likely have been taken off the cross and thrown into a mass grave like other villains.[75]

**§ 167b**
**Jesus' Body**
**Placed in a**
**Tomb**
(Mt 27:59-60;
Mk 15:46;
Lk 23:53-54;
Jn 19:39-42)

[JN 19:]39He was accompanied by Nicodemus, the man who earlier had visited Jesus at night. Nicodemus brought a mixture of myrrh and aloes, about seventy-five pounds.[a] 40Taking Jesus' body, the two of them wrapped it, with the spices, in strips of {cleanMT} linen {cloth.MT,LK} This was in accordance with Jewish burial customs. 41At the place where Jesus was crucified, there was a garden, and in the garden a {his ownMT} new tomb {cut out of rock,MT,MK,LK} in which no one had ever been laid. 42Because it was the Jewish day of Preparation and since the tomb was nearby, they laid Jesus there. {Then he rolled a big stone in front of the entrance to the tomb and went away.MT,MK}

a39 Greek *a hundred litrai* (about 34 kilograms)

Joseph is assisted by his friend and fellow Sanhedrinist, Nicodemus. This is the third time that he enters John's narrative (Jn 3:1ff; 7:45-52). While Joseph provides the tomb, Nicodemus provides the ointment, both at considerable expense. Myrrh was a gummy resin extracted from trees in Arabia. It was strongly aromatic and used as an expensive perfume. It could be mixed with other aloes to make a sort of paste which could be put in the folds of the linen cloth or strips of linen could be dipped in it. Its purpose was to overpower the stench of the decaying body, which seventy-five pounds could effectively do. Once it dried it would form a kind of stiff casing (cf. Jn 11:44), but it didn't have the preserving quality of Egyptian mummification.

According to the normal burial customs, these two men first washed the bloodied body. Then they wrapped it in clean linen. The text doesn't say just how they did this. But it was common to lay the body on a long sheet of linen which could then be folded over the front of the body (e.g., the shroud of Turin). Then more strips would be used to wrap around that linen sheet.

Because the Sabbath is quickly approaching, the two men have no time to waste. They carry Jesus a short distance to Joseph's tomb, which

---

[75]According to R.E. Brown, Pilate would probably not be eager to give Jesus' body over to his disciples lest they honor him as a hero. However, he would likely have no objections to placing it in the care of Joseph since he was a member of the Sanhedrin. (Cf. R.E. Brown, "The Burial of Jesus (Mark 15:42-47)," *CBQ* 50 [1988]: 233-245).

is in a nearby garden.[76] It is a private burial plot, not a public cemetery. (Hence, it would be nearly impossible for the women, as well as Peter and John, to go to the wrong tomb on Sunday.) The tomb is cut into white limestone rock. It has not yet been used. These burial caves were usually about nine feet square, with upwards of six "shelves" for bodies. Furthermore, there were often *loculi* tunnels carved into the sides of the cave. These were about a foot and a half wide and six feet deep, used for ossuary boxes. A year after a person was buried, the period of mourning would officially come to an end. Then a family member would re-enter the tomb and collect the remaining bones of the corpse.[77] These could be placed in a small box called an ossuary. Thus whole families could be buried in one small tomb.

Jesus' body is laid out on a rock ledge which has been carved for that purpose. Once the body is in place, a huge stone is rolled into a "v" shaped groove at the entrance. Although the entrance is low enough that even the women had to stoop to look into it (Jn 20:11), a rock that size, resting in a depression would still effectively detour scavengers and grave robbers.

---

[MT 27:]61Mary Magdalene and the other Mary {the mother of Joses[MK]} were sitting there opposite the tomb {[and] saw where he was laid.[MK]}

[LK 23:]55[These] women, who had come with Jesus from Galilee, followed Joseph and saw the tomb and how his body was laid in it. 56Then they went home and prepared spices and perfumes. But they rested on the Sabbath in obedience to the commandment.

**§ 168
Women Watch
the Tomb,
Soldiers Guard
It
(Mt 27:61-66;
Mk 15:47;
Lk 23:55-56)**

The women want to pay their respects to Jesus but they keep their distance from these two prominent members of the Sanhedrin. How could they know these two are sympathetic to Jesus? They also stand aloof due to the social stigma of men and women interacting. In addi-

---

[76]There are two proposed sites. One is the church of the Holy Sepulchre, inside the present walls of the city. The other is a small garden at the base of the hill that is presently called Golgotha, just outside the north wall of the city. While neither site can be proven beyond a doubt, the evidence is much stronger for the church of the Holy Sepulchre (cf. D. Bahat, "Does the Holy Sepulchre Church Mark the Burial of Jesus?" *BAR* 12/3 [1986]: 26-45; G. Barkay, "The Garden Tomb: Was Jesus Buried Here?" *BAR* 12/2 [1986]: 40-57; and J. McRay, "Tomb Typology and the Tomb of Jesus," *ABW* 2/2 [1994]: 34-42).

[77]This practice of "second burial" appears to be limited to the period of about B.C. 30 to A.D. 70. For further archaeological details on first century Palestinian burials, see R. Hachlili and A. Killebrew, "Jewish Funerary Customs During the Second Temple Period, in the light of the Excavations at the Jericho Necropolis," *PEQ* 115 (1983): 109-132.

tion, Carson states that Roman law forbade mourning executed criminals (p. 584). These two Marys want, in the worst way, to show their love for Jesus, but are simply not able to at this time. So they do the next best thing. They find out where Jesus is laid and plan to return at the first available opportunity. That will be at the crack of dawn on Sunday. For now, they must run back to town before sundown to prepare the necessary spices for anointing the dead.

Mt 27:62-66

⁶²The next day, the one after Preparation Day, the chief priests and the Pharisees went to Pilate. ⁶³"Sir," they said, "we remember that while he was still alive that deceiver said, 'After three days I will rise again.' ⁶⁴So give the order for the tomb to be made secure until the third day. Otherwise, his disciples may come and steal the body and tell the people that he has been raised from the dead. This last deception will be worse than the first."

⁶⁵"Take a guard," Pilate answered. "Go, make the tomb as secure as you know how." ⁶⁶So they went and made the tomb secure by putting a seal on the stone and posting the guard.

Pilate thinks that he is through with Jesus at 9 a.m. on Friday. But about 3 p.m. the Jews come and ask that he order Jesus' legs broken. Shortly after that Joseph arrives and asks for the body of Jesus. Now, Saturday morning a third delegation arrives asking Pilate to provide a guard for the tomb.

It's not that the chief priests believe Jesus could raise from the dead. They are merely afraid that his disciples will try to propagate a hoax by stealing Jesus' body and claiming a resurrection in fulfillment of Jesus' "supposed" prophecy. Now it should not surprise us that the chief priests were more perceptive than the disciples in interpreting Jesus' words. They were pretty good at hermeneutics, just miserably poor at faith.

They ask Pilate for a Roman guard for three days. Pilate's response is somewhat ambiguous: "You have a guard" [echete koustōdian]. Does he mean, "You got it. Take what you need" (as the NIV implies)? Or does he mean, "You have your own temple guards, use them!"? While both are possible, it seems that Pilate actually gives the Jews a Roman guard. First, he wants to avoid any potential conflicts which could flair into civil disorder. Second, after the resurrection, these guards are worried about the report getting back to Pilate (Mt 28:14). Temple guards wouldn't be concerned about that. The Roman guards, on the other hand, might very well report first to the Sanhedrin rather than to Pilate since it was the Sanhedrin's corpse that they "lost" (Mt 28:11). Third, Pilate puts his seal on the stone in front of the tomb. This is nothing more than a bit of clay or wax impressed with a signet ring, which holds a cord in front of the tomb. By moving the stone you would break the seal of clay/wax.

It is not hard to do, but by doing so you violate the authority of the one whose seal is on the clay/wax. In other words, with Pilate's seal on the stone, they would be trespassing against the authority of Rome — a violation of no small consequence. Thus, this little seal would dissuade would-be thieves. God, however, is not intimidated by it in the least.

# PART THIRTEEN
# THE RESURRECTION
# AND ASCENSION OF JESUS

We have finally come to the meat of the message — the resurrection. Throughout Acts and the Epistles, this event is proclaimed as the cornerstone of our faith (Acts 2:22-36; 4:2, 33; 23:6; 24:15; Rom 1:4; 6:5; 1 Cor 15; Eph 1:18; 2:4-7; Phil 3:10-11; 1 Thess 4:13-18; 1 Pet 3:18-22; Rev 20:5-6). Paul goes so far as to say that if Jesus didn't actually, factually, bodily raise from the dead, then we Christians are a pitiable lot (1 Cor 15:19). This event makes all the difference in the world. It validates Jesus as God's Son. We can then believe him implicitly and follow him completely. It validates Jesus' work on the cross. If he didn't raise from the dead, then he was nothing more than a valiant martyr, and we are still in our sins (1 Cor 15:17). It assures our own victory over the tomb and grants us hope for our own resurrection (1 Cor 15:21-22, 42-44, 51-54). Humanity's only unconquered enemy has now been defeated! These are not just theological acrobatics. The evangelists record for us the most important message of life and death (and life again!).

However, not everyone is eager to accept the bodily resurrection of Jesus as a historic fact. Some deny it for philosophic, religious, or even "scientific" reasons. But the testimony of the Gospels has to be accounted for in some way, and there are essentially only five theories which have attempted to deny the historic reality of Jesus' bodily resurrection.[1]

(1) A Stolen Body — the disciples came and stole Jesus' body and then propagated the hoax of his resurrection. This was the original theory concocted by the Jews (Mt 28:11-15). However, we are immediately confronted with two problems: motive and ability. How could eleven cowering disciples sneak past an armed Roman guard, roll away the stone (without waking them), remove the body, and then propagate

---

[1]For a longer defense of the historic, bodily resurrection see N.L. Geisler, *The Battle for the Resurrection* (Nashville: Nelson, 1989) and Josh McDowell's books on Evidences.

this hoax of a resurrection? Even if they could, why would they? None of the Eleven believed it even after someone claimed to see Jesus. And for a Jew to desecrate a burial site, especially one of such dignity, is unprecedented.[2] Furthermore, these would be colossally stupid thieves to rob the grave of a crucified peasant, unwrap a decaying corpse on site (ostensibly for the spices and ointment), and then tidy up the place before they left by folding up the linen wraps!

(2) The Swoon Theory (especially promoted in *The Passover Plot*) — Jesus never really died, but only swooned and then resuscitated. But consider the facts. After the flogging, Jesus was handed over to trained executioners and crucified. When Joseph of Arimathea asked for the body, Pilate had the centurion double check his work. They made sure of Jesus' death by lancing his side with a spear. The copious flow of blood and water indicated either a punctured or ruptured heart. Afterward, he was wrapped with linens and 75 lbs. of spices. Even if he was barely alive, this surely would have suffocated him. After that he was placed in a cool tomb which was sealed with a huge stone. Surviving such physical shock and then escaping from the tomb would, indeed, be almost as miraculous as the resurrection itself.

(3) The Wrong Tomb — The women, then Peter and John, went to the wrong tomb and mistakenly thought Jesus was raised. However, this was a private tomb, not a public cemetery. There were no other tombs with which it could be confused. Besides, it is difficult to think that Mary, Jesus' mother, would forget so quickly where they laid her son, especially when the tomb was marked by a huge stone and an armed guard. But the weakest point of this theory is that it doesn't explain where the body of Jesus was and why the Sanhedrin could not produce it on the day of Pentecost.

(4) Hallucination — The disciples wanted so badly for Jesus to be raised that they hallucinated his appearances. The study of psychology effectively demolishes this theory. Groups of people don't simultaneously see the same hallucination (cf. 1 Cor 15:6). Furthermore, it takes a certain psychosis to hallucinate. Now, we might believe that two or three of the disciples might be in such a state at some point in their lives, but not all of them at the same time. A worse problem is the fact that none of the disciples expected a resurrection and therefore could not have hallucinated one. Again, this theory also leaves the body of Jesus unaccounted for.

---

[2] D. Whitaker, "What Happened to the Body of Jesus?" *ExpT* 81 (1969-70): 307-311, suggests that grave robbers took it. However, he does not adequately account for the guards or the appearances.

A related theory is that Jesus' resurrection was spiritual and not physical. Thus, the disciples didn't actually see his body but a "Christophany" (a vision-type appearance). That's not what the Gospels say. They intend for us to believe that Jesus rose physically. Thus, any theory of a non-bodily resurrection can't be defended scripturally[3] or philosophically.[4]

(5) Myth — The Gospels are a literary "fiction" with little basis in historic reality. If this were a mere literary fabrication, however, we could almost certainly expect a number of differences from what we actually have in the Gospels. For example, the women would not likely have been the first witnesses.[5] And Peter & Company likely would have expected it and immediately believed. Surely somebody would have claimed to have seen the actual event.[6] The bottom line is that the evangelists write with "restrained sobriety of these accounts as compared with the later apocryphal Gospels (e.g., *Gospel of Peter*, 9:35-11:44)" (Carson, p. 588). What we are about to read is not literary fiction but a presentation of what the evangelists believed to be historic fact.[7]

The evidence in favor of the resurrection of Jesus is extremely compelling. There are a number of things that can only be accounted for by the literal, bodily resurrection of our Lord: (1) the conversion of 3,000 people on the day of Pentecost so close to the time and place of Jesus' death; (2) the transformation of Peter and Paul; (3) the martyrdom of the Apostles; (4) the continued sacraments of Baptism and the Lord's Supper; (5) the day of worship changed from the Sabbath (Saturday) to

---

[3]N.L. Geisler, "The Significance of Christ's Physical Resurrection," *BibSac* 146 (1989): 148-170.

[4]S.T. Davis, "Was Jesus Raised Bodily?" *CSR* 14/2 (1985): 140-152 and G.J. Hughes, "Dead Theories, Live Metaphors and the Resurrection," *HeyJ* 29 (1988): 313-328.

[5]It would be most unusual to portray women as the primary testimony since they were not legal witnesses in Jewish culture. Josephus says, "Let not the testimony of women be accepted because of the levity and presumption of their sex" (*Ant* 4.219). But as G. O'Collins and D. Kendall point out, Mary Magdalene in particular was a major witness to Jesus' resurrection. Of the six resurrection accounts (Mk 16:1-8, 9-20; Mt 28:1-20; Lk 23:56b-24:53; Jn 20:1-29; 21:1-23), Mary is mentioned (always first) in five of them. That certainly can't be first-century literary fabrication (cf. G. O'Collins & D. Kendall, "Mary Magdalene as Major Witness to Jesus' Resurrection," *TS* 48 [1987]: 631-646).

[6]Other potential literary additions might include more proof from prophecy, Jesus' descent into hell, a description of Jesus' resurrected body, and appearances of Jesus to the unbelieving Sanhedrin.

[7]W.L. Craig, "The Historicity of the Empty Tomb of Jesus," *NTS* 31 (1985): 39-67, shows how the evangelists present the resurrection as historic fact. Happily, the skepticism of the rationalists is quickly waning in current scholarly circles. The empty tomb is widely accepted as an historic fact. It even forms the basis of the original anti-Christian polemic against the reality of Jesus' resurrection.

Sunday (e.g., Acts 20:7); (6) the unswerving testimony of the early church that this event actually took place; and (7) the changed lives of millions of Christians throughout history.

At the same time, no part of the Gospels is fraught with so much textual difficulty or variation between the accounts.[8] Perhaps it is due to the excited nature of the events, compression of the narratives, the deeply personal accounts of Jesus' appearances, and the particular theological emphasis of each evangelist as he closes out his book. While these variations almost defy harmonization, they are neither irreconcilable contradictions nor do they impugn the historical veracity of the accounts. So, while we are perplexed, there is no reason to doubt the central truth of the Gospel: Jesus is alive and well!

**§ 169-171
The Women
Find the Empty
Tomb
(Mt 28:1-8;
Mk 16:1-8;
Lk 24:1-10;
Jn 20:1)**

[MK 16:]1When the Sabbath was over, Mary Magdalene, Mary the mother of James, {Joanna,[LK]} and Salome bought spices so that they might go to anoint Jesus' body.

[MT 28:]1After the Sabbath, at dawn on the first day of the week, Mary Magdalene and the other Mary went to look at the tomb.

2There was a violent earthquake, for an angel of the Lord came down from heaven and, going to the tomb, rolled back the stone and sat on it. 3His appearance was like lightning, and his clothes were white as snow. 4The guards were so afraid of him that they shook and became like dead men.

On Friday afternoon (Lk 23:56) and Saturday evening (Mk 16:1) these pious women busied themselves purchasing and preparing a fragrant ointment for Jesus' burial. By Sunday morning it would be a little late to cover up the stench of decomposition, and somewhat unnecessary since Nicodemus had already provided some 75 lbs of ointment for the job. Nonetheless, anointing a dead body was an act of devotion and love of which these women will not be deprived. The following chart shows which women each evangelist identifies at the tomb. Likely, they all went to the tomb together, but not necessarily.[9]

---

[8]C.E.B. Cranfield, "The Resurrection of Jesus Christ," *ExpT* 101 (1990): 167-172, lists ten apparent discrepancies in the resurrection narratives and gives reasonable explanations to each of them.

[9]J. Wenham, *Easter Enigma* (Grand Rapids: Baker, 1984), pp. 82-84, suggests that Mary Magdalene, Mary the wife of Clopas and Salome go to the tomb together, leaving from John's house. And Johanna and "Susanna" go together, leaving from the Hasmonean palace.

| Mt 28:1 | Mk 16:1 | Lk 24:10 | Jn 20:1-2 |
|---------|---------|----------|-----------|
| Mary Magdalene | Mary Magdalene | Mary Magdalene | Mary Magdalene |
| Mary, mother of James | Mary, mother of James | Mary, mother of James | |
| | Salome | | |
| | | Joanna | |
| | | Others | "we" (v. 2) |

While it is still dark, they set out for the tomb (Jn 20:1). Along the way the sun starts to peek over the Mount of Olives to the east. Suddenly there is a terrific earthquake, perhaps a strong aftershock of Friday's supernatural quake. This shaken band of women is now even more unnerved. But they are not nearly as frightened as the guards. We don't know exactly what these guys saw. Matthew only says they reported "everything that had happened" to the chief priests (28:11). According to Matthew 28:3-4, they likely saw this radiant angel descend from heaven, roll back this huge stone single-handedly, and sit on it. And based on their report to the Sanhedrin, they also observed that the tomb was empty. These guards are the only potential witnesses to the resurrection itself. If Jesus left the tomb when the angel rolled away the stone, the guards could hardly have missed it. Then again, Jesus could have exited the tomb even while the stone was in place (cf. Jn 20:26).

²Very early on the first day of the week, just after sunrise {while it was still dark,ᴶᴺ} they were on their way to the tomb ³and they asked each other, "Who will roll the stone away from the entrance of the tomb?"

⁴But when they looked up, they saw that the stone, which was very large, had been rolled away.

Mk 16:2-4 *with* Jn 20:1

³[B]ut when they entered, they did not find the body of the Lord Jesus. ⁴While they were wondering about this, suddenly two men {a young manᴹᴷ} in clothes that gleamed like lightning stood beside them {sitting on the right side.ᴹᴷ}

Lk 24:3-4 *with* Mk 16:5

These poor women have just pulled themselves together from the earthquake when reality sets in. "Who is going to move that boulder for us so we can anoint Jesus' body?" About that time they arrive at the site to find that the stone has already been rolled away. They don't yet know how.

As they enter the tomb, they find they have an even greater problem, more vexing than the stone. The body is gone! Who took it? And where did they put it?! Before they can come up with a decent hypothesis, they are floored (literally) by another ominous sight. Inside the tomb stood two men in white garments that shone like lightning.[10] Instinctively, the women drop to their knees with their faces to the ground.

Lk 24:5-8 *with*
Mt 28:5-6; Mk 16:6

[5]In their fright the women bowed down with their faces to the ground, but the men {angel[MT]} said to them, "{Do not be afraid, for I know that you are looking for Jesus[MT]} {the Nazarene, who was crucified.[MK]} Why do you look for the living among the dead? [6]He is not here; he has risen! {Come and see the place where he lay.[MT]} Remember how he told you, while he was still with you in Galilee: [7]'The Son of Man must be delivered into the hands of sinful men, be crucified and on the third day be raised again.'" [8]Then they remembered his words.

Mt 28:7 *with*
Mk 16:7

[7]Then go quickly and tell his disciples {and Peter[MK]}: 'He has risen from the dead and is going ahead of you into Galilee. There you will see him {just as he told you."[MK]} Now I have told you."

The angel comforts them saying, "Do not be afraid." Typically, these are the first words out of an angel's mouth (Mt 1:20; 28:5,10; Lk 1:13, 30; 2:10; Acts 18:9; 27:24). This angel is very "matter-of-fact." From the heavenly perspective this is all quite clear. Jesus predicted his resurrection several times (Mt 16:21; 17:23; 20:19; Lk 9:22, 43-45; 18:31-33). He is only doing what he promised and what his divine nature demanded. Why is that so hard to believe? The angel seems to be somewhat incredulous about the women's unbelief.

The angel orders them to quickly inform the men (especially Peter), what has taken place. They are to meet Jesus in Galilee. This is appropriate since Galilee is where it all began and it is a more appropriate place for launching his Gentile mission. But this does not mean that Jesus will not appear to them in Jerusalem. Indeed, for the next week, during the Passover celebration, he will make several appearances. After the Passover, these men are to return to their homes in Galilee and there await further instructions from the Lord. About a month later they would return to Jerusalem for the feast of Pentecost. Naturally, they will arrive early for the period of purification. It will be at that time that Jesus will ascend from the Mount of Olives, ten days before Pentecost.[11]

---

[10]Matthew comes right out and says that they are angels. Mark and Luke identify them as angels by their clothing (cf. Lk 24:23). Furthermore, Matthew and Mark concentrate on the angel who spoke, while Luke gives the fuller detail of two actual entities (cf. Jn 20:12). This is not uncommon (cf. Mt 8:28; 20:30 & parallels). Luke may be emphasizing the legality of the double witness.

[11]Luke's compressed narrative only tells of the appearances in Jerusalem. Matthew, on the other hand, stresses the appearances in Galilee. As C.F.D. Moule, points out, however, this certainly does not constitute a contradiction in light of the normal pilgrim commutes back and forth from Jerusalem to Galilee ("The Post-Resurrection Appearances in the Light of Festival Pilgrimages," *NTS* 4 [1957-58]: 58-61).

[8]Trembling and bewildered, {yet filled with joy[MT]} the women went out and fled from the tomb. They said nothing to anyone, because they were afraid.

Mk 16:8 *with*
Mt 28:8

[9]When they came back from the tomb, they told all these things to the Eleven and to all the others.

Lk 24:9

The women are frightened, confused, and dizzy with joy. They run as quickly as they can to tell the Eleven, without stopping to talk with anyone along the way.[12] Their report naturally is directed to Peter and John. The other nine are in a tight circle around them. Still other disciples are listening incredulously from the perimeter.

[JN 20:]2So she {Mary Magdalene, Joanna, Mary the mother of James, and the others with them[LK]} came running {from the tomb[LK]} to Simon Peter and the other disciple, the one Jesus loved, {to the Eleven and to all the others,[LK]} and said, "They have taken the Lord out of the tomb, and we don't know where they have put him!" {But they did not believe the women, because their words seemed to them like nonsense.[LK]}

**§ 172**
**Peter and John**
**Investigate the**
**Empty Tomb**
(Lk 24:9-12;
Jn 20:2-10)

There seems to be a discrepancy here between Luke and John. John focuses on Mary and her unbelief. She is convinced that Jesus' body has been stolen, not that Jesus has been raised as the angels (in Luke) have announced (Jn 20:2, 11-15). Luke, however, speaks of the whole group of women. As a whole, they believe the angels and remember how Jesus predicted his resurrection (Lk 24:6-8). We can account for these differences in one of two ways.

First, Mary may have looked at the empty tomb and run away quickly before the angels appeared. Thus, she reports to Peter and John, who then run to the tomb only hearing that it was empty. The other women report to the nine remaining Apostles and only later to Peter and John. They deliver the whole "scoop" which is, of course, rejected by the Apostles. Mary follows Peter and John to the tomb where she weeps bitterly and sees the angels for the first time (Jn 20:12). Just then, Jesus appears to her. She, of course, believes. She then runs and reports to the Apostles what turns out to be the first actual resurrection appearance (Mk 16:9-11).

---

[12]Mark 16:8 are likely the last words that Mark wrote himself. Verses 9-20 are not written in Mark's style or vocabulary and they are fraught with textual difficulties. But could Mark really have closed his book with verse 8? This would mean that Mark ends on a note of fear, with no actual appearances of the resurrected Jesus and the last word in his book would be the Greek conjunction *gar*, meaning "for" or "because." However, F.W. Danker, "Postscript to the Markan Secrecy Motif," *CTM* 38 (1967): 24-27, defends Mark 16:8 as the ending of the book. He suggests that this abrupt ending fits the book's abrupt beginning as well as its secrecy motif (cf. 1:45). Furthermore, P.W. van der Horst, "Can a Book End with *gar*? A Note on Mark 16:8," *JTS ns* 23 (1972): 121-124, shows that grammatically it is possible to end a sentence or even a book with the word *gar*.

A second explanation is that all the women, including Mary, see the angels and together they report it to the Apostles (Lk 24:9-10). However, not all the women are at the same level of belief. That, of course, would be natural; not all the Apostles believe at the same time either (cf. Lk 24:12 & Jn 20:8). Perhaps Mary is not as convinced as the others that Jesus is actually alive. Once she gets away from the garden, the empty tomb is a more ominous reality to her than the angelic message.

The narrative is so compressed, it is impossible to see just exactly where each of the pieces fit. But we really don't need to. We can be certain of the following: (1) Peter and John learn from Mary that the tomb is empty and they bolt for the door. (They may have stayed long enough to hear the report of the other women also). (2) At least nine Apostles hear the other women talk of an angelic announcement that Jesus has raised from the dead. (3) The women are growing in faith (Lk 24:8), but the men think their emotions have gotten the better of them.

**Jn 20:3-10** *with* **Lk 24:12**

³So Peter and the other disciple started for the tomb. ⁴Both were running, but the other disciple outran Peter and reached the tomb first. ⁵He bent over and looked in at the strips of linen lying there but did not go in. ⁶Then Simon Peter, who was behind him, arrived and went into the tomb. He saw the strips of linen lying there {by themselves,ᴸᴷ} ⁷as well as the burial cloth that had been around Jesus' head. The cloth was folded up by itself, separate from the linen. ⁸Finally the other disciple, who had reached the tomb first, also went inside. He saw and believed. {[But Peter] went away, wondering to himself what had happened.ᴸᴷ} ⁹(They still did not understand from Scripture that Jesus had to rise from the dead.)
¹⁰Then the disciples went back to their homes.

Both Peter and John head for the tomb *posthaste*. They run along side by side, but Peter just can't keep up and John is too excited to wait for him. Perhaps Peter is older than John or maybe just not quite as athletic. For whatever reasons, Peter is left behind. Poor Mary is further behind still. She apparently won't get to the tomb until these guys are already gone.

When John arrives at the site, sure enough, the stone is rolled away. He stops at the entrance and bends down to have a look inside. The body is gone! All that is left are the strips of linen which were lovingly wrapped around him. About that time, Peter, panting for breath, pushes past John, entering the tomb. He takes a closer look.¹³ Peter sees both the linen wrappings and the head cloth lying separately. Furthermore, the

---

¹³There are three different words in vv. 5-8 for "look," [v. 5, *blepei*; v. 6, *theorei*; v. 8, *eiden*]. Taken as a whole, John is saying that they carefully investigated the tomb.

head cloth is "folded." The word means "wrapped" (cf. Lk 23:53). "It implies that the cloth had been wound around the head into the shape of a sphere and not folded flat like a table napkin" (Tenney, p. 189). The text does not go so far as to say that the cloth is in the exact position it had been when on Jesus' face, as if he had just vanished through it, but it does indicate the burial clothes were in order. In other words, this is not the work of grave-robbers. Anyone who would steal or move the body would take the wrappings with it. After all, who would unwrap a rotting corpse? And considering the guards outside the tomb, no robber would dare take the time to neatly fold the garments, even if they did remove them from the body. This simply does not make sense! Peter is puzzled.

John finally straggles into the tomb and sees this strange sight. Although he does not yet connect it with fulfilled prophecy (cf. Ps 16:10; Isa 53:10-11; Hos 6:1-2; Lk 24:26-27), he believes Jesus rose as he said he would (cf. Jn 2:22; 11:25; 16:22).[14] Peter, on the other hand, needs more time and more evidence. He walks away confused. What a debate these two must have had on the way home!

---

[11][B]ut Mary stood outside the tomb crying. As she wept, she bent over to look into the tomb [12]and saw two angels in white, seated where Jesus' body had been, one at the head and the other at the foot.

[13]They asked her, "Woman, why are you crying?"

"They have taken my Lord away," she said, "and I don't know where they have put him." [14]At this, she turned around and saw Jesus standing there, but she did not realize that it was Jesus.

[9]When Jesus rose early on the first day of the week, he appeared first to Mary Magdalene, out of whom he had driven seven demons.

**§ 173**
**Appearance to**
**Mary**
**Magdalene**
([Mk 16:9-11];[15]
Jn 20:11-18)

Mk 16:9

---

[14]In his insightful article, "The Faith of the Beloved Disciple and the Community of John 20," *JSNT* 23 (1985): 83-97, B. Byrne analyzes the structure of John 20. He points out that Mary Magdalene (11-18), the Apostolic band (19-23), and Thomas in particular (24-29), believe after seeing Jesus. John, on the other hand, believes on the basis of this sign of the head coverings (perhaps in contrast to Lazarus' [11:44]) without seeing Jesus. Thus "the beloved disciple" alone demonstrates the paradigm of sign-faith that Jesus extols (20:29). In the end, this is what the entire book is all about (20:31). In this way, John models for his readers the proper response to Christ.

[15]From verse 9 to the end of Mark 16 is perhaps the most disputed text in all the Bible. The ancient manuscripts handle it in a variety of ways. (1) It is omitted by the Sinaitic (‎א) and the Vaticanus (B), although the latter leaves a blank column where it could be placed. Clement, Origen, Eusebius, Jerome, and Ammonius agree that it should be omitted. (2) It is included in a number of manuscripts (A, C, D, K, X, Δ, Θ, ω) from the Byzantine, Alexandrian and Western families. (3) It is included with an asterisk, obeli or some kind of critical note in several others (*f*1, 137, 138, 1110, 1210, 1215, 1217, 1221, 1241[vid], 1582). (4) Verses 9-20 are replaced by a shorter ending (it[k], k). (5) Both verses 9-20 and

Peter and John return home to give their report of the situation. They are wrapped up in conversation that appears to ignore Mary (which would be neither unusual nor rude in their culture). She is devastated as she stands in front of the tomb wailing [*klaiō*, Lk 8:58; Jn 11:31, 33]. When she stoops to look in the tomb to see what struck Peter and John, she sees something they did not. Two angels, apparently the same ones who were there earlier (Mt 28:5; Mk 16:5; Lk 24:4), are seated on the ledge where Jesus' body had lain. Surely she knows they are angels; Luke describes their white clothes as "gleaming like lightning." That's pretty hard to miss. In John, this is the first time Mary has seen these angels. This leads us to believe that Mary ran off from the other women before the angels appeared to them. On the other hand, the synoptics seem to place Mary at the scene when the angels first appeared. Therefore, we can't know with certainty if this is Mary's first or second encounter with these angels.

They ask Mary, "Why are you crying?" This was a glorious occasion if she would just listen to them and believe. These poor angels must be flabbergasted at the obtuse humans who won't believe what Jesus clearly told them. Mary, though, can't get over the thought that someone stole his body.

Before the angels have time to respond, Jesus appears behind Mary. We can't know what made Mary turn around to look at him. Perhaps the angels looked over Mary's shoulder at him or even pointed. Or perhaps Mary heard him walking up behind her. Whatever the reason, she turns around and looks at him without recognizing him. (The angels must be ribbing each other in unbelief.) Perhaps Jesus' appearance was veiled as with the two on the road to Emmaus (Lk 24:16, 31; Mk 16:12). Or perhaps her eyes were clouded with tears and an early morning mist. At any rate, she is not yet looking directly at him (Jn 20:16).

Jn 20:15-18 *with*
Mk 16:10

¹⁵"Woman," he said, "why are you crying? Who is it you are looking for?"

Thinking he was the gardener, she said, "Sir, if you have carried him away, tell me where you have put him, and I will get him."

¹⁶Jesus said to her, "Mary."

---

the shorter ending are included. Sometimes vv. 9-20 come first (L, Ψ, 099, 0112, 274^mg, 579, *l*1602, etc.) and sometimes the short ending comes first (274^mg, 1^961, 1602). (6) A long addition is inserted between vv. 14 and 15 (W). The bottom line is that we can't tell if Mark actually wrote this. Yet to omit it completely leaves a strange and difficult ending to the Gospel. S. Helton, "Churches of Christ and Mark 16:9-20," *RestQ* 36 (1994): 33-52, discusses an attractive option. While Mark probably didn't write it himself, it was added by a person of ancient authority and hence should be considered canonical. Therefore, Mark 16:9-20 will be treated here as having ancient authority, if not canonical status, even though we recognize that Mark likely did not pen these words himself.

She turned toward him and cried out in Aramaic, "Rabboni!" (which means Teacher).

[17]Jesus said, "Do not hold on to me, for I have not yet returned to the Father. Go instead to my brothers and tell them, 'I am returning to my Father and your Father, to my God and your God.'"

[18]Mary Magdalene went to the disciples {who had been with him and who were mourning and weeping[MK]} with the news: "I have seen the Lord!" And she told them that he had said these things to her.

[11]When they heard that Jesus was alive and that she had seen him, they did not believe it.

Mk 16:11

Jesus asks Mary the same question the angels had, "Why are you crying?" She assumes he is the gardener. Who else would be out there that early in the morning? Hoping this "insider" would help her, she asks him where he put the body. She even offers to take it off his hands for him.

When Jesus calls her name, as only he could, she instantly recognizes him. His tenderness and intimacy are unmistakable. She cries out "Rabboni" (a title of extraordinary honor), and latches on to him. Jesus tells her to let go [*mē mou haptou*], but not because she would "defile" him in his present state, for he invites Thomas to touch him (Jn 20:27). No, she must not get too attached to him because (1) he is not staying indefinitely, and (2) there is work to do. She is the first to see Jesus and she must quickly go tell the Apostles.

Jesus calls them "brothers" for the first time (in John). Times are changing. Jesus elevates them to new levels as he passes the baton of leadership and as he has now redeemed them from their sins (cf. Heb 2:11). They are no longer merely friends (Jn 15:15), but brothers. We will never be peers of Jesus, but we are his brothers and share in his inheritance (Rom 8:17). Yet Jesus differentiates between "my Father and your Father, my God and your God." While there is only one God, our relation to him is radically different than Jesus'. He is a Son by nature, we by adoption.

Mary bursts into the room where the confused Apostles are weeping. Surely they have heard the report of Peter and John. Some may have been leaning toward John's interpretation, others to Peter's. Mary clearly sides with John saying, "I saw him! . . . I touched him!" Still, she is "just a woman." They refuse to believe her.

[9]Suddenly Jesus met them. "Greetings," he said. They came to him, clasped his feet and worshiped him. [10]Then Jesus said to them, "Do not be afraid. Go and tell my brothers to go to Galilee; there they will see me."

**§ 174**
**Appearance to**
**the Other**
**Women**
**(Mt 28:9-10)**

We now return to Matthew's narrative. As the women leave the tomb to report to the Apostles, Jesus greets them with a cheery "Hello!" As they cling to his feet, he commands them to tell the disciples to meet him in Galilee.

This little piece presents a problem when we compare it to John 20:11-18. There, Jesus first appears to Mary Magdalene alone after she follows Peter and John back to the tomb. To harmonize Matthew and John we must do one of two things. First, we might say that Mary was not included in this group of women who saw Jesus. That would mean, of course, that she ran off quickly by herself to the Apostles. When she returned with Peter and John, Jesus appeared to her alone outside the tomb. And all this would take place *before* Jesus appeared to these other women since Mark 16:9 says "He appeared first to Mary Magdalene." Or we can chalk Mark 16:9 up to a textual variant or even interpret "first" as the first appearance to Mary, not the first appearance to anyone.

A second possibility is that Matthew 28:9-10 is speaking about Jesus' appearance to Mary, and Mary alone. Since she was the main representative of the group, and since the other women would later see Jesus anyway, Matthew compresses the narrative and includes the whole group of women here. This option is strengthened by the parallels in Matthew 28:9-10 and John 20:11-18. Both contain "clinging," "commissioning" and "brothers."

Another peculiarity of Matthew's rendition is his emphasis on Galilee. Reading verse 10 alone, we might get the impression that this appearance to the women was the only Jerusalem appearance. But this verse does not preclude other Jerusalem appearances. And from other parallels we know there were several more. But it would appear Matthew is emphasizing Jesus' continued work in Galilee, to *all* Israel, and even as a light to the Gentiles (cf. Mt 4:14-16).

**§ 175**
**The Soldiers**
**Report to the**
**Jewish**
**Authorities**
**(Mt 28:11-15)**

[11]While the women were on their way, some of the guards went into the city and reported to the chief priests everything that had happened. [12]When the chief priests had met with the elders and devised a plan, they gave the soldiers a large sum of money, [13]telling them, "You are to say, 'His disciples came during the night and stole him away while we were asleep.' [14]If this report gets to the governor, we will satisfy him and keep you out of trouble." [15]So the soldiers took the money and did as they were instructed. And this story has been widely circulated among the Jews to this very day.

While the women are making their report, the guards have to give a report of their own. These Roman soldiers are in big trouble. They would incur the penalty of the prisoner whom they had allowed to escape. So instead of going to Pilate, they go to the chief priests to whom the corpse belongs. These Jewish leaders are actually pretty understanding. But their plan was a dangerous one. If these guards confess to falling asleep on the job, it spells almost certain death. Then again, this was already their penalty for letting Jesus "get away." Both options are pretty grim. A large wad of money in each of their hands helps them make the "right" choice. Should Pilate hear about this episode, the chief priests promise to persuade him to let it go. Judging by Friday's events, they are perfectly capable of doing just that.

This story of a stolen body was still in circulation during Matthew's day. Indeed, some even suggest it today. But how credible is it? The disciples don't even believe the resurrection when they are told about it. Why would they steal a body to foist a lie which they didn't believe? Why would they later die a martyr's death for what they knew to be a lie?

We must also understand that Jesus received the most honorable burial that a Jew could have: 75 lbs of spices and repose in a wealthy tomb. Any other burial would be a step down. Besides, to move a corpse from its resting place was a horrific defilement to both the dead body and the one moving it. No friend of Jesus would ever do that, and his enemies certainly didn't want to. In addition, there was a posted armed guard. These disciples were cowering behind locked doors (Jn 20:19), not furtively moving boulders and removing linen strips. What is even more ridiculous is that the guards pinned the blame on the disciples. But how could they have known this if they were asleep? Why could they not stop them if they were awake? And why were the disciples never prosecuted or even questioned about the theft? Paradoxically, this theory would make the NT, the greatest body of moral teaching in all human history, a product of liars and thieves. This theory is not reasonable or believable. That's why just 50 days later, in this very city, 3,000 people accept Jesus as the Christ of God.

Not only does this pericope tell a true story, it is deeply spiritual and symbolic.[16] First, it epitomizes Jesus' post-resurrection appearances. We have two "legal" witnesses (cf. Lk 24:4), veiled sight, sorrow turned to joy, fulfilled prophecy, and a report to the Apostles. Second, it offers a

**§ 176**
**Appearance to the Two on Their Way to Emmaus**
**([Mk 16:12-13]; Lk 24:13-32)**

---

[16]B.P. Robinson, "The Place of the Emmaus Story in Luke-Acts," *NTS* 30 (1984): 481-497, shows how many of Luke's favorite themes play a prominent role in this narrative: Journey, prophecy, recognition and especially hospitality.

paradigm for handling the OT (i.e., Christologically). The NT handling of the OT was no mere literary invention. The writers learned it from Jesus' post-resurrection teaching. Third, it shows how Jesus fulfilled Luke 4:18-19, his mission statement for ministry.

Lk 24:13-16 *with* Mk 16:12

[13]Now that same day two of them were going to a village called Emmaus, about seven miles[a] from Jerusalem. [14]They were talking with each other about everything that had happened. [15]As they talked and discussed these things with each other, Jesus himself came up and walked along with them {[and] appeared in a different form[MK]}; [16]but they were kept from recognizing him.

[a] *13* Greek *sixty stadia* (about 11 kilometers)

The action begins Sunday afternoon. Two disciples, one named Cleopas,[17] but both virtually anonymous,[18] head toward the small village of Emmaus, seven miles from Jerusalem.[19]

There are two dominant thoughts here: Walking and talking. Each is represented by several different Greek words in the passage. As these two disciples make their sad journey home, they can't help but discuss these recent events. These two have been privy to the inner band of Jesus' followers. In fact, they heard the report of the women as well as Peter and John, their "companions," earlier that morning (vv. 22-24). Likely they had followed Jesus through his latter Judean ministry, right up through the Triumphal Entry. They had such high hopes. But these were dashed by the cruel murder of this great prophet. The Jewish leaders brutalized Jesus like the ancients had done to other great prophets of God. But these two had hoped for more . . . they were hoping for a Messiah.

Their steps, like their conversation, are sullen but deliberate. As they cast ideas back and forth [*antiballō*], Jesus joins them, almost unnoticed. They do not recognize him (lit., "their eyes were hindered from recognizing him"). This is likely a *divine passive*. In other words, it is God

---

[17]Eusebius (*Ecclesiastical History*, 3.11) identifies Cleopas as the brother of Joseph, hence Jesus' uncle by marriage. Cleopas is a variant form of Clopas, but that doesn't necessarily mean that he is the Clopas of Jn 19:25.

[18]Some have speculated that this unnamed disciple is Luke himself and that his hometown was Emmaus. While this would allow each of the four Gospels to bear the mark of their authors, there is absolutely no solid evidence for making such a claim. But this much we can say for certain about Luke as a witness to the resurrection: The evidence was compelling enough to convince Luke, both a medical doctor and a Greek, of the reality of Jesus' bodily resurrection.

[19]There are no less than four proposed sites for Emmaus, all of which are approximately the right distance from Jerusalem. For details, see W.L. Liefeld, "Exegetical Notes: Luke 24:13-35," *TrinJ* 2 *ns* (1981): 223-229.

who closes their eyes. Mark's addition seems to support this interpretation by saying that Jesus appeared in a different form.

> [17]He asked them, "What are you discussing together as you walk along?" They stood still, their faces downcast. [18]One of them, named Cleopas, asked him, "Are you only a visitor to Jerusalem and do not know the things that have happened there in these days?"
> [19]"What things?" he asked.
> "About Jesus of Nazareth," they replied. "He was a prophet, powerful in word and deed before God and all the people. [20]The chief priests and our rulers handed him over to be sentenced to death, and they crucified him; [21]but we had hoped that he was the one who was going to redeem Israel. And what is more, it is the third day since all this took place. [22]In addition, some of our women amazed us. They went to the tomb early this morning [23]but didn't find his body. They came and told us that they had seen a vision of angels, who said he was alive. [24]Then some of our companions went to the tomb and found it just as the women had said, but him they did not see."

Lk 24:17-24

When Jesus asks them about the topic of the day, they are shocked, even scandalized by his ignorance. In fact, it stops them dead in their tracks. Cleopas breaks the silence by asking a rhetorical question, "You're not from around these parts, are you?" Jesus responds with a Socratic question, "What things?" The floodgates open. They tell Jesus all about himself and their hopes for him. They recognized Jesus as a prophet from Nazareth (cf. Lk 4:24) and a great miracle worker. In fact, they expected that he would redeem Israel (cf. Lk 1:68). Paradoxically, they had no idea of the true redemption Jesus has accomplished.

Now to pour salt in the wound. Three days have passed. That was significant to the Jews. They believed the spirit of the dead person hovered about the corpse for three days and then left. Now Jesus is *completely* gone. Furthermore, while they are grieving over the death of their potential deliverer, someone comes and steals his body. As if that isn't bad enough, these women "flip out." They claim that angels told them Jesus was alive. Now Peter and John verify the report of an empty tomb, but they saw no angels and they saw no body, dead or alive.

> [25]He said to them, "How foolish you are, and how slow of heart to believe all that the prophets have spoken! [26]Did not the Christ[a] have to suffer these things and then enter his glory?" [27]And beginning with Moses and all the Prophets, he explained to them what was said in all the Scriptures concerning himself.
> [28]As they approached the village to which they were going, Jesus acted as if he were going farther. [29]But they urged him strongly, "Stay with us, for it is nearly evening; the day is almost over." So he went in to stay with them.
> [30]When he was at the table with them, he took bread, gave thanks, broke it and began to give it to them. [31]Then their eyes were opened and they recognized

Lk 24:25-32

him, and he disappeared from their sight. [32]They asked each other, "Were not our hearts burning within us while he talked with us on the road and opened the Scriptures to us?"

[a]*26* Or *Messiah*; also in verse 46

Cleopas charges Jesus with being socially ignorant. Jesus charges both of them with being Scripturally ignorant. By their selective reading of the OT, they have ignored passages like Psalm 22 and Isaiah 53. These were essential to Jesus' glorification which included, among other things, the resurrection and ascension (cf. Phil 2:6-11).

For the rest of the trip Jesus expounds on the whole OT (summarized by "Moses and the Prophets"), showing how it all refers to the Messiah. When they arrive at Emmaus, Jesus acts like he's going on. Jesus isn't trying to trick them. This is normal social procedure. The host would invite the visitor to stay; the visitor would refuse. The host would urge the visitor to stay; the visitor would refuse. The host would insist that the visitor stay; the visitor would accept.[20] Hence, they finally persuade Jesus to stay with them. Their seven mile journey ends late that afternoon.

As they sit down to supper Jesus assumes the role of host. "He took the bread, gave thanks, broke it and began to give it to them." There is something so characteristically Jesus in the way he does it that they instantly recognize him. Some have suggested they recognized him through the Lord's Supper. However, there is no reason for these guys to take the Lord's Supper. In fact, they probably didn't even know about it since they were likely not even in the upper room last Thursday night. Furthermore, Jesus said that he would not participate in that celebration until the establishment of the kingdom. Another suggestion is that they saw the scars in his wrists. Yet another, that there was something unique about the way he prayed and/or distributed the bread (cf. Lk 9:10-17). While these may be true, it seems that God is responsible for opening their eyes at just that moment.[21]

Jesus mysteriously (and probably miraculously) vanishes from their sight. Then all the pieces fall into place. They remembered how their hearts burned (cf. Lk 12:35; Jn 5:35) as Jesus explained the Scriptures en route to Emmaus. "Of course this was Jesus," they might say. "Only he could teach like that! We should have known."

---

[20]The verb translated "urged him strongly" [*parebiasantō*] can even mean "to compel by force." For other such "strong" invitations see Gen 24:55; Judg 19:9; Tobit 10:8; Acts 16:15.

[21]Again we assume that their eyes "were opened" is a *divine passive*.

[33]They got up and returned at once to Jerusalem. There they found the Eleven and those with them, assembled together [34]and saying, "It is true! The Lord has risen and has appeared to Simon." [35]Then the two told what had happened on the way, and how Jesus was recognized by them when he broke the bread.

It is now early evening. Cleopas and his partner make a beeline back to Jerusalem. They cover the seven miles in record time. It is dark as they race through the streets of Jerusalem to the secret gathering place of the Apostles. They know the place; they had been there that morning.

The Apostolic band had been called "The Twelve." Since Judas was now apostate and dead, the official title becomes "The Eleven." Luke uses this new title for the Apostolic band. We learn from John that there are actually only ten there (Thomas is absent for some unexplained reason). Luke leaves out that incidental detail since it would only confuse his readers who might not know about the Thomas incident, only later recorded by John. (Paul does the same thing in 1 Cor 15:5 when he refers to the Apostolic band as the Twelve when the actual number was only eleven.)

No doubt Cleopas and his partner think they might encounter some resistance to their story. Happily, Peter has now seen Jesus and his testimony carries the day. This was now at least the third individual account of Jesus' appearance. We don't know when or where Jesus appeared to Peter. How kind it was of Jesus to do it privately. Peter was surely still stinging from his denial in Caiaphas' courtyard.

§ 177
**The Two Report to the Ten**
(Lk 24:33-35; cf. 1 Cor 15:5a)

[LK 24:]36While they were still talking about this {on the evening of the first day of the week . . . with the doors locked for fear of the Jews,[JN]} Jesus himself stood among them {the Eleven as they were eating[MK]} and said to them, "Peace be with you."

[37]They were startled and frightened, thinking they saw a ghost. [38]{He rebuked them for their lack of faith and their stubborn refusal to believe those who had seen him after he had risen.[MK]} He said to them, "Why are you troubled, and why do doubts rise in your minds? [39]Look at my hands and my feet. It is I myself! Touch me and see; a ghost does not have flesh and bones, as you see I have."

[40]When he had said this, he showed them his hands and feet. [41]And while they still did not believe it because of joy and amazement, he asked them, "Do you have anything here to eat?" [42]They gave him a piece of broiled fish, [43]and he took it and ate it in their presence.

§ 178
**Appearance to the Ten**
([Mk 16:14]; Lk 24:36-43; Jn 20:19-25)

The Apostles have sat down for their evening meal when suddenly it is interrupted by these two ecstatic disciples. About the time they all get calm and sit back down, their meal is interrupted again. This time there is no knocking at the door, no loosening the lock. He is just there! It appears as though Jesus simply passes through the walls. Of course, if he could walk on water and transfigure in his incarnate state, it shouldn't come as such a shock if his resurrected body passes through walls or "materializes" in certain locations. Jesus catches their attention with a simple greeting. Obviously, the disciples are startled and frightened.

Jesus rebukes them for their unbelief. Even now, as he stands before them, they think they are seeing a ghost. Even though they have just said they believed (Lk 24:34), they now demand proof. It may well be that there are still levels of belief. Some are fully convinced, others are not quite there yet. Furthermore, they all doubted when the women told them they had seen Jesus alive. Perhaps the only one who believed in the resurrection prior to having seen Jesus was John (Jn 20:8). But none of them should have needed to see Jesus. None should have needed the reports of the women or even the angels. Jesus told them that he was going to rise again (Mt 12:40; 16:21; 17:9; 17:22-23; 20:18-19; 26:32; Mk 14:28; Jn 2:19-22). That should have been enough.

Even after Jesus showed them his hands and his feet and allowed them to touch him (cf. 1 Jn 1:1) to prove he was no mere apparition, they still had trouble believing. They were giddy with joy and dizzy with astonishment. It's not so much that they are unbelieving as that they just can't believe it. In other words, it hasn't quite sunk in yet. So Jesus drives reality home by eating a piece of broiled fish they are serving for dinner. Now it is clear. Jesus is unmistakably, undeniably, bodily alive!

Jn 20:20-23

²⁰The disciples were overjoyed when they saw the Lord.
²¹Again Jesus said, "Peace be with you! As the Father has sent me, I am sending you." ²²And with that he breathed on them and said, "Receive the Holy Spirit. ²³If you forgive anyone his sins, they are forgiven; if you do not forgive them, they are not forgiven."

Jesus repeats his opening greeting, "Peace be with you," as if to say, "OK, boys, now let's get down to business." He didn't come primarily to prove that he was alive. He came to reiterate his commission. His words, "As the Father has sent me, I am sending you," must remind them of so many words Jesus spoke during the Passover meal just three days ago (Jn 14:2-5, 18-19; 15:20-27; 16:5-7, 16-23). It would remind them that they will be opposed and persecuted as Jesus had been. It would remind them of the promise of the Holy Spirit. And it would remind them of the painful truth that Jesus is going back to the Father. They had better not get too attached to him. Jesus predicted this moment:

Some of his disciples said to one another, "What does he mean by saying, 'In a little while you will see me no more, and then after a little while you will see me,' and 'Because I am going to the Father'?" I tell you the truth, you will weep and mourn while the world rejoices. You will grieve, but your grief will turn to joy (Jn 16:17, 20).

With this simple commission Jesus breathes on them and says, "Receive the Holy Spirit." This is apparently a symbolic "promissory note." For the Holy Spirit will come only after Jesus ascends to the Father (Jn 7:39; 16:7). Now Jesus represents this future coming of the Spirit by breathing on the disciples.[22] The words "breath" and "spirit" are the same in both Hebrew and Greek. Thus, the meaning of this action would be obvious to the Eleven. They may, in fact, have connected it with Genesis 2:7, when God breathed life/spirit into Adam. The Holy Spirit will be the necessary "life-force" for the Apostles to carry out their commission.

Not only will the Eleven have the responsibility of the commission and the special empowerment of the Holy Spirit, but they will have the right to declare forgiveness of sins. This is not arbitrary absolution of sins by an ecclesiastical authority. It is not the right to point a finger at someone and say, "You are forgiven . . . You are not forgiven." Jesus' words here must be read alongside his words in Matthew 16:19 and 18:18-20. There we discover that ecclesiastical forgiveness of sins is performed in two ways. First, Apostolic preaching sets the parameters of salvation. Their doctrine would express Jesus' will and authority for the church. In other words, Apostolic preaching determines who is in and who is out. Second, the church leaders, as a body, are responsible for exercising discipline, including excommunication (e.g., 1 Cor 5). This interpretation also accounts for the unusual verb tense of v. 23. The perfect verbs could be translated something like this:[23] "Whatever sins you forgive, *they stand as already having been forgiven*; and whatever sins you retain, *stand as having been unforgiven*." Thus this passage bestows three things on the disciples and probably specifically the Eleven

---

[22]R.W. Lyon, "John 20:22, Once More," *ATJ* 43/1 (1988): 73-85, discusses a number of interpretive options, including that this was the moment that the Apostles actually became Christians through the indwelling of the Spirit. But ultimately he suggests that Jn 20:22 functions in John as Acts 2:4 does in Luke. For both of them, the bestowal of the Spirit is connected to mission, power and authority. M.B. Turner suggests a simpler, yet less attractive, option. He purports that "receiving the Spirit" is not a one-time event. Rather, people received the Spirit at different levels at different times for different purposes ("The Concept of Receiving the Spirit in John's Gospel," *VE* 10 [1977]: 24-42). While this fits well the OT pattern of the Holy Spirit's work, this event seems to have a deeper significance, especially as a "preview" of Pentecost.

[23]Cf. J.R. Mantey, "Evidence That the Perfect Tense in John 20:23 and Matthew 16:19 is Mistranslated," *JETS* 16 (1973): 129-138.

Apostles. They have (1) the commission to preach, (2) the promise of persecution and (3) Jesus' authority over the church.

Jn 20:24-25

²⁴Now Thomas (called Didymus), one of the Twelve, was not with the disciples when Jesus came. ²⁵So the other disciples told him, "We have seen the Lord!"

But he said to them, "Unless I see the nail marks in his hands and put my finger where the nails were, and put my hand into his side, I will not believe it."

Thomas, the twin (a.k.a. Didymus), for whatever reason, was absent from the assembly that evening. The next time they see him, they are obviously going to tell him about it. Now it's not just a few giddy women who say they have seen Jesus, it is also Peter, the two on the road to Emmaus, and the other Apostles. The evidence is mounting. But Thomas remains steadfastly skeptical. We can see from the other two glimpses of Thomas (Jn 11:16; 14:5) that he was a committed follower of Jesus, even willing to die with him. But he also has a pessimistic bent.

He knew that Jesus was dead. And though he lived in a "pre-scientific" age, he knew that dead men don't walk and talk. He was neither gullible nor expectant of a resurrection. He would have to be shown. No, more than that, he would have to touch Jesus in the very spots he had been wounded.

**§ 179**
**Appearance to**
**Thomas with**
**the Eleven**
(Jn 20:26-31;
1 Cor 15:5b)

[JN 20:]26A week later his disciples were in the house again, and Thomas was with them. Though the doors were locked, Jesus came and stood among them and said, "Peace be with you!" ²⁷Then he said to Thomas, "Put your finger here; see my hands. Reach out your hand and put it into my side. Stop doubting and believe."

²⁸Thomas said to him, "My Lord and my God!"

²⁹Then Jesus told him, "Because you have seen me, you have believed; blessed are those who have not seen and yet have believed."

The following Sunday night (lit., "after eight days," counting inclusively), the Eleven were again assembled. This time Thomas was present. Just as before, Jesus appears in the room in spite of the locked doors. Again Jesus greets them with "Peace be with you." He goes straight over to Thomas who was probably picking his jaw up off the floor. Thomas had demanded three things: To see the nail prints, to put his finger in one of them, and to put his hand in the spear wound in Jesus' side. Although Jesus wasn't there (bodily) when Thomas made these demands, he is well aware of them. Using Thomas' own words, Jesus commands him to put his finger in his nail scars and his hand in his spear wound. We don't know if Thomas actually did, but according to 1 John 1:1 somebody touched Jesus!

Jesus orders Thomas to stop doubting. And he did! He utters one of the most powerful acclamations that Jesus has ever received. For a Jew to say to another man, "My Lord and my God," was blasphemous. Thomas has crossed the line; he now believes in the incarnation of God.

"Doubting" Thomas has received kind of a bum rap. Sure, he doubted. Yes, he demanded empirical proof before he believed. But so did all the others. Perhaps they had less testimony than Thomas had. But the error of the others is essentially the same as Thomas'. They wouldn't believe until they saw Jesus. Because Thomas saw Jesus he believed. But what blessings are in store for those who believe without seeing. The testimony is true. The witnesses are credible. If we will but trust their reliable accounts we will receive a commendation from Jesus and life in his name.

[30]Jesus did many other miraculous signs in the presence of his disciples, which are not recorded in this book. [31]But these are written that you may[a] believe that Jesus is the Christ, the Son of God, and that by believing you may have life in his name.

Jn 20:30-31

[a]31 Some manuscripts *may continue to*

This is the conclusion of the book. As John says, "There is so much more that could be said; so much more that could be written." Apparently, by the time John writes this book near the close of the first century, the written gospel records were multiplying. But John writes these few miraculous signs[24] so that people could read about them and believe in Jesus. By believing in Jesus they could have eternal life.

Chapter 21 seems somewhat out of place. After all, the Gospel "proper" has already ended with John's purpose statement (20:30-31). In addition, this chapter does contain some unusual vocabulary for John, a mention of the family name (v. 2), and an odd "we" in v. 24. This evidence has led some to conclude that John did not write this chapter. However, because there is no manuscript evidence that John 21 was ever separate from the rest of the book, and because it is in John's typical style, we hold that John, or at least his amanuensis, did, in fact write it.[25] This chapter plays a vital role in the book and in the first century church.

**§ 180**
**Appearances**
**to Seven**
**Disciples While**
**Fishing**
**(Jn 21:1-25)**

---

[24]John records seven signs of Jesus: (1) changing water into wine; (2) healing the official's son; (3) healing the man at the pool of Bethesda; (4) feeding 5,000; (5) healing the blind man; (6) raising Lazarus; and (7) the Resurrection. To these one might add the cleansing of the temple, the Triumphal Entry, walking on the water, and the great catch of fish. But each of these are qualitatively different than the seven other "signs."

[25]For an excellent evaluation of the evidence, see S.S. Smalley, "The Sign in John 21,"

It functions to: (1) show that Peter was restored, (2) show that Jesus did, indeed, make a Galilean appearance, and (3) dispel the rumor that John would not die (v. 23).

Jn 21:1-6

¹Afterward Jesus appeared again to his disciples, by the Sea of Tiberias.ᵃ It happened this way: ²Simon Peter, Thomas (called Didymus), Nathanael from Cana in Galilee, the sons of Zebedee, and two other disciples were together. ³"I'm going out to fish," Simon Peter told them, and they said, "We'll go with you." So they went out and got into the boat, but that night they caught nothing.

⁴Early in the morning, Jesus stood on the shore, but the disciples did not realize that it was Jesus.

⁵He called out to them, "Friends, haven't you any fish?"

"No," they answered.

⁶He said, "Throw your net on the right side of the boat and you will find some." When they did, they were unable to haul the net in because of the large number of fish.

ᵃ 1 That is, Sea of Galilee

After the feast of Passover ends, the Apostles return to Galilee as they are directed. They wait for Jesus to appear to them there (Mt 28:7; Mk 16:7; Lk 24:6). Instead of just vegetating, Peter decides to go fishing in the Sea of Galilee (John calls it Tiberias). For years Peter had made his living on this lake and is perhaps now thinking about taking up his old occupation again (cf. Jn 16:32). The fishing business has been carried on by Zebedee and the family servants for the last two years. Peter gets in his old familiar vessel and heads out. Six men come along with him. Two of them are not named. Likely candidates are Andrew, Peter's brother, and Philip, who, like Peter and Andrew, lived in this small fishing village of Bethsaida just outside Capernaum.

They fish throughout the night and don't catch so much as a minnow. As the sun begins to rise, they start thinking about docking the boat to begin the tedious task of cleaning their nets. A solitary figure stands on the shore. He calls out to them from about one hundred yards away, "Friends, haven't you any fish?" They don't realize who they are talking to. Their answer is short and to the point, "NO!" (characteristic of unsuccessful fishermen). The stranger says, "If you'll throw your nets on the other side of the boat, you'll catch a bunch of fish." Well now, that was a stupid suggestion! What difference could fifteen feet make? But why not? They've tried everything else. And when they cast to the other side, they land a whole school of big ones. (If this weren't Scripture, we

*NTS* 20 (1974): 275-288. Smalley points out that Jn 21 not only summarizes the theology of the whole book, but follows the typical cyclical pattern of the other seven signs: Statement, sign, witness.

would have to wonder if it weren't the product of a fish story combined with a preacher's count.)

Jn 21:7-14

⁷Then the disciple whom Jesus loved said to Peter, "It is the Lord!" As soon as Simon Peter heard him say, "It is the Lord," he wrapped his outer garment around him (for he had taken it off) and jumped into the water. ⁸The other disciples followed in the boat, towing the net full of fish, for they were not far from shore, about a hundred yards.ᵃ ⁹When they landed, they saw a fire of burning coals there with fish on it, and some bread.

¹⁰Jesus said to them, "Bring some of the fish you have just caught."

¹¹Simon Peter climbed aboard and dragged the net ashore. It was full of large fish, 153, but even with so many the net was not torn. ¹²Jesus said to them, "Come and have breakfast." None of the disciples dared ask him, "Who are you?" They knew it was the Lord. ¹³Jesus came, took the bread and gave it to them, and did the same with the fish. ¹⁴This was now the third time Jesus appeared to his disciples after he was raised from the dead.

ᵃ8 Greek *about two hundred cubits* (about 90 meters)

John is the first to identify the *deja vu*. He's been here before. In fact, it was when they first heard the call to vocational discipleship. After the first miraculous catch of fish, Jesus said, "Follow me and I will make you fishers of men" (Lk 5:1-11; § 41). That stranger was unmistakably Jesus. When John says, "It is the Lord," impetuous Peter realizes John is right. He snatches his fishing jacket and dives in. (Fisherman often stripped down to a "loin cloth" to work; but such attire would be unpresentable on shore.) He swims the one hundred yards to shore. The boat trails behind. In tow behind the boat is this net bulging with fish. It is simply too big to haul into the boat.

On shore Jesus has already stoked up a little charcoal fire and cooked some small fish [*opsarion*]. They make a dandy relish on the bread he has. We're not told if they add their fish to the fire or if Jesus provides the whole meal. (Given Jesus' track record, one little sardine and a single tortilla was enough to feed seven hungry fishermen.)²⁶ But they are commanded to fetch their catch. Peter, surely helped by the others, drags the wriggling bundle to shore. When they count them (and possibly throw back the little ones), they have one hundred and fifty-three keepers.²⁷ Oddly enough, the nets aren't even broken.

---

²⁶The absence of a definite article may indicate that Jesus only had one small fish and only one little round "loaf" of bread.

²⁷The number 153 has had a number of allegorical interpretations attached to it, none of which appear valid: (1) There were supposedly 153 varieties of fish in the Sea of Galilee. Thus, this is a veiled reference to Mt 13:47-48, showing that all kinds of people will be saved. This estimate comes from Oppian via Jerome. However, Jerome is somewhat "loose" in his counting of Oppian's categories. Besides that, Oppian wrote c. 176-180

Verse 12 makes it seem that Jesus' resurrected body is somehow different in appearance (cf. Mk 16:12; Lk 24:16; Jn 20:14). But there is no mistaking Jesus. They know by his actions that it was the Lord. Had they any doubt, they could surely look at his hands as he broke the bread and distributed the fish. This is his third appearance to the group of disciples. (It is actually Jesus' seventh appearance, but individual appearances to Mary, Peter, the women, and the two on route to Emmaus are not included in this count). It is an interesting observation that Jesus only appears to his associates and not to his antagonists (cf. Acts 10:41). If they tried to kill Lazarus after he had been raised from the dead, they likely would have done the same to Jesus (Jn 12:10). As Abraham said, "If they do not listen to Moses and the Prophets, they will not be convinced even if someone rises from the dead" (Lk 16:31).

Jn 21:15-19

[15]When they had finished eating, Jesus said to Simon Peter, "Simon son of John, do you truly love me more than these?"

"Yes, Lord," he said, "you know that I love you."

Jesus said, "Feed my lambs."

[16]Again Jesus said, "Simon son of John, do you truly love me?"

He answered, "Yes, Lord, you know that I love you."

Jesus said, "Take care of my sheep."

[17]The third time he said to him, "Simon son of John, do you love me?"

Peter was hurt because Jesus asked him the third time, "Do you love me?" He said, "Lord, you know all things; you know that I love you."

Jesus said, "Feed my sheep. [18]I tell you the truth, when you were younger you

---

and therefore cannot adequately account for John's usage of 153. (2) The total represents the sum of all the numbers from 1-17. 17 = 10 commandments plus the 7 gifts of the Spirit. Or, according to R. Grant, "'One Hundred Fifty-Three Large Fish' (John 21:11)," *HTR* 42 (1949): 273-275, there are seven Apostles present at the catch and ten who received the Holy Spirit (John 20:24). Thus, 153 functions here as 144,000 does in Rev 7:4 to represent all of God's redeemed. (3) Peter's name in Hebrew, *Simon Iona*, numerically is 153. (4) 153 = 100 (Gentiles) + 50 (Jews) + 3 (Trinity). (5) The Hebrew word for Mt. Pisgah has a numerical value of 153. This shows how Jn 21 is Jesus' farewell address to the leaders of the New Israel, just like Moses' (cf. Num 11:16-25; 27:17). (Cf. O.T. Owens, "One Hundred and Fifty Three Fishes," *ExpT* 100 [1988]: 52-54). (6) The Hebrew for "The Children of God" has a numerical value of 153. Hence, Jn 21 is a reference to the new "children of God" (cf. J. A. Romeo, "Gematria and John 21:11 — The Children of God," *JBL* 97/2 [1978]: 263-264). (7) The 153 fish in the net, plus the one Jesus had cooked make 154 fish. This matches the numeric value of the Greek word "day," which was one of the titles for Jesus in the early church (cf. K. Cardwell, "The Fish on the Fire: Jn 21:9" *ExpT* 102 [1990]: 12-14). (8) 153 is geometrical Atbash. If you reverse the numerical value of the Hebrew alphabet, then take the numbers 70, 3, and 80, you get the Greek letters "I," "X," and "Θ." These are the first three letters of the Greek word "fish" which was, of course, a significant symbol in early Christianity. This word was an acrostic for early Christians which signified: "Jesus Christ, God, Son, Savior" (cf. N.J. McEleney, "153 Great Fishes [John 21:11] — Geometrical Atbash," *Biblica* 58 [1977]: 411-417).

dressed yourself and went where you wanted; but when you are old you will stretch out your hands, and someone else will dress you and lead you where you do not want to go." ¹⁹Jesus said this to indicate the kind of death by which Peter would glorify God. Then he said to him, "Follow me!"

It is time for Jesus to rebuke and restore Peter. Three times Jesus asks, "Do you love me?" Three times Peter answers, "Lord, you know that I love you. Three times Jesus responds by saying, "Feed my sheep." That's in the English. In Greek, there are some subtle synonyms. They may merely reflect rhetorical variation. Or they may suggest a deeper meaning. The reader is left to decide. The following chart shows the subtle changes:

| Jesus' Question: | Peter's Reply: | Jesus' Response: |
|---|---|---|
| Do you love [*agapaō*] me more than these? | You know [*oida*] that I love [*phileō*] you. | Feed [*boskō*] my lambs [*arnia*] |
| Do you love [*agapaō*] me? | You know [*oida*] that I love [*phileō*] you. | Take care of [*poimainō*] my sheep [*probata*] |
| Do you love [*phileō*] me? | You know [*ginōskō*] that I love [*phileō*] you. | Feed [*boskō*] my sheep [*probata*] |

We have here four sets of synonyms:
- (A) Love — divine love of the NT [*agapaō*] vs. a dear friendship [*phileō*].[28]
- (B) Knowledge — to know intellectually [*oida*] vs. a personal and experiential knowledge [*ginōskō*].
- (C) Feed/Care — mere feeding [*boskō*] vs. shepherding or overseeing [*poimainō*].
- (D) Sheep — Little lambs [*arnia*] vs. adult sheep [*probata*].

The fact that so many synonyms appear side by side here leads some to look for deeper meanings in them. Perhaps that is appropriate. However, there is no contextual indication that these synonyms are used with different meanings. Therefore, we should be cautious about importing too much significance into them. The obvious meaning of the passage is enough to occupy our attention.

After breakfast, Jesus addresses Peter by his old name, his pre-Apostle name. It is a subtle statement but Peter hears it loud and clear. His question is simple but painful: "Do you love me more than these?"

---

[28]However, in John's Gospel these two words are used in reference to both God and men without any clear distinction (cf. 3:16; 5:20; 14:21; 16:27).

"These" probably refers to the other Apostles as opposed to the fishing paraphernalia. Jesus is taking Peter on a painful journey back to Thursday evening when he said, "Even if all these other guys betray you, I will not!" (Mt 26:33; Mk 14:29). Peter realizes what a foolish boast that had been. But surely the Lord could not deny Peter's deep love for the Master. When Jesus repeats the question the second and third times, it is even more painful for Peter, since there is no comparison of Peter's love with the rest. He simply asks, "Do *you* love me?" Peter responds with identical words as before, but surely a bit more emphatically. Then comes round three; more penetrating than before. It isn't so much that Jesus changes the word from *agapaō* to *phileō*, although this couldn't have helped. The pain comes from the fact that Jesus presses Peter three times with the same question. It is a subtle reminder of Peter's triple denial on the evening of the Passover.

Although this is painful for Peter, it is kind of Jesus. In the presence of these prominent men, he charges Peter with the oversight of his flock. Yes, Peter had failed Jesus, miserably. But that doesn't mean that he is no longer valuable. It doesn't mean Peter will no longer be given the keys of the kingdom. Peter has been duly chastised by Jesus for his error. No one else needs to do that any more.

At last Peter is a full-time fisher of men. His nets are hung out to dry for the last time. He will have a long and prosperous career as a preacher. And his boisterous, independent life will come to a cruel yet glorious end. Jesus predicts here that Peter would become a martyr by crucifixion. According to tradition, Peter was crucified in A.D. 68 under the rule of Nero. He felt unworthy to die as the Lord had so he requested to be crucified upside down. His wish was granted.

Jn 21:20-25

²⁰Peter turned and saw that the disciple whom Jesus loved was following them. (This was the one who had leaned back against Jesus at the supper and had said, "Lord, who is going to betray you?") ²¹When Peter saw him, he asked, "Lord, what about him?"

²²Jesus answered, "If I want him to remain alive until I return, what is that to you? You must follow me." ²³Because of this, the rumor spread among the brothers that this disciple would not die. But Jesus did not say that he would not die; he only said, "If I want him to remain alive until I return, what is that to you?"

²⁴This is the disciple who testifies to these things and who wrote them down. We know that his testimony is true.

²⁵Jesus did many other things as well. If every one of them were written down, I suppose that even the whole world would not have room for the books that would be written.

John has been following them. When Peter turns and sees him, he has to ask what John's fate will be. Jesus simply says, "That's none of

your business. You take care of your own obligations." But the way
Jesus phrases it gave rise to the rumor that John would not die.
According to tradition, John was the only Apostle not to die a martyr's
death, but he did die. This little addition should have effectively
squelched the rumor even in John's day.

Without naming himself, John is identified as the author of the book.
He is the beloved Apostle, the one who laid next to Jesus at the Passover
meal, the one who supposedly would not die. He was an eyewitness of
Jesus' ministry.[29] While he could have written seemingly infinite volumes on the words and deeds of Jesus, he selected these few incidents
and described them only briefly. But even these should be sufficient to
bring the reader to faith in Jesus.

§ 181
**The Great
Commission in
Galilee**
(Mt 28:16-20;
[Mk 16:15-18])

The great commission is repeated in some form in each of the four
Gospels as well as in the book of Acts (Mt 28:18-20; Mk 16:16-18; Lk
24:45-49; Jn 20:21; Acts 1:8). In a nutshell, these are our marching
orders. Based on the fact that Jesus has *All* authority, we are to evangelize *All* nations, by baptizing them and teaching them to obey *All* Jesus'
teachings. If we do, Jesus will be with us at *All* times.

Mt 28:16-17

¹⁶Then the eleven disciples went to Galilee, to the mountain where Jesus had
told them to go. ¹⁷When they saw him, they worshiped him; but some doubted.

In obedience to Jesus' instructions, the disciples make their way
back to Galilee after the Passover feast (Mt 28:7, 10). "Galilee of the
Gentiles" was an appropriate place for such a global commission.
Apparently, Jesus prearranges this meeting. As he has done so often
before, he uses a mountain as a platform for delivering lofty truths to his
disciples (Mt 4:8; 14:23; 15:29; 17:1; 24:3; 26:30). When they see Jesus,
there is a mixed response. Some worship, while others doubt.

If we are only talking about the Eleven, then it seems odd that they
would have doubted since they had already seen him twice in Jerusalem
and some of them had seen him a third time when they went fishing.
However, the words "but some" [*hoi de*] seem to indicate a group of disciples distinct from the Eleven. It would be natural for large crowds to
follow the Apostles when they returned to Galilee. It was their home territory and they had been away for the better part of nine months. Paul
confirms this in 1 Corinthians 15:6, "After that, he appeared to more

---

[29]The "we" of v. 24 is rather odd for John. It may be explained in one of several ways. First,
it might be a rhetorical "we," essentially equivalent to "I." Or *oidamen* "we know" may be
divided as *oida men*, "I *surely* know." Or it may be the work of John's amanuensis.

than five hundred of the brothers at the same time." That may, in fact, be this very instance. So we interpret the verse this way: The Apostles and probably a good portion of the other disciples believe and worship Jesus. But some of them doubt. Perhaps they doubt because Jesus appears in a different form (cf. Mk 16:12; Lk 24:16, 37, 41; Jn 21:12). Or perhaps this was the first time these disciples have seen the risen Lord. After all, even the Apostles had a hard time believing when they first saw Jesus (Lk 24:37-43).[30] Matthew's honesty here is impressive. His point is simply that this is not fiction but reality. Sure, some have a hard time believing it at first. But Jesus provided ample evidence for a sure faith in the resurrection.

Furthermore, the word "doubt" [*distazō*], does not mean that they refuse to believe, but that they waver in their belief.[31] They are hesitant, not resistant. While it would have been better for them to believe the credible testimony of the Apostles, they are neither hardheaded nor hardhearted.

Mt 28:18-20

[18]Then Jesus came to them and said, "All authority in heaven and on earth has been given to me. [19]Therefore go and make disciples of all nations, baptizing them in[a] the name of the Father and of the Son and of the Holy Spirit, [20]and teaching them to obey everything I have commanded you. And surely I am with you always, to the very end of the age."

[a]*19* Or *into*; see Acts 8:16; 19:5; Romans 6:3; 1 Cor. 1:13; 10:2 and Gal. 3:27.

In the face of wavering disciples, Jesus sets the record straight. He is supreme. While he has talked frequently about his authority (Mt 9:6, 8; Lk 9:1; 10:19; Jn 5:27; 10:18; 17:2), his resurrection now establishes the fact. Jesus is God incarnate and rules as God in heaven and on earth. He will remain in submission to his Father, of course, but that is all (1 Cor 15:27-28).

Based on Jesus' authority, we are to make disciples of all nations. Verse 19 has one main verb and three supporting participles. The main verb is imperative: Make Disciples! The other verbs describe how we do that. First, we are to go. Now it is true that the participle "go" could be rendered "as you go, make disciples." Some have stressed, therefore, that the commission is simply to make disciples where you are.[32] But this

---

[30]Cf. E.M. Howe, "'. . . But Some Doubted.' (Mt 28:17): A Re-Appraisal of Factors Influencing the Easter Faith of the Early Christian Community," *JETS* 18 (1975): 173-180.

[31]I.P. Ellis, "'But some doubted,'" *NTS* 14 (1967-68): 574-580.

[32]E.g., R. Duncan Culver, "What is the Church's Commission? Some Exegetical Issues in Matthew 28:16-20," *BETS* 10 (1967): 115-126.

can't be all Jesus means. Linguistically, a participle "adopts" some of the force of the imperative main verb.[33] In other words, we are commanded to go. Besides, the context seems to demand it. How can we reach all nations unless we intentionally cross borders for the purpose of evangelism? Jesus is clearly commanding a global missionary endeavor. At the same time, we need to be cautious not to create an unscriptural dichotomy between local and foreign missions by exalting missionary work above evangelism where we are. Both are commanded by Jesus and both are necessary for accomplishing the task Jesus gives us here.

The second and third participles in verse 19 are "baptizing" and "teaching." Together they describe the process of making disciples. These were the marks of conversion and cultivation, the pilgrimage of every believer. In the NT church there was no such thing as a Christian who was either unbaptized or untaught.

Much "to-do" has been made over this baptismal "formula": "In the name of the Father and of the Son and of the Holy Spirit." This text is great support for the Trinity. In Acts and the Epistles, however, we only find people baptized into the name of Jesus, not all three. This has led to a variety of practices. For example, some have insisted that one must be baptized *only* in the name of Jesus, others immerse three separate times, one for each person of the Godhead.[34] Such hagglings are misguided for two reasons. First, there is no reason to believe that Jesus was giving us a formula here. The words we say when we immerse someone are not what is important. What does matter is that a person puts their faith in Jesus as Savior and Lord, that they die to themselves, and are raised together with Christ. Second, to be baptized in (or into) the name of Jesus has nothing to do with a certain appellation. The "name" of Jesus represents his authority, purpose, and character. The "effectiveness" of baptism, therefore, is not in a magical incantation used in the ceremony. Baptism "works" because of the power and authority of Jesus to cleanse us from our sins (1 Pet 3:21; Acts 2:38) and bring us into his kingdom. The same error is made when we pray, "In Jesus' name, amen," thinking that because we have said those words, we have actually prayed in Jesus' name. The verbal formula may have little correspondence to a person actually praying or being baptized in the name of Jesus.

Just as baptism represents the entire conversion process, so is teaching a simplification of the growth of a Christian. There is so much

---

[33]For other examples of this construction in Matthew see 2:13, 20; 5:24; 11:4; 21:2. Cf. C. Rogers, "The Great Commission," *BibSac* 130 (1973): 258-267.

[34]E.g., D.R. Plaster, "Baptism by Triune Immersion," *GTJ* 6/2 (1985): 383-390.

involved; it is a lifelong process. But at least this much should be said: (1) Church leaders must preach the whole counsel of God. In order for a church to grow spiritually, there must be opportunity to delve into the deeper waters of theology and the more difficult passages of Scripture. (2) Christian education is the primary task of the church. It may take the form of preaching, Sunday Schools, home Bible studies, camps, conventions, TV, computers, etc., but Christian education is the purpose of the church. Jesus didn't commission us to invite people to church to learn about him. We are to take this message to the world. When believers do gather, it is for edification through education. (3) Christian education must never merely be academic. Our goal is not to know more Bible but to be more like Jesus. Most of us know far more than we practice already. It is unlikely that yet more knowledge will make us live more like Jesus. Therefore, Christian education must focus on implementing the knowledge we learn. It must be practical and applicable.

Now Matthew draws his story to a close. Rather than focusing on our command, he concludes with Christ's promise. This is the full promise of Immanuel, "God with us" (Mt 1:23). He will be with us until the end of time through the presence of his Holy Spirit. But then, O glorious thought, face to face!

Mk 16:16-18

¹⁶"Whoever believes and is baptized will be saved, but whoever does not believe will be condemned. ¹⁷And these signs will accompany those who believe: In my name they will drive out demons; they will speak in new tongues; ¹⁸they will pick up snakes with their hands; and when they drink deadly poison, it will not hurt them at all; they will place their hands on sick people, and they will get well."

This ending of Mark is fraught with textual difficulties, which were discussed earlier. Even beyond these textual difficulties, this is a peculiar text. Verse 16 contains "Mark's rendition" of the great commission, with an especially strong statement about immersion. He then goes on to list a number of miraculous signs which would accompany the believers (not just the Apostles). Now, we are not surprised that they would drive out demons. Both the Twelve and the seventy-two did that during Jesus' ministry (Mk 6:13; Lk 10:17). And Paul did it in the book of Acts (16:18). In fact, the power of Jesus' name over demons was well-known in Ephesus (Acts 19:13). Neither are we surprised that they would speak in tongues. This phenomenon touched the Apostles (Acts 2:1-4); Cornelius' house (Acts 10:44-48); the twelve disciples at Ephesus (Acts 19:1-4); and the church at Corinth (1 Cor 14). And, of course, we would expect miraculous healings to take place in the name of Jesus. Healing was one of the gifts of the Spirit (1 Cor 12:9).

What we do not necessarily expect is picking up snakes and drinking deadly poison. It just seems weird. Then again, Jesus said earlier that the disciples would trample on snakes and scorpions (Lk 10:19 — likely an allusion to demonic powers). And Paul was not harmed when a viper bit him at Miletus (Acts 28:3-6). While there is no example in Scripture of anyone drinking a lethal dose of poison, it falls into the same category as surviving a venomous snake bite. Now, if we could, for a moment, overcome our penchant for spectacular exhibitions, this text is not so bizarre as it first appears. It is hardly advocating testing God or tempting fate by purposely handling snakes or drinking strychnine. Essentially, all it is saying is that supernatural phenomena, and at times supernatural protection from harm, would accompany Christians.

We must remove this text from the circus and put it back in the Roman arena where Mark's readers would encounter it. Because Christians were taking an evangelistic stand for Christ, they were subjected to lethal opposition. Sometimes they were forced to drink poison as a form of execution, sometimes they faced deadly animals. The specific details can vary. You could replace the snakes with lions or wild dogs. You could replace the poison with a sword or a cross. But the meaning is still the same: When you serve a supernatural God who loves his people, you can expect some wonderful surprises when he makes his presence known among his people.

This text is not saying that every Christian will manifest miraculous signs, nor even that miraculous signs will always accompany the body of believers. Rather, it is saying that when the church stands for God, he will stand with his church. In effect, Mark 16:17-18 functions in the great commission as does Matthew 28:20b (& Acts 1:8). It is a promise of God's presence among us. Hence, this passage provides great comfort, especially to beleaguered believers trying to take Christ to a hostile world. Matthew says that when we evangelize the world, Jesus will be with us (Mt 28:20). Luke says that when we evangelize the world, the Holy Spirit will empower us (Acts 1:8). Mark says that when we evangelize the world, God will protect us.

[6]After that, he appeared to more than five hundred of the brothers at the same time, most of whom are still living, though some have fallen asleep. [7]Then he appeared to James, then to all the apostles.

**§ 182**
**Appearance to**
**James and**
**Five Hundred**
**(1 Cor 15:6-7)**

At some point Jesus also appears to his half-brother, James, and to a group of more than five hundred brothers. The way it reads, Jesus first appears to the five hundred then to James and then to the Apostles.

While this is an accurate list of appearances, it is surely not chronological. That would mean that Jesus appeared to James and to the five hundred on Sunday afternoon before appearing to the Apostles on Sunday night. Actually, an inverse order would be more likely: Apostles, then James, then the five hundred (likely in Galilee).

No matter what the exact time of these occurrences, they provide us with startling evidence of the reality of the resurrection. First, James became a leader in the Jerusalem church (Acts 12:17; 15:13; 21:18; Gal 2:9), and likely the author of the NT letter bearing his name. But he wasn't always committed to Jesus. In fact, even at the cross, Jesus delivers Mary into the care of John, as if he had no living brothers. And six months before that, Jesus' brothers, probably including James, challenged Jesus to go up to Jerusalem and prove himself (Jn 7:1-5). They had already decided that Jesus was crazy, and they wanted to take hold of him and bring him home (Mk 3:31-32). What changed James from a skeptic to a pillar of the church? Nothing short of the resurrection.

There is also this huge crowd of five hundred who all see him at once. This is no mere hallucination. There are multiple witnesses. Furthermore, Paul claims that most of them are still alive when 1 Corinthians was written (c. A.D. 55). In other words, this is no fraudulent myth. They could talk to the people who were there.

**§ 183
Appearance to
the Apostles in
Jerusalem**
(Lk 24:44-49;
Ac 1:3-8)

We have combined Luke 24:44-49 with Acts 1:3-8 as if they were one incident. But notice, the Luke account begins with v. 36, which took place on Resurrection Sunday. The Acts account seems to have taken place toward the end of the forty days. Luke, the author of both accounts, is using a literary device which pulls the two books together. It is kind of like when a soap opera gives you a preview of the next episode at the end of a show and then gives you a recap of the previous episode at the beginning of the next show. What we probably have here is not a single incident, but a synthesis of several appearances. Luke may be combining all the "table talk" of Jesus in his forty days of appearances. The ending of Luke stands at Resurrection Sunday and "telescopes" forward forty days, while the beginning of Acts stands at the Day of Ascension and "telescopes" backward forty days.

Ac 1:3

[3]After his suffering, he showed himself to these men and gave many convincing proofs that he was alive. He appeared to them over a period of forty days and spoke about the kingdom of God.

Lk 24:44-48 *with*
Ac 1:4

{On one occasion, while he was eating with them[AC]} [44]He said to them, "This is

what I told you while I was still with you: Everything must be fulfilled that is written about me in the Law of Moses, the Prophets and the Psalms."

⁴⁵Then he opened their minds so they could understand the Scriptures. ⁴⁶He
told them, "This is what is written: The Christ will suffer and rise from the dead on
the third day, ⁴⁷and repentance and forgiveness of sins will be preached in his
name to all nations, beginning at Jerusalem. ⁴⁸You are witnesses of these things.

Jesus' first appearance was on Sunday after the Passover. His last
appearance was forty days later on the Mt. of Olives. Now, Pentecost
began on Sunday, fifty days after the resurrection. Hence, Jesus ascended
ten days before that feast began.

During those forty days he demonstrates that he is alive in a variety
of ways. Luke calls them "convincing proofs," [*tekmerion*, Acts 1:3].
Aristotle used the same word to indicate "a necessarily convincing
proof" (*Rhetoric* I. 2.16). He speaks with them, eats with them, appears
to them, lets them touch his wounds, and teaches them as only Jesus can.
John puts it this way: "That which was from the beginning, which we
have heard, which we have seen with our eyes, which we have looked at
and our hands have touched — this we proclaim concerning the Word of
life" (1 John 1:1).

During those forty days Jesus had much to teach his disciples about
the kingdom of God (Acts 1:3). A catalogue of his post-resurrection
teachings shows that Jesus spoke specifically about three things:

1. Interpretation of Messianic prophecies (Lk 24:26-27, 44-45; Acts
   1:5)
2. World evangelism (Mt 28:18-20; Mk 16:15-16; Lk 24:47-49; Jn
   20:21)
3. His continued presence with the church (28:20; Mk 16:17-18),
   especially through miraculous powers (Mk 16:17-18; Lk 24:49;
   Acts 1:4)

On one occasion, while Jesus was eating with them, they had a Bible
study. Jesus not only taught them the content of the OT, he taught them
how to interpret it properly. From this passage we learn at least three
things about proper Bible interpretation. First, it must be Christocentric.
In other words, we are to look for Jesus everywhere, even in the OT
(which was, of course, the only Scriptures Jesus had). Jesus covered the
whole thing. The phrase, "The law of Moses, the Prophets and the
Psalms," represents the three major divisions of the Hebrew Bible. In
our vernacular, Luke is saying, "Jesus explained the OT from cover to
cover." This is not to say that every single verse points to Jesus. But it is
to say that every book prepares for, predicts, or foreshadows Jesus.

Second, Luke 24:45 teaches that Jesus will help us understand the Bible. That job has now been taken over by the Holy Spirit (Jn 16:13-15; 1 Cor 2:10-16). This does not mean that the Holy Spirit will give us new, objective revelation. His job is to show us how to apply the Scriptures more than exegete them. He helps us understand the Bible by giving us God's heart. When we prioritize what God prioritizes, when we share his purpose and appreciate his grace, it is then that his Word opens up to us. There are many well-educated people who aren't committed to Christ who know all too well what the Bible meant, but they have no idea what it means. "The man without the Spirit does not accept the things that come from the Spirit of God, for they are foolishness to him, and he cannot understand them, because they are spiritually discerned" (1 Cor 2:14).

Third, interpretation must be evangelistic. That means it centers on the death and resurrection of Jesus which cleanses our sins and raises us in righteousness. It also means we take what we learn to a waiting world. There is no room for narcissistic Bible study in the kingdom of God. God has little use for academic religious research which spirals ever inward on itself, questioning and debating, refining and rethinking, but never communicating to a lost world. God is not glorified through endless Bible studies where believers pat themselves on the back for attending, discuss the latest theological trends, and leave quietly, imagining that this exercise has accomplished the will of God. Luke, like the other evangelists, presses us to proclaim this good news globally.

Lk 24:49 *with* Ac 1:4

⁴⁹I am going to send you what my Father has promised; but stay in the city until you have been clothed with power from on high, {wait for the gift my Father promised which you heard me speak about.^AC}"

Ac 1:5-8

⁵For John baptized with^a water, but in a few days you will be baptized with the Holy Spirit."

⁶So when they met together, they asked him, "Lord, are you at this time going to restore the kingdom to Israel?" ⁷He said to them: "It is not for you to know the times or dates the Father has set by his own authority. ⁸But you will receive power when the Holy Spirit comes on you; and you will be my witnesses in Jerusalem, and in all Judea and Samaria, and to the ends of the earth."

^a5 Or *in*

The disciples need Jesus' leadership, companionship and teaching. But Jesus needs to return to the Father. So Jesus passes the mantle to the Holy Spirit. He will be even more effective than the incarnate Jesus in accomplishing the Great Commission.

The Apostles return to Jerusalem for the celebration of the Pentecost. They are instructed to remain in the city, rather than to return to Galilee, at least until they have been baptized in the Holy Spirit. They won't have to wait long. Ten days later, the Holy Spirit comes on them bodily (Acts 2:1-4), and manifests his power visibly. Peter uses his keys to unlock the front door to the church, 3,000 enter, and the church of Jesus Christ is born. Thus, Christ's global conquest begins.[35]

§ 184
**The Ascension**
([Mk 16:19-20];
Lk 24:50-53;
Ac 1:9-12)

This glorious event completes Jesus' glorification, and exaltation. He was raised not only from the dead but to the right hand of the Father. There he is sitting down on the job; of course, all judges do (Heb 1:3; 12:2). He is not only a judge but also our defense attorney (Rom 8:34) or as the book of Hebrews puts it, our high priest, making intercession for us (4:14; 8:1ff; 9:11; 10:12). God has exalted him (Phil 2:9-11), granting him rule over the galaxies (Eph 1:20-23). But the most amazing thing is yet to come. Because Jesus ascended, so shall we (Col 3:1)! Just as we share in his resurrection, so also we share in his glorification. Indeed, this is the icing of the gospel.

[50]When he had led them out to the vicinity of Bethany, {after the Lord Jesus had spoken to them,[MK]} he lifted up his hands and blessed them. [51]While he was blessing them, he left them and was taken up {before their very eyes,[AC]} into heaven {and a cloud hid him from their sight.[AC]} {And he sat at the right hand of God.[MK]}

Lk 24:50-51 *with*
Mk 16:19; Ac 1:9

[10]They were looking intently up into the sky as he was going, when suddenly two men dressed in white stood beside them. [11]"Men of Galilee," they said, "why do you stand here looking into the sky? This same Jesus, who has been taken from you into heaven, will come back in the same way you have seen him go into heaven."

Ac 1:10-12 *with*
Lk 24:52

[12]Then they {worshiped him and[LK]} returned to Jerusalem {with great joy[LK]} from the hill called the Mount of Olives, a Sabbath day's walk from the city.

[53]And they stayed continually at the temple, praising God.

Lk 24:53

Ten days before Pentecost, Jesus leads the disciples out toward [*pros*] Bethany (Lk 24:50). They stop atop the Mount of Olives where the triumphal procession began about six weeks earlier (Acts 1:12).

---

[35]There is much in this passage from Acts that deserves comment. With great restraint, we'll leave that to one of the many good commentaries on Acts. However, this much should be noted: The book of Acts is the continuation of the Gospel story. Acts 1:1 says, "In my former book, Theophilus, I wrote about all that Jesus **began** to do and to teach . . ." (emphasis added). Although Acts is categorized as history and not gospel, and while it is separated from its first volume by the Gospel of John, we should not lose sight of what Luke was doing. In volume one he tells of the work of Jesus through the Incarnation. In volume two he tells of the work of Jesus through his Helper, the Holy Spirit. Without the book of Acts, the message of the four Gospels is incomplete.

There he speaks to the Apostles for the last time. Most likely the one hundred and twenty are there as well (Acts 1:15). He lifts up his hands and blesses them.[36] With that, he closes out his earthly ministry.

In the middle of the blessing Jesus floats away. They know that Jesus' incarnational body could walk on water. They know his resurrection body is not hindered by locked doors. But this still takes them by surprise. The disciples, like children who've lost a helium balloon, stare at the sky as Jesus drifts away. Finally, he is lost in the clouds, but they still continue to gaze into the heavens. None of them notice the two angels that appear next to them, dressed in white.

We wonder how long the angels stand there waiting for the Galilean disciples to notice them. Finally, they break the silence by asking, "How long are you fellows gonna just stand there looking up?" Then they say, "He'll be back!" The implication is obvious: Get busy! There's work to do before he returns. Naturally, they worship Jesus and return to the Holy City with great joy and anticipation of what God will do next.

The ascension is obviously a wondrous and miraculous event. Yet it is only recorded by Luke (and Mark's longer ending). Predictably, some are skeptical that it really happened. But Stott presents a reasonable argument for the historical reality of the ascension:

1. It was predicted (Ps 110:1; Lk 22:69).
2. It is claimed in the NT (Mk 16:19; Lk 24:50-51; Acts 1:9-11).
3. It is assumed in the NT (Jn 20:17; Acts 7:55; Rom 8:34; 1 Cor 15:1-28; Eph 1:18-23; Phil 2:9-11; 3:10, 20; Col 3:1; Heb 1:3; 4:14ff; 8:1; 9:11ff; 10:12; 12:2; 1 Pet 3:21-22).
4. It is presented with sobriety, not like apocryphal literature.
5. There were witnesses present.
6. Nothing else accounts for the sudden cessation of the resurrection appearances.[37]

So we accept the ascension as a historically true event. Big deal! What does it matter? First, Jesus' work was finished (Jn 17:4-5; 19:30; Phil 2:6, 9-10). He accomplished what he came to do and it was time to go home. Second, he has to get busy with his new work of interceding for the saints at the right hand of the Father (Rom 8:34; Heb 7:25). Third, he promised to go and prepare a place for us (Jn 14:2). Finally,

---

[36]Liefeld (p. 1058) notes that Luke uses the word "bless" [*eulogeō*] only at the beginning and end of his book (1:22, 42, 64; 2:28, 34; 24:30, 51, 53). Thus Luke may intend that this word serve as the "book ends" for volume one.

[37]J. Stott, *The Spirit, the Church and the World* (Downers Grove: IVP, 1990), pp. 47-49.

and perhaps most importantly, the Holy Spirit would come only after Jesus ascended (Jn 7:39; 16:7). Jesus was the only one who could do his job. But now it is time for Jesus to pass the baton to the Holy Spirit. It is the ascension of Jesus that promises his return and thus empowers us to live in eternity in the present absence of our Lord.

[20]Then the disciples went out and preached everywhere, and the Lord worked with them and confirmed his word by the signs that accompanied it.

Mk 16:20

Thus, the story of Jesus ends and the annals of his bride begin. May his power continue to pervade our preaching until his glorious appearing in the clouds. Come Lord Jesus!

# BIBLIOGRAPHY OF CITED SOURCES

Alford, Henry. *The Greek Testament*. Vol. 1. Chicago: Moody Press, 1958.

Ash, Anthony L. *The Gospel According to Luke*. 2 Vols. Austin, TX: Sweet, 1972.

Barclay, William. *The Gospel of Matthew*. 2 Vols. Philadelphia: Westminster Press, 1975.

Beasley-Murray, George R. *John*. Vol. 36: *Word Biblical Commentary*. Waco, TX: Word Books, 1987.

Blomberg, Craig L. *The New American Commentary: An Exegetical and Theological Exposition of Holy Scripture*. Nashville: Broadman, 1992.

Brooks, James A. *The New American Commentary: Mark*. Nashville: Broadman, 1991.

Brown, Raymond E. *The Gospel According to John XII-XXI*. New York: Doubleday, 1970.

Bruce, F.F. *The Hard Sayings of Jesus*. Downers Grove: InterVarsity Press, 1983.

Butler, Paul T. *The Gospel of John*, Vol. 1. Joplin, MO: College Press, 1961.

_____. *The Gospel of Luke*. Joplin, MO: College Press, 1981.

Carson, D.A. *Matthew*. Vol. 8: *The Expositor's Bible Commentary*. Ed. by Frank E. Gaebelein. Grand Rapids: Regency Reference Library, 1984.

_____. *Sermon on the Mount: An Evangelical Exposition of Matthew 5-7*. Grand Rapids: Baker, 1978.

Crowther, Duane S. *Atlas and Outline of the Life of Christ*. Bountiful, UT: Horizon Publishers & Distributors, 1982.

Dodd, C.H. *Interpretation of the Fourth Gospel*. Cambridge: University Press, 1955.

Edersheim, Alfred. *The Life and Times of Jesus the Messiah*. McLean, VA: MacDonald, n.d.

Evans, Craig A. *Luke*. Peabody, MA: Hendricksen, 1990.

Ferguson, Everett. *Backgrounds of Early Christianity*. Grand Rapids: Eerdmans, 1987.

Foreman, Dale. *Crucify Him: A Lawyer Looks at the Trial of Jesus*. Grand Rapids: Zondervan, 1990.

Foster, R.C. *Studies in the Life of Christ*. Joplin, MO: College Press, 1995.

Green, Joel B., Scot McKnight, and I. Howard Marshall, eds. *Dictionary of Jesus and the Gospels*. Downers Grove: InterVarsity Press, 1992.

Guelich, Robert A. *Mark 1-8:26*. Vol. 34A: *Word Biblical Commentary*. Ed. by David A. Hubbard, Glenn W. Barker, John D.W. Watts, and Ralph P. Martin. Dallas: Word Books, 1989.

Gundry, Robert H. *Matthew: A Commentary on His Handbook for a Mixed Church Under Persecution*. Grand Rapids: Eerdmans, 1994.

Hendriksen, William. *New Testament Commentary: Exposition of the Gospel According to John*. Grand Rapids: Baker, 1953.

Johnson, Luke Timothy. *The Gospel of Luke*. Ed. by Daniel J. Harrington. Collegeville, MN: The Liturgical Press, 1991.

Lane, William L. *The Gospel According to Mark*. Grand Rapids: Eerdmans, 1974.

Lewis, Jack P. *The Gospel According the Matthew*. 2 Vols. Austin, TX: Sweet, 1976.

Liefeld, Walter L. *Luke*. Vol. 8: *The Expositor's Bible Commentary*. Ed. by Frank E. Gaebelein. Grand Rapids: Regency Reference Library, 1984.

Linnemann, Eta. *Is There a Synoptic Problem?* Grand Rapids: Baker, 1992.

Longenecker, Richard N. *Acts*. Vol. 9: *The Expositor's Bible Commentary*. Ed. by Frank E. Gaebelein. Grand Rapids: Regency Reference Library, 1981.

*The Lost Books of the Bible*. New York: Bell Publishing, 1979.

MacArthur, John. *The MacArthur New Testament Commentary: Matthew 16-23*. Chicago: Moody Press, 1988.

*Matthew-Mark*. Vol. 8. *The Broadman Bible Commentary*. Ed. by Clifton J. Allen, et al. Nashville: Broadman, 1969.

McGarvey, J.W. and Philip Y. Pendleton. *The Fourfold Gospel or A Harmony of the Four Gospels*. Cincinnati: Standard, 1914.

Meserve, Albert D. *The Olivet Discourse: A Study of Matthew 24*. San Jose, CA: San Jose Bible College, 1970.

Morris, Leon. *Expository Reflections on the Gospel of John*. Grand Rapids: Baker, 1988.

Mounce, Robert H. *New International Biblical Commentary: Matthew*. Peabody, MA: Hendrickson Publishers, 1991.

Nolland, John. *Luke 1-9:20*. Vol. 35A: *Word Biblical Commentary*. Ed. by David A. Hubbard, Glenn W. Barker, John D.W. Watts, and Ralph P. Martin. Dallas: Word Books, 1989.

_____. *Luke 18:35-24:53*. Vol. 35C: *Word Biblical Commentary*. Ed. by David A. Hubbard, Glenn W. Barder, John D.W. Watts, and Ralph P. Martin. Dallas: Word Books, 1993.

Rogers, Cleon L., Jr. *The Topical Josephus: Historical Accounts that Shed Light on the Bible*. Grand Rapids: Zondervan, 1992.

Ryle, John C. *Ryle's Expository Thoughts on the Gospels: Matthew*. Greenwood, SC: Attic Press, 1974.

Shepard, J.W. *The Christ of the Gospels*. Grand Rapids: Eerdmans, 1939.

Stott, John R.W. *Christian Counter-Culture: The Message of the Sermon on the Mount*. Downers Grove: InterVarsity, 1978.

Tenney, Merrill C. *John*. Vol. 9: *The Expositor's Bible Commentary*. Ed. by Frank E. Gaebelein. Grand Rapids: Regency Reference Library, 1981.

Walvoord, John F. *Matthew: Thy Kingdom Come*. Chicago: Moody Press, 1974.

Wenham, John. *Easter Enigma: Are the Resurrection Accounts in Conflict?* Grand Rapids: Baker, 1984.

Wessel, Walter W. *Mark*. Vol. 8: *The Expositor's Bible Commentary*. Ed. by Frank E. Gaebelein. Grand Rapids: Regency Reference Library, 1984.

Westcott, Brooke F. *The Gospel According to St.John*. Grand Rapids: Eerdmans, 1954.

Wieand, A. *A New Harmony of the Gospels*. Grand Rapids: Eerdmans, 1947.

*The Works of Flavius Josephus*, Tr. William Whiston, four volumes. Grand Rapids: Baker, 1974.

# TABLES FOR FINDING PASSAGES IN THE *HARMONY*

# SUBJECT INDEX